JP CAMPBELL:

PICTORIALIST PHOTOGRAPHER

AT HOME AND AT WAR

JP CAMPBELL:

PICTORIALIST PHOTOGRAPHER
AT HOME AND AT WAR

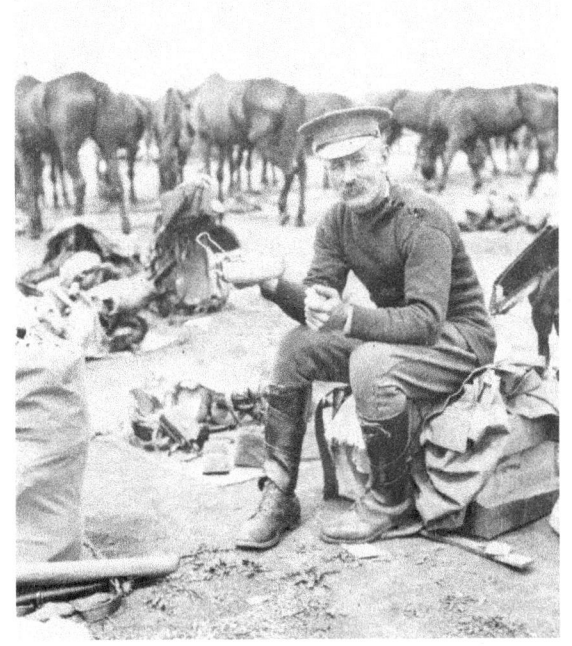

JP Campbell at Broadmeadows army camp, 1915.
(Courtesy of Australian War Memorial, image HO3037)

ALAN HARDING

CONNOR COURT PUBLISHING

Published in 2015 by Connor Court Publishing Pty Ltd

Connor Court Publishing Pty Ltd.
PO Box 224W
Ballarat VIC 3350
sales@connorcourt.com
www.connorcourt.com

ISBN: 9781925138825 (pbk.)

Front cover photo: JP Campbell (c.1918) as featured on a postcard.
Postcard provided by the author.

Cover design by Maria Giordano

Printed in Australia

CONTENTS

ABBREVIATIONS

AIF Australian Imperial Force

ASP Australian School of Photographers

AWM Australian War Memorial

AWRS Australian War Records Section

EAD External Affairs Department

MCG Melbourne Cricket Ground

NAA National Archives of Australia

NGA National Gallery of Australia

NLA National Library of Australia

NTL Northern Territory Library

PROV Public Record Office Victoria

RMIT Royal Melbourne Institute of Technology

RSL Returned and Services League

SECV (often shortened to SEC) State Electricity Commission of Victoria

SLNSW State Library of New South Wales

SLV State Library of Victoria

UNESCO United Nations Educational Scientific and Cultural Organization

WMC Working Men's College

WMCPC Working Men's College Photographic Club

ACKNOWLEDGEMENTS

Researching and writing the life of JP Campbell would not have occurred without the involvement and cooperation of the Tyson family. Nance Tyson had the foresight to keep material relating to her aunt, Lilian Pitts, and JP Campbell. Nance's daughters, particularly Anne Tyson, have given me continuous access to this material and have supported this project, for which I am grateful. I would like to thank Roger Ries for giving me the opportunity to research and write the history of Toongabbie, Victoria, in conjunction with himself. This provided me with the grounding to tackle the biography of a relatively unknown photographer in JP Campbell.

Many individuals have contributed to my research. Noel Fethers gave me valuable background information on the Campbell family. Rod Falconer and his mother Wendy have been kind, hospitable stalwarts throughout the project, giving me full access to their collection of JP Campbell photographs. Jim Nicholas and Marjorie Mossop supplied me with Campbell photographs of the Upper Murray district of Victoria. Gordon McMillan, and later Graham Godber, assisted me with an album held by the Mansfield RSL, and Mansfield Masonic Lodge records. Alan Elliot of the Melbourne Camera Club explained the intricacies of the glass plate camera and suggested avenues of research. Francis Ebury forwarded me his articles on Australian pictorialism and shared with me his knowledge and ideas on the work of JP Campbell and his cousin, Archibald Campbell. Greg Gillespie granted me access to a Campbell Light Horse album, and to the First World War letters of the Mack brothers. Jeff Pickerd's day-by-day, work-in-progress history of the 8th Light Horse was of great value. Laurie Geary and Heather Francis provided me a copy of William Burne Campbell's memoirs. Lt Col Doug Hunter of the 8th/13th Victorian Mounted Rifles Museum kindly showed me a JP Campbell 8th Light Horse album held by the museum. Others to contribute were: Stella Andrews, Bryan Campbell, Joyce Evans, Steven Evans, Chris Harding, Gary Harding, Ken Harding, David Hibbert, Jean Lester, Peter Pinkerton, Frank Pitts, Geoffrey Ritchie, Alice Tyson and Don Wilson.

I utilised the resources of many archival institutions in Australia and I appreciate the service they delivered. I would particularly like to thank Ian Affleck, the former curator of photography at the Australian War Memorial,

Gael Newton, former senior curator of photography at the National Gallery of Australia, John Cudmore of the State Electricity Commission of Victoria, Office of the Administrator, and the staff of the State Library of Victoria, National Library of Australia, State Library of New South Wales, National Archives of Australia, Northern Territory Library, Public Records Office Victoria and Royal Melbourne Institute of Technology Archives. Members of the Mansfield and Euroa Historical Societies were generous with their supply of material on JP Campbell.

This book was originally a Monash University PhD thesis completed externally via their Gippsland campus at Churchill in the Latrobe Valley (now a campus of Federation University). During part of my research period I was the recipient of a Monash departmental scholarship, and I thank those responsible for instigating and administrating the scholarship. Particular thanks go to my supervisors, Dr Meredith Fletcher and Dr Karen Crinall. I am indebted to Dr Fletcher for her perceptive reading of drafts, astute advice, and for her continuing involvement in a supervisory role after taking semi-retirement. Her experience as an historian and writer informed her comments on the thesis. Dr Crinall brought other, particularly relevant skills to overseeing a thesis on a photographer, skills regarding the visual media, in particular image interpretation. I thank her for her encouraging comments and for steering me through to the completion of the thesis. Patrick Morgan has kindly edited the manuscript, completing its transition from thesis to book. I am very grateful for his contribution.

I would like to express my gratitude to my wife Eunice who has tolerated my indulgence in pursuing Campbell's life under trying circumstances. I also thank our sons, James and Timothy, for their support and restraint as they listened to all things JP Campbell *ad nauseam* over the years. Both helped with computer issues, of which there were many.

MAPS AND ILLUSTRATIONS

The photographs were taken by JP Campbell unless otherwise indicated. Campbell's original captions are in inverted commas. Many of the images have had their size altered to allow reproduction and placement amidst the text of the thesis. Some have been cropped slightly. In cases where an image has been replaced by a sharper one from another source, both the source of the caption and the photograph will be acknowledged.

Maps

Illustrations

INTRODUCTION

During his lifetime James Pinkerton Campbell (1865-1935) was a committed photographer, with a career spanning from the 1890s to the 1930s. An Australian of Scottish heritage, Campbell grew up in small rural towns in central Gippsland, Victoria, where he developed a lasting love of the bush and scenic landscapes. As a young man he moved to Melbourne to work as a clerk, and developed a passion for photography and bicycle riding, which he combined when he became a travelling salesman in the mountains of eastern Victoria. This robust, physical life, coupled with a driving ambition to travel, led Campbell to become the first Commonwealth Government photographer, then to Gallipoli and to the Middle East as an official war photographer, and back to Yallourn in central Gippsland, where he documented the beginnings of the massive brown coal project for the State Electricity Commission of Victoria (SECV). Campbell, a sensitive, intelligent man who saw the world through the lens of a camera, made a considerable contribution to Australian photography. His work, however, has gone largely unacknowledged.

I first came across JP Campbell's photographs in the 1970s, in the house of my mother-in-law, Annie Catherine 'Nance' Tyson, in the small central Victorian town of Merrigum. Nance lived in a cottage formerly occupied by her aunt, the teacher and photographer Lilian Pitts. When Lilian died Nance had the foresight to rescue some of her possessions from the inevitable cleansing fire, including loose photographs, albums and postcards. Among them were more than sixty postcards sent to Lilian by Campbell during his period of service overseas with the Australian Imperial Force (AIF), many with his neat pencilled hand writing on the back. Campbell had taught Lilian photography and they were close friends, corresponding for many years.

Nance stored the postcards loosely, tucked away in drawers and cupboards, safe from harmful light. As a regular visitor I was shown these treasures, including an album of Campbell's early photographs which he presented to Lilian Pitts and is now in the possession of the National Gallery of Australia. Campbell had worked for Vallan Studio in Mansfield on the edge of the Victorian high country, a place I visited regularly during the course of my work. My interest intensified.

The twelve volumes CEW Bean's *Official History of Australia in the War of 1914-1918* listed a JP Campbell as an official photographer. An enquiry to staff at the Australian War Memorial, who at the time knew little about him, confirmed this, and turned up an early 1920s address of Campbell's at Yallourn in Gippsland's Latrobe Valley, which I later found out he photographed from its beginnings. This was my territory, near where I grew up, and I was hooked. Who was Campbell? How did he come to see the world through the lens of a camera? Work and family commitments prevented me pursuing the matter, so my JP Campbell file was put away.

Years later, in October 2003, photography expert Helen Ennis appeared on the ABC's *7.30 Report* to promote an exhibition of photographs about to open at the National Library of Australia.[1] I watched in amazement as Ennis, curator of the exhibition, appealed to the television audience for information about a soldier by the name of JP Campbell, first names unknown, some of whose photographs appeared in the exhibition. These images, regarded by Ennis as extraordinary, were from a World War One album of Campbell's held by the National Library.[2] I rang Helen Ennis to inform her of what I knew about JP Campbell, and over the next few weeks I corresponded with staff at the National Library of Australia regarding Campbell. I was now more than ever convinced of the need to research Campbell thoroughly, and perhaps write about him. Having just finished writing a local history, I was keen to start another project. I visited the Centre for Gippsland Studies at the Churchill campus of Monash University in the Latrobe Valley, to commence researching the mysterious photographer's life in Yallourn. The general idea of writing on Campbell came from that visit.

I set out to document his intriguing life, and to delve into why he photographed what he did, and under what circumstances. Because current knowledge of Campbell and his work is fragmented, as Helen Ennis's appeal shows, I decided to present a cohesive, biographical account of Campbell's career as a photographer documenting crucial events in Australian history. Campbell immersed himself in the world of photography when he began studying at the Working Men's

---

1 The exhibition of photographs, part of the National Library of Australia's Photography Collection, was titled *In a New Light: Australian Photography 1850s-1930s*, and on display at the National Library Exhibition Gallery from 9 October 2003 to 26 January 2004. See Helen Ennis, *Intersections: Photography, History and the National Library of Australia*, National Library of Australia, Canberra, 2004, p. 272. Helen Ennis appeared on the '7.30 Report' on 7 October 2003.
2 'The Great War 1914-1915: a Collection of Photographs taken by Signaller J.P. Campbell whilst on Active Service with the The Glorious 3rd Brigade of Light Horse (Whose Heroic Deeds will long be remembered)', PIC PIC/6109/1-184 LOC Album 1009, National Library of Australia.

College (now RMIT University), and in many ways his approach to photography reflected his early rural life. He was influenced by 'pictorialism', or photography as art, and I have relied upon art historian Francis Ebury's analysis of Australian pictorialist photographers to illuminate this important aspect of Campbell's art.[3] Campbell's photographs are themselves a major resource in reconstructing his life. The challenge has been to locate Campbell's photographs, albums, negatives and postcards scattered around Australia in public and private collections. As little was known about him, a great deal of his work in public collections has not been attributed to him.

From the late 1890s Campbell contributed photographs to the Melbourne pictorial weekly newspapers, so these are also an important source of his images. This association with newspapers was to continue for the rest of his life. My newspaper research involved combing through the Melbourne pictorial weeklies and photography journals from the1890s to the 1930s. Official records relating to Campbell's war service and his employment as a Commonwealth photographer are held in the Australian War Memorial and the National Archives of Australia. Campbell was a prolific writer, but only a few of his private letters have survived, so the search for his official correspondence was crucial. His postcards to Lilian Pitts helped, and in local, rural newspapers I was able to find some of his letters reproduced.

As photography developed in Australia it was increasingly used to promote landscapes and attract tourists. Predominantly a landscape photographer, Campbell became involved in producing postcards for the commercial market. Around 1900 photographs began appearing in official publications to promote agricultural pursuits or to attract immigrants to Australia with luring images of a fertile, productive land.[4] Campbell became involved in these promotional schemes when he commenced work as a photographer/cinematographer with the Commonwealth Department of External Affairs in 1911. The First World War loomed at an opportune time, propelling him into the Light Horse and as a soldier-photographer on the tragic shores of Gallipoli where he watched (and

3 Francis Ebury, 'Pictures: Australian Pictorial Photography as Art 1897-1957', Doctor of Philosophy Dissertation, University of Melbourne, 2001, and 'Illuminating the Subject: Towards a Distinctive Australian Pictorial Photography', *History of Photography*, Volume 26, Number 1, Spring 2002, pp. 34-41.
4 Paul Ashton, 'Illustrating Evidence: Photography & the Bush', *Locality*, Volume 6, Number 5, 1994, pp. 207-8.

recorded) his regiment all but destroyed at the charge of the Nek. Wounded, he marked time in Cairo as a clerk in the Australian Army Pay Corps before joining the Australian War Records Section (AWRS) and linking up with the renowned photographer, Frank Hurley, who anointed him as his successor in the role official war photographer with the AIF in Egypt.

Except for Frank Hurley and Hubert Wilkins, few biographies of Australia's official World War One photographers exist.[5] As Campbell's experiences were very different from theirs, his story offers new insights into the role. As official photographer in the Middle East, Campbell documented a number of military actions in 1918, leading up to and including the 'Great Ride' to Damascus. This was another highlight of his career, but he clashed with officialdom and lost his post. After the war he continued his photography career with the SECV at Yallourn, but this settled lifestyle presented difficulties for him, as he persisted in doing things his own way. He was a determined and courageous man, confident in himself and his obstinate in his beliefs. During his working life disagreements with government and bureaucratic bodies over his private photographic interests and philosophy resulted in conflict.

JP Campbell's life was enticing for a potential biographer: the bush childhood, the early amateur photographer and cyclist recording landscapes and streetscapes around the time of Federation, the Commonwealth photographer travelling Australia, the soldier-photographer in the Middle East, and the chronicler of industrial progress back home. These experiences formed the basis of a fascinating life at a time of immense change in Australia. My challenge was to fill in the unknowns in his life to get to the essence of Campbell the man and his photography. This book attempts to do this.

---

5 Alasdair McGregor, *Frank Hurley: A Photographer's Life*, Viking, Camberwell, 2004, and Simon Nasht, *The Last Explorer: Hubert Wilkins Australia's Unknown Hero*, Hodder Australia, Sydney, 2005. Because of the lack of knowledge on other World War One official war photographers, the Australian War Memorial has been supportive of any research on JP Campbell.

1

EARLY YEARS IN GIPPSLAND

*The Campbell and Pinkerton Families – The Central Gippsland
Plain – School and Seaton – Heyfield and Newry – To Melbourne –
Clerical Career and Marriage*

JP Campbell spent the best part of his first twenty years in comparative
isolation in central Gippsland, growing up in small selector communities.
Five of these years were spent in Seaton near the foothills of the Great Dividing
Range. Mary Fullerton, a renowned writer, is particularly remembered for the
depiction of her childhood near Seaton in her book *Bark House Days*.[1] She
described the bush as she remembered it in the 1870s, at the time JP Campbell
was also living in the district:

> It came down close all round us, dark and stern, along the ranges, lighter
> timbered toward the valley, where the fertile land followed the rambling
> creek. The massed foliage of the ranges flowed back and back; the sombre
> greens made a deep blue by the alchemy of the atmosphere in distance.[2]

It was in this landscape that Campbell spent some of his most formative years.
Was it his bush childhood that led him to become a photographer – part alchemist,
part artist – who was obsessed with landscape and the camera as an instrument to
capture the scenes that absorbed his attention?

James Pinkerton Campbell, born in Ralston Street, South Yarra, on 4 July
1865, was the first child of William Campbell and Margaret (nee Pinkerton), who
had married in early 1864. The birth took place at the home of William's brother,
Archibald, who himself had married Margaret Pinkerton's sister Catherine in
1852.[3] JP Campbell's heritage from both sides of his family was Scottish. His
father came from a prosperous Scottish merchant family. His father's brother
Archibald had arrived in Australia in 1840 and immediately sought to establish

---

1 Mary E Fullerton, *Bark House Days*, Melbourne University Press, Melbourne, Paperback Edition, 1964.
2 Ibid., p. 59.
3 Marriage certificate for William Campbell and Margaret Pinkerton, and birth certificate for JP Campbell,
Registry of Births, Deaths and Marriages, Victoria. On Campbell brothers marrying Pinkerton sisters,
Pinkerton and Campbell family history manuscript, author and date unknown, courtesy of Rod Falconer.

himself on a squatting run, but with little success. He battled to survive in the harsh frontier environment. Low on funds, he welcomed his brother's arrival in 1842, along with the money he brought with him. Well educated and now with sufficient capital to establish themselves in the colonies, they launched themselves into various ventures.[4] Unfortunately their capital was quickly lost on, among other things, 'unfortunate sheep deals'.[5] William lost substantially on a horse-buying deal in Sydney orchestrated by his brother. In about 1849 Archibald took up a squatting run, 'Fern Hill', on the Broken River near Benalla.[6] William joined him there in 1853. Archibald also leased the adjoining run to the north, 'Kilfeera'.[7] Both ventures failed. For a short period William managed a station called Kings, which gave him valuable experience.[8] Archibald and Catherine's first child, Archibald James Campbell, was born in Collingwood in 1853 while they struggled to make a go of 'Kilfeera' (Fig. 1).[9] He was to become a renowned naturalist and ornithologist, and was an important influence on JP Campbell's career as a photographer.

After the Broken River venture ended in 1855, the brothers occasionally worked for James Pinkerton, Archibald's father-in-law, which is when William presumably began his relationship with his future wife Margaret.[10] Archibald stated that the Pinkerton family had been 'near neighbours at home [in Scotland]'

---

4 Their father, also William, was a textile merchant, and his wife Jane Campbell (nee Burne) had given birth to William junior in Lisbon, Portugal in 1822. William snr represented the family's textile business in Lisbon at that time. He died when William and Archibald were young, leaving them in the care of their grandparents in Glasgow where they were educated. When their grandfather died it was left to a step grandmother to look after them and it seems it was this that gave them the impetus to migrate to Australia, along with trust money received as they 'came of age'. Margaret Kissock, 'A Pioneering Family', a short Pinkerton and Campbell family history manuscript, 1931, provided by the Falconer family, who also allowed me access to a similar, shorter manuscript, author and date unknown; also, 'The Diary of Archibald Campbell, 1817-1872: An Early Port Phillip Resident, 1840-1872', foreword by Archibald Bryan Campbell, December 2005, p. 3, 20-21, 24 (unpublished manuscript, Courtesy of Archibald Bryan Campbell). Interview with Noel Fethers, 20 April 2005. Noel believed the family was involved in the weaving business.

5 Author unknown, Pinkerton and Campbell family history manuscript.

6 'The Diary of Archibald Campbell, 1817-1872', p. 25

7 Ibid, p. 30.

8 'The Diary of Archibald Campbell, 1817-1872', p. 27.

9 Margaret Kissock, 'A Pioneering Family', and *Argus*, 21 February 1853. The Births, Deaths and Marriage Index, Victoria, Birth Reg. No. 20800, 1853, states Archibald James Campbell was born on the Broken River. Other sources state he was born in Fitzroy, e.g. *Australian Dictionary of Biography*, Vol. 7, A-Ch, MUP, 1979, p. 543.

10 Author unknown, Pinkerton and Campbell family history manuscript, probably taken from the booklet Founders of Australia and their Descendants, author unknown.

to the Campbells, and he had been best friends with the eldest son.[11] Archibald struggled to provide for his growing family, which he settled in rented premises in the Werribee district, before finally settling in South Yarra in the early 1860s. The brothers drifted about seeking work in the latter half of the 1850s and early 1860s, Archibald writing in June 1862 that '[William] arrived from the country only being a short time at Riddell's Creek and had been wandering about for weeks, without a shadow of employment'.[12]

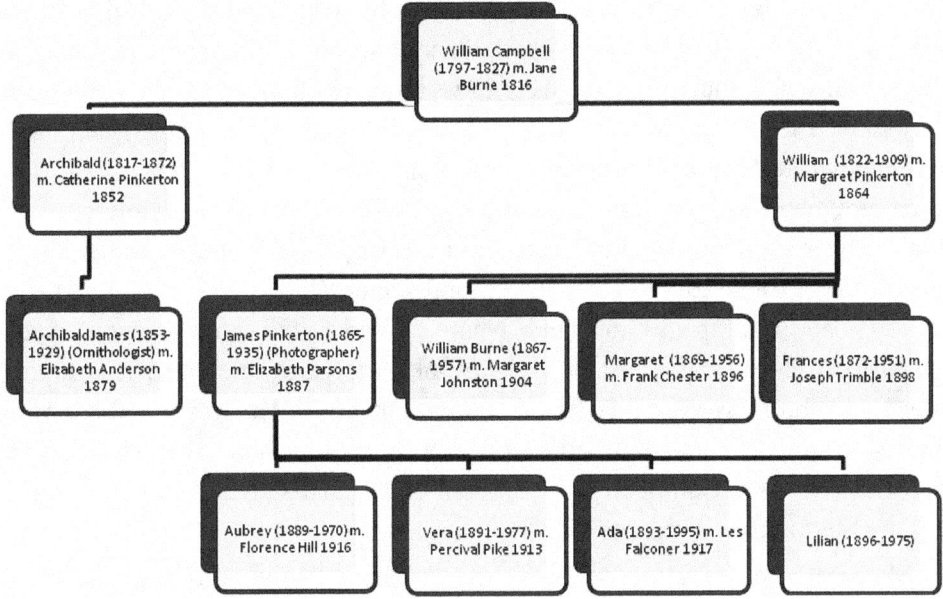

Fig. 1. The Campbell family tree including the principal family members mentioned in this book. (Courtesy of the Falconer family and Noel Fethers)

JP Campbell's mother Margaret was born in Glasgow, Scotland, in 1829 to James and Margaret Pinkerton. The Pinkerton family arrived in Port Phillip Bay from Glasgow in December 1839. James Pinkerton obtained land along Kororoit Creek in the Keilor district, where the family prospered until their home burnt down in 1848 and the property was sold. They re-settled on a new property, 'Yaloke', on the Werribee River near the present suburb of Rockbank. They did well for a time until fire, drought, floods and stolen sheep, coupled with a shortage of labour brought on by the gold-rushes, caused financial disaster. James Pinkerton's wife Margaret died in 1855, and he was declared insolvent

---

11 'The Diary of Archibald Campbell, 1817-1872', p. 24.
12 Ibid, p. 50.

in 1856 having incurred extensive debts.[13] Later, in 1862, 'Yaloke' fell into the hands of the voracious land baron WJT ('Big') Clarke of Sunbury.[14] After his financial troubles it would have been a relief for James Pinkerton (now retired, in his seventies and a widower) to see another daughter, Margaret, become part of the Campbell family.

At the time of his marriage to Margaret Pinkerton in 1864, William Campbell's occupation was given as 'settler', his residence 'Bolindavale' near Sunbury, where he had taken up a fencing contract with 'Big Clarke'. [15] William was still on Clarke's estate in the Sunbury district when JP Campbell was born in July 1865, where the family seems to have remained until February 1866 when they moved to his brother Archibald's home in South Yarra, baggage in hand. William, wrote Archibald, who was struggling to feed his own family, was 'Out of employment. Bad job very difficult for he [William] couldn't get anything. He handed over some money, but I am afraid I must provide for an infinite period. Hope I may be able to do so'.[16] Three months later William departed for Ligar's station, Cape Liptrap in Gippsland, where he had found work at 15/- a week. Much to Archibald's disgust he did not take Margaret and James, as money was 'very short'; weeks later he complained that William was not forwarding money to support them. William returned at the end of September 1866, and in mid-October 'Wm Campbell, wife and child and goat sailed to Bass enroute to Ligar's Station for 12 months'.[17]

Margaret and William's second child, William Burne, was born about 17 October 1867 at Bald Hills near Cape Liptrap. After the twelve month stint on the Cape Liptrap station the Campbell family moved to Yanakie Station on Wilson's Promontory.[18] From here yet another move occurred, deeper into Gippsland. JP Campbell's sister, Margaret, was born in December 1869 near Toongabbie, a small town north of Traralgon. This settlement served as a base for packers ferrying

---

13 Ibid, Margaret Kissock, 'A Pioneering Family', and *Argus*, 20 July 1855, 19 July 1856, 25 July 1856, 25 September 1856, 7 March 1857, 16 June 1857 and 10 May 1919.

14 Margaret Kissock, 'A Pioneering Family', and Author unknown, Pinkerton and Campbell family history manuscript.

15 'The Diary of Archibald Campbell, 1817-1872', p. 52. Marriage and birth certificates. 'Bolindavale' is a Clarke property not far north of Sunbury on the road to Romsey.

16 'The Diary of Archibald Campbell, 1817-1872', p. 53.

17 Ibid.

18 WB Campbell's birth is documented in the family bible which gives the 17 October date. His birth is mentioned in Archibald Campbell's diary entry of 16 September 1867. 'The Diary of Archibald Campbell, 1817-1872', p. 54. The isolation meant no official registration was made.

supplies to the gold mining town of Walhalla. William had taken a job as station overseer with Edward Jones, grazier and hotelier, one of the largest landholders in the district.[19] In this drier, flatter part of Gippsland, European settlement was more established, with selections being carved out of large squatting runs. In 1866 all the land between Seaton and the Latrobe River, an area estimated at 100,000 acres, with Toongabbie at its centre, was surveyed. Some was considered 'good agricultural land' and the rest 'good for grazing purposes'.[20] A web of post and rail fences had begun spreading across the red-gum studded plains. The land, once the domain of the Aboriginal inhabitants, the Ganai, and then of the squatters, was now being divided into small farms with orderly straight lines. Scrub was cleared, trees ring-barked and the bush subdued.[21] The young JP Campbell was witnessing a major transformation of the landscape.

Another daughter, Catherine, was born in June 1871 at Fells Creek near Toongabbie. Sadly, she died of pneumonia three months later and was buried in the Toongabbie cemetery.[22] The family moved again in early 1872 to Upper Cowwarr (Fig. 2). It was here that William Campbell, utilising his good, sound Scottish education, started a night school for people unable to attend day school.[23] In April 1872 he signed a petition supporting a request for state government aid to the Cowwarr Church of England School, established in 1869. He named James and William, aged six and four, as his two children eligible to attend the school.[24] When JP Campbell's third sister, Frances, was born in October 1872 at Cowwarr, William's occupation was recorded as 'Schoolmaster'.[25]

---

19 Alan Harding and Roger Ries, *Toongabbie, Gippsland: A Gateway to the Walhalla Goldfields*, Roger Ries, Toongabbie, 2003, p. 30, 33.

20 *Gippsland Times*, 5 April 1866.

21 For a full account of land settlement on the Central Gippsland Plain and particularly on its western edge, see Chapter 2 of Harding and Ries, *Toongabbie, Gippsland*.

22 William Burne Campbell, 'Doings and Experiences', Unpublished, East Malvern, 1955, p.1. These are autobiographical notes, courtesy of his granddaughters, Laurie Greary and Heather Francis. The memoir is untitled, but William wrote at the beginning: 'This is a rough outline of my "doings and experiences" from as far back as I can remember', so I have adopted this as a title. Also: Harding and Ries, *Toongabbie, Gippsland*, p. 138, and Birth, Deaths and Marriages, Pioneer Index Victoria, CD ROM. There was a small settlement east of the town where the Toongabbie-to-Sale Road crosses Fells Creek. This may have been where the Campbells lived initially.

23 William Burne Campbell, 'Doings and Experiences', p. 1. It was a lifelong ambition of William Campbell to open a school. Interview with Noel Fethers, 20 April 2005.

24 Ivan T Maddern, *History of Cowwarr 1866-1971*, Back to Cowwarr committee, Cowwarr, 1971, p. 5.

25 Birth certificate for Frances Catherine Campbell, and the Campbell family bible. Birth, Deaths and Marriages, Pioneer Index Victoria, CD ROM, birth certificate for Frances Catherine Campbell and Campbell family bible.

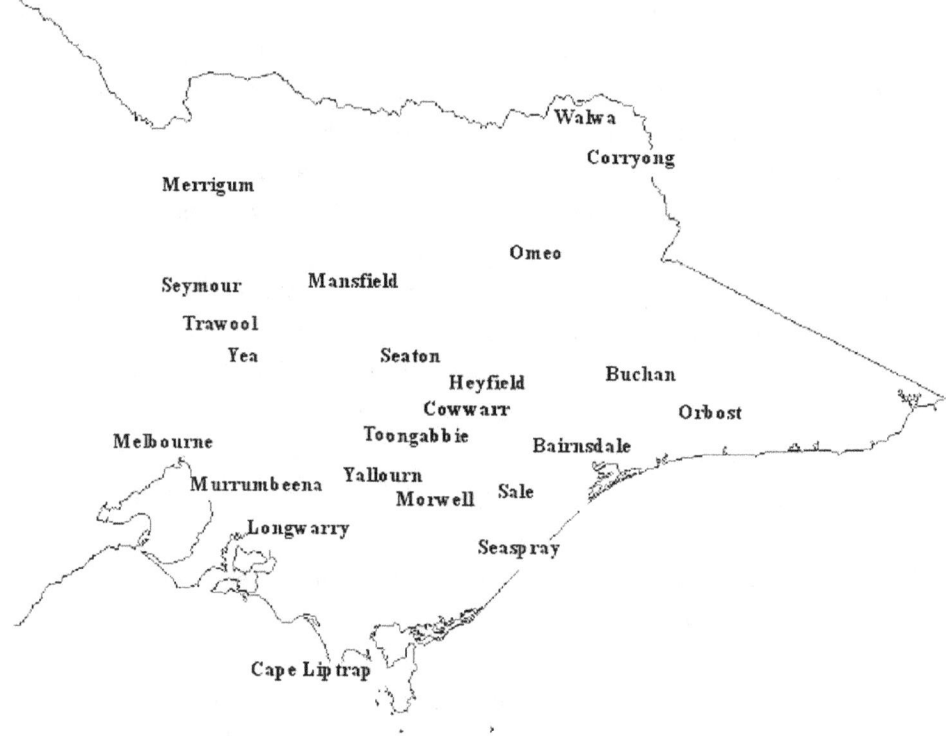

Fig. 2. Map of central and eastern Victoria showing places frequented by JP Campbell.

In 1873 the family moved to Lower Cowwarr where they had 'some anxious times because of flood waters from the Thomson River'.[26] Towards the end of 1875 the Campbell family made yet another move, this time to Seaton, six miles north of Cowwarr. The town's first school had opened in 1866, but soon folded as Seaton quickly declined due to Toongabbie becoming the predominant base for packing supplies into the booming Walhalla region. Despite this setback, Seaton township survived because of its position on a stock route and through agricultural activity in the district.[27]

By the mid 1870s the population had increased so William Campbell was requested 'to build up a school class with a view to the Education Department providing a school'.[28] Seaton pioneer Carl Rumpff donated part of his general store for the purpose. The post office was at one end of the store and the

---

26 William Burne Campbell, 'Doings and Experiences', p. 1.
27 Brian Howell, *The Seaton Story*, Brian Howell, Croydon North, 1998, pp. 51-2.
28 William Burne Campbell, 'Doings and Experiences', p. 2.

Campbells lived in three rooms at the other end. Another large room was used as the school.[29] William was busy in December 1875 mustering student numbers for its opening in January 1876, snaring only twelve out of a potential sixty or more children within two miles of Seaton.[30] On opening, however, there were upwards of ninety children attending the school, and the ten year old JP Campbell was sitting alongside some students over nineteen years of age, many of whom had never been to school before.[31]

The Campbell family settled down to life in this small community. Today, looking down from Seaton on the valley of Glenmaggie Creek to the north-east where Mary Fullerton lived provides a glorious view of the rolling range to the north, dominated by Ben Cruachan. Such views from elevated positions later became bread and butter to Campbell as a landscape photographer producing postcards. Mary Fullerton recalled there was always 'chopping or splitting, sawing or adzing going on in the bush around us', and the ever present 'ringing sound of axe and maul and wedge, and the glorious odour of broken green gum or box wood.'[32] European style farms were being carved out of the bush.

In the 1870s and 1880s the world of the Campbells and Fullertons was limited. As Mary Fullerton relates, there were 'red letter' days: the opening of a bridge, school or church, attending school for the first time, the excitement of horse races, or other momentous social occasions. It was a rare event when a doctor ventured into the district, and people gathered at a selector's house for vaccinations against smallpox.[33] Itinerant workers brought stories of the outside world to the selector community in the shadow of the hills. Hawkers would occasionally arrive in the settlement with a covered waggon loaded with a variety of goods. They were rushed by eager settlers anxious to see the latest fashion or obtain the necessary equipment to tame the land.[34]

People were often too busy surviving to be able to visit anyone other than their near neighbours. For children, the school was their main social contact, with a student age range from toddlers to young adults, a potpourri of the literate and almost-illiterate. Living initially in a section of Rumpff's general store in the

29 Brian Howell, *The Seaton Story*, p. 60.
30 *Gippsland Mercury*, 23 December 1875.
31 Brian Howell, *The Seaton Story*, p. 60.
32 Mary Fullerton, *Bark House Days*, p. 67.
33 Ibid., p. 96.
34 Ibid., pp. 93-4.

township, close to a track leading to the mining settlements in the hills, and in the vicinity of the hotel, the Campbell children must have been exposed to the rough and tumble of country life. For the young James this would have been an education in itself. Like Mary Fullerton, books for JP Campbell were an escape into another world beyond the bush environment.[35] One of his school books survives: *First French Course* by Dr. Ahn & S. Barlet, a small, well preserved hardback with 'JPC, Seaton, Gippsland' written neatly in ink on the inside cover. William Campbell taught James both French and German.[36]

The two Campbell boys roamed the bush and burgeoning selections in their spare time. Their father taught them to use a shotgun and an Enfield rifle, both of the muzzle-loading variety, with which they shot possums and kangaroos. Near their former home at Lower Cowwarr they had some 'hair-raising experiences' hunting wild pigs, wallabies, bandicoots and snakes with their ever-present dog. William described a hunting expedition in the scrub near the Thomson River, where their dog got on the scent of a wallaby:

> We mounted a fence nearby to see what we could of the hunt as the scrub was well over our heads. Presently the wallaby came within a few yards of us and made to get through the 3-rail fence but in its hurry it struck a rail with its head and was partly stunned. As it fell through to the opposite side my brother [James] was off the fence in an instant and had it by the tail. Off they went – the fall at the fence had let the dog get nearer and with a hefty boy on its tail the wallaby was slowed down. All I could see from my grandstand position on the fence was a fair head, cap gone, appearing now and then. Finally I heard the dog at the kill and off I went to see what I could get. When I got there, boy, dog and wallaby were tangled up in raspberry scrub – the boy with no cap and the dog worrying the wallaby which was breathing its last.[37]

Like the generations of country youths to come after them, growing up in the bush often involved killing wildlife for food, or as a recreational pursuit. In doing so they learnt the habits of the creatures they hunted, and developed a closer attachment to the land as a consequence. Their hunting skills were mainly applied to the native wildlife, as the rabbit and the fox had yet to arrive, but the fleet-footed hare was becoming established. Twelve year old James would use

---

35 Mary Fullerton, *Bark House Days*, Chapters 2, 11, 15 & 17.
36 Interview with Noel Fethers, 20 April 2005.
37 William Burne Campbell, 'Doings and Experiences', p. 1.

his brother William as a resting post for the heavy Enfield rifle.[38] Their father tutored them well in hunting and horsemanship, skills which were to stay with both.

Another Australian photographer, Jack Cato, spent some of his formative years in a similar environment. Cato was to become enamoured with photography in the same decade as Campbell, the 1890s, although he was some twenty-four years younger. Cato's early years were spent in Tasmania at Trevallyn on the Tamar River. His parents' fruit orchard, like Seaton, was the 'last outpost before the virgin bush began'.[39] Their house was situated above the river 'with a magnificent view of our varied world'.[40] Cato was second generation Tasmanian born, and said of his immigrant ancestors that 'if England was their home, Tasmania was ours'. We 'grew from the product of its soil, and we loved this land with the sincere belief that it was the most beautiful place in the world'. He likened the forest to a temple, the bush track being the aisle between the trees or columns, their canopy the roof, and the sun streaming down through the foliage 'like rays from stained-glass windows'.[41] This was a very European image of light and form.

Campbell may have been influenced in a similar way in the much less grand bush of the Seaton district. The Great Dividing Range to the north, ever changing depending on the light, must have stayed with him. Campbell's parents being Scots responded to the alien environment according to their cultural background. The Australian born, like JP Campbell and Jack Cato, knew no other world, and although they were heavily influenced by their parents and immigrant community through processes of socialisation and education, they were more able to adapt to the natural environment, learning quickly the ways of the bush. Europeans also brought to Australia an interest in the landscape as scenery, an aesthetic sense developed from exposure to landscape painting and the gardens in Europe. These settlers had preconceived notions as to what was picturesque.[42] The Campbells

---

38 Ibid., p. 2.

39 Jack Cato, *I Can Take It!: The Autobiography of a Photographer*, Georgian House, Melbourne, 1947, p. 15.

40 Ibid., p.16.

41 Ibid., pp. 18-19.

42 RL Heathcote, 'Early European Perception of the Australian Landscape: the first hundred years', in George Seddon, and Mari Davis (eds.), *Man and Landscape in Australia: Towards an Ecological Vision*, Papers from a symposium held at the Australian Academy of Science, Canberra, 30 May – June 1974, Australian National Commission for Unesco, Canberra, 1976, pp. 40-1.

were well educated, so the young James would have been exposed to such aesthetic ideas from an early age. But as an Australian-born youth growing up in the rugged Gippsland landscape, JP Campbell would have absorbed the bush environment, while his father's Scottish landscapes were known only in story. The bush, coupled with his European heritage, and ideas of the picturesque, seems to have nurtured within him an interest in the visual world.

William Campbell senior, who had commenced teaching in Seaton for the Education Department on 1 January 1876, was 'removed' from the school on 30 September 1877 'in consequence of failure at exam (was extremely poor)'. This was despite a community petition supporting his retention which asserted his intelligence, 'great effective manner of teaching' and his 'good work in the school'.[43] It is possible that William, accustomed to operating as a private teacher, and set in his ways, may not have been able to handle the bureaucratic Education Department. JP Campbell's immediate forbears displayed certain personality characteristics: inability to settle down, lack of business success and difficulty in dealing with official bodies. He himself was to show traces of these traits during his adult life.

William junior did not mention his father's removal from the Education Department in his memoirs, stating only that 'after a [new] school was built and a full-time teacher appointed we lived for a time on Wells creek'.[44] JP Campbell completed sixth class at the Seaton School, aged fifteen, successfully passing his examinations.[45] One of his projects was drawing a large coloured map of Victoria on canvas showing all the counties and railway routes, quite a cartographic masterpiece.[46] He seems to have applied himself as a student, in contrast to his brother William who 'would far sooner go hunting possums or play moonlight football than improve [his] learning'.[47] Their two sisters are not mentioned in

---

43 Teacher Record Number 7505, Seaton Roll No. 1649, Teacher Record Books, VPRS13718, Public Record Office Victoria.

44 William Burne Campbell, 'Doings and Experiences', p. 2, *Gippsland Mercury*, 28 June 1877, and *The Baillieres Post Office Directory* of 1880-81, which lists a 'William Campbell, School Master, Seaton', although he had almost certainly left for Heyfield by then.. I have not been able to find the location of Well's Creek. They may have returned to Fells Creek before moving to Heyfield.

45 *Gippsland Mercury*, 4 May 1880. Interestingly, Mary Fullerton is listed as one of the nine children obtaining their certificate.

46 I was fortunate to view this map courtesy of the Falconer family.

47 William Burne Campbell, 'Doings and Experiences', p. 3.

William junior's memoir for this period; Margaret Campbell, their mother, is also absent. One newspaper report shows she catered for school functions.[48]

Around 1879 the Campbell family moved to the nearby town of Heyfield, where William senior resumed teaching night classes.[49] James commenced work as an apprentice blacksmith with William Tulloch of Newry, a small farming community about six miles from Heyfield.[50] Whilst working in Newry, JP Campbell befriended the local teacher, Arthur Liddelow, and his family, starting a lifelong friendship.[51]

Whether through a desire to experience city life, or occupational dissatisfaction, or a combination of both, JP Campbell moved to Melbourne around 1886, starting work as a timekeeper-clerk with the Board of Land and Works in the Railways Construction Branch.[52] In this transition from country to city he was assisted by a supportive family, particularly his teacher-father who had provided him with a good education. In December 1887 he married Elizabeth Blanche Parsons at St John's Church, Melbourne. He was twenty-two years of age and Elizabeth was thirty-five. London born, she had arrived in Melbourne in 1853 with her parents. Her father, John, a wealthy builder in North Melbourne, was killed in an accident in March 1887, and her mother had died in 1883. She had one close relative, her brother. The inheritance Elizabeth received after her father's death, including land and four houses, helped sustain the Campbell family comfortably and later

---

48 *Gippsland Mercury*, 28 June 1877.

49 William Burne Campbell, 'Doings and Experiences', p. 3. The report in the *Gippsland Mercury* of May 1880 mentioning James Campbell's exam results, presumably sat for at the end of 1879, supports this. William senior appears in *Wise's Post Office Directory* of 1884-85 as a School Master in Heyfield, and in *Middleton & Maning's Gippsland Directory 1884-85* as a teacher in Heyfield, so his teaching career must have continued for some time.

50 NAA: B2455, Campbell JP. Tulloch was believed to be the first blacksmith in the town. *Newry and Upper Maffra: 1842-1975* by the 'Back to Newry' committee (foreword by Max Rowley), 1975, p. 4. JP Campbell commenced employment with Tulloch sometime in the early 1880s. He was to say later that he left for Melbourne in his 'late teens', (*Gippsland Mercury*, 18 March 1919).

51 Liddelow arrived in the town in October 1883 to replace a temporary teacher at Newry State School, and stayed to 1888. *Gippsland Mercury* 28 July 1883, 4 September 1883, 13 September 1883, 27 September 1883, 11 October 1883 and 3 July 1888.

52 Letter, JP Campbell to the Secretary, External Affairs Department, 16 October 1911, in NAA: A1, 1913/14458.

allowed JP Campbell to pursue photography more or less unhindered by financial constraints.[53]

James and Elizabeth lived in Kensington where their first three children were born. James arrived in September 1888, but was stillborn, and then a second son, Aubrey, was delivered safely in 1889, followed by Vera in 1891. Still in his mid twenties, JP Campbell had made the transition from the relative isolation in Central Gippsland to working in Melbourne seemingly with ease (Fig. 3). He leapt into marriage and family responsibilities with a much older wife at an early age.

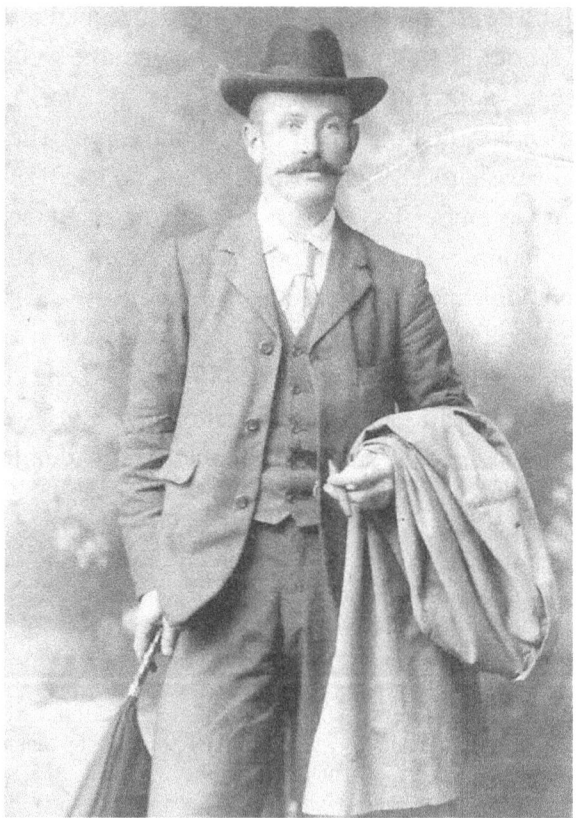

Fig. 3. A young, debonair JP Campbell.
(Courtesy of Falconer collection)

53 Births, Deaths & Marriages, Victorian Pioneer Index, full marriage certificate, and interview with Noel Fethers, 20 April 2005. Elizabeth inherited four houses and land in Peel Street, Hotham (North Melbourne), as well as her father's household furniture, providing a substantial financial base on which to build her marriage to JP Campbell. Will of John Parsons late of 50 Peel Street, Hotham, VPRS 7591/ P0002/122, Public Record Office Victoria, and Probate and Administration Files for John Parsons, VPRS 28/P0002/216, Public Record Office Victoria.

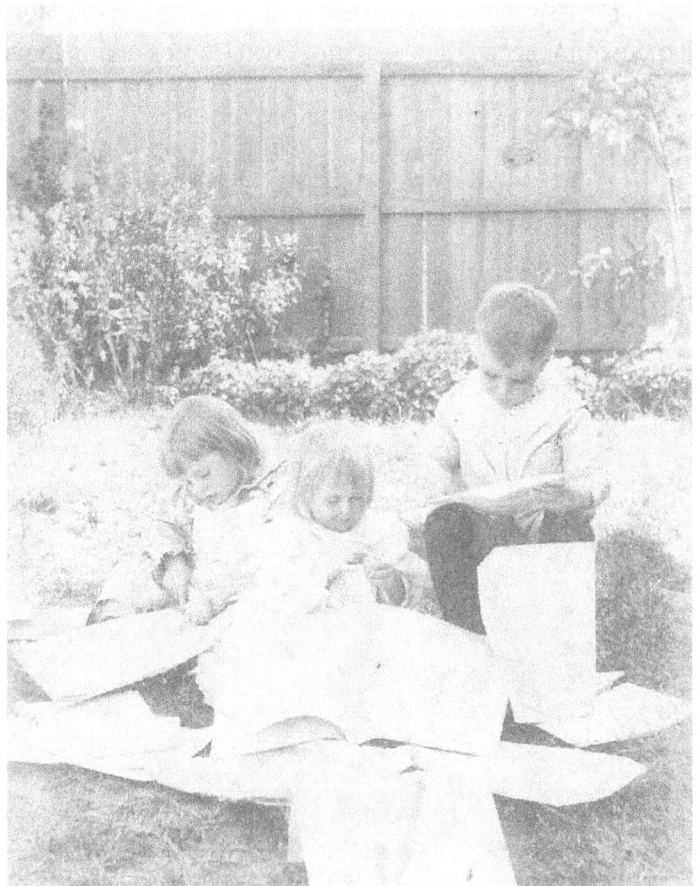

Fig. 4. Left to right: Vera, Ada and Aubrey Campbell, 1895.
(Courtesy of Falconer collection)

However, there must have been some dissatisfaction with city living, for in the early 1890s the Campbells had a house built in Neerim Road, Murrumbeena, now a suburb of Melbourne, but then a separate township. The call of the bush may have been strong in Campbell, with Elizabeth's inheritance enabling them to move into a semi-rural country setting within easy travelling distance of Melbourne. In addition his old friend from Newry, the teacher Arthur Liddelow, had been posted to nearby Rosstown (now Carnegie) in 1888.[54] The Campbell's moved into their new house in 1893. Soon after, their daughter Ada was born, so they called the house Ava after the children, Aubrey, Vera and Ada (Fig.4). Ada

54 *Gippsland Mercury*, 3 July 1888 and Teacher Record No. 5003, Arthur Liddelow, VPRS 13718, Teacher Record Books, Public Record Office Victoria.

later attended the Rosstown school where Arthur Liddelow was teaching.[55] The family settled down in the small community, with James taking the train to work in the city.

---

55 Interview with Noel Fethers, 20 April 2005.

2

A PASSION FOR PICTORIALISM

*Henry Berry and Co. – Working Men's College Photographic Club
– Campbell the Cyclist – Pictorialism – The Australian School of
Photographers – A Travelling Salesman – 'Across the Alps to Omeo' –
Corryong and District – East Gippsland – Herbert Vallance*

In 1892 Campbell left the Board of Land and Works and obtained a job in the commercial sector as a clerk with Henry Berry and Co. Pty Ltd.[1] This company, with its offices in Collins Street, Melbourne, dealt in general groceries, specializing in butchers' and bakers' requisites.[2] He may have been a victim of the 1890s economic downturn.[3] Campbell also enrolled at the Working Men's College (later known as RMIT), primarily to study bookkeeping and to boost his clerical skills.[4] Established in 1887, the main aim of the Working Men's College was to provide learning in the evenings for disadvantaged students, so they could continue earning a living at the same time.[5] Although he had enrolled in bookkeeping, it was not long before Campbell started studying photography at the College.

Archibald Campbell, JP Campbell's cousin, was also studying photography at the College, having commenced a three year course in 1891.[6] Archibald's main motivation for taking up photography was to illustrate his forthcoming book *Nests and Eggs of Australian Birds*.[7] His enthusiasm for photography may have stimulated his cousin to take it up, as in 1892 James commenced studying

---

1 *The Camera House Beacon* , 25 November 1909, p. 262.

2 *Birthday 100, Henry Berry & Company (Australasia) Limited*, The Company, Melbourne, 1959, p. 1.

3 Donald S Garden, *Victoria: A History*, Thomas Nelson Australia, Melbourne, 1984, pp. 204-5, and Geoffrey Blainey, *A History of Victoria*, Cambridge University Press, Melbourne, 2006, p. 144.

4 Interview with Noel Fethers, 20 April 2005.

5 Alan Elliot, *A Century Exposed: One Hundred Years of The Melbourne Camera Club*, The Melbourne Camera Club, Melbourne, 1991, pp. 2-4.

6 Papers of Archibald James Campbell, MS 9650, Box 4, Folder 20, National Library of Australia, Canberra.

7 *The Camera House Beacon*, 25 November 1909, p. 261. *Nests and Eggs of Australian Birds* was published in England in 1900, profusely illustrated with photographs taken by the author, AJ Campbell.

photography under the tutelage of the Instructor in Photography, Ludovico Hart. Both Campbells also joined the Working Men's College Photographic Club, formed by Hart in 1891, which became the influential Melbourne Camera Club in 1919.[8] Campbell's brother was undertaking night courses, studying bookkeeping and surveying. Family ties were important to Campbell – to have family members around him as he strove to learn creative photography would have provided added encouragement.[9]

Ludovico Hart was a cultured man with great charisma, a vast technical knowledge of photography, and a broad range of interests in the scientific and art worlds. Students responded to his warm personality and problem-solving skills.[10] JP Campbell studied under Hart for two or three years, completing the photography course with honours.[11] The Working Men's College photography syllabus, as well as covering the mechanics of photography such as focusing, the structure of camera, making negatives, use of the lens, retouching, developing and printing, also looked at composition and how to study nature.[12] Campbell, with his bush background and practical bent, thrived on such tasks.

Hart's later comments on photography shed some light on his photographic philosophy. Writing in 1904, Hart made it clear that he disapproved of the emphasis on art in photography exhibitions of the time 'to the detriment of the technical side' of photography. He regarded the painter as a creator and the photographer as a copier, and considered both perceive beauty, but interpret it in different ways. For Hart, after taking into account light, angle and composition, the photographer should:

> make the very best of his photographic materials so as to produce a negative as perfect in technique as possible. Such a combination in my opinion would be immensely nearer artistic (natural) effect than the hazy,

---

8 Ibid., pp. 261-2; Letter, JP Campbell to the Secretary, External Affairs Department, 16 October 1911, in file 'JP Campbell – Commonwealth Photographer', Item 16281, National Archives of Australia; Alan Elliot; *A Century Exposed*, p. 2, 6, and the *Argus*, 17 April 1891 & 1 August 1919.

9 Interview with Noel Fethers, 20 April 2005, and William Burne Campbell, 'Doings and Experiences', p. 5.

10 Alan Elliott, *A Century Exposed*, p. 3.

11 Letter, JP Campbell to the Secretary, External Affairs Department, 16 October 1911, in file 'JP Campbell – Commonwealth Photographer', Item 16281, National Archives of Australia; *The Camera House Beacon*, Nov. 25, 1909, p. 262. RMIT Archives was not able to find details of JP Campbell's enrolment at the Working Men's College, due, they believed, to gaps in the records.

12 *Prospectus of the Working Men's College, Melbourne, 1901: The Technical College and School of Mines for the Metropolitan District* , pp. 73-4.

blurred productions one unfortunately has seen of late years, called by some "natural effects".[13]

JP Campbell's involvement in photography intensified through club membership, serving on committees, competing in exhibitions and writing articles. He was elected a member of the Amateur Photographic Association of Victoria at their 1893 meeting at the Royal Society's Rooms, Melbourne.[14] In 1896, when the Working Men's College Photographic Club was given the bulk of the responsibility for organising an Intercolonial Photographic Exhibition and Congress of Australasian Photography, held at the Exhibition Buildings in Melbourne, JP Campbell was elected joint honorary secretary to the Exhibition, along with Ludovico Hart.[15] It was opened by the Governor of Victoria, Lord Brassey; nearly 3,200 photographs were hung for the public to peruse. JP Campbell was successful in the competitive side of the Exhibition, winning the 'Invicta' and 'Austral' prizes, gaining a first in the 'Humorous' class, and a third in the 'Landscape' class.

JP Campbell gave a lecture on carbon printing during the Congress, demonstrating the technical skills he had acquired under Hart's tutelage.[16] He was described as 'a very successful carbon printer'.[17] In August he gave a demonstration of carbon printing to the Working Men's College Photographic Club, where papers on photography were regularly presented by members. In September the Ballarat Photographic Association awarded JP Campbell a first class certificate for a landscape photograph taken using a half plate, and shown at an exhibition held in the School of Mines.[18]

---

13 *The Australian Photographic Journal*, 20 February 1904, p. 30.

14 *The Photographic Review of Reviews*, Australian Edition, June 15, 1894, page number unclear.

15 *The Camera House Beacon*, 25 November 1909, p. 262. JP Campbell would have completed his photography course in 1895, if it was a three year course similar to that completed by his cousin, AJ Campbell.

16 His cousin, AJ Campbell, was even more successful at the Inter-colonial Photographic Exhibition, winning in a 'Landscape' class, a 'Special Processes' class, and, topping off a triumphal effort by the Campbell family, winning the overall champion prize at the exhibition. *The Australian Photographic Journal*, 28 April 1896, p. 77, and an unpublished piece by Alan Elliott, 2001.

17 *The Australian Photographic Journal*, 20 July 1896, p. 173. Early photographers could be described as alchemists. They had to be familiar with the basics of chemistry, at the very least. For further details see: Gordon Baldwin, *Looking at Photographs: A Guide to Technical Terms*, J. Paul Getty Museum, California, and British Museum Press, London, 1991, pp. 19-20.

18 Certificate courtesy of Noel Fethers.

In a further indication of his influence in photographic circles, JP Campbell was offering prizes for competitions held at the Working Men's College Photographic Club during 1896.[19] He was elected press correspondent for the club in August 1896 and added the role of assistant secretary in May 1898. The editor of *The Australian Photographic Journal* stating that 'our correspondence with this gentleman in the past [proves] he is well fitted for the position he has undertaken'.[20] JP Campbell's ambitions were being fulfilled.

The *Australian Photographic Journal* reviewed a paper by Archibald Campbell 'What is pure landscape?' in which he railed against waterfalls and 'choice little nooks' being regarded as 'pure landscape'.[21] These were subjects his cousin James photographed, so there may have been some philosophical differences between them. Both were constant prize winners within the Working Men's College Photographic Club and in the wider photography world. The photography club held a competition in 1898 for the most original artistic compositions, in which fifty prints were shown. AJ Campbell won the figure section with a nude posing in a forest setting, entitled "The Maid of Mullum Mullum". JP Campbell tied with another photographer with an image called 'Tramps', a brown carbon half-plate, a 'typical' bush scene, the type of photograph which was becoming his signature.[22] JP Campbell attended the Intercolonial Photographic Congress of Australasia in June 1898, demonstrating his commitment to photography.[23]

Camera clubs nurtured amateur photographers like Campbell, providing a supportive environment for like minds. In his study of Australian pictorial photography as art, Francis Ebury discussed the importance of photographic clubs in Australia. In 1907 there were about 30 clubs; this number had nearly doubled by 1910. Apparently, there were only about 60 clubs in the USA, so Australia was doing well given the differences in population.[24] The camera clubs which formed in the 1880s and 1890s in Australia were not exclusive, in contrast with many overseas camera clubs which were undemocratic.[25]

---

19 *The Australian Photographic Journal*, 20 July 1896, p. 173.

20 *The Australian Photographic Journal*, 20 August 1896, p. 179, and 20 May 1898, p. 122.

21 *The Australian Photographic Journal*, 20 October 1896, p. 247.

22 *The Australian Photographic Journal*, 20 May 1898, p. 123.

23 Ibid., p. 148.

24 Francis Ebury, 'Pictures: Australian Pictorial Photography as Art 1897-1957', Doctor of Philosophy Dissertation, University of Melbourne, 2001, p. 289.

25 Ibid., pp. 298-9.

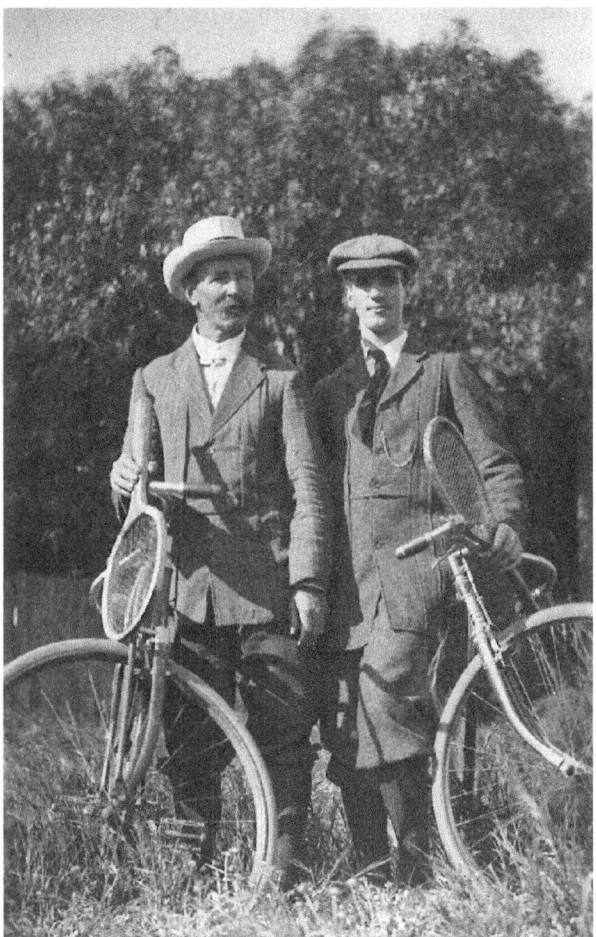

Fig 5. Anyone for tennis? JP Campbell (left) and his
son Aubrey prior to the First World War. Photographer
unknown. (Courtesy of Falconer collection)

The Working Men's College Photographic Club had a predominantly working
class membership.[26] Initially, membership was restricted to College students and
graduates, but in 1896 this was extended to outside membership, which diluted
the working class base. Under the influence of Ludovico Hart, the Club enjoyed
an early reputation for commercial and technical rather than artistic work.[27] The
Working Men's College Photographic Club was also open to women, despite
the name, making it different from other clubs. The Club's objectives included

26 Ibid.
27 Ibid., p. 306.

promoting the study of photography, comparing Australian photography with that overseas, and discussing learned papers on photography. Members had the use of a dark-room and free access to library facilities, and could exhibit in annual exhibitions. Many working class camera enthusiasts were upwardly mobile, destined to become part of the urban middle-classes.[28] JP Campbell certainly looked every inch a middle-class gentleman. (Fig 5).

Throughout the 1880s and 1890s people were settling down after the selection acts. Tourism grew, despite the economic depression of the 1890s, with outdoor recreational activities like cycling and photography gaining in popularity for city dwellers. The introduction of dry photographic plates and silver bromide gelatin coated papers saw photography take off as a hobby, with a booming market for rural landscapes.[29] Photography journals sprang up.[30] In vain did the professional photography studios looked down their noses at this new popular wave of photographers.

In 1898 Campbell wrote an article for the *Australian Photographic Journal Annual* on holidaying in 'the "Queen City" of the South'.[31] Readers were asked to imagine they were taking their annual holidays in Melbourne with, of course, their cameras. On arrival they were to first avail themselves of the hospitality of the Working Men's College Photographic Club and its facilities. The tour was planned around the need to have handy dark rooms at various locations to process the exposed glass plates to obtain 'photographic souvenirs'.[32] In the article, Campbell provided a running commentary on visits to the Exhibition Building, the Museum, Melbourne University, the Zoo, Government House and the Botanic Gardens. The Melbourne's docks, its Yarra bridges and Dight's Falls were cited as worthy photographic subjects. He described the valley of Glen Iris as 'one of the prettiest of suburban districts . . . but sparsely populated, beautiful undulating country, ti-tree scrub and marshy flats, well timbered in places, rustic foot-bridges, grazing cattle etc., etc., all tending to delight the heart of the cameraist'.[33]

---

28 Alan Elliott, *A Century Exposed*, p. 3, and Francis Ebury, 'Making Pictures', p. 307.

29 Gael Newton, *Shades of Light: Photography and Australia 1839-1988*, Australian National Gallery and Collins Australia, Canberra, 1988, pp. 68-9.

30 Ibid., p. 70.

31 James P. Campbell, 'How to Spend your Holiday in the "Queen City" of the South and its surroundings' in *The Australian Photographic Journal Annual*, Harrington and Co., Sydney, 1898, pp. 163-172.

32 Ibid., p. 163.

33 Ibid., p. 166.

The tour continued by steamer to Williamstown, Geelong and back to Melbourne by train via Footscray 'crossing the Saltwater River near the famous Flemington racecourse' where photographers would 'note that the vicinity of the river has not much charm for the visitor's point of view by reason of it being the "noxious trades" stronghold'. He then described photogenic locations out of Melbourne, including the Mornington Peninsula, Ferntree Gully, Lilydale, Healesville, Yan-Yean, Whittlesea, Melton and Bacchus Marsh. At the end, reflecting his devotion to the bicycle, Campbell classified the roads to these places by the degree of difficulty for the 'cyclist photographer'. He claimed to have 'ridden them all, and often with a ½-plate [camera] rig out'.[34]

This article indicates that Campbell had an outgoing personality and liked outdoor physical exercise. The descriptions of 1890s Melbourne are evocative and vivid. Campbell welcomed interaction with strangers, particularly those who shared his passion for photography. Jack Cato, using the language of his time, believed a photographer's personality to be

> a contradiction in all its terms [requiring] the sensitiveness of an artist and the hide of an elephant, the patience of Job, the delicate touch of a woman, strength of character to command any situation, a mind that dreams of life in pictures, and the calculating brain of an accountant – altogether a freak "oil and water" combination of the dreamer and the man of action.[35]

Campbell was developing such traits. It was a time of enhanced nationalism, with emerging art movements such as the Heidelberg School. Capturing the Australian light and the feel of the bush became important to the formation of Australian identity.[36] The earliest photograph of Campbell's I have found is titled 'EVENING (Pool at Heidelberg), Victoria,' a picture published in the *Australian Photographic Journal* in 1898.[37] This is a dark image of a dam framed by trees with protruding dead tree branches and an ominous sky in the background, a foreboding scene, perhaps displaying Campbell's attitude that the bush had a darker, brooding, dangerous side to it. The branch reflections appear exaggerated, suggesting intervention of some sort during the printing stage. Campbell used

---

34 Ibid., p. 172.
35 Jack Cato, *I Can Take It*, p. 30.
36 Gael Newton, *Shades of Light*, p. 70.
37 *The Australian Photographic Journal Annual*, 1898, p. 79.

locals to help find such scenes; he referred tourists to Warrandyte and its local postmaster, 'an old identity, being one of the earliest on the [gold] fields of the colonies, is excellent company, and has above all an eye for the picturesque'.[38]

He was a keen cyclist, which complemented his photography. Campbell competed at the highest level at a time when bicycle racing was popular. In December 1898 he won the Flying Stakes over half a mile at the Melbourne Bicycle Club's Austral Carnival at the Melbourne Cricket Ground in front of thirty thousand people (Fig. 6).[39] Campbell also competed in heats of the Austral Wheel Race over the longer distance of two miles at the Austral Carnival in 1897 and 1898 but was unplaced both times.[40] The fitness gained from cycling allowed him to pursue his landscape photography with vigour. The bicycle, being portable, was easily loaded on to a train, and allowed access to rugged, scenic country.

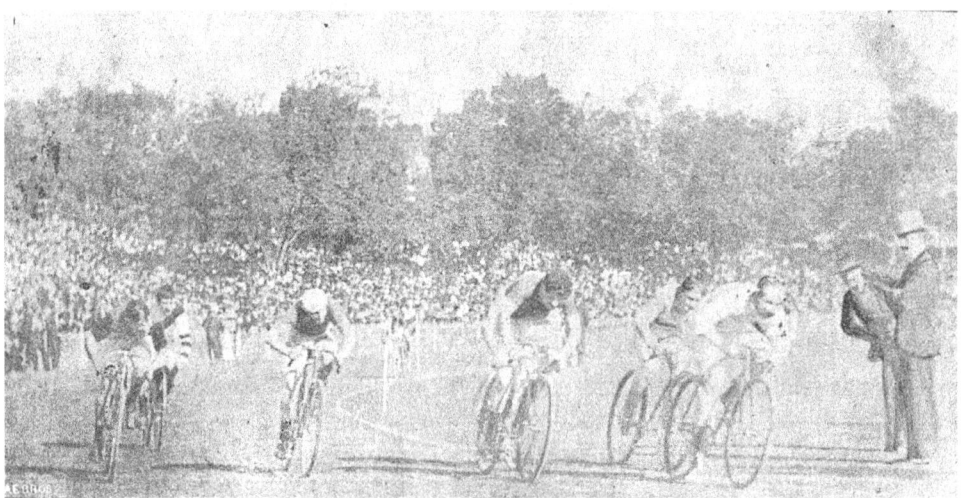

Fig. 6. JP Campbell wins the Flying Stakes on the MCG in 1898, under close scrutiny from the judges. Note the crowd and trees in the background.
(*Australian Cyclist*, 15 December 1898, p. 20)

JP Campbell and his cousin Archibald were swept up in the pictorial movement which emerged in the 1890s under the influence of French

---

38 Ibid., p. 169.

39 *Australian Cyclist*, 15 December 1898, p. 15, 20.

40 *Australian Cyclist*, 9 December 1897, p. 30. In his Austral Wheel Race heat of 1898 'J.P. Campbell made a big effort to get away from the field and win. If he had a mate [pacemaker], J.P. might have accomplished the feat'. *Australian Cyclist*, 8 December 1898, p.17.

Impressionism. The traditional school of photography had sought a 'sharp-focus realism' which practitioners believed was synonymous with fine art. 'Pictorialists' believed a straight, unaltered photograph was not art; interference with the image equated with creativity. Inspiration came from such painters as Whistler and his 'etched tonal work . . . characterised by impressionistic, soft-focus effects'.[41] As Gael Newton has pointed out, this style arrived in Australia in 1897 with John Kauffmann, who returned to Adelaide from Europe where he had been won over by the new pictorial photography movement. He was soon winning praise for his soft-focus, bromide enlargements, regarded as 'works of art' and lacking the 'sharp' and 'hard' lines usually associated with photography.[42] Using gum bichromate and carbon processes, the photographer/developer could achieve a low-tone or low effect like an etching.

The Campbells considered themselves photographic artists, but they were less prepared to manipulate an image to achieve an artistic effect. Within the movement known as 'pictorialism', or photography as art, Francis Ebury identifies two distinct schools emerging in Australia in the late 1890s. Put simply, these were the 'fuzzo-wuzzos', and the 'straights'. Both believed photography could be an art: the fuzzo-wuzzos 'were more interested in how their photographs looked than what they were of, the 'straights' emphasised the primacy of the subject'.[43] Ebury places the two Campbells into the straight camp. They took clear, artistic photographs, which illuminated the subject; they were more interested in what the picture was of, than how it looked. In contrast the 'fuzzo-wuzzos' produced artistic images of a misty, more abstract nature.[44]

With up to fifty members in 1903, the Working Men's College Photographic Club focussed on the commercial side of photography. This influence led to a style of 'pictorialism' emphasising the 'natural' as opposed to the 'impressionist' qualities in photography. Both Campbells became members of the short-lived Australian School of Photographers. Formed in August 1907 and based in Melbourne, it disappeared by 1910.[45] This school was devoted to the 'natural pictorial' style, photographing landscape and scenery using natural rather than

---

41 Francis Ebury, 'Illuminating the Subject: Towards a Distinctive Australian Pictorial Photography', *History of Photography*, Volume 26, Number 1, Spring 2002, p. 34.
42 Gael Newton, *Shades of Light*, pp. 70-1.
43 Francis Ebury, Web Page, *About My Thesis*, viewed 2004, <http://febury.com./My%20Thesis.htm>
44 Ibid., and Francis Ebury, 'Illuminating the Subject', pp. 34-41.
45 Francis Ebury, 'Illuminating the Subject', pp. 5-7.

impressionist effects. Nicholas Caire (1837-1918), famed for his scenes of the Australian bush, was an influential member of the school.[46] Campbell published articles demonstrating the attention to detail which was to stay with him for the rest of his photographic career as a photographer.[47]

Campbell resigned as press correspondent with the Working Men's College Photographic Club in May 1900 because in 1899 he had transferred from a clerical position to one as a travelling salesman with Henry Berry and Co.[48] His new job gave him access to a world of scenic vistas, the dream of any photographer, pictorialist or otherwise. This may be why he took the job because it allowed him to combine his amateur pursuits of photography and cycling with paid employment. On a bicycle specially built for the purpose he travelled through north-east Victoria, Gippsland and the Riverina making sales and taking photographs.[49] This move marked his first major step on the way to becoming a professional photographer.

While working as a travelling salesman, Campbell compiled hundreds of photographic glass negatives of all sizes. These were likely taken with a Thornton-Pickard camera mounted on a tripod, chosen for the quality of picture it produced. [Note 50] The popular Kodak pocket camera was not for Campbell.[50] The camera and tripod were relatively light; it was the glass plates that posed weight problems, as well as being expensive and fragile. When using his bicycle, especially made for the purpose of carrying photography equipment and sales material, Campbell probably used a leather container strung under the crossbar of the bicycle frame, called a framebag. In this way Campbell could often access country for purposes of sales and photography, although he also used a buggy for

---

46 Ibid., p. 34-5.

47 *The Australian Photographic Journal*, 20 September 1900, pp. 195-6.

48 By the time Campbell transferred to a travelling sales job with Henry Berry and Co it employed six hundred people in Australia and New Zealand. Berry was a philanthropist and Methodist lay-preacher, and these values infused the company and its employees. J. Ann Hone, entry for 'Berry, Henry (1836? – 1923)', in *Australian Dictionary of Biography*, Volume 3, Melbourne University Press, 1969, p. 156. Presumably Campbell's job involved verbal selling and presenting catalogues to prospective buyers who would order goods through Campbell or by mail, as Campbell travelled frequently by bicycle and could not carry the goods with him.

49 *The Australian Traveller*, 7 October 1935, p. 28, *The Camera House Beacon*, 25 November 1909, p. 262, and the *Gippsland Mercury*, 18 March 1919.

50 Anne-Marie Willis, *Picturing Australia: A History of Photography*, A & R, North Ryde, NSW, 1988, p. 127.

more accessible destinations.[51] He wore leggings to prevent his trousers tangling in the bicycle chain and to prevent scratching.[52] Bicycles were cheaper and much easier to maintain than a horse.[53]

In 1902 the Campbells moved from Murrumbeena to 12 Hunter Street, Malvern, nearer to larger, more suitable schools for the children, and closer to Elizabeth's preferred church, St John's Anglican in East Malvern.[54] James joined the Commercial Travellers' Association.[55] Membership of this club opened up a new social world for Campbell. From that time on, when in Melbourne, he alternated between staying at the club's Flinders Street premises and his home in Malvern. He also began contributing photographs to the journal *The Australian Traveller*.[56] Campbell was soon lecturing to meetings of the Working Men's College Photographic Club on his travels. He gave one presentation on 'Gippsland and Omeo' to a packed house. He showed photographs depicting the problems of using a trap on country roads, difficulties with ruts and logs, and the indignity of the trap 'coming to rest with wheels in the air' – Campbell liked to inject amusement into his shows. Another series of pictures featured his bicycle going up hills, over stones, across corduroy roads, and with the wheels clogged with mud. For extra drama he threw in a snake story, how he was lying in a stream when he heard a splash in the water a few inches from his head and was confronted with a snake. He scared off the startled reptile by squirting water at it out of his mouth.[57] The Working Men's College Photographic Club regarded Campbell as one of their 'most skilled fieldsman'.[58] Club members may have been envious of their colleague's occupation. He not only used a bicycle, as later legends suggest, but on some trips utilised a 'light buggy' and 'heavy horses', perhaps carrying the bicycle aboard, much like tourists today might carry a

---

51 Jim Fitzpatrick, *The Bicycle and the Bush*, Oxford University Press, Melbourne, 1980, pp. 74-5, and *The Australian Traveller*, 7 October 1935, p. 28.

52 Ibid., p. 90.

53 Ibid., p. 195, 199. The first cycling in the Mount Hotham area occurred in 1894, and in late 1898 the first bicycle ascent of Mount Kosciusko took place. This was the beginning of cycling tourism in the Australian Alps, so Campbell was not alone in his meanderings through the hills. Ibid., p. 124.

54 Interview with Noel Fethers, 20 April 2005.

55 *The Australian Traveller*, 7 October 1935, p. 28, and interview with Noel Fethers, 20 April 2005.

56 Australian Traveller, 7 October 1935, p.28.

57 *The Australian Photographic Journal*, 20 February 1903, p. 47. 'Corduroy roads' refers to wood placed across muddy roads so that wheeled conveyances could gain purchase.

58 *The Australian Photographic Journal*, Volume XV, 21 May 1906, p. 119.

bicycle on their car.[59] Campbell photographed his beloved bicycle propped up on wooden slats lying across a dirt road in the bush in eastern Victoria, a picture titled 'Corduroy' (Fig 7). The bag in the foreground was probably used to carry his photographic equipment. Note the valise in the middle of the bicycle frame.

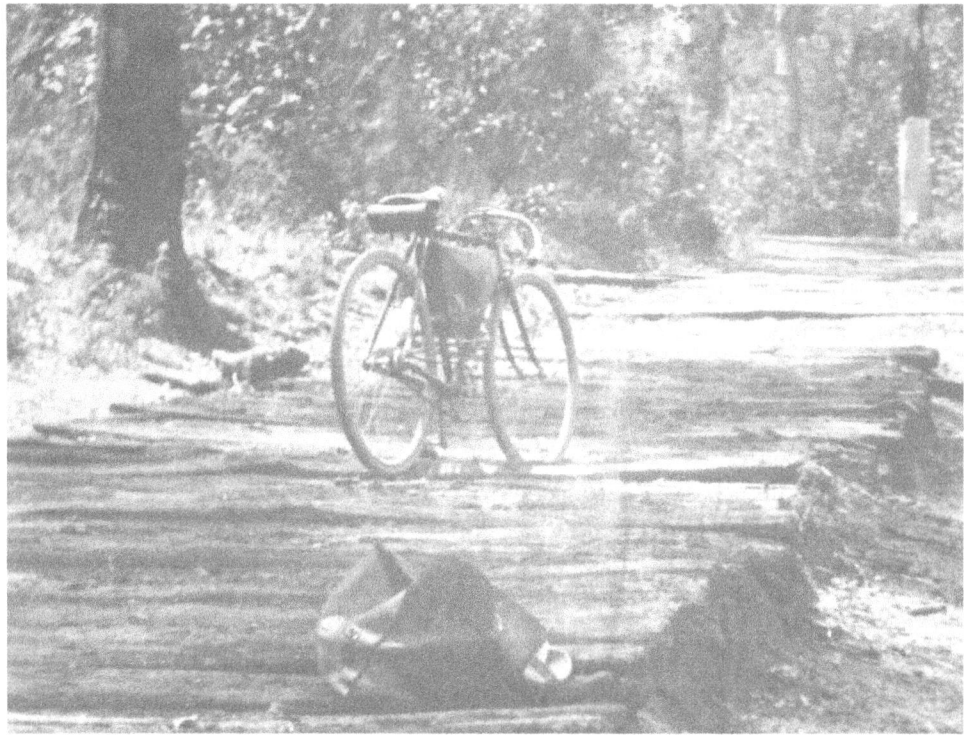

Fig. 7. Detail of a JP Campbell photograph titled 'Corduroy'. His bicycle is propped up on corduroy on a bush track, c.1907. (Courtesy of Falconer collection)

Campbell's love affair with the township of Omeo started as a result of his sales job. While in the district in 1900 he competed in cycling events at the Omeo Easter Show, narrowly winning the two mile race.[60] James found his brother William a job as an assistant storekeeper in a hardware store in Omeo. Both men were to have an extended association with the Omeo-Benambra district.[61] Nestled in the hills of north-east Gippsland, Omeo, like many other townships

59 Ibid.
60 *Bairnsdale Advertiser*, 21 April 1900.
61 William Burne Campbell, 'Doings and Experiences', Introduction and pp. 15-16.

in Victoria, owed its origins to mining.[62] As the gold petered out, the economic focus turned to farming; by the time the Campbell brothers were associated with the town it had all the institutions necessary for survival in its isolated, mountainous location.

The Omeo association coincided with Campbell's first forays into publication in the weekly pictorial newspapers, exposing his high country images to a wider audience. His work appeared in the *Australasian* pictorial weekly in June 1902, the first time, as far as I can ascertain, his photographs appeared in a popular newspaper. They were two Omeo and district scenes, one outcome of three years travelling as a salesman with Henry Berry and Co.[63] The *Australasian* was the weekly rural digest of the Melbourne *Argus* and, because cost and time factors prohibited the reproduction of photographs in the daily paper, it functioned as its illustrated arm, as did the *Leader* pictorial weekly for the Melbourne *Age*. The weekly papers were aimed at developing markets in country towns as agriculture expanded.[64]

The *Australasian* had a reputation for attracting ambitious photographers, having commenced a photographic competition in 1894. The lure of good prize money, along with the status attached to publication of one's work, attracted entries from all the Australian colonies and New Zealand.[65] JP Campbell's cousin, AJ Campbell, had been contributing ornithological articles to the *Australasian* since 1893, illustrated with his own photographs. This may have helped JP Campbell's appearances in the paper. Publication in a pictorial newspaper was a natural step in his gradual transition from amateur to professional.

JP Campbell's second contribution to the *Australasian* was not until October 1903, a picture of Agnes River Falls in South Gippsland, an entry in the paper's photographic competition.[66] Thereafter his contributions accelerated considerably, and by 1909 he had contributed over forty photographs to the *Australasian*, the majority being alpine landscapes. In early 1905 the picture 'Toil and Dust', an image of a wagon, driver and horses shrouded in dust,

---

62 Alby Adams, *The Chinese Ingredient: A History of the Chinese at Omeo*, A. Adams, Toongabbie, 1997, p.5.

63 *Australasian*, 28 June 1902, p. 1482.

64 Peter Dowling, *The Culture of Newspapers: The Slow Birth of the Modern Newspaper in Australia, 1890-1940*, paper presented to the History of the Book in Australia conference, Sydney, August 1996, p. 2.

65 *Australasian*, 2 February 1895.

66 Ibid., 10 October 1903, p. 835.

appeared in the paper. This was to become his signature composition – his pictorialist trademark – exemplifying his fascination with atmospherics and light. Australia being a dry continent it is hard to avoid photographing horses and wagons churning up dust on dirt and gravel tracks, so it was not necessarily a subject sought out by Campbell for its atmospherics. However, he worked in a relatively wet part of South Eastern Australia, where he photographed fog and mist-shrouded scenes. Both dust and fog were in his images because he sought them out.[67]

Campbell's association with north-east Victoria led to his first significant publication as a landscape photographer in *Across the Alps to Omeo*, a tourist booklet with an eye-catching naive painting of mountains on the front cover, published in November 1906 (Fig. 8).[68] The booklet was published by the Omeo Tourist Association, an organisation promoting the beauties of the Alps.[69] Of the forty-two photographs included in *Across the Alps to Omeo*, ten were attributed to Campbell. He was in illustrious company, with Nicholas Caire contributing three images.[70] Campbell knew Caire, having met him at John Lindt's home, 'The Hermitage', where Campbell was a regular visitor with his daughter, Ada.[71]

Caire and Lindt were famous professional photographers, having started out in the 1860s when Campbell was a toddler, going through the various evolutionary developments of the camera, including the wet plate phase of photography, and adapting quickly to the new dry plate technology.[72] Caire, in particular, held great reverence for the bush, and promoted it to city dwellers with haunting fern scenes and pictures of rustic shacks and bush dwellers. The company of such skilled photographers must have stimulated Campbell to greater heights.

---

67 Ibid., 7 January 1905, p. 27. This image was a precursor to his 1907 photograph 'Heavily Laden' of a horse team hauling timber in a forest environment. Unfortunately the newspaper image is of poor quality and thus cannot be reproduced here.

68 *Omeo Standard*, 23 November 1906. The introduction of the dry plate in photography had made possible the use of photographs in commercial advertising in such booklets, replacing the line drawings and lithographs used previously. Francis Ebury 'Making Pictures', p. 378.

69 *Across the Alps to Omeo*, The Omeo Tourist Association, Omeo, 1906, (facsimile edition published by Max Bridges, Toongabbie) p. 5.

70 The other images in *Across the Alps to Omeo* were by HD Bulmer, WH Johnson and Manning. Fourteen of the scenes were not attributed.

71 Interview with Noel Fethers, 20 April 2005. Caire and Campbell may also have associated with one another as fellow members of the Australian School of Photographers.

72 By the time Campbell took up photography the dry glass plate was in common usage, allowing much more flexibility in regard to outdoor photography.

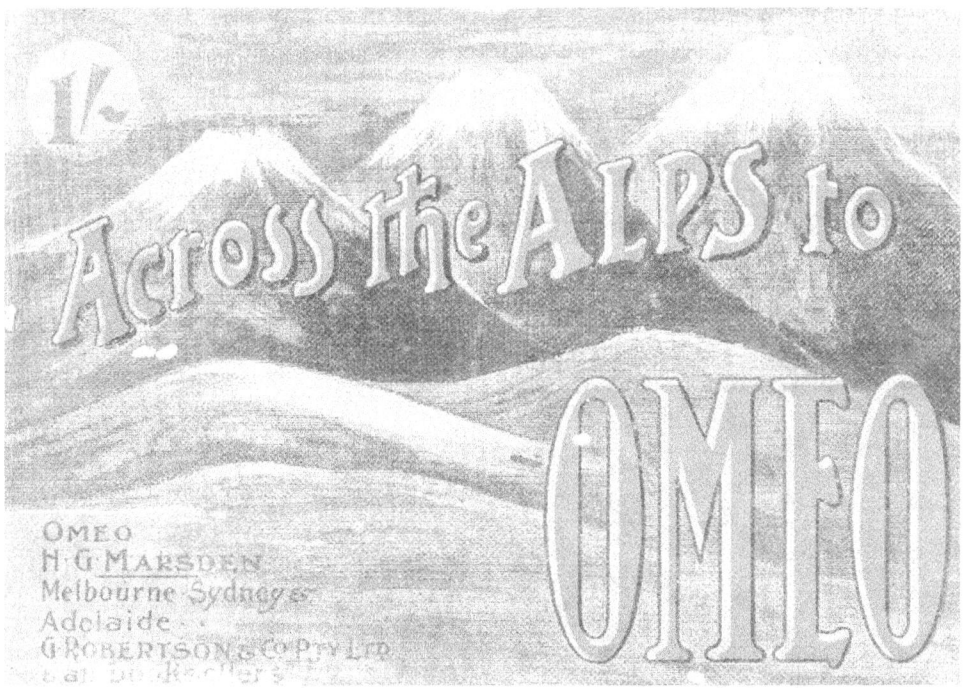

Fig. 8. The front cover of the original edition of the 1906 tourist booklet
Across the Alps to Omeo. (Courtesy of Gary Harding)

Are Campbell's images in *Across the Alps to Omeo* 'picturesque records' as opposed to 'pictorialist' images, as suggested by Francis Ebury in assessing some of Lindt and Caire's tourist work. Pictorialists of the impressionistic school created 'artistic' pictures for their own gratification, or for exhibition, but not usually for commercial purposes, as in advertising.[73] Members of the Australian School of Photographers, however, like JP Campbell, had a more commercial outlook. In *Across the Alps to Omeo* Campbell manages, in some cases, to merge the artistic with the commercial using 'natural' effects such as smoke, light, and elements of the landscape. Four of Campbell's photographs are of bush towns: Swift's Creek, Cassilis, Omeo and Glen Wills, mostly plain but picturesque scenes.[74] The Glen Wills image has a more pictoralist look, smoke drifting from chimneys across the centre of the image behind a strangely shaped tree set against the dark outline of the bush. Timber buildings stand to the left; stumps and frost-covered scrubby ground dominate the foreground. Of his other images only one, captioned 'The

---

73 Francis Ebury, 'Making Pictures', pp. 378-9.
74 *Across the Alps to Omeo*, pp. 22, 27-8 & 45.

Mitta Mitta, near Omeo', has a person in it, a woman sitting holding a stick next to a stream and framed by trees.[75] This photograph won Campbell equal first prize in a landscapes section of the *Australasian's* photographic competition in 1904.[76] It clearly demonstrated his artistic qualities.

One of the images, 'Mammoth Flume, Lightning Creek' is taken from below the large, 150 ft high spindly structure (Fig. 9). The text on the facing page explains how it is 'one of the most remarkable monuments to the industry, the pluck, and the enterprise of the miner'.[77] The flume had been built to take water from the creek to the mine only to find, as happened in many cases, that the venture was not economically viable.[78]

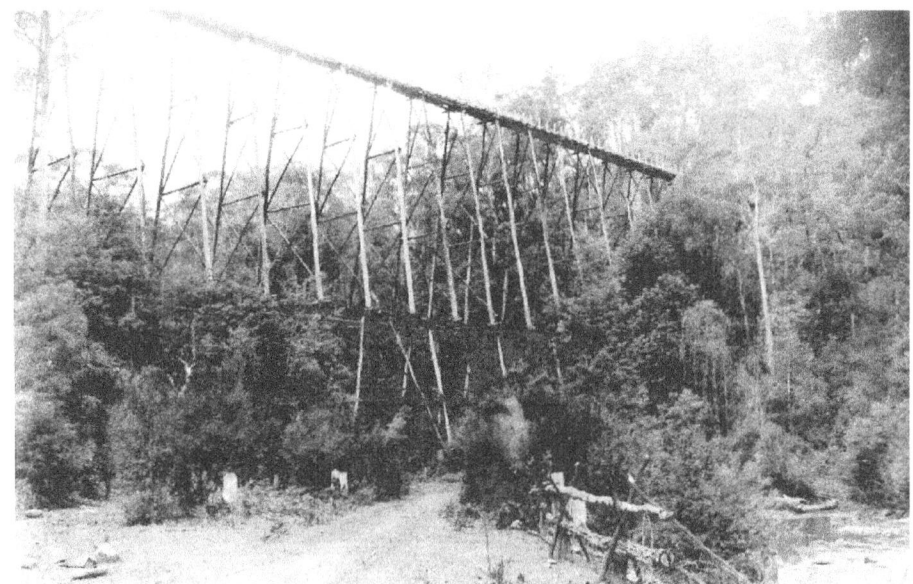

Fig. 9. 'Mammoth Flume, Lightning Creek', c.1905. (Courtesy of Jim Nicholas)

---

75 Ibid., p. 41.

76 *Australasian*, 19 November 1904 & 17 December 1905. The caption in the *Australasian* is 'On the Banks of the Mitta'. The other prize winning photograph, 'While the Sun Shines', is in an album presented to LL Pitts by JP Campbell and now held by the National Gallery of Australia. Campbell received £2 for each photograph. Both were entered under the name 'JP Campbell, Commercial Travellers' Club'. In the same competition he also received honorable mentions in Class 4, Station or Township Life, and Class 5, Flower Subject, showing his versatility. His only other prize winning effort in the *Australasian* came in August 1909 when he came second in the Landscape Class with 'Winter', the study of a tree bent with the weight of snow in the Omeo area (described later in this chapter).

77 *Across the Alps to Omeo*, pp. 46-7. I have used a sharper, clearer identical image, courtesy of Jim Nicholas, for illustration purposes here because the *Across the Alps to Omeo* booklet image is not clear enough to be reproduced.

78 Ibid., p. 47.

'Near Tallandoon' is of interest as it shows what is probably Campbell's bicycle lying in the right hand corner, advertising his means of transport. It is, in a sense, a 'self portrait'. The photo reveals a wide, open bend in a creek framed by a large double-leader tree bole to the left, with a house up on the creek bank above it to the right, a beautifully balanced scene. (Fig. 10).[79]

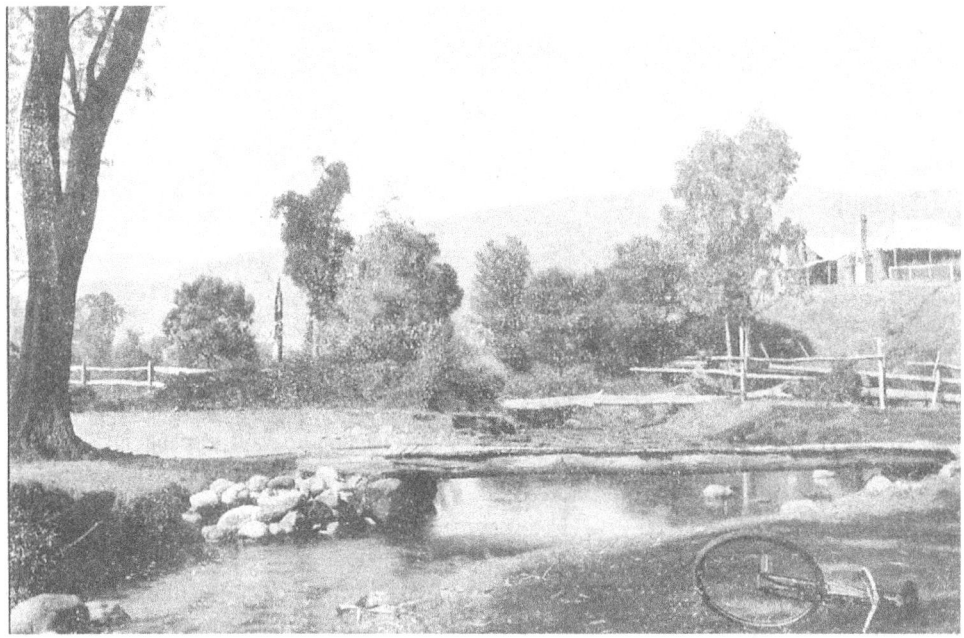

Fig. 10. 'Near Tallandoon'. Note the bicycle in bottom right hand corner.
(Courtesy of Gary Harding)

The 'Tallangatta-Glen Wills Coach' (Fig.11) also has pictorial elements.[80] It is an absorbing image because of the contrasting shade and light, the tree as a dividing and framing device, the lurching, splashing horse and coach, and the sweeping line of hills. Collectively the Campbell photographs in *Across the Alps to Omeo* are representative of the clear, sharp, technically correct images of the 'straight' Australian School of Photographers. There are no blurred, 'fuzzy' images created by manipulation of the lens or in the developing process – any atmospheric effects in Campbell's work are provided naturally by smoke, fog, dust or splashing water.

---

79 Ibid., p. 51.

80 *Across the Alps to Omeo*, p. 54, and the late Frank Pitts' collection. Many of the Campbell images in *Across the Alps to Omeo* were released as coloured postcards and are held by the State Library of Victoria.

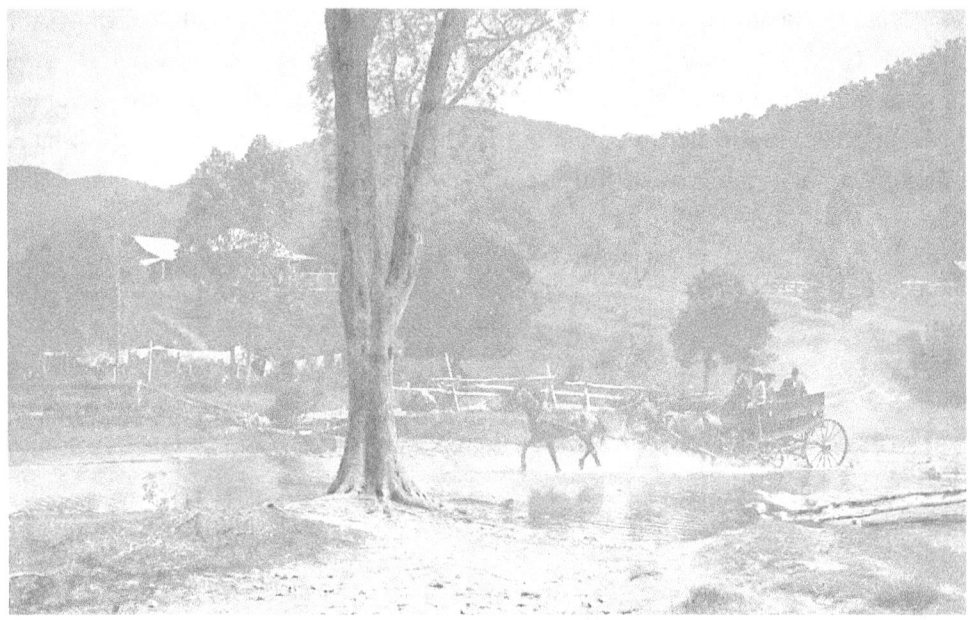

Fig. 11. Postcard 'The Mitta Valley', c 1905. This photograph appears in
Across the Alps to Omeo as 'Tallangatta-Glen Wills Coach'. (Courtesy of Frank Pitts)

Complementing Campbell's *Across the Alps to Omeo* images is a series of
cards of the Omeo district, produced around 1907, demonstrating Campbell's
decorative skills and his dedication to detail and presentation. The cards, on rather
thick cardboard and exemplifying his artistic ability, were probably produced as
gifts for people (Figures 12 & 13).

As with the Omeo region, Campbell's association with the Upper Murray
began as a result of his work as a traveller with Henry Berry and Co. By 1905
he had established a close relationship with John Bramley and Clara Coghill of
the Walwa/Corryong district, taking their wedding photographs at Berringama
near Corryong that year. He was close to this family for many years; they called
him 'Kam', and the children knew him as Uncle Jim. He took a series of family
photographs as well as views of the Walwa and Guy's Forest area. The Bramleys
moved to Walwa homestead close to the Murray River near Walwa after their
marriage; their homestead appears to have served as a base for Campbell in the

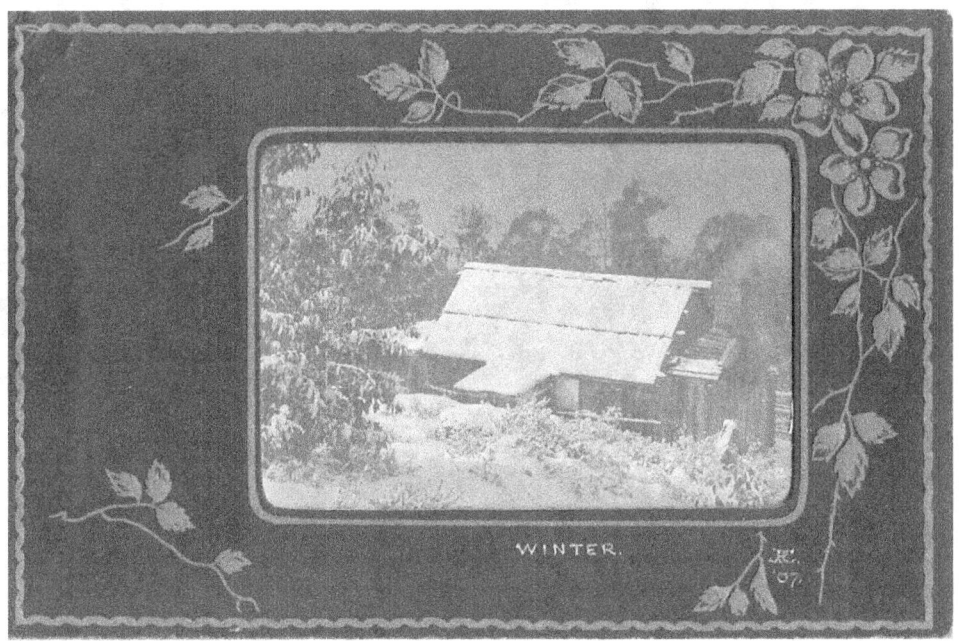

Fig. 12. 'Winter'. Mt Wills, 1907. (Courtesy of Falconer collection)

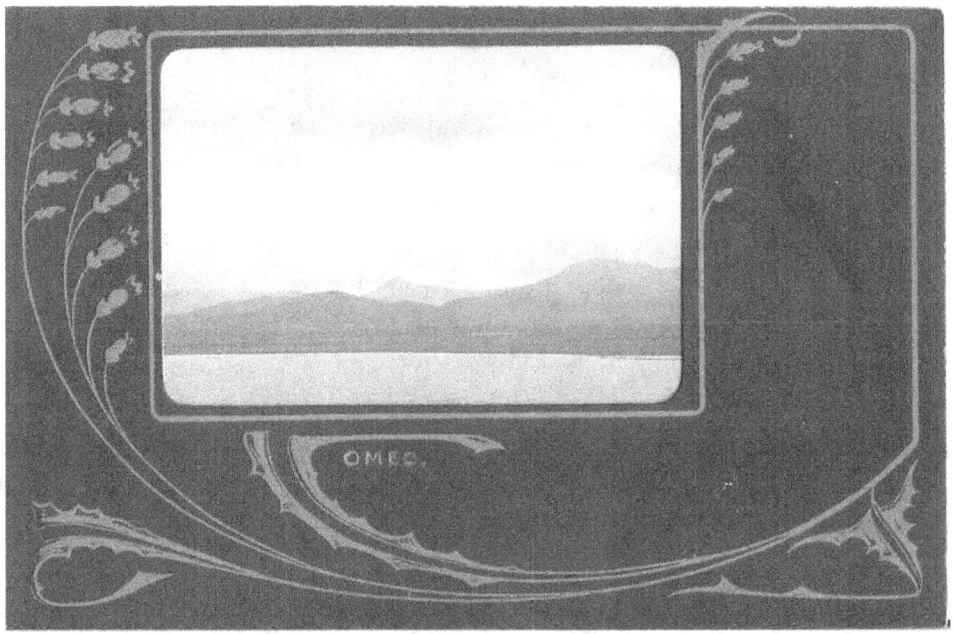

Fig. 13. 'Omeo', c.1907. A thick, decorative card simply titled.
(Courtesy of Falconer collection)

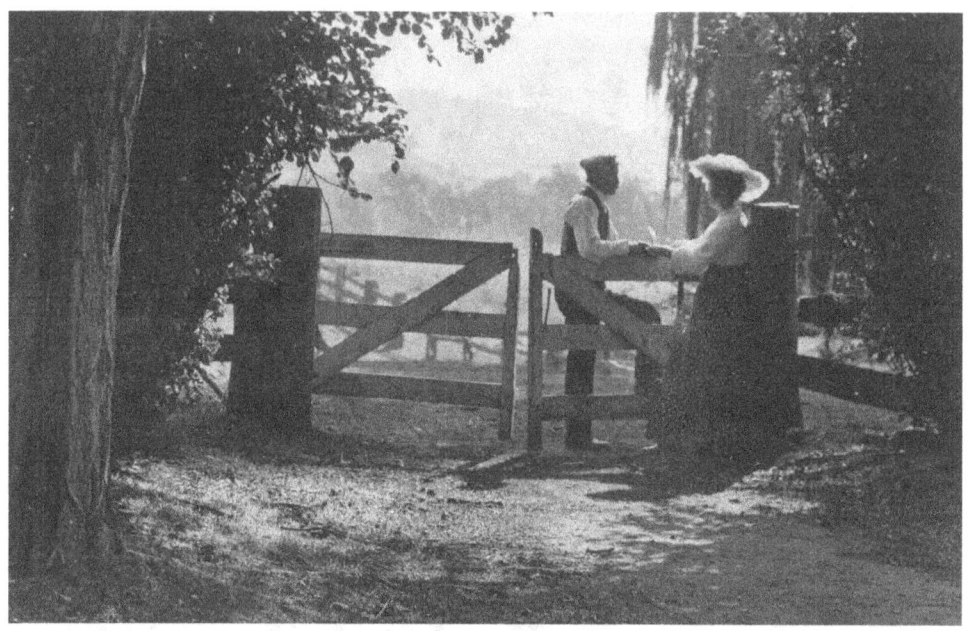

Fig.14. 'What tales the moon could tell!'
Campbell's friends the Bramleys at Walwa Station, c.1905.
(Courtesy of Australian National Gallery)

district up to his enlistment in 1914.[81] He took a rather romantic photograph of
the couple near Walwa homestead (Fig. 14).

European settlement of the Upper Murray dates from 1837 when the Tintaldra
squatting run was taken up on the Murray River, followed by the Corryong run
in 1838. Other runs were soon occupied, including Berringama and Walwa.[82]
Campbell was to photograph all these areas some sixty-five to seventy years later
when the inevitable scars of activities, such as farming and mining, were only too
apparent. The town of Corryong was about twenty-five years old when Campbell
first saw it.[83] Situated close to the Murray River and at the base of the Australian
Alps, it was a beautiful spot that appealed to Campbell's need to photograph
grand, picturesque landscapes. Fortunately a number of these early images of
Omeo and the Upper Murray districts, taken before he became a professional
photographer in 1909, have survived.

81 Conversations with Marjorie Mossop (nee Bramley), 15 December 2003, 28 December 2003 and 22
January 2004, and with Jack Bramley, 30 December 2003. Also Susie Zada, *Memories of the Bramley
& Coghill Families*, 1994.
82 Jean Carmody, *Early Days of the Upper Murray*, Shoestring Press, Wangaratta, 1981, p. 3.
83 Ibid., p. 63.

Some of the same Omeo and Upper Murray images published in *Across the Alps to Omeo* and the *Australasian*, also appeared in a 26-leaf album of Campbell's photographs now held by the National Gallery of Australia.[84] The album contains 45 photographs in print and postcard form. It may have been compiled by Lilian Pitts of Merrigum, the original owner of the album and a photographer friend of Campbell's as he gave her prints of his photographs and sent her postcards. Or it may have been initially assembled by Campbell and then given to Lilian who added to it.[85]

This album is significant as it is a representative sample of Campbell's early pictorial work. Most of the photographs are north-eastern landscapes, but there are also eight coastal images. One of these, an evening seascape with no caption, is an atmospheric picture with haunting, contrasting dark and light. This image has been designated by the National Gallery of Australia as having 'Archival Permanence' and was included in a travelling exhibition in 1996-7 called 'Time and Timelessness in 100 Years of Australian Photography'.[86] Trees are the subject in eight photographs in the album, for example a tree on the side of a snow-covered hill sweeping in an arc in the middle of the picture and silhouetted against the sky, its foliage weighed down with snow, with snow-covered hills. The image is beautifully balanced but has the rather sentimental caption: 'Burdened with its weight of Purity'. Twelve of the photographs in the album include people. One is a self portrait of Campbell at his working table, a postcard sent to Lilian Pitts with 'Very Busy! but not chasing a dish of Jelly' written on the back (Fig 15).[87]

There are also genre photographs, images of children involved in various forms of activity, popular in the early twentieth century.[88] One three-image narrative

84 "Untitled album", Campbell, J.P., Accession Number 83.1372.1-24, NGA IRN 91540, National Gallery of Australia. This album was donated to the National Gallery of Australia by Mrs AC (Nance) Tyson in 1983. All the photographs in the album were taken before the First World War.

85 The evidence for Lilian Pitts compiling the album from photographs given to her by Campbell, or adding to an album partially compiled by him, is the inclusion of postcards sent to Lilian by Campbell.

86 National Gallery of Australia, 83.1372.17, "evening seascape", Campbell, J.P., viewed 2004. <http://cms.nga.gov.au/web/pages/nga/Display.php?irn=7103&QueryPage=%2Fpages%...>

87 Campbell is wearing leggings for bicycle riding. The postcard(s) leaning against the table leg also appear in the National Gallery of Australia album with the caption 'On The Hill. Corryong'. A detail of this portrait of Campbell appeared in the photography journal *The Camera House Beacon*, 25 November 1909, part of the biographical background on Campbell's contribution to the Dresden International Exhibition of Photography. Of the eleven mini portraits of the Dresden exhibitors Campbell's is the only one actively doing something, reflecting his manic energy. The rest are austere bust portraits of men gazing to the side or glaring solemnly at the camera.

88 Francis Ebury, 'Making Pictures', pp. 43-5

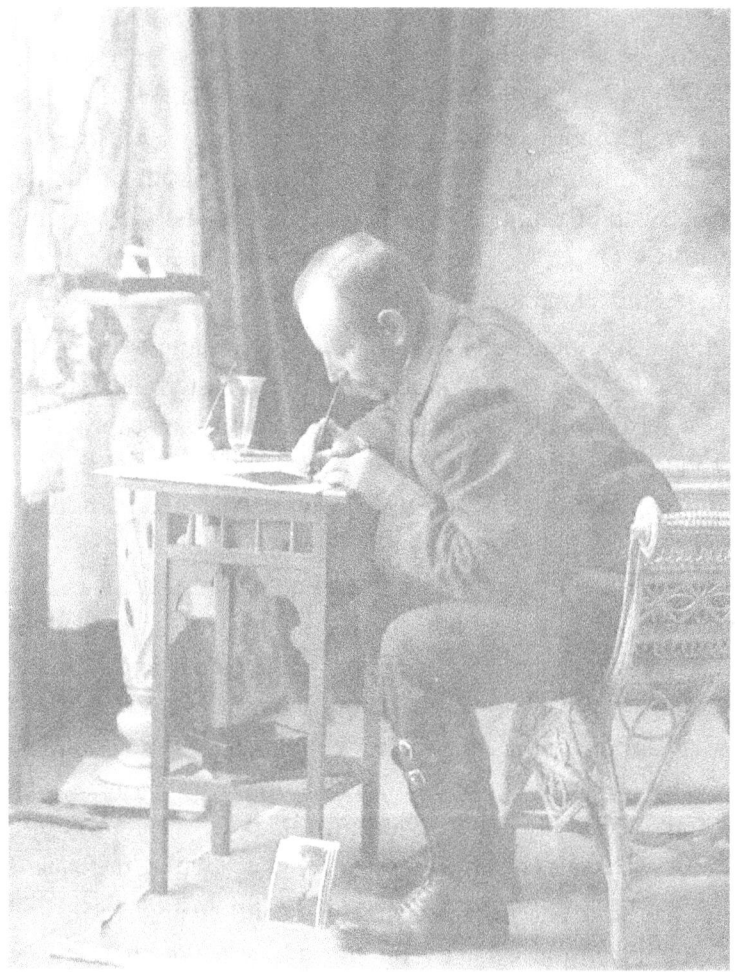

Fig. 15. JP Campbell working at a table, c.1909.
(Courtesy of Falconer collection) Photographer unknown.

is of a little boy, a nephew of JP Campbell, playing beside a creek. In the first he is playing in the sand, 'His First Sand Patch'. In the second he throws sand into the water, 'Splish', and in the third he is looking cheekily at the camera, 'He! He! He! I'nt it Funny Unkajim!' Other genre pictures in the National Gallery of Australia album involve the Trimble family of Nambrok in central Gippsland. When Campbell's sister, Frances, married Joseph Trimble they settled on a farm at Nambrok, south of Heyfield. Two images show Campbell's nieces and nephews having what looks like an outdoor bath in a copper boiler filled with well water by their mother, Frances. Their clothes are strewn on bushes in the background.

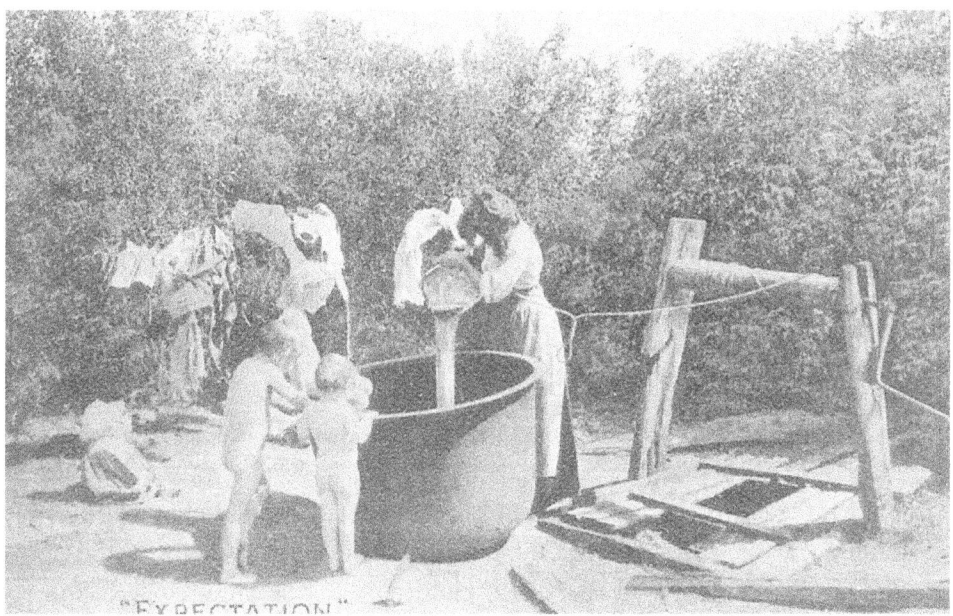

Fig. 16. 'Expectation'. An example of narrative photography. Postcard version of the first of two images of JP Campbell's sister Frances and her children on a farm in Nambrok, central Gippsland, c1905. (Courtesy of Falconer collection)

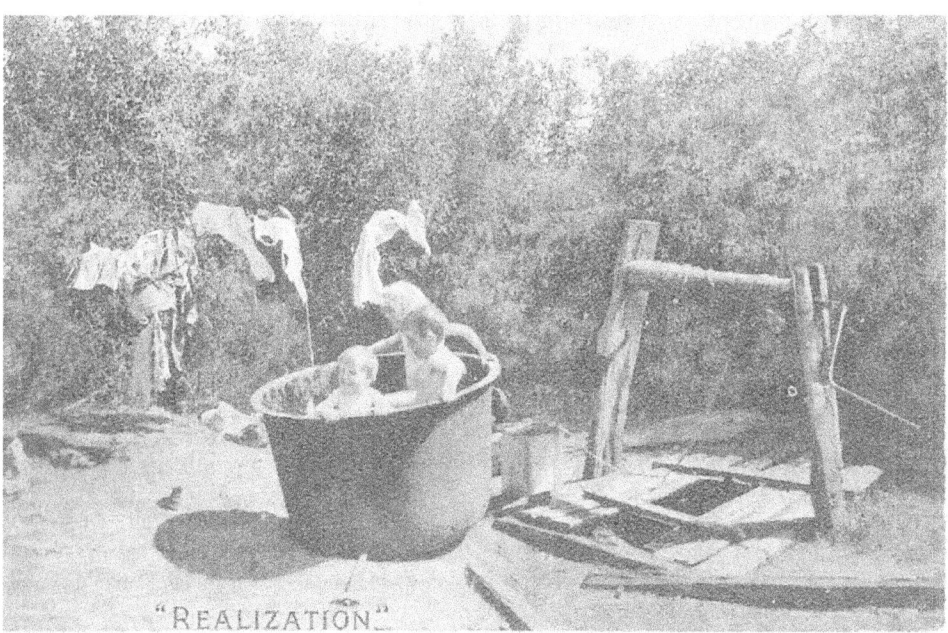

Fig. 17. 'Realization'. The second of two images in the Trimble family Nambrok bathing narrative by JP Campbell. (Courtesy of Falconer collection)

37

The first image of the boiler being filled while the children wait impatiently is called 'Filling the Boiler', or, in other prints produced as commercial postcards, 'Expectation' (Fig. 16). The second, with the three children in the boiler, is called 'The Boilerfull' or 'Realisation' (Fig. 17). 'Filling the Boiler' was reproduced in *Pioneer of the Bush and Outback* by Jennifer Isaacs, published in 1998, and interpreted as children about to have their weekly bath, It was included in a chapter on housekeeping under the sub-title 'Carting water and washing'.[89] The idea was to show the difficulties faced in performing these tasks in the isolation of the bush, particularly with a scarcity of water.

Campbell's granddaughter, Noel Fethers, believes these two images wrongfully depicted the Trimble family as poor. Citing the clear memory of her elderly mother Ada, Noel stated that 'Joseph Trimble was a prosperous landholder, the family house very comfortable and very well equipped [meaning the children washed indoors, not out]. There was a holiday house at Seaspray and the family were early owners of a motor car'.[90] The children were merely playing and cooling down on a hot summer's day in 1905, a popular pastime in the hot weather, and observed by their uncle with his camera. The clothes were not washing hanging out to dry, but stripped off quickly in anticipation of play. Thus the photograph 'had nothing to do with hardship in the bush as suggested by J. Isaac's book'.[91] This shows how easily a photograph can be misinterpreted when taken out of context.

How does this album reflect Campbell the person? It reveals his physicality, his ability to put himself in a position to take photographs in isolated places. As Francis Ebury points out, successful outdoor photography entailed considerable time, effort and sometimes danger.[92] He exposed his playful side in his family images, as opposed to the serious, fastidious photographer. His love of landscape is also displayed as almost a pristine entity, devoid of the dark side of the bush, like fire, flood and human suffering on the land. In this respect he conformed with other pictorialists of the time.[93] Campbell's love of family is displayed in the National Gallery of Australia album with the two narrative works on his

---

89 Jennifer Isaacs, *Pioneer Women of the Bush and Outback*, Lansdowne, Sydney, 2nd Edition 1998, p. 50.

90 Letter, Noel Fethers to Gael Newton, Acting Curator of Photography, Australian National Gallery, 19 August 1992. Copy of letter courtesy of Noel Fethers.

91 Ibid.

92 Francis Ebury 'Making Pictures', p. 202.

93 See discussion on the Kyabram series of postcards in chapter three.

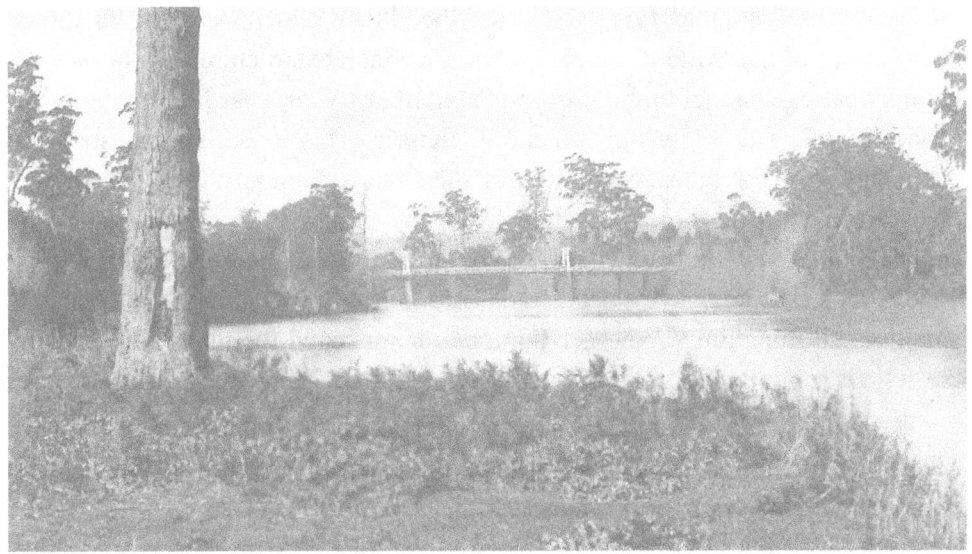

Fig. 18. Postcard: 'Snowy River and Bridge. Orbost'. This beautifully balanced
image is one of nine of Campbell's which appeared in the *Australasian* in late 1906.
(Courtesy of Falconer collection)

nieces and nephews. The album as a whole displayed Campbell's best amateur
photography prior to his employment with Vallan Studio. It reflected his technical
training in photography at the Working Men's College, and particularly the
pictorialist influence of the Australian School of Photographers. He also used
these skills for commercial and later documentary photography.

Campbell continued to submit photographs to the weekly pictorial newspapers.
Three sets of images with associated text published by the *Australasian* were
probably commissioned. The first of these incorporates two photographs taken
in 1905 of the new manse at the Church of England in Ferntree Gully with
descriptive text. It is a strange departure from Campbell's normal work as a
landscape photographer.[94] The second set was of nine photographs of Orbost and
district in 1906, with a lively, descriptive text directed at prospective tourists and
settlers (Fig. 18).[95] His forays into East Gippsland included at least two visits
in 1907 to Buchan, already attracting tourists to its famed caves. However, no
Campbell photographs of the Buchan caves have been found.[96]

---

94 *Australasian*, 14 October 1905, p. 927.

95 *Australasian*, 29 December 1906, p. 1535.

96 Brian Hansford, *Always Believe Your Grandfather*, Post Pressed, Teneriffe, Queensland, 2008,
pp. 44, 62 & 74.

The third set of photographs were published in the *Australasian* in 1907, three photographs of the 'Muddy Creek Syphon', a concrete structure built to take the main irrigation channel running from the Goulburn Weir, near Nagambie, under Muddy Creek near Moorilim in central Victoria. This irrigation infrastructure was significant for the development of the State's economy. The siphon was constructed by the Monier Concrete Company run by engineer and part-time soldier John Monash, a man who was to be significant in Campbell's working life in the 1920s. The text gave a detailed description and explanation of the siphon's structure and function.[97] Whether Campbell contributed the text is unclear, but the style is reminiscent of his writing style in later articles.

In August 1904 Campbell gave an illustrated lecture at the Longwarry Mechanics Institute in west Gippsland. Shopkeeper Herbert Vallance, local photographer and operator of the Longwarry Photo Studio, had arranged for his fellow photographer to give a 'show', with the proceeds going to the Mechanics Institute. With Vallance's assistance Campbell showed lantern slides of Australian scenery, with his own narration. He concluded his lecture with his own verse describing the bush, which, according to the local newspaper, he had 'splendidly illustrated' with pen drawings.[98] Campbell was displaying his talent for drawing in his young days at Seaton. Three years later he was still putting on fund-raising shows, on this occasion at the Tinamba public hall in central Gippsland. Promoted as 'The Popular Entertainer (By Special Request)' he showed 'Over 200 Lantern and Bioscope Views, full of Funny Incidents [and] Interesting Descriptions'.[99]

From 1906 Herbert Vallance, who became a life-long friend of Campbell, published photographs in the *Australasian* and *Leader* newspapers, mainly views of agricultural shows and forestry activities. Campbell and Vallance had two things in common: a passion for photography and a belief in private enterprise. In combination these drives determined their future as professional photographers.

---

97 *Australasian* , 3 August 1907, p. 287.

98 *Gippsland Independent*, 1 September 1904 and Sandy Barrie *Australians Behind the Camera: Directory of Early Australian Photographers 1841 to 1945*, Published by the Author, 2002, p. 192.

99 *Maffra Spectator*, 29 April 1907.

3

VALLAN STUDIO

Vallan Studio, Mansfield – The Upper Murray – Lilian Louisa Pitts –
Professional Rural Photographer – The Pictorial Weekly Newspapers

In October 1907 Herbert Vallance, JP Campbell and a friend, Thomas Bergin, went on a bicycle tour across the Victorian Alps via Dargo and Grant to Bright.[1] Seven of the photographs they took were published in a two page spread in the *Australasian*. There were sweeping views of a snow covered landscape and scenes of the cyclists pushing their bicycles through the snow.[2] It must have been an arduous, physically demanding journey, but it may have been on this trip that they decided to open a photography studio near the Victorian Alps. A few months later Herbert Vallance left Longwarry with his family, moved to Mansfield in north-east Victoria, and opened his newly built premises near the Mansfield railway station in November 1908, calling it Vallan Studio, with Campbell joining him as a partner in 1909, a momentous year for Campbell.[3] He resigned from his sales position with Henry Berry and Co. midyear, receiving 'handsome trophies and expressions of good will from the salesroom staff and lady employees of the house', indicating he had done his job well despite the distraction of photography.[4]

In 1909 the Victorian Photographic Affiliation had eight photographs accepted at the International Exhibition in Dresden, Germany, held to celebrate the seventieth birthday of photography. These photographs were drawn from affiliated clubs, one of which was the Working Men's College Photographic Club.

---

1 *Argus*, 7 October 1907 and *Australasian*, 21 December 1907.

2 *Australasian*, 21 December 1907. They started in Traralgon astride 'variable-speed and rim-braked machines', each carrying 'a 50 lb. "bluey"', and rode north through Toongabbie, Cowwarr, Heyfield, Maffra, Boisdale, Briagolong and into the hills to Dargo. Snow was first encountered on the edge of the High Plains at Lankey's Pinch. They arranged for a 'huge bonfire [to be] kindled' to guide them to St. Bernard Hospice, situated on the northern slopes of Mount Saint Bernard, where they stayed before descending to Harrietville and Bright.

3 *Gippsland Independent*, 10 September 1908, and *Mansfield Courier*, 24 October 1908 and 19 December 1908.

4 *Camera House Beacon*, Vol. 3, No. 11, 25 November 1909, pp. 262-3.

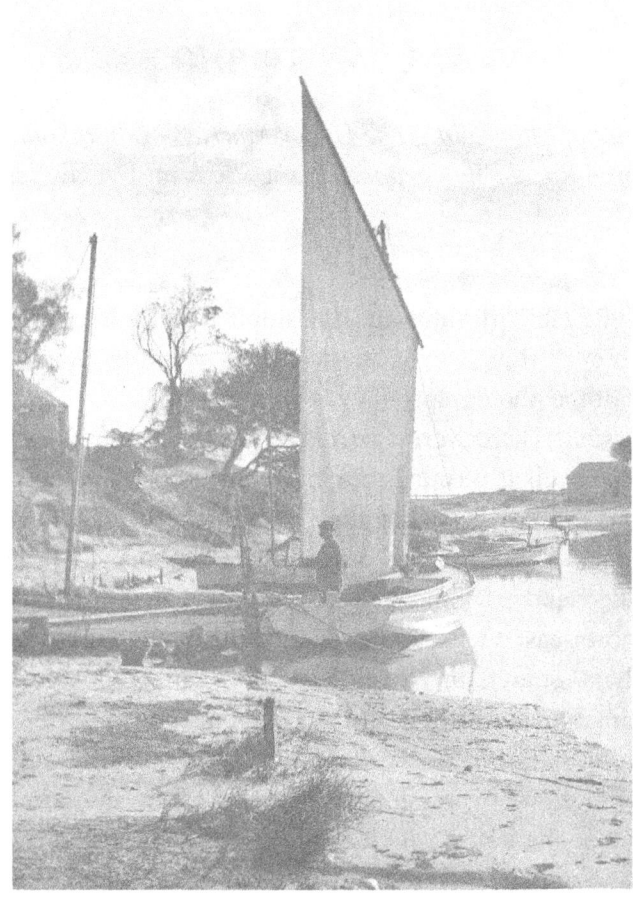

Fig. 19. 'Fisherman's Nook', c 1908, JP Campbell's entry in the Dresden Exhibition
(Courtesy of Australian National Gallery,
see also *The Camera House Beacon*, 25 November 1909, p. 257)

Both AJ and JP Campbell had photographs selected for exhibition. JP Campbell's contribution was the 'Fisherman's Nook' (Fig. 19).

It was a very competitive event, so the Campbells had done well to be exhibited. The *Camera House Beacon* published brief observations on Campbell, revealing how he was viewed by his contemporaries. Known simply as 'JP' by his college mates, he was regarded as a 'good sort', never suffering from a 'swelled head', nor did he brag about his work to the disadvantage of his competitors.[5] Another of his achievements at this time was coming second in the landscape section of a

---

5 Ibid, p. 243, and Vol. 3, No. 8, 25 August 1909, pp. 171-2.

competition held by the *Australasian* in mid 1909. The *Australian Photographic Journal*, reporting on this achievement, described him as 'the energetic J.P. Campbell', a fitting description of his physicality and lifestyle.[6] He carried this energy with him when he joined his friend Herbert Vallance at Vallan Studio in September 1909, primarily as the 'outdoor' photographer, buoyed by his success at being exhibited at Dresden. He was now a professional photographer and a partner in a growing business.[7]

Sadly, in November of that year his father died, another emotional event in a year of change for Campbell. He most likely saw the Vallan Studio venture as a money-making enterprise, freeing him from the tedium of sales work. Vallance had capital from his Longwarry business to start afresh in Mansfield, a district at the foot of the mountains well suited to a photographic enterprise.[8] Campbell would do the bulk of the landscape photography on his bicycle, Vallance the bulk of the indoor portrait work. According to his granddaughter, Campbell never liked indoor work and did little portraiture.[9] Vallance was the younger man by about six years, thirty-eight to Campbell's forty-four, but Campbell's energy knew no bounds. Vallance and Campbell shared another interest: they attended the Mansfield Masonic Lodge together. Campbell had joined the Masons in Melbourne in 1902 – the organization was to remain important to him until his death.[10]

There was an element of financial risk for both men in forming a business partnership. Campbell had the bigger family, but with his wife and children in Malvern, the youngest thirteen years of age, and a financial cushion provided by Elizabeth's inherited money, he was free to take the risk. Just how much capital

---

6 *The Australian Photographic Journal*, 22 September 1909, p. 285.

7 Letter, JP Campbell to Department of External Affairs, 2 October 1911, in 'JP Campbell – Commonwealth Photographer', Item 16281, National Archives of Australia; Appearance Book, Mansfield Masonic Lodge No. 158; and *The Australasian Photo-Review*, 22 January 1912, p. 45.

8 Vallance was in partnership with a Mr Edney in the Longwarry store, and was able to sell his interest in the business, thus financing his new venture. *Gippsland Independent*, 10 September 1908.

9 Interview with Noel Fethers, 20 April 2005.

10 Vallance proposed Campbell as a member in November 1910. After a character check he was accepted into the Mansfield Lodge in December 1910 after having been classed as a visiting member from Kent Masonic Lodge, Melbourne (where he had been initiated in May 1902), since October 1909. Minute Book entries for 27 October 1909, 16 November 1910 and 14 December 1910, Mansfield Masonic Lodge No. 158. Also, JP Campbell's 'United Grand Lodge' book, courtesy of Noel Fethers. Campbell's initial attendance as a visitor at the Mansfield Lodge confirms his commencement with Vallan Studio in 1909.

each man put into the new venture is unknown – Campbell may have had only his expertise in landscape photography to offer. It is also possible that his marriage was under strain, and his new job was a means of being closer to his family than his previous occupation had allowed, but far enough away to give him space.

By the time Vallance and Campbell arrived in Mansfield it was a thriving town serving the surrounding farming community. The township, surveyed in the 1850s, was at the base of Mt Battery between the Broken and Delatite Rivers. Importantly for Vallance and Campbell, it was 'a beautiful setting: a sheltered valley surrounded by hills with in the distance the mountains, snow covered in winter – Buller, Howitt, Skene, Feathertop, part of the chain of the Australian Alps'.[11] Campbell designed a Vallan Studio business 'card' featuring district scenes and a portrait of one of his daughters, Ada, then sixteen years of age, covered in what looks like snow, but which was actually cotton wool (Fig 20).[12] Campbell was close to his children, particularly Ada, who had left school because of ill health in 1907, and thereafter spent a lot of time with her father, before obtaining full time employment in 1913. She accompanied her father on many photography trips.[13]

Vallance promoted the scenic nature of the Mansfield district in his Vallan Studio advertisements, asking the public to come to the studio for 'views of the beauty spots'.[14] He offered 'all kinds of photography' in his new 'spacious and well lighted studio'.[15] Vallance threw himself into Mansfield affairs, being a member of the Progress Association, treasurer of the Manchester Unity Independent Order of Oddfellows, and secretary of both the Church of England management committee and the Mansfield Hospital Board.

In contrast Campbell's name does not appear on any list of people attending meetings, nor on committee member lists, in line with his transient nature. He did attend St Andrew's Presbyterian Church and the Masonic Lodge, displaying a lifelong commitment to conservative values. Caught between Mansfield, Malvern and the roaming demands of his work, Campbell was obviously too busy to put down roots in Mansfield. He would ride from Mansfield to Malvern

---

11 Joan Gillison, *Colonial Doctor and his Town*, Cypress Books, Melbourne, 1974, pp. 24-9.
12 Interview with Noel Fethers, 20 April 2005. Although serving the same purpose as a modern business card it actually consisted of flimsy paper.
13 Ibid.
14 *Mansfield Courier*, 13 October 1909.
15 *Mansfield Courier*, 11 August 1909.

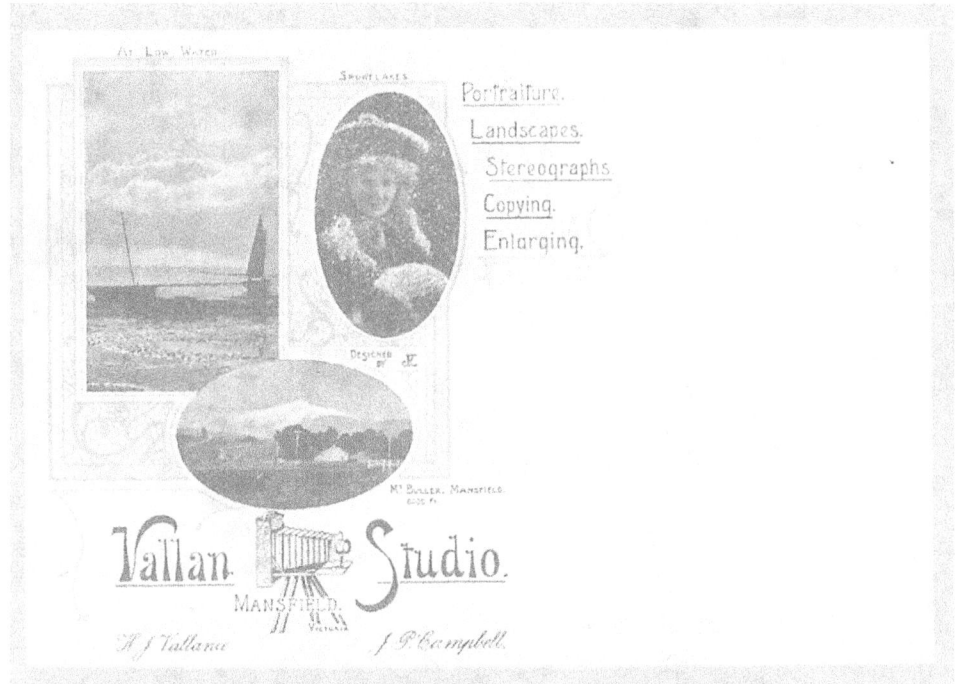

Fig. 20. The Vallan Studio business 'card' designed by JP Campbell.
(Courtesy of Falconer collection) Photograph by the author.

on his bicycle. In March 1910 he told Lilian Pitts that he had 'attended a picnic [near Mansfield] per bike and camera yesterday – Roads gorgeous in dust – think I'll wait for some rain to lay it before tackling the ride city-wards'.[16]

His out-of-doors work for Vallan Studio involved views for postcards, the communication fad gripping the nation at the time. Postcard enthusiast David Cook claims that every facet of life was captured on the postcard, 'from the lawn at Flemington on Melbourne Cup day to the slab hut on a new selection in the bush'.[17] Picture postcards filled a need for fast communication. They were cheap to buy and post. For people who did not travel, they provided images of a world beyond, and for those who did, they were cheap 'convenient souvenirs of places visited and remembered'. They crossed class barriers, as there was no need for refined literary skills in filling in the limited space on the back of a postcard. Postal reforms, mass printing techniques, increased leisure time, and

---

16 JP Campbell, postcard to LL Pitts, 29 March 1910.
17 David Cook, *Picture Postcards in Australia 1898-1920*, Pioneer Design Studio, Lilydale, 1986, p. 10.

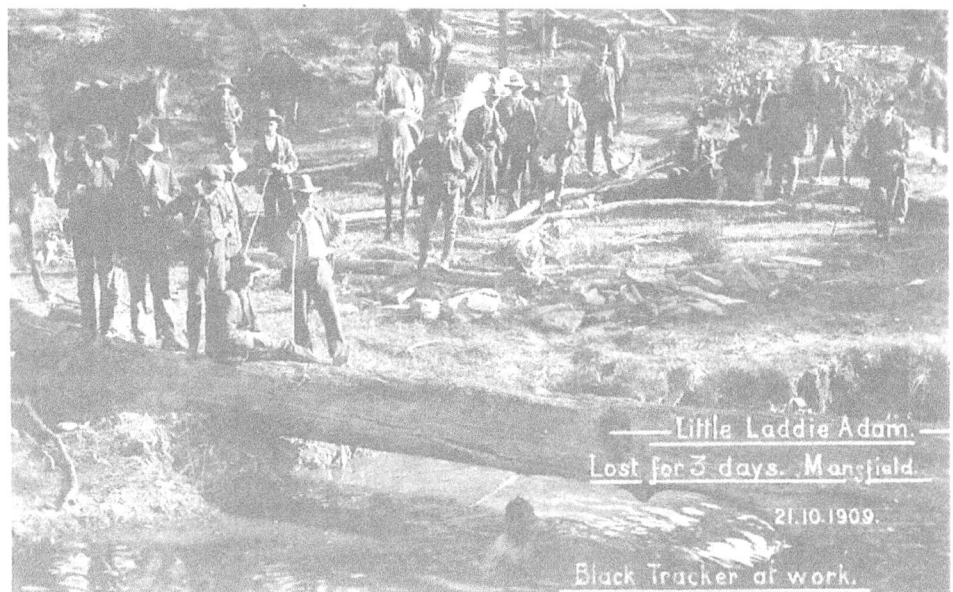

Fig. 21. Postcard. Searching for 'Little Laddie Adam' in a waterhole.
Note the figure in the water under the log.
(Courtesy of Mansfield Historical Society)

an expanding public transport system all contributed to the rise of the postcard.[18] Indeed the creators of postcards 'crawled into every nook and cranny of society for a new angle on life' and they remained popular until about 1910 when their use gradually began to decline, picking up again briefly during World War One, but fading away after the war as the telephone became the medium for short, immediate messages.[19]

Vallan Studio did not limit itself to producing pretty views, becoming involved in documentary photography, that is, taking images with content instructive to the viewer, pictures conveying information on aspects of society.[20] Visiting dignitaries and local dramas were common subjects in Vallan Studio postcards. When a little boy became lost in the bush in late 1909 Campbell was there to photograph one of the search parties about to set off, with co-opted 'black'

18 Ibid., p. 13.

19 Ibid., p. 16.

20 Documentary photography was 'invented' in the mid 1930s where it was used to record the lives of poverty-stricken rural Americans. Arthur Rothstein, *Documentary Photography*, Focal Press, Boston, 1986, pp. 1-3.

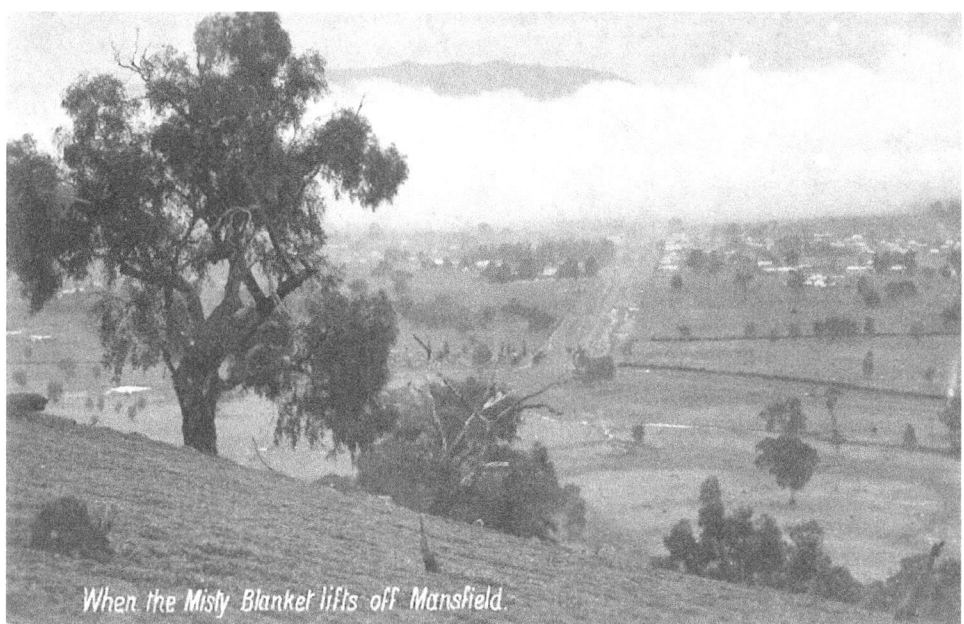

Fig. 22. 'When the Misty Blanket lifts off Mansfield'. A Vallan Studio Photo Card, Mansfield, c.1909. (Author's collection)

trackers from Dandenong as part of the contingent. He took a documentary photograph of searchers watching on as a black tracker looked for the missing boy in a waterhole (Fig. 21).[21]

Campbell and Vallance photographed buildings and institutions, streetscapes, monuments, citizens and sporting activities in Mansfield and district. Campbell, in particular, took photographs of the town from elevated points around it, using his pictoralist skills, for example 'When the Misty Blanket lifts off Mansfield', showing a mass of fog floating above the town and gradually exposing it (Fig. 22). Landscape photographs of local rivers like the Delatite, and images of the mountains, particularly views of a snow-capped Mount Buller, were popular. Campbell went further afield in order to produce marketable postcards. One of these places was the Upper Murray River district to the north of Mansfield, a place he knew well from his travelling salesman days.

Campbell kept in contact with the Bramley family of Walwa and often stayed with them, using Upper Murray photographs to produce postcards for the Vallan

21 *Mansfield Courier*, 27 October 1909, and the 'Little Laddie Adam' series of postcards held by the Mansfield Historical Society. The boy, Frank Adam, was found 'safe and well'.

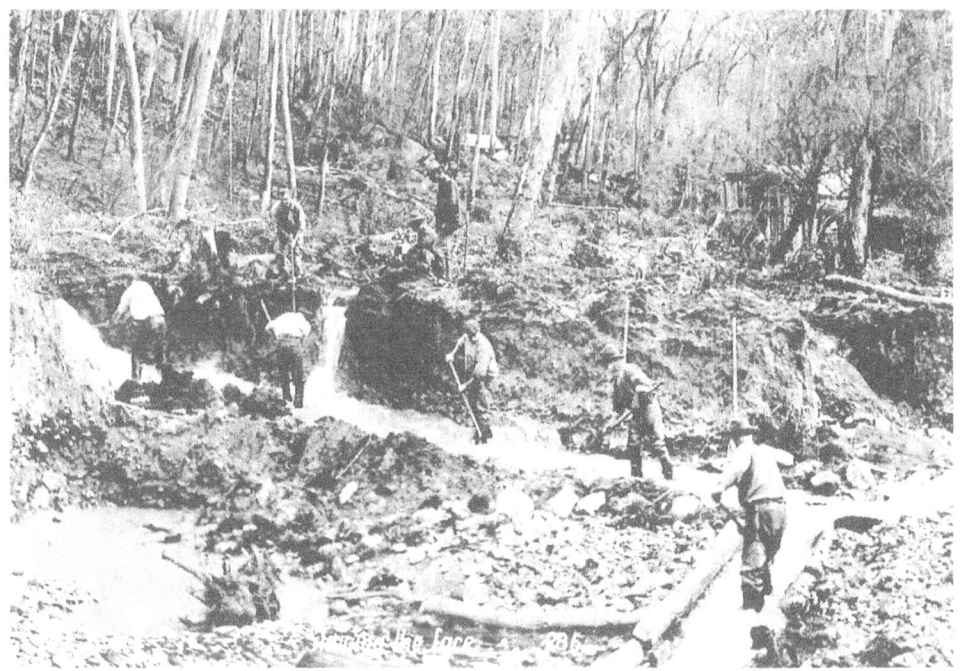

Fig. 23. 'Sluicing the face', c.1910. Tin miners at work, Surveyor's Creek.
(Courtesy of Jim Nicholas)

Studio business. Many of Campbell's postcards can be found today, held by postcard dealers, collectors and archival institutions. He established a business relationship with the Corryong shopkeeper Arnold Playle who acted as an agent for Campbell's photographic work.[22] These Upper Murray images are more abundant than Campbell's earlier work, and as a result are over-represented in the sample of his Upper Murray work I have compiled.

Although landscape scenes predominated among Campbell's Upper Murray images, he did take photographs of various rural industries, including tin mining. Tin mining first began in the district in the early 1880s at Mt Alfred, Koetong and Walwa, its intensity regulated by the fluctuating tin market. It gathered pace again at Koetong in 1905, then a few years later attention turned to Surveyor's Creek south of Corryong.[23] It was there that Campbell took a series of photographs

22 Arnold Playle (1857-1941), a newsagent, watchmaker and jeweller, as well as an amateur photographer, had established himself in Corryong in 1883. Jean Carmody, *Early Days of the Upper Murray*, pp. 63-4, and the *Corryong Courier*, 18 March 1914.

23 Robyn Annear, *Historic Mining Sites Assessment Project*, Department of Conservation and Natural Resources, August 1994.

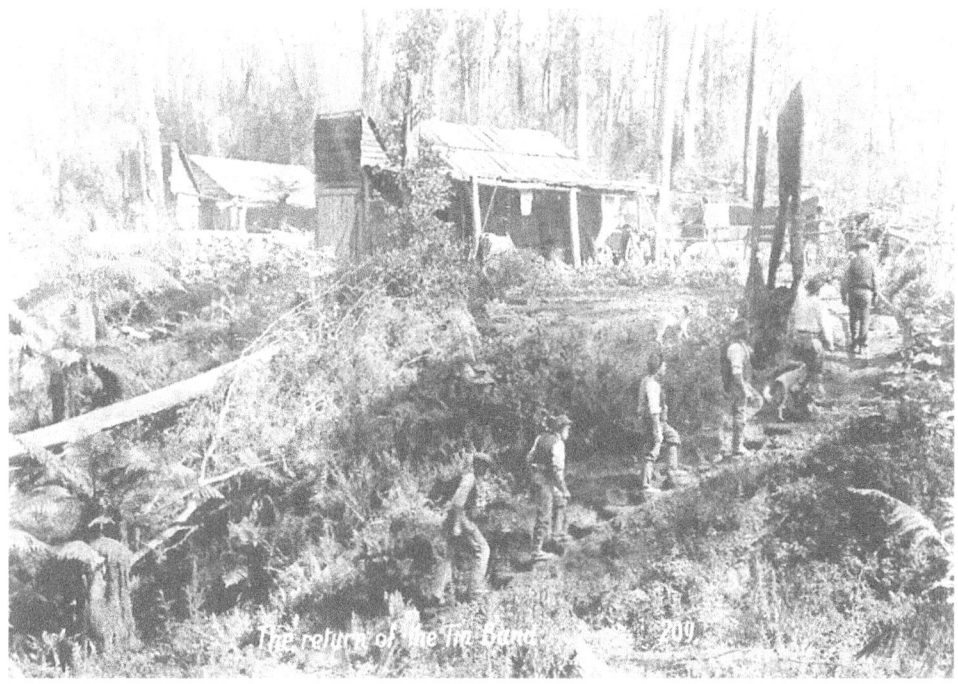

Fig. 24. 'The return of the Tin Band', c.1910. (Courtesy of Jim Nicholas)

of the Australian Tin Mining Co. employees working the company's claim, and the site itself. The photographs are numbered, starting at 201 through to approximately 215, with some in the series missing. The images shown here are 'Sluicing the face' (Fig. 23), 'The Return of the Tin Band' (Fig. 24) and 'The Bushman's friend – Roofing Bark' (Fig. 25).[24]

They are all clear, sharp images. The first two show the dependence of the mining industry on hard, manual work. The last two were contrived as Campbell stood by with his camera mounted and ready. In the second the miners return to their huts, trudging wearily up the steps in the hillside. The site is scarred by clearing but the remnants of tree ferns can be seen, and the structure of the huts is wonderfully clear. The bush stands silently in the background.

Isolation, rough conditions and hard physical work are prominent in the photographs. In 'The Bushman's friend' two men balance on a log, pipes in mouth, a sheet of bark curved over their backs. They are using the plentiful

---

24 These images were printed from the original glass plates and then the computer program Photoshop was used to 'enhance' them further. I was assured that the negatives produced sharp, clear prints in any case, so little adjustment was necessary.

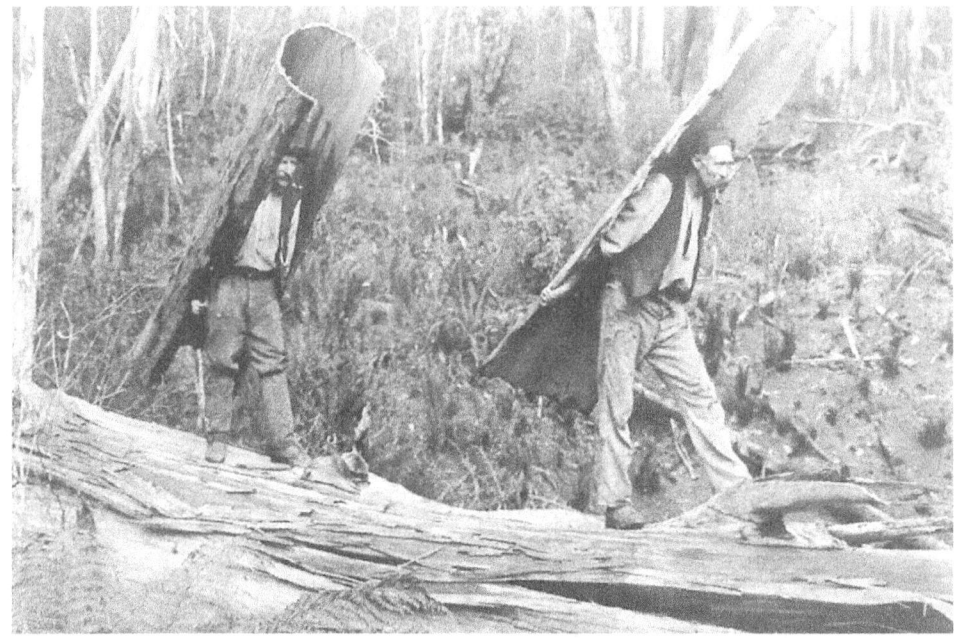

Fig. 25. 'The Bushman's friend – Roofing Bark', c.1910. (Courtesy of Jim Nicholas)

materials at hand, possibly to patch up their hut roof, as settlers and miners had done since European settlement. Bark had been used for thousands of years by the Aboriginal people as a material for constructing shelters.

While these images are rich in historical evidence for the viewer today, for Campbell at the time it was a matter of recording the miners at work in a clear and interesting way, which would produce commercially saleable photographs. This was 'subject' photography which produced 'realist' prints sharp in focus. Ebury raises a point made by Susan Sontag, 'that the identification of the subject of a photograph always dominates the viewer's perception'. This is important, he states, for subject photography, 'but the photographer has a creative role to play through choice, framing and lighting'.[25]

Campbell's scenic views are characteristic of the postcard producers of the time. The image 'Corryong. Murray River and Mt. Kosciusko from Towong' (Fig. 26) is an outstanding example of his landscape views.

In a different category is 'Walwa. Fording the Murray' (Fig. 27). It is an attractive enough scene, the river shallow and seemingly benign, but a reading

25 Francis Ebury, 'Making Pictures', pp. 152-3.

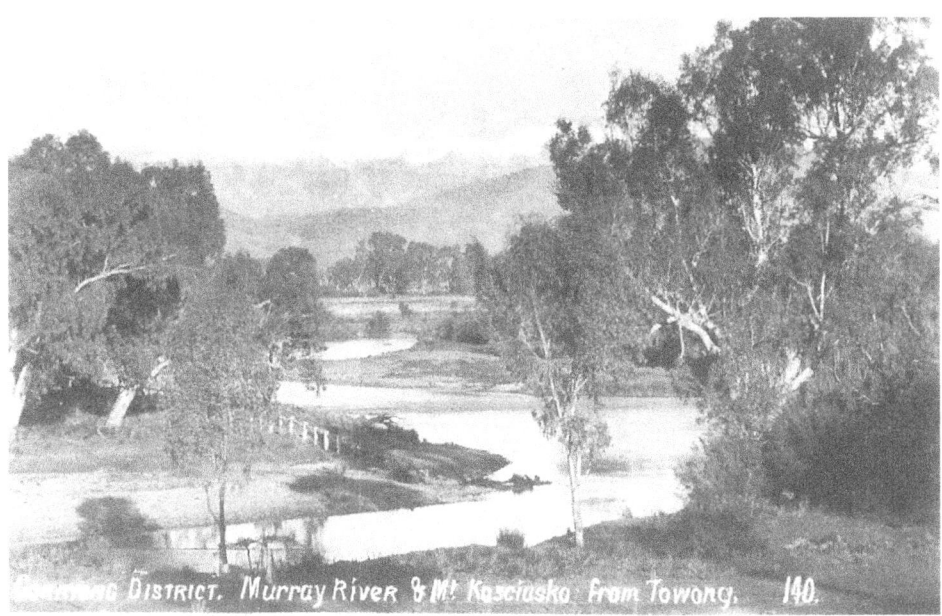

Fig. 26. 'Corryong District. Murray River & Mt. Kosciusko from Towong'. Mt Kosciusko
was a common subject in Campbell's views of the Corryong area.
(Courtesy of Marjorie Mossop)

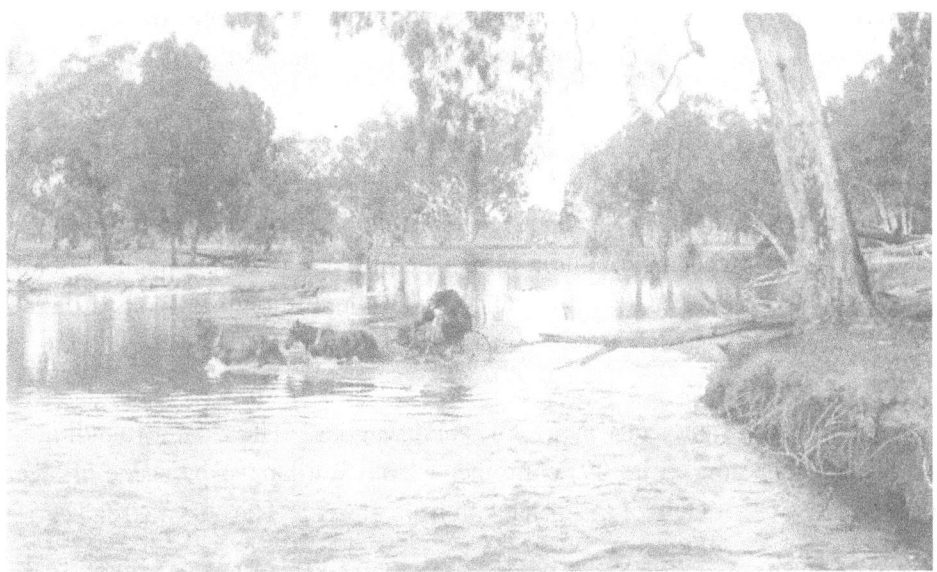

Fig. 27. 'Walwa. Fording the Murray at Everards'. Crossing the Murray in this manner was
a dangerous business, although in this scene the river looks quite benign.
(Courtesy of Marjorie Mossop)

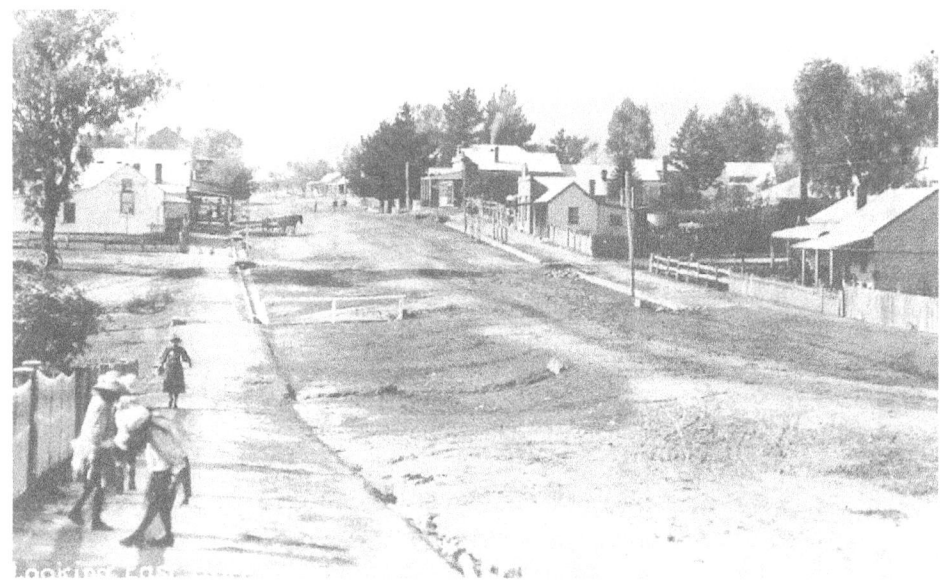

Fig. 28. 'Looking East. Corryong'. (Courtesy of Jim Nicholas)

of the *Corryong Courier* at the time shows that such crossings were hazardous, and a number of people lost their lives in its swirling, unpredictable waters over the years. The purchaser of such a postcard, a tourist, may not have made the connection, but the locals certainly knew, as would Campbell. It is a picture with an 'edge' to it, as we might say now.

Streetscapes of country towns were a favourite subject of Campbell's. He developed a formulistic approach to their creation. There would be either people (often children) in them, or a lone gig, often dogs nosing about, and usually a relatively quiet street lined with buildings leading you into the image. 'Looking East. Corryong' (Fig. 28) is an excellent example, although it lacks a defined row of buildings, and not a dog can be seen. Street scenes sold well on the postcard market.

Another regular subject was coaches and wagons. 'The Coach rounding the Needles. Berringama' (Fig. 29) combines a dramatic landscape scene of steep, forested hills with a view of a coach taken from above.[26] The curving road carries

---

26 This photograph is also one of eight under the creator 'Vallan Studio' published in the *Leader*, 4 July 1914, with the overall caption 'Valley Scenes of the Upper Murray Railway: Now being constructed'. The caption on the coach scene sets the picture in a different context: 'Line, Road and Cudgewa Creeks meet in the narrow confines of the Cudgewa Valley at "The Needles"'. The eight photographs are accompanied by a numbered map showing the locations where the photographs were taken.

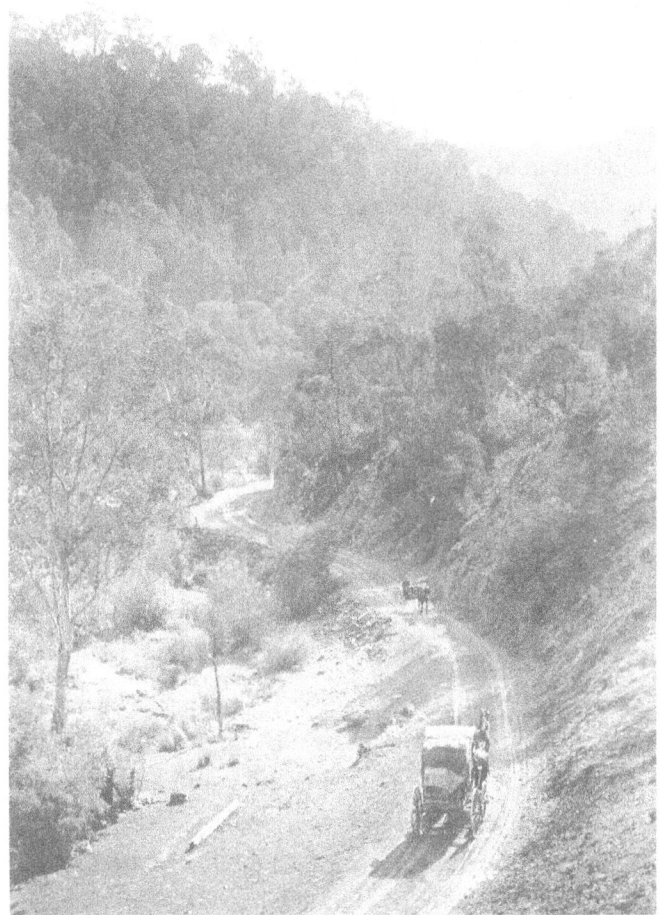

Fig. 29. 'The Coach rounding The Needles. Berringama'.
(Courtesy of Jim Nicholas)

you into the picture along with the coach, and the approaching gig adds interest. Will it have enough room to pull over and let the coach pass?

Not all of Campbell's photographs were taken in the far north-east of the state during his years with Vallan Studio. Other regions he went to included south-west Gippsland, central Victoria and East Gippsland. I have found Campbell photographs of places within these regions at random, the majority are on postcards, most numbered sequentially, probably relating to a series in a particular district, and in the case of the Upper Murray they could go well beyond the highest number in a series, 289, so far found.

Another area frequented regularly by Campbell and his camera was Trawool in the Goulburn River Valley between Seymour and Yea. He took many photographs in this district, and as a result his postcards of this spot are not hard to find. Trawool was easily accessible by train from Mansfield, so he could load his bicycle onto the train and use it as his form of transport when he arrived at his destination. The Trawool images (see figures 30 and 31) show Campbell's never-flagging energy in getting into rugged locations.

Some of these Trawool photographs were printed on cards with 'J.P. Campbell, 12 Hunter Street, Malvern' on the back, suggesting they may have been taken before he joined Vallan Studio. Or he may have been using up old card stock. Local historical societies in these areas hold a number of Campbell photographs, usually in the form of postcards. Most districts favoured by Campbell's camera are scenic places either in the hills or close to forests and rivers. I have found no Campbell images of the western part of Victoria – he was not a fan of predominantly flat country. The only time he appeared to have ventured on to the plains with his camera during his Vallan Studio days, was when visiting his photographer friend Lilian Pitts at Merrigum in the Goulburn Valley, hence photographs of Shepparton, Tatura, Kyabram and Merrigum itself.

Campbell had a significant relationship with Lilian Pitts, but there is conflicting evidence on the nature of that relationship and when their friendship began. Lilian, like Campbell, grew up in Gippsland. Noel Fethers, Campbell's granddaughter, believes he met Lilian through his wife Elizabeth who had known her via the Potton family of Bairnsdale, East Gippsland, a family close to Elizabeth's parents, John and Frances Parsons.[27] As mentioned in chapter one, John Parsons was a builder, and although based in North Melbourne did work elsewhere, including Bairnsdale. The Pitts family had lived in Maffra and Bairnsdale for a number of years before moving to Merrigum.[28]

Lilian was born in Bairnsdale in 1872 where her father, Frank, was variously a flour miller, insurance agent and shopkeeper.[29] Frank was also heavily involved in the community life of Bairnsdale, including the Wesleyan Church.[30] This was to have an influence on Lilian for the rest of her life. The Pitts family left

27 Interview with Noel Fethers, 20 April 2005.
28 Valda Cook, 'Unremarkable Women? The Life and Times of Lilian Louisa Pitts, Photographer', Master of Arts Thesis, Monash University, 1992, p. 7.
29 Ibid., pp. 8-18.
30 Valda Cook, 'Unremarkable Women?' p. 12.

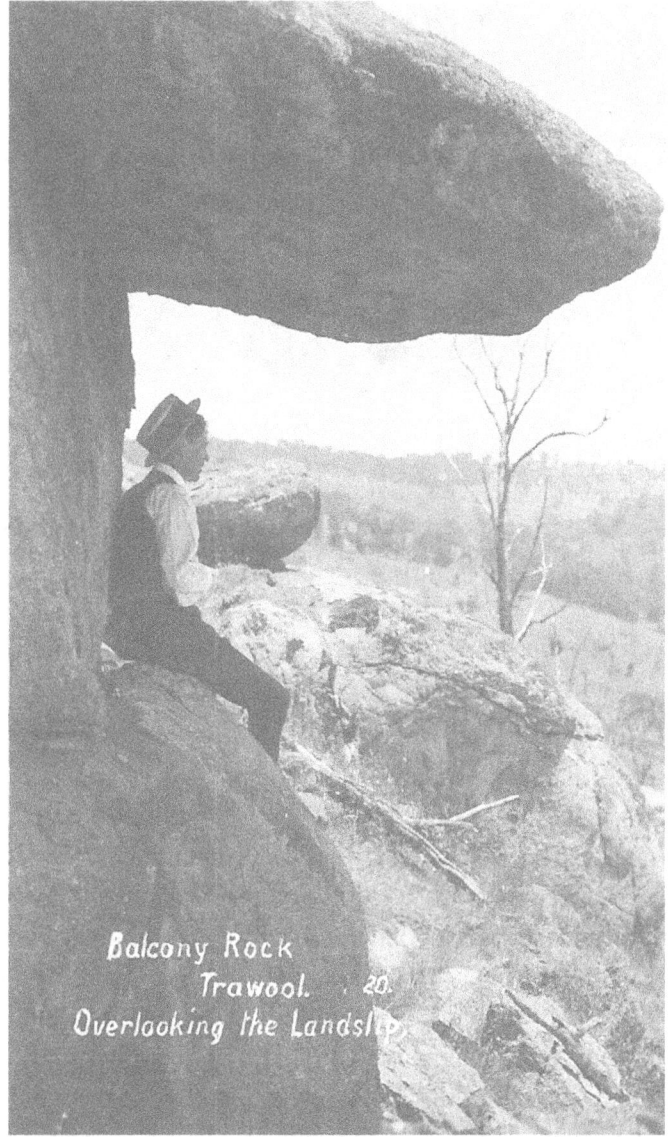

Fig. 30. 'Balcony Rock Trawool'. (Author's collection)

Bairnsdale in 1888 to take up a drapery business in Dandenong, a venture that failed in 1893 due to the depression.[31] They resurfaced in Merrigum where Frank became a pioneer orchardist in an irrigation district. They built a large, plain weatherboard house called Othery, and threw themselves into work, church and

31 Ibid., pp. 20-5.

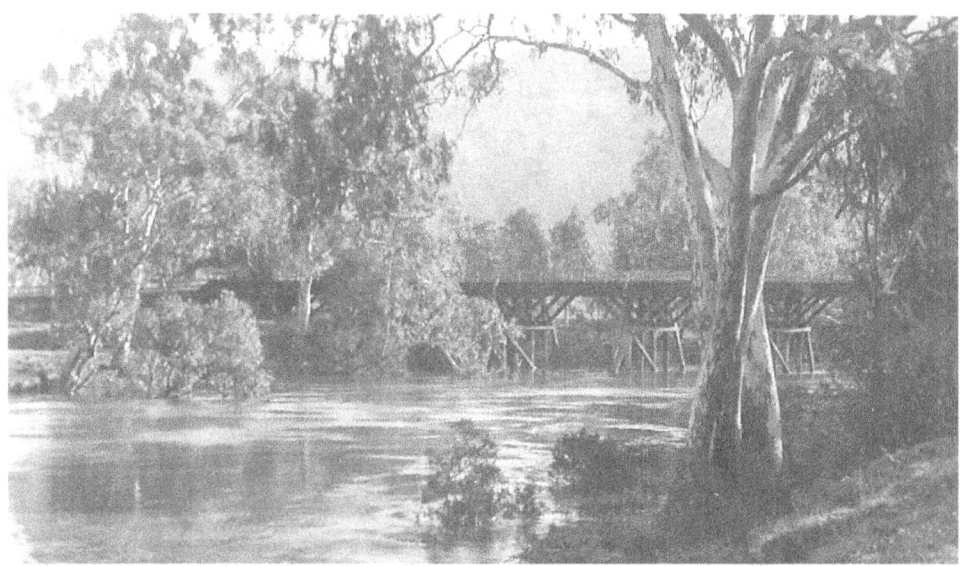

Fig 31. 'Goulburn River Bridge. Trawool'. (Author's collection)

community activities in the small farming town (Fig. 32).[32] By this time Lilian had three sisters and two brothers.

Unlike her siblings, Lilian never married. Instead she carved out a living teaching music, singing and crafts. She organised and conducted choirs and was deeply immersed in the activities of the Methodist Church.[33] Valda Cook, Lilian's biographer, believes her private school education in Bairnsdale provided a model 'of a woman of some gentility supporting herself by teaching' and 'may have influenced Lilian to [later] eschew the traditional woman's role in the private sphere and ultimately to take up a self-supporting life in the public sphere in contradiction of education, religious training and the views of her father'.[34] She went on to become a significant photographer in the early 1900s, but it was not until the 1970s that her work received wide recognition, when her photographs were included in the Museum of Victoria's 'The Biggest Family Album in Australia' project. Some of her best images were also included in an Australia-wide touring exhibition of work by Australian women photographers,

---

32 Ibid., pp. 37-42.

33 Ibid., pp. 56-7.

34 Ibid., pp. 33-4. In her thesis Cook analyses Lilian's life 'within the framework provided by the ideology of the separate spheres for men and women which colonists had brought with them from Europe'. Ibid., p. 5. To this she adds the private sphere of the home and public sphere of the community.

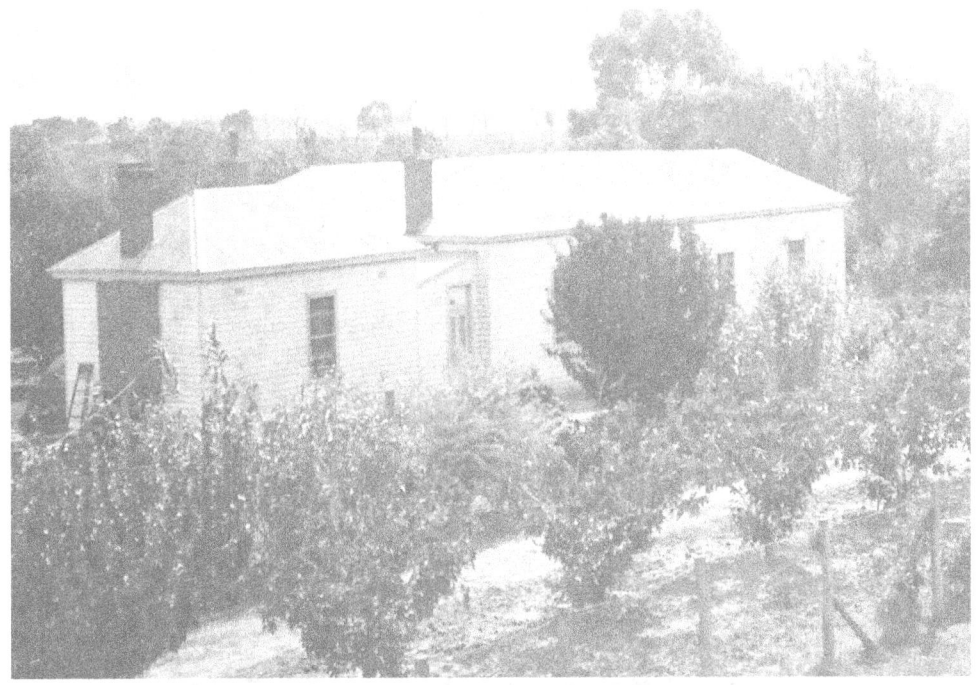

Fig. 32. Othery, the home of the Pitts family at Merrigum, north-central Victoria.
Probably taken by LL Pitts from the windmill. Note the young fruit trees.
(Courtesy of Nance Tyson collection)

covering the period 1890 to 1950.[35] Lilian's relationship with Campbell was a close one for him as his photography career unfolded (Fig. 33).

Despite extensive research, Valda Cook could not find any record of Lilian learning photography. Noel Fethers believes her grandfather, JP Campbell, taught Lilian at Vallan Studio in Mansfield, before the First World War.[36] Although close to her family and living at home, Lilian remained in a sense aloof from them.[37] Cook found that Lilian had a network of friends in artistic circles in Melbourne, seemingly unknown to her family at the time. This included the Campbells.[38]

35 Jenni Mather, Christine Gillespie and Barbara Hall, Catalogue titled *Australian Women Photographers: 1890-1950, Australian Tour 1981-1982*, George Paton Gallery, Melbourne University Union, Parkville, 1981.
36 Interview with Noel Fethers, 20 April 2005.
37 Valda Cook, 'Unremarkable Women'? pp. 79-80.
38 Ibid., p. 73. An 'A. Campbell' sent her a Christmas postcard dated 8 January 1911, a 'compliments of the season' note written in a flourishing, artistic hand. Was this AJ Campbell, the ornithologist, photographer, founder of the Wattle League in Victoria and JP Campbell's cousin, or Aubrey, JP Campbell's son?

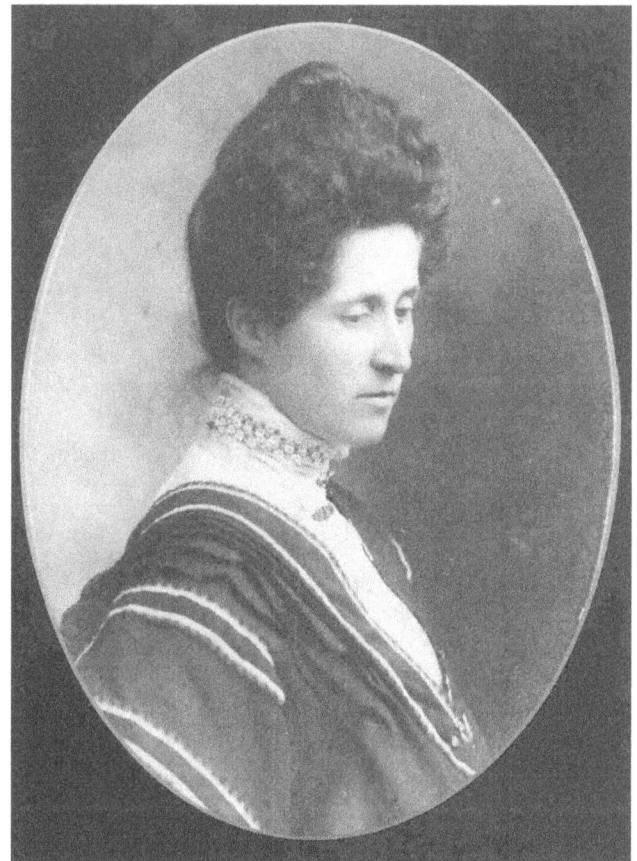

Fig. 33. Lilian Louisa Pitts.
(Courtesy of Nance Tyson collection, photographer unknown)

Cook believes Lilian's photography dates from 1904, but if Noel Fethers is right, it is more likely 1909.[39]

There are a number of factors which, when combined, suggest Lilian had a strong connection with Vallan Studio and JP Campbell from 1909 onwards. Campbell visited Lilian in Merrigum. There is a photograph of him taken by her, camera and tripod across his shoulder, a shadowy figure alighting from a train at Merrigum Station.[40] Both exhibited photographs at the Merrigum Flower Show in May 1909, competing against one another. The *Kyabram Guardian* reporter wrote

---

39 Vallan Studio began in 1908: had Lilian left Merrigum under some pretense to go to Mansfield and learn photography there? It may be that she went off with the family's blessing, but nobody alive at the time of Cook's research in the early 1990s knew much about Lilian's life prior to the First World War.
40 Courtesy of Nance Tyson collection. It is not clear enough to be reproduced here.

that 'the collection of amateur photography work surpassed anything we have seen in a country show'.[41] It was 'Miss Pitts 1st, Mr. Campbell 2nd' in the '6 local views' category, but Campbell prevailed in the 'humorous photograph' category, coming first and second.[42] In November 1910 they again exhibited together at the Merrigum Flower Show, where Lilian's work was highly commended. This time Campbell did not compete with her, instead presenting a collection of Vallan Studio photographs for display only.[43] Just what Lilian's family and the small Merrigum community thought of Campbell's association with her is unknown.

In correspondence between them, it is clear they were close friends by 1909. The earliest postcard from Campbell to Lilian is dated 20 September 1909, about the time Campbell joined Herbert Vallance at Vallan Studio. He wrote in a tone suggesting he had known her for quite a while, his opening sentence being: 'Will reply to correspondence soon'. He was 'to leave for Mansfield Thursday [presumably from Malvern]'. He told Lilian that he will 'take Val's face' for her. 'Val' is HJ Vallance. Campbell claimed his eye was good and that he was not 'teasing' it.[44] It was an intimate note between two people who were very comfortable with one another. On the back of another postcard titled 'Merrigum Station. Arrival of Train from Echuca', taken from the top of an open railway truck loaded with what looks like bags of wheat, Campbell wrote this opening line to Lilian: 'There are 8 pages of a letter written which you'll get completed some day'.[45] They were clearly good friends.

On the back of a postcard captioned *What tales the moon could tell!* (see Fig. 14) are a few telling words hinting at Campbell's relationship with his wife and Lilian:

Mansfield Tuesday. 4/9/10

Dear Miss Pitts,

I couldn't come [on a trip to Mt Buffalo]. The olive branch I've been waiting for for ages was strewn in my path at No. 12 [Hunter St., Malvern] and I hung on. I know you'll be glad – and also sorry I couldn't join the Alpiners. I did think I'd have one day at least and stay a few days after.

---

41 *Kyabram Guardian*, 7 May 1909.

42 Ibid. They may have been the only photographers to exhibit.

43 *Kyabram Guardian* and *Kyabram Free Press*, 4 November 1910.

44 Postcard, JP Campbell to Lilian Pitts, 20 September 1909, courtesy of Frank Pitts.

45 Ibid., 29 March 1910, courtesy of Frank Pitts.

> I wired you on Friday morning the offices being closed Thursday. Did a few Alpine prints so as not to be quite out of it. Hooray. James J.P.C.[46]

This seems to indicate there had been some estrangement between Campbell and his wife, whilst at the same time indicating that Lilian would be pleased to see the couple patching things up. It goes some way to suggesting a platonic relationship between Campbell and Lilian, reinforcing the view of Noel Fethers that they were nothing more than friends, and that Elizabeth had a good friendship with Lilian prior to Campbell and Lilian meeting. On the other hand, it showed that Campbell was quite happy to go on a trip to Mt Buffalo with three women, the 'Alpiners', if he could. It is worth pointing out that Elizabeth was thirteen years older than Campbell, and Lilian was seven years younger than him. Noel Fethers insists Elizabeth and Campbell were close, despite the fact he was rarely at home. Lilian may have visited 12 Hunter Street Malvern. In a postcard to Lilian that Campbell sent in February 1916 he wrote: 'thought those Buffalo negs went back to you – my memory faileth – Maybe they are at Mansfield or did I bring them down *for you to collect at Malvern* [my emphasis]'.

There may also have been a commercial side to the Campbell/Lilian relationship. In a postcard to Lilian dated 17 March 1910 Campbell wrote: 'Am mailing to you today your enlarged print and including the one for Mr. Clements and am advising him'. This suggests that Vallan Studio was doing work for Lilian and perhaps other people in the district. In a postscript on the same card he wrote: 'A repeat order from Byrneside', suggesting that the Byrneside store, not far from Merrigum, had ordered items (probably postcards) from Vallan Studio.[47] Was Lilian acting as an 'agent' for Vallan Studio? She was a single woman trying to make a living teaching music, drawing and painting. This was a respectable occupation for an educated woman of her class and situation at the time. Photography provided another string to her bow. By selling her photographs in the form of postcards she could turn a hobby into an income generating sideline,

---

46 Gelatin silver photograph, postcard print 'What tales the moon could tell!', Accession No. 83.1372.6A, in 'Untitled album', Creator: J.P. (James Pinkerton) Campbell, Accession No. 83.1372.1-24, Accession Date 09/05/1983, NGA IRN 91540, National Gallery of Australia, and Camerratic [Lilian Pitts], Clumsy Creature [Olive Pitts] and Adult Child [Irene Palamountain], *Three of us and Mt. Buffalo*, Published by the Authors, G.H. Wilson & Co., Printers, Kyabram, c1911. The three women had travelled to Mt Buffalo Chalet by train and coach the year it opened, leaving on 25 August 1910 and returning on 1 September. Lilian recorded their adventures with her camera and the three published the diary of their trip.

47 JP Campbell postcard to LL Pitts, 17 March 1910, courtesy of Frank Pitts.

or at least pay for the cost of equipment. She was known to be shrewd with her finances, and on her death had a substantial amount of money in the bank.[48]

Lilian did not have the facilities to produce postcards, given her darkroom was the cellar under the kitchen at Othery.[49] Vallan Studio did have the means to produce postcards from Lilian's photographs. On a postcard in late 1910 Campbell wrote: 'This is my latest idea – toned cards [the photo on the card is of a scene entitled 'Fairy Pool' arranged by Campbell, using what looks like porcelain figurines with roses decorating the foreground]'.[50] He included storage and quantity details of photographic materials, discussing these as if Lilian would want to give her opinion on the venture.

The series of twelve Kyabram postcards now in the Museum of Victoria's 'Biggest Family Album in Australia' collection, with each postcard captioned on the front in Campbell's distinctive printing, have been attributed to Lilian by the Pitts family and Valda Cook.[51] Did Vallan Studio produce them from Lilian's negatives, or were the photographs taken by Campbell on one of his visits to see Lilian at Merrigum? They are certainly in his pictorial style, and the same subjects and angle of view are replicated in many photographs he took of other towns. One photograph in particular, 'The Weighbridge is busy, Kyabram' (Fig. 34), is reminiscent of the image 'Heavily Laden', previously discussed, and also of a photograph he was to take a few years later at the railway goods yard in Darwin. The dust kicking up around the wheels of a horse drawn vehicle in motion is a JP Campbell signature. I believe the Kyabram series is Campbell's.[52]

Valda Cook is quick to observe that the 'neatness and quiet prosperity' of the Kyabram Street scenes do not quite line up with the written descriptions in a history of the town, describing a raw, dirty, primitive settlement in 1890.[53] As Francis Ebury points out, pictorialists and camera club participants like Campbell were not inclined to depict the darker side of life.[54] They sought the

---

48 Valda Cook 'Unremarkable Women?' p. 82.

49 Ibid., p.65.

50 Postcard, JP Campbell to Lilian Pitts, 8 November 1910, courtesy of Frank Pitts.

51 Valda Cook, 'Unremarkable Women?' p. 85. For the Biggest Family Album in Australia, see the Museum of Victoria's website, <www.museum.vic.gov.au>

52 I have come to this conclusion after looking at hundreds of JP Campbell's photographs, and those of Lilian Pitts.

53 Valda Cook 'Unremarkable Women?' pp. 86-90. To be fair to the town and photographer, these scenes were taken twenty years later and the streets were far more developed.

54 Francis Ebury, 'Making Pictures', p. 331.

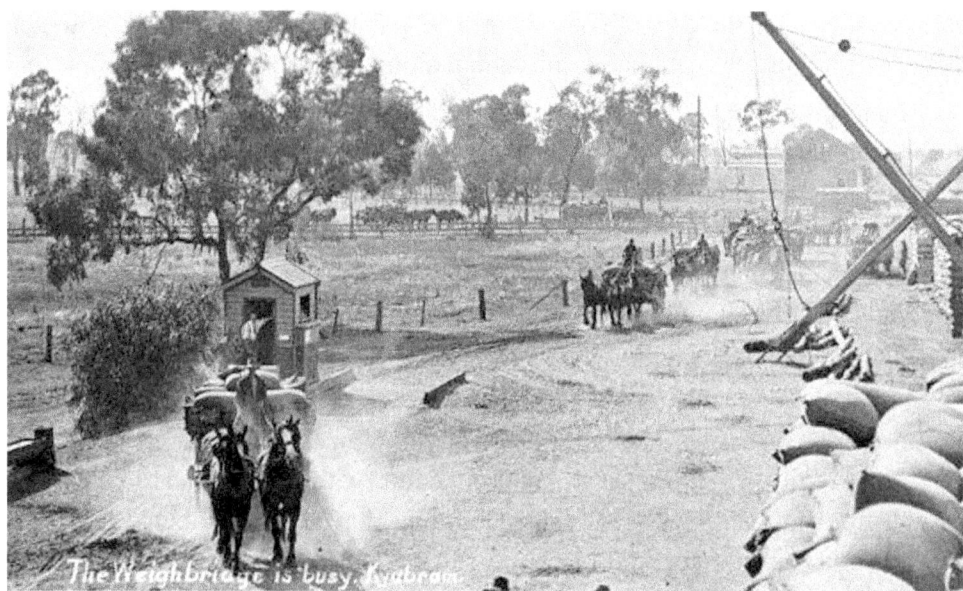

Fig. 34. 'The Weighbridge is busy. Kyabram'. One of the Kyabram series of postcards, c.1910, attributed to LL Pitts, but which has all the attributes of a JP Campbell scene, including the printed caption. (Courtesy of Museum Victoria)

picturesque and the serene. Campbell rarely used dust in streetscapes, but sought it in 'working horse' scenes, so horse, rider or vehicle could be shrouded in it, giving the artistic effect he desired.

Lilian's photographic output ranged across a number of categories. Many images are family portraits, both of the Pitts' and other families. Some of these are humorous and it is here that Campbell's influence is discernable. Like other pictorialists he enjoyed taking pictures of children, although his images were animated, his subjects playing naturally, acting out or posing. He would photograph a short narrative series, adding humorous captions to the images. Lilian's series of photographs of the visit of her mischievous nephew, the young Frank Stephenson, to Merrigum, later published as *Merrigum Frank* by the Museum of Victoria, has these qualities.[55] She sold landscape views to newspapers, took photographs of work activities and buildings in the Merrigum district, and travelled further afield in Victoria and Tasmania pursuing her hobby. Barbara Hall and Jenni Mather, authors of *Australian Women Photographers,*

---

55 Lillian (sic) Louisa Pitts, *Merrigum Frank*, compiled by E McGillivray and M Nickson, Museum of Victoria, 1990.

1840-1960, found Lilian's photographic work 'exceptional', but hard to assess for style, seeing the influence of early pictorialists in some of it, although they thought 'she was reluctant to use an overall soft focus'.[56]

Lilian was exposed to the pictorialist style through JP Campbell. Not only did he teach her at Vallan Studio, but they went on photography field trips together before the First World War.[57] One of the features of Lilian's work was to often include people, a technique Campbell used, particularly in his streetscapes and narrative photography. There were, however, other photographers who may have influenced her. Hall and Mather believe Lilian attended painting classes in Melbourne run by AME (Alice) Bale, a leading painter at the time, and it was here she may have met prominent women photographers of the day, although Cook largely discounts the 'painting/pupil' angle.[58] Lilian did know the Bales, but this may have been through some other artist-contact like the wood carver John Blogg, who visited the Pitts family in Merrigum.[59] Bale moved in a circle of artists including photographers, and the Campbells, AJ and JP, may have also been in this group. Lilian Pitts corresponded with Campbell until the 1930s.[60] Some of his correspondence to her survives on postcards, revealing they frequently swapped notes on photography. None of her correspondence to him survives. Their relationship was a limited one, constrained by social mores and distance.

Campbell carried out a variety of commissioned work for Vallan Studio, photographing activities at country agricultural shows for the metropolitan weekly newspapers, or compiling albums for station owners and town progress associations.[61] This was like the work of the Sydney based photographer Charles Kerry (1858-1928), whom Campbell's path in photography resembled, although Kerry was much more successful commercially. The pastoral element in the bush where they grew up influenced their subject matter as photographers, such as views of properties, shearing activies and agricultural shows. Both went into

---

56 Barbara Hall and Jenni Mather, *Australian Women Photographers 1840-1960*, Richmond, Vic., 1986, p. 15.

57 Ibid., p. 17.

58 Valda Cook, 'Unremarkable Women?' pp. 72-3.

59 Ibid., pp. 73-4.

60 Hall and Mather, *Australian Women Photographers*, p. 16.

61 Letter, application for Commonwealth photography job, JP Campbell to Secretary, Department of External Affairs, 2 October 1911, in file 'JP Campbell – Commonwealth Photographer', Item 16281, National Archives of Australia.

the postcard trade, an extension of the 'views' market, when it took off after the turn of the century. Kerry instituted a style of 'pioneer photojournalism' with his staff of photographers, capturing anything topical and getting it out to the public.[62] He also conducted what he called his "Squatters' Service" in New South Wales, travelling about the countryside taking commissioned pictures of homesteads and their inhabitants, livestock and rural outlooks.[63] Campbell completed similar work but on a smaller scale in north-east Victoria.

As well as his Vallan Studio commitments, Campbell continued to enter images in exhibitions held by the Working Men's College Photographic Club, winning prizes in June 1911.[64] Both Campbell and Vallance were published in the weekly pictorial newspapers as individual photographers, and in the *Leader* in the years 1910-11 forty-two images were published under Campbell's name and eight under Vallance's. This compared to only twenty-one under the name of Vallan Studio for the same period. The first photographs attributed to Vallan Studio were published in the *Leader* on 21 May 1910, a series of five images of the Powlett River Coal Field at Wonthaggi. The *Leader* probably paid well for photographic contributions, and may have commissioned individuals and studios. This would have generated extra income for Vallan Studio, but just as important was exposure of their work to the public. Many of the Vallan Studio photographs appearing in the newspapers were taken by Campbell.[65] The number of Campbell's photographs published in newspapers indicates his ambition as a photographer.

Two examples of the type of photographic work Campbell completed on behalf of Vallan Studio, both commissioned in 1911, give an idea of how the studio operated from its small country town base. Campbell took external and internal photographs of the Agricultural High School, Mansfield, for inclusion in its prospectus. The headmaster was so pleased with the quality he forwarded the images to the Education Department for inclusion in their annual report.[66]

---

62 Gael Newton, *Shades of Light*, p. 82.

63 Anne-Marie Willis, *Picturing Australia: A History of Photography*, Angus and Robertson, North Ryde, NSW, 1988, p. 79.

64 *Argus*, 13 June 1911.

65 Some photographs appeared in both forms, i.e. on postcards and in the newspapers. Campbell's distinctive printing of the caption in white ink on the postcards (and often his distinctive style) allows identification of the same Vallan Studio images in the newspaper which are not written on.

66 Letter, Mansfield Agricultural High School headmaster to JP Campbell, Vallan Studio, 16 August 1911, in 'JP Campbell – Commonwealth Photographer', Item 162811, National Archives of Australia.

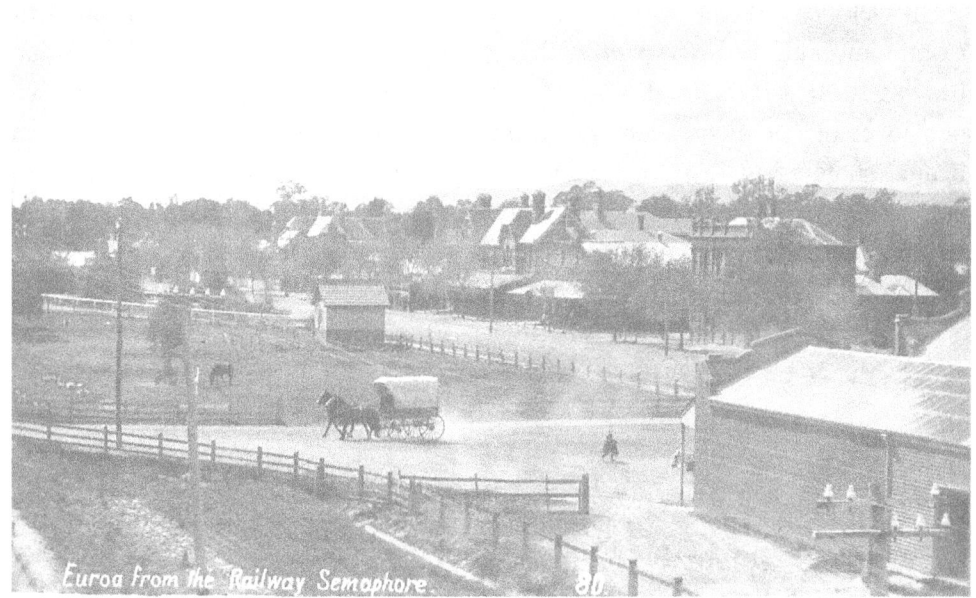

Fig. 35. 'Euroa from the Railway Semaphore'. This is one of a series of photographs taken of Euroa by JP Campbell in 1911. (Courtesy of the Euroa Historical Society)

In addition, the Euroa Hotel requested an album of photographs to promote Euroa and its district. Campbell produced a 'handsomely bound [album] in green cloth, and each leaf [contained] two or more high-class photographs, set off by a neat handwork illuminated border.'[67] It included views of waterfalls, rocks, cascades and fishing pools on district creeks, street scenes and town buildings. Many postcards were produced from this work, an example being an image taken near the Euroa Railway Station (Fig. 35). This is a good example of Campbell's pictorial clarity, sharp and balanced, with his trademark dust kicking up round the horse-drawn cart.

The Euroa and District album was Campbell's last major commission with Vallan Studio. While he was in Euroa he applied for a job as Commonwealth Photographer. He had been with Vallan Studio for only two years. He was capable of 'directing' his human subjects to get his desired result in an image. Although an outgoing man he liked working on his own and being his own boss. His relationship with Lilian Louisa Pitts was problematic, but important to him. He isolated himself from the city 'intellectuals' of the Australian School of Photographers to some degree by working in the country.

---

67 *Euroa Advertiser*, 1 March 1912.

In October 1911 he was able to write in his application for the position of Commonwealth Photographer with the Department of External Affairs that he was 'well versed in all branches of photography' and '[a] Victorian native and lover of our own scenery', and that he had 'always boosted up our own beauty spots as against other States and proved my contentions when lantern entertaining'.[68] This experience ensured he went into the next phase of his career as a photographer with confidence.

---

68 NAA: A1, 1913/14458.

4

COMMONWEALTH PHOTOGRAPHER/ CINEMATOGRAPHER

Becoming a Public Servant – Travelling North – 'The White Ant Funk' – Pine Creek and Katherine – Daly River – Melville, Bathurst and Thursday Islands – Parliamentary Visit Aftermath

JP Campbell arrived at the Port of Darwin on the steamer *Eastern* on 22 April 1912, on his first major assignment as photographer/cinematographer with the Commonwealth Department of External Affairs, accompanying the minister of that department and a group of Commonwealth parliamentarians and 'hangers-on', on a fact-finding visit to the Northern Territory. Drenching in the humidity, he was 'first ashore over the steerage bulwarks, and was soon dancing along railway tracks with the reflex [camera], and my word I perspired some, though a silk shirt was my only top gear, I was wet as if I dipped into the sea'.[1] Campbell, aged forty-six, was displaying his usual energy and prowess with a camera in the heat of the tropical north. (Fig. 36). His photographs from this venture were published in 1913 as *Views of the Northern Territory of Australia*. Albums with similar content are held by the National Library of Australia, the Northern Territory Library, the State Library of Victoria and in private collections.[2]

---

1 *Heyfield Herald*, 1 August 1912.

2 This photograph, and a number of other JP Campbell images reproduced in chapters four and five, are part of the album 'Souvenir of the Visit of the Federal Parliamentary Party to the Northern Territory, April-May, 1912', held by the Northern Territory Library, Darwin, and accessible via their Internet site and PictureNT. The National Library of Australia has almost identical contents to the album in the possession of the Northern Territory Library ('Souvenir of the visit of the Federal Parliamentary Party to the Northern Territory, April – May, 1912', PIC PIC/7459/1-133 LOC Album 1017, National Library of Australia, hardcopy viewed 1 December 2004, digital copy first viewed 2004, <http://nla.gov.au/nla.pic-an23605285>). Another important source is the official government promotional publication produced from Campbell's photographs, *Views of the Northern Territory of Australia*, 1913. Complementing these are photographs held in private collections, especially the Northern Territory component of the Falconer family's collection of Campbell's photographs. There is also a substantial number of Campbell's 1912 Northern Territory photographs held by the State Library of Victoria in an album called the Kirkbride collection (Accession no. H27744), named after its original owner Charles Kirkbride. Dr Sophie Couchman, a researcher into Chinese settlement in the NT, recognised that this album contained JP Campbell images after I completed the thesis on which this book is based. It is very fragile and the photographs are poorly captioned.

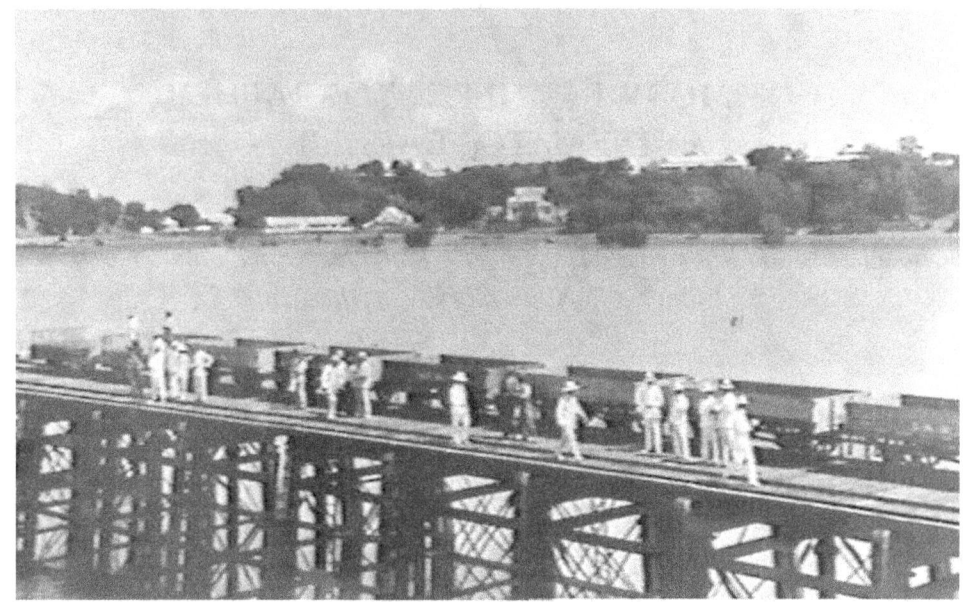

Fig. 36. 'Arrival scene at Darwin'. (Northern Territory Library,
<http:hdl.handle.net/10070/6196>)

In October 1911 the Commonwealth Department of External Affairs had advertised in the Melbourne *Herald* for somebody to take on 'Photographer and Cinematograph Operation in connection with Commonwealth Advertising'. The Department wanted 'an experienced photographer, able to travel continuously throughout the Commonwealth and have experience of rural life and industries to supply still and movie photography for promoting Australia in the UK'.[3] The Department at that time used State governments photographs to promote Australia as a desirable place to settle, but the supply of images from this source was inadequate. In addition these State photographs were mainly of technical subjects for their respective agricultural departments, and had already been used extensively for promotional purposes.[4]

In his application for the Commonwealth photographer/cinematographer position, Campbell emphasised his numerous prize-winning efforts in the *Australasian* photographic competition and his knowledge of rural life, sending

3 External Affairs Department advertisements in the Melbourne *Herald*, 30 September 1911 and *Age*, 2 October 1911, in NAA: A1, 1913/14458. The successful applicant was to be added to the temporary public servants' list. The Commonwealth had a scheme in place to promote Australia abroad, not only in the UK but in America and Europe as well.
4 Ibid.

samples of his work. He put his age down from forty-six to forty-three. To support his application he drew on a strong battery of referees.[5] In a letter to the Department he indicated he had experience with movie cameras, stating that he would 'be leaving for the City [at the] end of this week to do some cinematography'.[6]

Campbell was appointed ahead of thirty-nine other applicants, so his work must have been outstanding. Because of his wandering habits he read of his appointment in a newspaper before receiving official notification by mail. He then had to negotiate a starting date in order to complete photography assignments already arranged. As the position was on a trial basis, he was put on a contract starting from 6 December 1911 for a period of twelve months, at £4 per week with a small daily travel allowance.[7] On top of this wage he had his transport costs paid, giving him free rail, coach and steamer transit across borders, but he was not provided with an office or darkroom. When not in the field Campbell had to work from his family home in Malvern or the Vallan Studio in Mansfield, with the generous permission of HJ Vallance, although the Commonwealth did pay Vallance for services rendered.[8]

In April 1912 Campbell joined a Federal parliamentary party group led by Josiah Thomas, Minister for External Affairs in Prime Minister Andrew Fisher's Government, on a trip to the Northern Territory. His main task was to capture movie and still photographic views to promote the Territory as a place for mainly British migrants to settle. In the process he was to record the trip as a memento for the participants, and to produce a souvenir album. The Department provided him with a hand camera and one lens for taking still pictures, inadequate photographic equipment in Campbell's mind, so he took his own large glass plate camera and

5 These references are in NAA: A1, 1913/14458. They included: the secretary of the Commercial Travellers Association of Victoria; the State Government Tourist Officer; the manager of Kodak (Australasia) Limited, Melbourne; ER Peacock, a friend of twenty years and a Consulting Expert in Modern Business Methods and Devices; the management of Henry Berry and Company; the Director of the Working Men's College, FA Campbell (no relation), and E Kernot, Chief Engineer of the Railways Construction Branch of the Board of Land and Works.

6 Letter, JP Campbell to the Secretary, External Affairs Department, Melbourne, 16 October 1911, in NAA: A1, 1913/14458. This is the only evidence I have found to indicate Campbell had anything to do with cinematography prior to his employment with the External Affairs Department. It may be he was quickly getting lessons and experience before tackling what he hoped would be his new job, but it is also quite plausible that he was already familiar with the medium, given his obsession with film and his propensity to absorb new technology.

7 Ibid.

8 Presumably Campbell relinquished his partnership with HJ Vallance once he obtained his job with the External Affairs Department.

lenses.[9] He was later to complain bitterly about the meagre resources provided to perform a demanding job.

The administration of the Northern Territory had been taken over by the Commonwealth from South Australia on 1 January 1911 after protracted negotiations of nearly ten years.[10] Various schemes to populate the region with settlers of different nationalities and to develop it economically had failed. From the time of early white settlement, development had been driven by a fear of forcible occupation by Australia's northern neighbours. The Territory was considered to have untapped riches waiting exploitation, produce that could be exported to the vast markets of Asia and beyond.[11] In the 1870s the South Australian Government had even hatched a scheme involving the mass immigration of Japanese free settlers to the Territory, but this failed at the last minute due to a domestic uprising in Japan.[12] As historian Libby Robin points out in *How a Continent Created a Nation*, the South Australian Government's main achievements in the Territory had been the construction of the Overland Telegraph from Adelaide to Darwin in 1872, which dramatically improved communication between Australia, the Far East and England, and the construction of the railway from Darwin to Pine Creek. The telegraph helped unify continental Australia and put the 'North' on the map, but the railway was expensive, creating a large debt for South Australia, a burden handed on to the Commonwealth.[13]

The harsh climate continued to be a barrier to attracting white settlers. In 1912 the touring parliamentarians hoped to see at first-hand what was hindering the development, and to use this knowledge to make informed legislative decisions for its future. Fourteen parliamentarians went on the tour, along with five others, including Campbell, who were specialists in various fields relevant

9 Letter, JP Campbell to Patrick Glynn, Minister for External Affairs, 11 July 1913, in NAA: A1, 1913/14458.

10 Alan Powell, *Far Country: A Short History of the Northern Territory*, Melbourne University Press, Carlton, First Edition, 1982, pp. 138-42.

11 Bruce Davidson, *The Northern Myth: A Study of the Physical and Economic Limits to Agriculture and Pastoral Development in Tropical Australia*, Melbourne University Press, Melbourne, Third Edition, 1972, pp. 1-3.

12 Stephen H Roberts, *History of Australian Land Settlement*, Macmillan, South Melbourne, 1968, pp. 379-381. Roberts, in his thorough chapter on land settlement in Northern Territory, gives a terrific account of these early schemes (an oldie but a goody!).

13 Libby Robin, *How a Continent Created a Nation*, University of New South Wales Press, Sydney, 2007, p. 127.

to the aims of the trip.[14] They set out amid press protests of a 'jaunt'; the trip was labelled as the 'principle picnic' of the parliamentary recess.[15] Campbell enjoyed the leisurely trip north and the pampering the passengers received on the steamer *Eastern*. He boarded the boat in Sydney, a city that captured his imagination, particularly the harbour, which he photographed extensively. The first stop on the journey up the east coast was Brisbane, where the Minister for External Affairs, Josiah Thomas, the dapper solicitor George Wise, MHR for Gippsland, and the dashing peer Sir Walter Barttelot, aide-de-camp to the Governor General, joined the party.[16]

Part of the itinerary involved a stop off at Cairns and a brief sojourn inland by train to the Barron Falls, a scenic gorge in mountainous country which Campbell likened to the Mount Buffalo gorge in Victoria. He excitedly described the 'real tropical verdure now, mangrove swamps, palms, cocoanut [sic], bananas, etc., and the ascending of the gorge [as] one of Australia's best sights'. (Fig. 37).[17] Campbell was in his element, the pictorialist landscape photographer let loose on this spectacular train journey and paid to do it, as he passed through tunnels and crawled slowly 'round precipitous gullies and steeper spurs'. The train halted to obtain views of the country and the harbour below, and to view the huge falls, which Campbell, showing his parochialism, regarded as impressive 'but not pretty like plenty of small Victorian falls I have photographed'.[18] The *Eastern* continued north, its progress slowed by the hazardous Great Barrier Reef. Campbell was captivated by the scenery rounding Cape York and the Whitsunday passage –

---

14 *Argus*, 1 April 1912, p. 6. There were three senators and eleven members of the House of Representatives, the majority Labor Party members. Others to participate along with JP Campbell, 'Commonwealth Government photographer', were: Sir Walter Barttelot, aide-de-camp to the Governor General; Captain Matthews, the chief inspector of mines, South Australia; H Farrands, secretary to the minister of external affairs; and G McLeod, a customs official with Northern Territory expertise. Most caught the steamer *Eastern* in Sydney when it departed for Darwin on 10 April 1912, others at stops on the way north. The Commonwealth Government's first Administrator of the Territory, Dr John Gilruth, former Professor of Veterinary Pathology at the University of Melbourne, had left on a steamer for the Territory earlier that month. See also Alan Powell, *Far Country*, pp. 144-5.

15 Adelaide *Advertiser*, 27 March 1912.

16 *Heyfield Herald*, 25 July 1912.

17 Ibid.

18 Ibid.

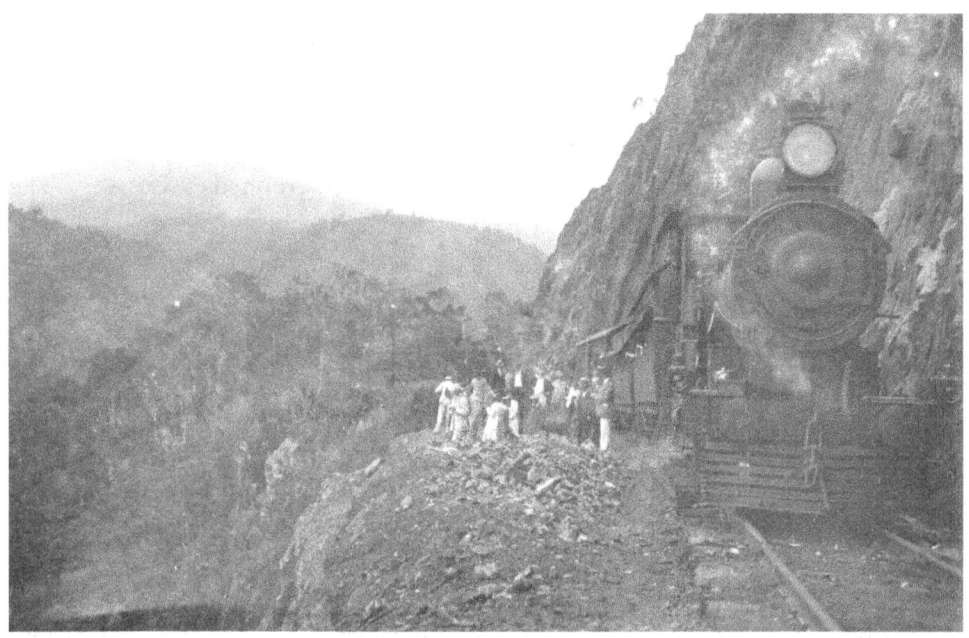

Fig. 37. 'Viewing the Gorge'.
(Northern Territory Library, <http://hdl.handle.net/10070/264>)

Northern Australia was turning out to be a photographer's delight.[19]

Back in Victoria, the *Heyfield Herald* published 'interesting extracts from [letters] written to his relatives by an old Heyfield boy, Mr J.P. Campbell, who has a responsible position as photographer for the Commonwealth Government in the Northern Territory'.[20] Whether Campbell knew extracts from his letters to his family in Gippsland were going to be published is unknown. News may have filtered back to him in correspondence from family and friends that his opinions on the Northern Territory were being aired in the *Heyfield Herald*. It was a chance for Campbell to show his writing skills, and to demonstrate to

---

19 His photographs of the trip to Darwin included a group portrait of the parliamentary party, the *Eastern* itself, scenes of Sydney Harbour, Pinkenba on the Brisbane River, Cairns and its hinterland on the train excursion, coastal views as they slipped northwards, Asian deckhands swabbing the deck, and still pictures and movie film of Cape York and environs as they rounded the top of Australia. He captured party members at rest and play: John West asleep in a deck chair; George Wise reading, likewise Sir Walter Barttelot; and Minister Josiah Thomas versus Colonel Granville Ryrie, 'keen rivals' (Labor versus Conservative) in a game of deck quoits. See album 'Souvenir of the Visit of the Federal Parliamentary Party to the Northern Territory, April-May, 1912', Northern Territory Library, <http://handle.net10070/213546>. See also the *Heyfield Herald*, 25 July 1912 & 1 August 1912, and the *Barrier Miner*, Broken Hill, 26 May 1913.

20 *Heyfield Herald*, 18 July 1912.

family, friends and acquaintances from his childhood how far he had come in the world. Having Campbell's words complements the images, providing insights into his views on a number of Territory issues such as race, class and gender. The first letter published began with Campbell's impressions of the social and racial makeup of the North, revealing the prejudices of the time:

> The Never-Never, or the land of heaps of time and wait-a-bit, has a microbe, and that is indolence and the white ant funk, and the curse is the two gins and tobacco. The 'national' drink is gin in the square bottle, the other gin being the black one, the lady of the bush. The white population away from Darwin is composed mostly by those pushed out from elsewhere, and not game to face some "accident", and they eventually descend to the level of the gin, and that level applies to many who have not been "pushed out", and to many of the Darwin population. Malays, Chinese and blacks are as one, and plenty of whites have only the difference in color.[21]

Even so, he was pleasantly surprised with the physical appearance of Darwin:

> The Territory is quite different to what I expected, though I had read Searcy and Gunn. Dense jungle, snakes, mosquito ad lib, 'gaitor [crocodile] likewise, game everywhere, wicked lagoons, etc. But it is not so. The town I had pictured as low-lying, with malarial mangrove swamps around, but the harbor shore is quite picturesque, as there are semi-cliffs of a couple of hundred feet, like part of Sydney harbour, with the town on top.[22]

This passage complements his 'Arrival scene at Darwin' (Fig. 36). With a photographer's eye for detail Campbell described the Chinese quarter and the rest of the town, commenting on the quietness of the white quarter, writing 'except when there is something special on, [it] seems to be deserted most of the day. The "something" being the bi-weekly train to and from Pine Creek, a day's journey each way, and the steamers. At such time the town does the pier and swarms into the saloon for ice drinks'.[23] As a southerner there is a derisive tone to his assessment of a small outpost of Empire, isolated in an unforgiving climate. Any

---

21 *Heyfield Herald*, 18 July 1912.
22 Ibid. 'Searcy and Gunn' refers to Alfred Searcy (1854-1925) and Mrs Aeneas Gunn (1870-1961), both authors of books on Australia's north. Campbell was most probably referring to their main, well received publications, Searcy's *In Australian Tropics*, 1907, and Gunn's *We of the Never-Never*, 1908.
23 Ibid.

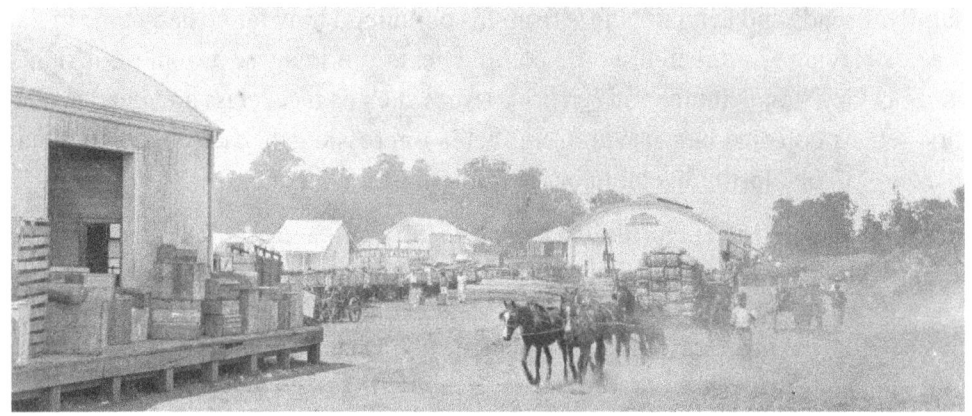

Fig. 38. 'Railway Goods Yard, Darwin',
(Northern Territory Library, <http://hdl.handle.net/10070/249>)

contact with the world outside Darwin was of interest to the locals.

The visiting southerners spread themselves between two of the main hotels, Campbell staying at the Club. Minister Thomas and Sir Walter Barttelot stayed with the Gilruths in the Administrator's Residency. The day of arrival was hectic: 'A drive to the hospital, gaol, railway workshops etc., was duly accomplished, a couple of smoke socials attended to, and the Minister hardly had breathing time on shore owing to numerous deputations demanding attention.' (Fig. 38). There was a garden party at the residency the next day, 'and all "it" of Darwin assembled, male and female, white and yellow, of which I have due records'.[24] Campbell was conscious of his roles of capturing the activities of the parliamentary party, and documenting industrial and farming practices.

The visitors were following a strict itinerary, but the organisational skills of their hosts were not quite up to the challenge. Called 'Number One Fiasco' by Campbell, a scheduled party excursion around the harbor was cancelled due an unsuitable boat for a trip on choppy waters. As a result,

> it was decided to broach the liquid portion of the lunch, drown the disgust, and abandon the trip. A little diversion was occasioned by the Minister's nice new helmet taking wings to the sea, and the resultant capture by a fisherman per boat gave material for a snapshot or two.[25]

Campbell was quick to capitalise on any embarrassing or humorous

---

24 *Heyfield Herald*, 1 August 1912.
25 Ibid.

incidents, happenings which did not always put the parliamentarians, or the local administrative officials, in a good light.

The real business of the trip began when the party boarded the special train in Darwin for the journey to Pine Creek. From Pine Creek they undertook an eighty mile slog by horse and buggy to the small settlement of Katherine, to assess its progress. (Fig. 39). The party's conveyances, mainly poorly sprung buckboards, were loaded on to flat railway carriages, and Campbell made sure he 'commandeered the best buggy for my outfit, as if carried in a bucker there would have been some choice second hand cameras, etc., at the finish'.[26] Transporting cameras and glass plates safely over rough country was a perennial concern throughout his career as a photographer.

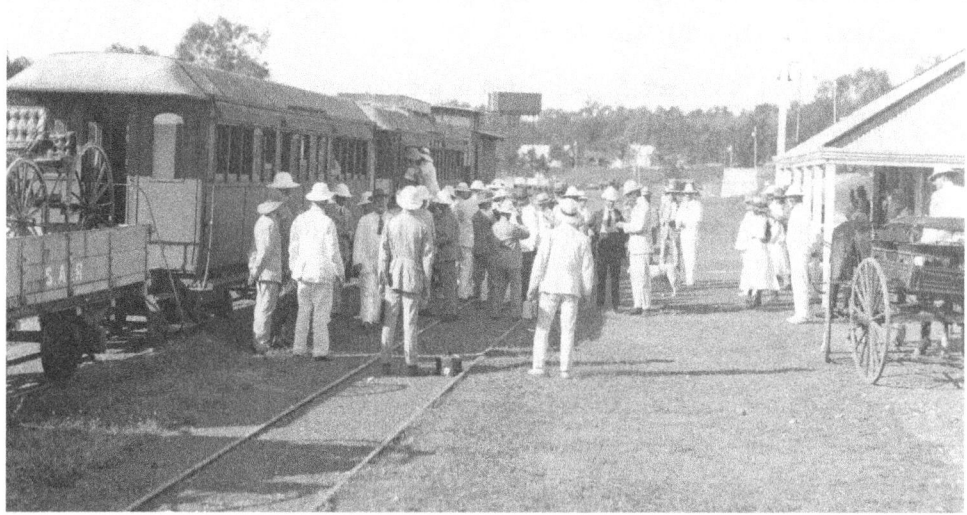

Fig. 39. 'On the way to the Katherine. The party boarding the train at Darwin for Pine Creek', (Northern Territory Library, (<http://hdl.handle.net/10070/8554>)

Two government-run experimental farms at Rum Jungle and Daly River were on the itinerary for inspection. The Rum Jungle Demonstration Farm, the result of advice from touring agricultural experts, had commenced operation only two months earlier, but, according to Campbell,

> very good work had been done in the time, as several acres had been cleared and some under cultivation, the plants looking well . . . [and] no expense is being spared as regards machinery and labor, the main

---

26 Ibid.

idea being to show what the country can and cannot do as a guide to prospective land seekers.[27]

Campbell was optimistic that farming would be successful, but seemed less enamoured with the expensive labour force brought in from the south, some of whom proved unfit for the climate. Others he called 'useless agitators', out for 'a picnic at the expense of the Labor party they profess to be proud of'. He went on:

> My sympathy is with the labourer, as I have done my fair share in days gone by, but I have no time for 'pointers,' and it would do some of these coons good to have to crack a certain quantity of stones on the roads under a slave driver for a lengthy period.[28]

The word 'coons' probably referred to the mixed races performing labouring work in the Territory. Campbell's preference for private enterprise, the result of his employment with Henry Berry and Co., and Vallan Studio, as opposed to government run ventures, was clear:

> Commercial brains are sadly needed in the compilation of departmental staffs, and the sooner the country is handed over to the Commercial Travellers Association the better! The Minister of any department may be the keenest of business men, but the staff is a permanent one and cannot be sacked for a flourishing display of individual or collective brainless red-tape incapacity.[29]

There was some hypocrisy in his attitude here – he was happy to be a contracted public servant himself, with opportunities to travel and take photographs at the taxpayer's expense. He also fancied himself as an economist. The 'labor problem' in the Territory, he believed, would benefit if poor economic conditions down south arose and caused unemployment (Fig. 40).[30] Campbell was adamant that the Territory could not be worked successfully with white labor alone because of the climate, which he thought:

> will never suit the average white woman, and I maintain that the success in any land is where the white woman will be happy and comfortable – the comfortable first please – then the man will be alright. [31]

---

27 Ibid.
28 *Heyfield Herald*, 1 August 1912.
29 Ibid.
30 Ibid.
31 *Heyfield Herald*, 18 July 1912.

Only the wives of the well-to-do who could afford servants would find it bearable, he considered, and in addition they could also escape for holidays down south or north into Asia.[32]

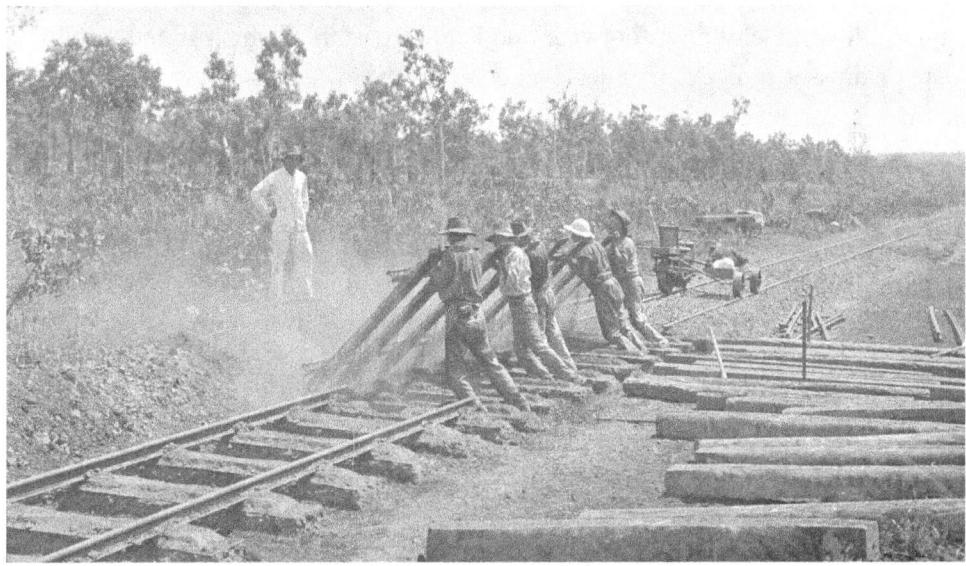

Fig. 40. 'Unloading farm goods and putting in new siding for the farm, the first break in the line for16 years'. Railway siding construction at Batchelor. Note the dust, Campbell's trademark pictorial effect. (Northern Territory Library,<http://hdl.handle.net/10070/5404>)

Campbell turned his mind to other aspects of Territory life. Servants were hard to get, 'though Chinese or Japanese make excellent waiters, but then that is not the White Australia Policy'. He believed the Territorians had a poor diet, with the prevalence of meat and a dearth of fruit and vegetables. The Chinese grew plenty of the latter, which they sold at dear prices to the whites who were 'too lazy to grow any'. Indeed the whites treated the Territory as a rubbish tip:

> Tinned dog, damper, and Beecham's pills is the menu of many out back, whose lot is of course much harder, but tinned everything of tip-top quality can be had now-a-days, and the influx of Southerners causes a trail of empty tins which eventually becomes useful to the blacks to boil yams, etc, in.[33]

He had not eaten meat since leaving Sydney 'excepting some goat at Daley's

32 Ibid.
33 Ibid.

River, which was excellent, but a goat chop at Brock's Creek I could not mark, notwithstanding I had fine new tusks'.[34] Despite his criticism of the Territorians he wrote to his sister stating with some surprise that: 'There is not a snob in the Territory. Think of that'. He remarked on the high cost of living and the dress styles, all white clothing, footwear and hats as was the fashion in the tropics. A dapper dresser himself, he even had a removable washing cover made for his helmet hat, so he could keep it white and clean.[35]

After the inspection of the Rum Jungle farm it was renamed 'Batchelor' by the Minister Josiah Thomas, in honour of a former Minister for External Affairs, Egerton Batchelor, a pioneer of developmental schemes in the Territory, who had died in October 1911 climbing Mount Donna Buang in Victoria.[36] The party continued on another train to Pine Creek, where the railway terminated, 235 km from Darwin. They arrived after dark to a tumultuous welcome by the town's population 'down to the smallest piccaninny'.[37]

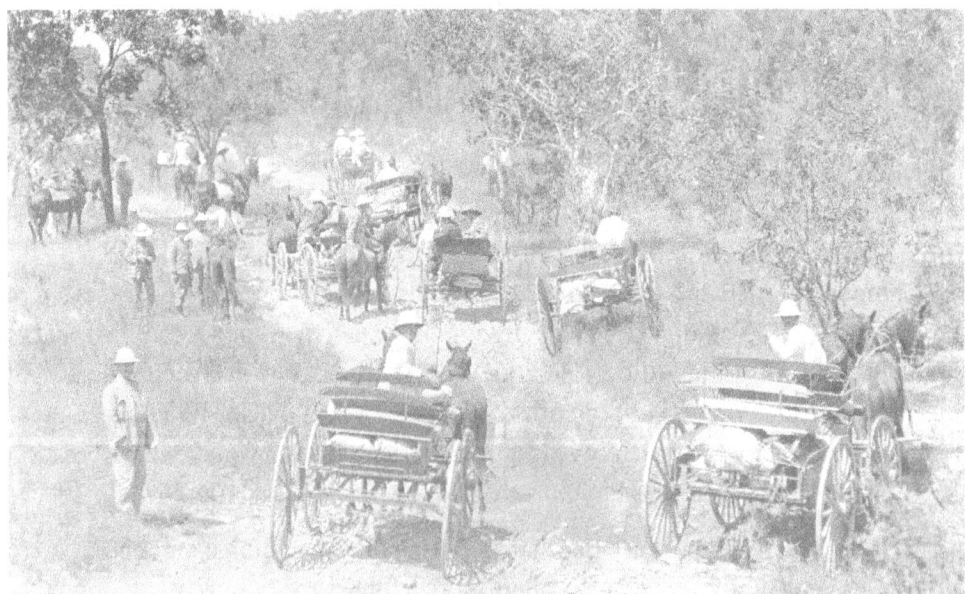

Fig. 41. The parliamentary party 'Leaving Pine Creek for Katherine and the first halt on the way', (Northern Territory Library, <http://hdl.handle.net/10070/3331>)

---

34 Ibid.

35 Ibid.

36 *Leader*, 14 October 1911.

37 *Heyfield Herald*, 1 August 1912, and Ian R Stevenson, *The Line that Led to Nowhere: The Story of the North Australia Railway*, Rigby Limited, Adelaide, 1979, p.77.

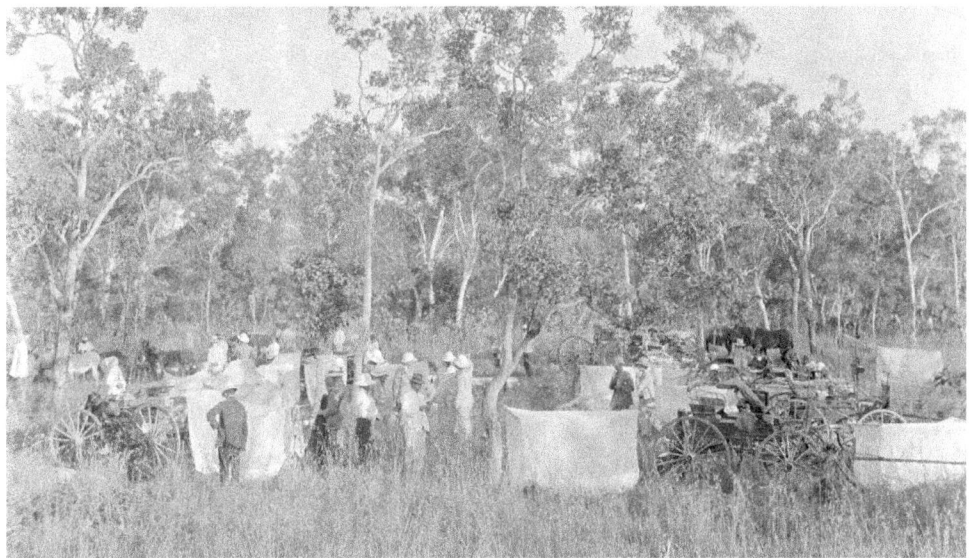

Fig. 42. 'The first morning camp'. The parliamentary party camp with mosquito nets over swags, (Northern Territory Library, <http://hdl.handle.net/10070/5321>)

Next morning, 25 April, was chaotic as horses ('such a scratch lot of gee gees one never sees down south', wrote Campbell) were organised and conveyances loaded. (Fig. 41) The party rode out through a triumphal arch of greetings erected across the street, some of the wild horses shying, resulting in:

> disaster to the guy ropes, and at one time I had doubts as to the safety of my cinema, as I was busy twirling on the moving scene. The cinema wanted constant watching as the road bumps used to loosen some of its teeth, notwithstanding it was lying on all my bedding on the floor of the buggy.[38]

On their first night in the bush they used their new mosquito nets-cum-tents designed to keep out the many creatures of the Territorian nights (Fig. 42). Campbell described this camping equipment in great detail, and was perturbed that the parliamentarians got to keep theirs as a memento of the trip. However, as he regarded himself 'as good as a member [of parliament] any day, and as entitled to Government perquisites, as I work for mine instead of skite', he kept his as well. In a one sentence line he had summed up his attitude to the travelling parliamentarians he was with. His compensation for being with these 'skites' was

---

38 *Heyfield Herald*, 8 August 1912.

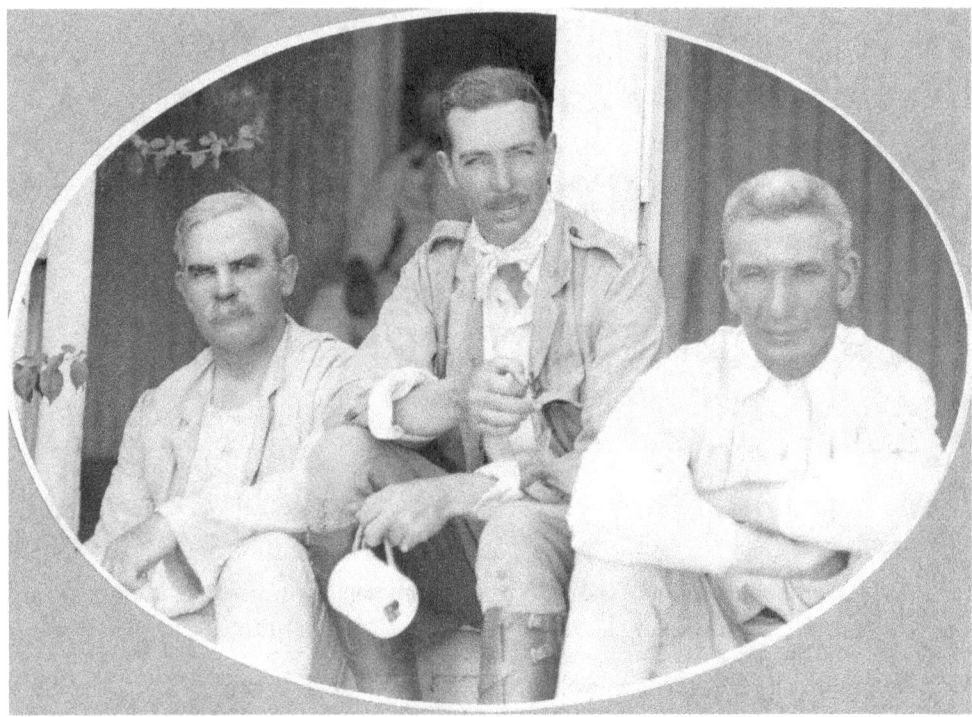

Fig. 43. 'On the verandah of the Katherine Telegraph Station, [from left] Minister [Josiah] Thomas, Sir Walter Barttelot, [and Northern Territory administrator] Dr [John] Gilruth'. (Northern Territory Library, <http://hdl.handle.net/10070/787>)

the bush, which he loved, and the opportunity to photograph it: 'The nights were glorious moons, never a light was needed beyond that, and almost every instance my outlook from under the net was facing the Southern Cross'.[39]

Their visit to Katherine was brief. Tongue in cheek, Campbell described the embryo township 'on the edge of the Never Never', as a 'boomer city, comprised of an overland telegraph station, police station, and pub and store combined'. The Katherine River was 'a little drain about ¼ mile wide from top to top of the banks'. They used the Telegraph Station's 'official shower house, its fire, and lunched on [its] official verandah', Campbell wrote sarcastically.[40] At this point Sir Walter Barttelot left the party to travel overland through Queensland and map out a future trip – scheduled for the dry season of 1913 – for his boss, the Governor General (Fig. 43). Campbell, it seems, did not lament his departure:

39 Ibid.
40 Ibid.

He amused me once. I had closed a metal box of vestes [matches] . . . and the lot caught fire, and in my eagerness to get rid of the fiery furnace I flung it on his lying on the ground valise. From his manah, don't you know, he would rather I had got fried to the bone than there should have been the risk of singing (*sic*) his cashmere bouquet soap.[41]

Another incident on this visit to Katherine shows Campbell's impatience with official authority, particularly when it interfered with his restless drive to photograph subjects of his own choosing. A government veterinarian attached to the party asked Campbell to come with him to photograph a foal with deadly swamp cancer in the hotel yards. Campbell complied, but was reluctant,

as there was a blacks' camp a half-mile the opposite way, and there was only 1½ hours to spare, and I hadn't yet seen a camp. Policeman Turner, who escorted us, also came with the Vet. and I, so I saw the pub, the police station, and had two lemon squashes, which treat I didn't return, as drinks are 1s each. I didn't get to the camp, and the other item was a waste of time as far as I am concerned, as I've seen the vet. several times since and he hasn't mentioned the snap.[42]

One can imagine Campbell avoiding to pay for his round of drinks, horrified at the cost and frustrated as time drifted away and he lost his chance to take photographs in the Aboriginal camp. This social misdemeanour would not have gone unnoticed by his companions, and one wonders how popular he was among the members of the touring party.

They returned to their camp north of Katherine, driving through head-high long grass in country Campbell regarded as monotonous. Used to the tall trees in the forests of eastern Victoria, Campbell thought the 'timber . . . miserable, one stack of firewood I saw looked more like drain pipes than wood'.[43] They passed a settlement of Chinese and stopped for refreshments at a vendor's establishment, enjoying a joke at his expense and buying beer from his unlicensed premises. Thus 'law makers patronised a law breaker', Campbell perceptively observed.[44]

The road took them past Constable Turner's Police Station at Horseshoe Creek (Fig. 44). Campbell was struck at the poor quality of the structure

---

41 Ibid.
42 *Heyfield Herald*, 8 August 1912.
43 Ibid.
44 Ibid.

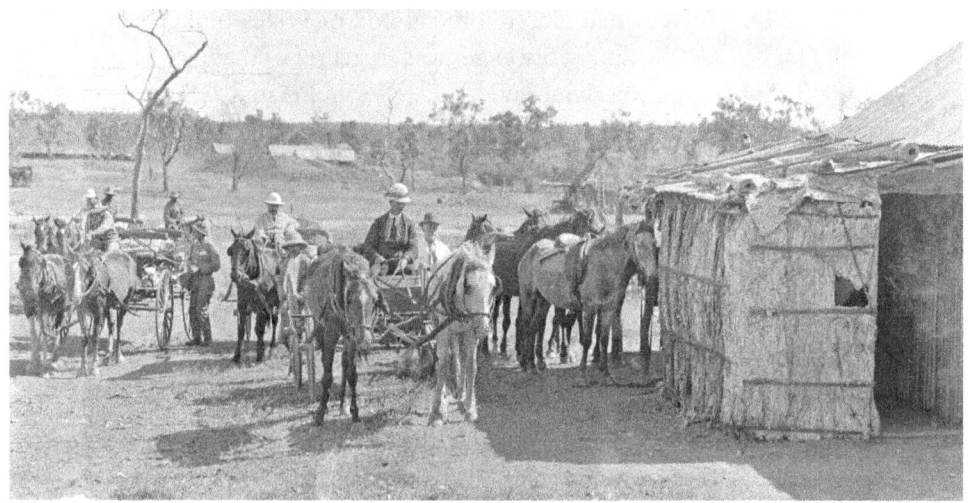

Fig. 44. The parliamentary party arrives at the fragile Horseshoe Creek Police Station
(Northern Territory Library, <http://hdl.handle.net/10070/2131>)

and the gaol nearby, both constructed 'of bark and sticks'. He castigated the
politicians:

> Now, if the party who received good treatment at the station cannot see
> its way to return the shout by getting a white man's dwelling for a white
> man servant living under a White Australia policy, then the party had
> better haul down its flag in favor of the Yellow man'.[45]

In making this comment on the police station and its inhabitant, Campbell
echoed the views of many Australians. At the Darwin citizens' welcoming
function for the parliamentary party in April 1912, the Minister for External
Affairs declared himself a passionate believer in the White Australia policy. But,
conscious of the large percentage of Asians in the Northern Territory community,
and with no doubt many Asians in the audience he was addressing, he declared
'that aliens admitted before [the White Australia] policy was adopted must
receive justice'.[46] Eleven years earlier the new Federal Parliament had passed the
Immigration Restriction Act in its first parliamentary session, the linchpin of the
White Australia Policy.[47] Some of the weekly newspapers at the time thought the

---

45 Ibid.
46 *Northern Territory Times*, 26 April 1912.
47 Alexander T Yarwood, *Asian Migration to Australia: The Background to Exclusion, 1896-1923*,
Melbourne University Press, Melbourne, 1964, p. 1.

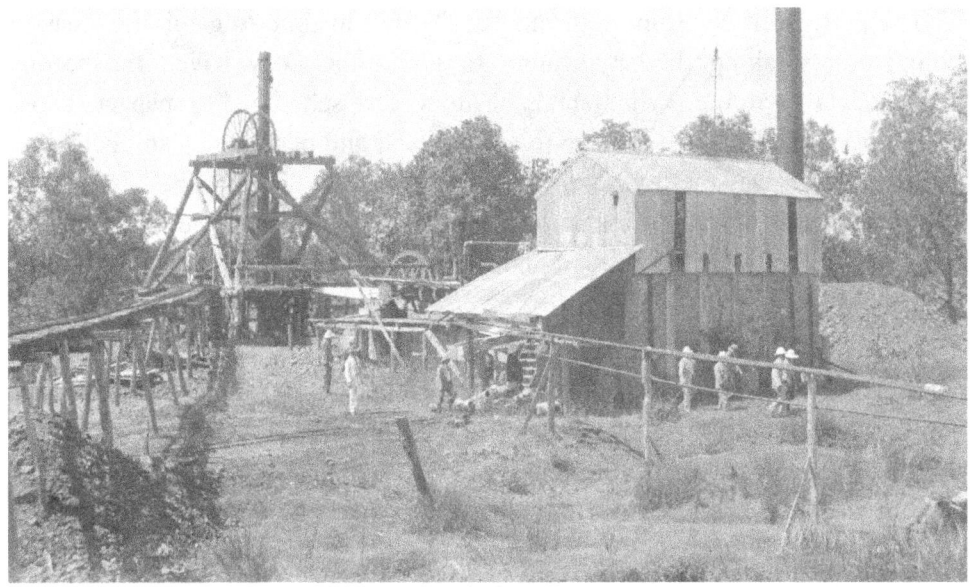

Fig. 45. Inspecting the Commonwealth Government owned Zapopan gold mine near Brock's Creek (Northern Territory Library, <http://hdl.handle.net/10070/4725>)

policy unrealistic in regard to tropical northern Australia, where white labour was either reluctant to go or regarded as unsuitable in the climate, and they suggested importing coloured workers, as happened with the Kanakas in Queensland. Not even the urgent push to populate the Northern Territory was enough to provide political support for a weakening of the Act.[48] But when it came to practicalities it was another matter. Someone had to do the backbreaking work in northern Australia, and more often it was people of Asian descent.

Due to another organisational error the party arrived back in Pine Creek a day earlier than expected, causing friction between visitors and hosts.[49] Campbell gave a 'cinematograph display', mainly for the children of the town.[50] The party inspected the Zapopan gold mine at (Fig. 45) north of Pine Creek the next day, but a proposed trip to the Daly River was in doubt because of the lack of a launch to take them down the river to its mouth where they were to be picked up by the coastal steamer *en route* from Wyndham to Darwin, and to go round via Bathurst and Melville Islands.[51]

---

48 Ibid., p. 33.
49 *Heyfield Herald*, 8 August 1912.
50 *Northern Territory Times*, 3 May 1912 and *Argus*, 4 May 1912. He also did this in Darwin.
51 *Heyfield Herald*, 8 August 1912.

The party split up, some returning to Darwin in time to catch the steamer home, others taking the opportunity to go to the Daly River, the second experimental farm the parliamentary visitors were scheduled to inspect. Those travelling to the Daly River were to go overland and back, and Campbell, ever the adventurer, was the first to volunteer, followed by five others.[52] This small party spent their first night in camp *en route* to the Daly River 'in the very best of country, and by far the best we had seen up to date'.[53] The luxurious growth after the wet could be deceptive.

In her book *How a Continent Creates a Nation*, particularly in her chapter titled 'The Empty North' which focuses on the failed development of the Northern Territory, Libby Robin concentrates on the Daly River area. She examines the relationship between nature and nation, focusing on the application of the sciences to the natural world and the triumph of the latter despite the effort by successive governments to sell the Territory to the world as a suitable, profitable place to settle.[54] The Daly River area, approachable only by boat, was first farmed in a tentative fashion in the 1870s, and in the 1880s became involved for a time in sugar production. Around the same time a cattle station was established, but late in the decade disease decimated the stock. Missionaries arrived but were eventually driven out by floods.[55] Past failures, however, were not taken into account, and the experimental farms went ahead under the Administrator, Dr John Gilruth.[56] As Libby Robin documents, this history of the failure of agriculture was to continue for the rest of the century in the Northern Territory, including on the Daly River, with the harsh climate and sheer isolation triumphing over science.[57] In May 1912 Campbell was still trying to capture images that would promote the Territory to the world as an agricultural paradise awaiting enterprising settlers.

There was a near disastrous attempt by members of the parliamentary party

---

52 Ibid. These were: the Director of Agriculture, WH Clarke; Senator Allan McDougall; MHR Alfred Ozanne; miner Mr A Kelly of Broken Hill; and Mr Ramsay, the farm manager for the government's proposed Daly River Demonstration Farm.

53 Ibid. This is the end of Campbell's written account of his Northern Territory experiences, or at least what was provided in the way of letters to the *Heyfield Herald*. The last letter, written in Darwin on 17 June 1912 and published on 8 August 1912, ended with: 'This is all for the present, as I've got to the end of my rough notes'.

54 Libby Robin, *How a Continent Created a Nation*, pp. 123-51.

55 Ibid., pp. 129-30.

56 Ibid., p. 131.

57 Ibid., pp. 141-9.

who had returned to Darwin from Pine Creek, including the Minister, to get to the mouth of the Daly River by sea. They were attempting to pick up the party members, including Campbell, who had travelled overland to the Daly, and at the same time view that part of the Territory themselves. They left on 2 May in three relatively small boats from Darwin, but the attempt was abandoned when one of the vessels, which happened to be carrying the only two Liberals, David Gordon and Colonel Granville Ryrie, was cast adrift on the open sea after a rope broke. They survived, but failed to enter the Daly River, leaving the other party no choice but to return to Darwin overland. The Minister's party then visited Melville and Thursday Islands instead.[58]

Colonel Ryrie inspected Thursday Island with an eye to defence, finding the established fort (not photographed by Campbell) obsolete. Later, back in Federal Parliament, Ryrie demanded that Australia increase its population for defence purposes, particularly in the north. He was sceptical about the development of the Northern Territory, attacking the application of agriculture, stating that the Government experimental farm at Batchelor would be a dismal failure, the soil being sand and gravel and generally miserable land for farming.[59]

The Minister's seafaring party returned to Darwin on Sunday 5 May, and the over-landing group from the Daly River (including Campbell) arrived back by special train from Brock's Creek (they were forced to retrace their tracks overland to Brock's Creek from the Daly River) on 8 May, just in time to catch the steamer *St Albans* for the journey south and home. Of all the members of the parliamentary party only Alfred Ozanne, MHR, and JP Campbell remained behind in Darwin.[60] Five days later Campbell left again for the Daly River, this time on the steamer *Waihoi* with, among others, the administrator, Dr John Gilruth and Professor Baldwin Spencer, Chief Protector of Aborigines.[61] Gilruth reported positively to the Minister of External Affairs on their return, stating that we 'had a good look at the country, and I am satisfied from results obtained from settlers there that there is [a] good future for the district'.[62]

---

58 Ibid., pp. 511-12, 523, and *Northern Territory Times*, 10 May 1912.

59 *Commonwealth of Australia Parliamentary Debates*, House of Representatives, 5 July 1912, pp. 508-9, 512.

60 *Argus*, 1 April 1912 & 9 May 1912.

61 *Northern Territory Times*, 17 May 1912. Others on this trip were: A Kelly, miner; Alfred Ozanne, politician; a Mr Carey, private secretary to the administrator; and WH Clarke, Director of Agriculture. Baldwin Spencer's contact with JP Campbell is discussed later in next chapter.

62 *Daily Herald* (Adelaide), 23 May 1912.

Once the official parliamentary party had departed, Campbell could concentrate on compiling a portfolio of images for promotional purposes. In addition to the Daly River district, Campbell toured Melville and Thursday Islands, and the Stapleton area, and it was in these places that he was able to photograph and film Aboriginal people, as well as some of the legendary European figures of the Northern Territory, like Joe Cooper, 'lord' of Melville Island. Campbell took an iconic photograph of Cooper which has been much reproduced, an image for which he is not acknowledged (Fig. 46). Cooper also featured in a Campbell photograph taken of the Brothers Quarters at the Bathurst Island Mission Station (Fig. 47).

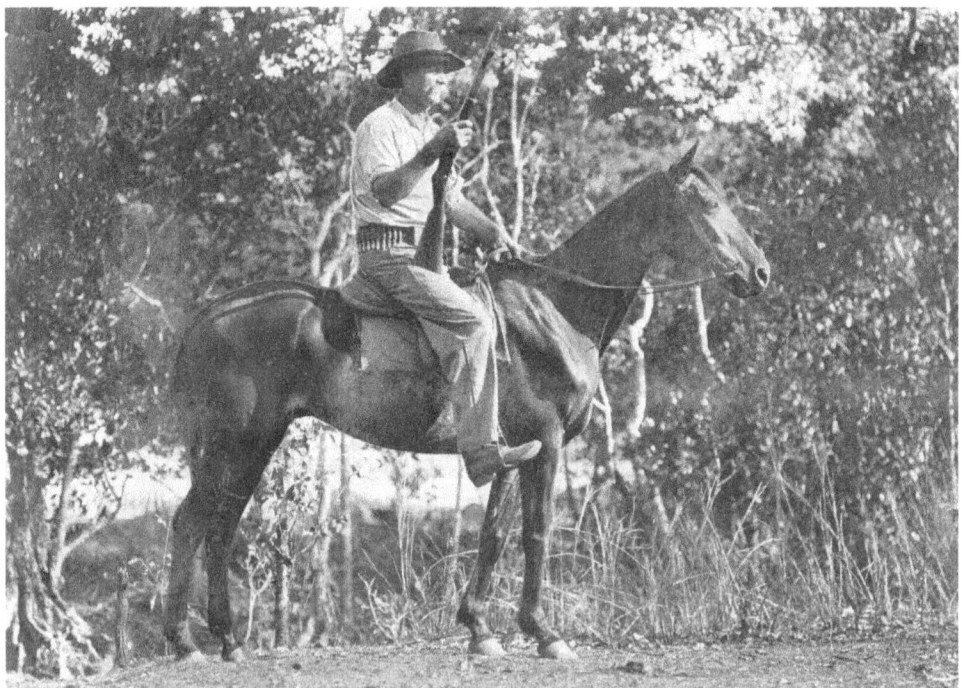

Fig 46. 'Joe Cooper on his favorite hunter'.[63]
(Northern Territory Library, <http://hdl.handle.net/10070/9844>)

This image appeared in both the Northern Territory Library and National Library of Australia souvenir albums, but not with the names of the two European men appended. However, they were named in the Melbourne *Leader*

---

63 The caption continues: 'Cooper has sole use of the Island 2400 square miles. He is the only white man thereon, and accounts for about 1000 Buffalo Hides per annum. (May to October the Dry Season)'. This picture appeared in the *Leader* of 17 May 1913.

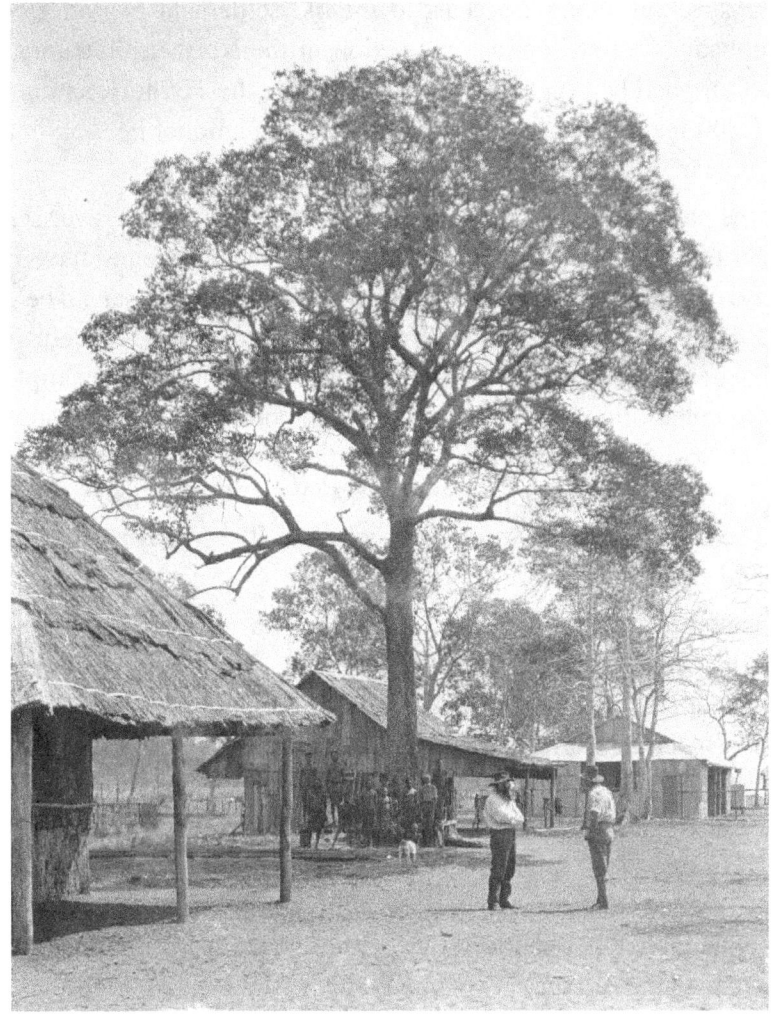

Fig 47. Father Gsell and Joe Cooper, and Aboriginal Group, Bathurst Island
Mission (Northern Territory Library, <http://hdl.handle.net/10070/7832>)

weekly illustrated newspaper of 22 March 1913, where the photograph appeared
alongside other Campbell Northern Territory photographs. They are 'Father Gsell
on the Left, Joe Cooper on the Right'. A group of Aboriginal people look on from
under the large tree, centre.[64] In early July 1912 Campbell left Darwin in a small
boat with the Administrator, Dr Gilruth, and two other officials on a week-long

64 RJ Cooper (1860-1936), Father FX Gsell and their relationship with the islander people is discussed
in DJ Mulvaney and JH Calaby, *So Much That Is New: Baldwin Spencer 1860-1929, A Biography*,
Melbourne University Press, Carlton, 1985, pp. 269-71, and Alan Powell, *Far Country*, p. 164.

'visit of inspection' along the coast to the old settlement of Port Essington.[65] It was probably Campbell's last expedition in the Northern Territory with his cameras. Campbell had spent over three months in the Territory, and in that time he took 3,800 feet of movie film, 23% of the total amount he took in Australia for the whole of 1912.[66]

After the parliamentary party had departed, the Territorians, ever sensitive to southern criticism, waited for the true thoughts of the politicians, having listened to what was generally glib and polite rhetoric during their stay. The *Northern Territory Times and Gazette* monitored with glee, via the southern press, the outpouring of the parliamentarians as they journeyed home. For example Senator Blakey, disembarking in Brisbane, said the Zapopan gold mine, purchased by the Federal Government from a private syndicate, was no good, but thought the country offered 'excellent opportunities'. Mr West, MHR, 'had much to say in favor of the country, *but little for its inhabitants* [the *Northern Territory Times and Gazette* emphasis]'.[67]

Campbell became caught up in this bitter war-of-words in the aftermath of the parliamentary visit. Back in Victoria the *Walhalla Chronicle* reprinted three of his letters from the *Heyfield Herald*, and one found its way to Darwin. The *Northern Territory Times and Gazette* did not reprint the letter, but named Campbell and identified him as 'the Federal Government photographer who has for some time past been taking views in the Territory'.[68] The newspaper described the letter as containing 'some amusingly frank and not too flattering statements respecting various matters Territorian', but refrained from further comment, stating Campbell had not intended the letter to be published. It noted, with some sarcasm, that Campbell thought white women could not cope in the climate.[69] Campbell returned south sometime in July or August.

---

65 *Northern Territory Times and Gazette*, 12 July 1912.
66 Memorandum, DB Edward to Atlee Hunt, 8 March 1913, in NAA: A1, 1913/14458.
67 *Northern Territory Times and Gazette*, 24 May 1912.
68 Ibid., 23 August 1912.
69 Ibid. It is possible that Campbell did not know his letters were being published, given he was away from Darwin a lot, and the mail from down south would have taken some time to get to him.

5

PROMOTING THE NORTHERN TERRITORY

Promoting the Northern Territory – The Souvenir Album – The Views Booklet and Postcards – Campbell and the Aborigines – Campbell's Demise as Commonwealth Photographer/Cinematographer

Between June 1912 and May 1913 a show of Campbell's movie film and photographs of the Northern Territory toured Australia, visiting cities including, Melbourne, Sydney, Adelaide, Hobart, Launceston and Broken Hill. It drew large crowds and had mixed reviews. The Melbourne show was held in mid June 1912 at the Salvation Army hall in the presence of the Minister for External Affairs and other ministers and their friends. Both the *Age* and the *Argus* criticised the movie film for 'lacking in general interest' and focusing too much on the camping and social activities of the parliamentary party.[1] The Northern Territory trip had not occupied all Campbell's time as Commonwealth photographer. His movies of the sheep and timber industries in Victoria were also shown, along with his 'long film of some of the methods of amusement in Sydney'. Indeed the *Age* reviewer believed the best film shown did not concern the Northern Territory, but 'was one which gave an excellent idea of the timber industry at Warburton and the grandeur of the mountain scenery' (Fig. 48).[2] Campbell was at his creative best in his home-state, particularly the hills of eastern Victoria.

South Australia, having not long relinquished control of the Northern Territory, and being more familiar with it, received the touring picture show with more enthusiasm. The Adelaide show was held in January 1913 at West's Olympia Theatre. The Governor of South Australia, the Minister for External Affairs and other luminaries attended, along with hundreds of school children. An orchestra accompanied the moving pictures, and the 'set views' were 'entertainingly explained from the stage', possibly by their creator, JP Campbell, who had travelled from Mansfield to attend.[3] The *Adelaide Register* praised the show:

---

1 *Age* and *Argus*, 18 June 1912. The Salvation Army biograph department developed the films.

2 *Age*, 18 June 1912.

3 *Adelaide Register*, 16 & 23 January 1913 and a JP Campbell postcard dated 16 January 1913 and held by Peter Pinkerton, showing a water buffalo pulling a plough guided by a man, with details on the back of Campbell's plans to travel to Adelaide and his offer of tickets to anyone wishing to attend the Northern Territory show.

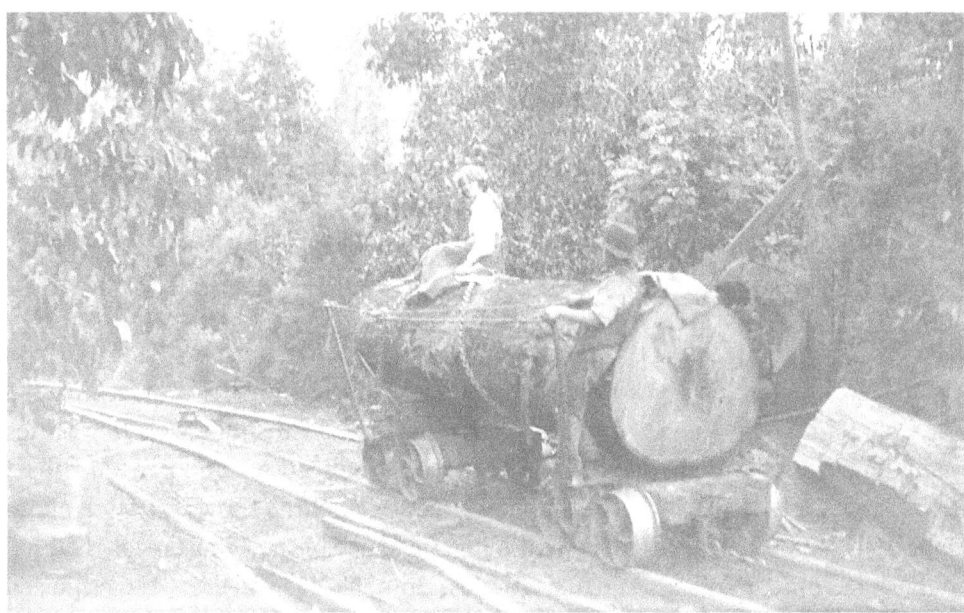

Fig. 48. Ada Campbell, JP Campbell's daughter, sitting on a log and trolley on a timber tram line as part of a promotional film for the timber industry in 1912.[4] The man controlling the trolley is well camouflaged. (Courtesy of Falconer family collection)

To launch upon detailed description of that avalanche of scenes would be an unwarrantable task. They left one main indelible impression upon the beholder, however, namely that northern Australia is truly a wonderful country, tropically luxuriant. To cull a vignette from the mass, one of the most magnetic of the motion scenes described a grass fire. Billowing white clouds ballooned upwards from long lines of rushing flames. Next came a view of that stretch of denuded country, only a few weeks afterwards, yet showing a superb growth of fresh young grass, and all without moisture other than the bounteous dew that falls by night.[5]

Smoke and fog, trademarks of Campbell's still photography, featured in the moving films. He captured Melville Island buffalo hunting, sawmilling, and tropical fruit and vegetable gathering industries on movie film. Movie film was, of course, still in its infancy, so in Adelaide as in other locations, the audience was

4 This is a 'still' from the movie film. As previously mentioned, Ada left school early because of illness and between 1907 and 1913 she often accompanied her father on photographic expeditions. Part of the movie showed Ada's skirt caught in blackberries, which provided some amusement for the audience when it premiered in Melbourne. Conversation with Noel Fethers, 7 February 2006.
5 *Adelaide Register*, 23 January 1912.

transfixed by the technology. The *Adelaide Register* appreciated the promotional content in the film, concluding 'that Australia's northern inheritance is a veritable wonderland, rich below and above its surfaces of unending plain and rugged mountain – a land which must be kept and held, and above all immensely developed for Australia and Empire'.[6] The Register's opposition, the Adelaide *Advertiser*, was, however, dismissive of the Northern Territory promotional film, almost sneeringly so:

> This is to be shown throughout the British provinces, doubtless not on account of its display of the Territory's products – there are no pretensions in that regard – but to convince possible immigrants that the Commonwealth legislators are accustomed to the rigors of the bush.[7]

The Launceston show also received criticism, the *Examiner* pointing out that the 'party evidently had a glorious time of it', with the movie film showing little 'from the development [of the Northern Territory] point of view', thus negating its purpose. The pictures were 'interesting' and in many cases 'charming' and 'beautiful . . . but that is the most that can be said'.[8] Campbell's pictorialism was shining through. When the show rolled in to Broken Hill the local paper was more positive in its reporting. Its reviewer was captivated by the scenes on Melville Island of buffalo and turtle hunting, as well as the wildlife:

> One of the finest views exhibited was a picture showing an enormous rookery of seagulls. Thousands and thousands of these birds were seen, and when they rose from the ground their wings almost obscured the sun from the camera.[9]

Campbell's cousin, the amateur ornithologist Archibald Campbell, would no doubt have been pleased with this effort by James. It may be one of Australia's first movie film scenes of such profuse wildlife.

In April 1913 Campbell's 'cinematograph pictures' of the Northern Territory were shown for the first time in England, in Camborne, Cornwall, the home town of the Australian Minister for External Affairs, Josiah Thomas. It was an invitation

---

6 Ibid.

7 Adelaide *Advertiser*, 8 July 1912.

8 The Launceston *Examiner*, 5 April 1913.

9 The Broken Hill *Barrier Miner*, 26 May 1913. The last image in *Views of the Northern Territory of Australia* is of a Crested Tern rookery at Cape Van Diemen in the far north-west corner of Melville Island. Terns are massed on the ground with hundreds of others whirling above them against a cloudy sky.

only affair at the behest of the Commonwealth Government of Australia and in the name of Mr Thomas, who had a number of relatives in the audience of 1500. The show was designed to attract immigrants, but was also a celebration of a favourite son. The London correspondent of the Sydney *Daily Telegraph* crowed 'that these pictures are the finest yet shown by any Dominion Government in the United Kingdom', and they would 'unquestionably give a decided impetus to emigration'.[10] The demand for Campbell's Northern Territory photographs, albums and lantern slides was high. The Prime Minister and Governor General were given copies. Ministers and other parliamentarians borrowed the movie film and showed it in their electorates. There were enough favourable press reports to buoy Campbell's spirits considerably.[11]

Whatever the criticisms of the quality of Campbell's work, the Department of External Affairs made good use of his images. In June 1913 it published *Views of the Northern Territory of Australia*, a 52-page book of photographs, with no acknowledgement of the photographer, Campbell, as was the practice with government organisations. The images focused on primary industry, infrastructure and landscape, all designed to show the Territory in the best possible light to attract prospective settlers from abroad and within Australia. Only eight of the forty-eight images appearing in *Views* also appear in the *Souvenir* album, the album compiled as a record of the Northern Territory parliamentary visit. Many of the other forty images were taken by Campbell after the parliamentary party departed Darwin.

Campbell and his employer, the External Affairs Department, used various forms of image presentation to depict the Northern Territory. The meaning of Campbell's photographs changed depending on the medium they appeared in and the caption attached. Campbell's pictorialist aesthetic influenced what he chose to photograph in the Northern Territory and in Australia as a whole during his time as a public servant. The tension between art and record partly determined the photographic product.[12]

The 133 images in the souvenir album titled *Souvenir of the Visit of the Federal Parliamentary Party to the Northern Territory, 1912* provided a record

---

10 Sydney *Daily Telegraph* report dated 18 April 1913 and reprinted in the Broken Hill (NSW) paper, the *Barrier Miner*, 27 May 1913.

11 Letter, JP Campbell to Patrick Glynn, 11 July 1913, in NAA: A1, 1913/14458.

12 This conflict between art and record may also have manifested itself in Campbell's movie film footage, but unfortunately none of the movie film has survived.

of the trip for its participants, other members of parliament and relevant officials. Campbell produced a souvenir album for the Minister of External Affairs, and was directed to compile three similar albums to be distributed to the Governor General and the Governors of New South Wales and South Australia.[13] The photographs in these albums are presented in chronological order, plotting the narrative from the steamer leaving Sydney to its departure from Darwin. They show the party *en route* in trains, boats, buggies and on horses, with camping, swimming, landscape and street scenes, interesting characters (whether black or white), and mines, agricultural activity, schools and police stations. The captions, in Campbell's handwriting, are informative, and not worded solely for advertising. The *Views* booklet had a more formal structure. The blurb at the front attempted to promote the Territory to prospective settlers. It stated that, although land in the Territory varied in quality, much of it was suitable for farming when combined with grazing. The Territory was described as mineral rich, free of tropical diseases and with a climate which offered no barrier to white settlement. Even so, only enterprising people willing to overcome hardships were invited to apply for land. The government was prepared to help those interested in farming and mining with 'cheap land and liberal assistance'.[14]

To illustrate the government's assertions landscape photographs were included in *Views* alongside rural and mining scenes. Newly constructed schools demonstrated the existence of a civilised society. Selected by the Department, the images were clear and concise, not too much Campbell smoke or dust. But in 'Pine Creek Gold Mine – Carting Timber' (Fig. 49) Campbell was able to satisfy his employer while indulging himself as an artist. The image provides evidence of a gold mining industry to potential immigrants, and at the same time depicts a scene artfully divided in two by the river, with the curve of the road and the wood-carrying cart below, juxtaposed with the wood piles and mine structures above, and the hills and sky beyond.

The captions in *Views* were concise, such as 'Large cattle in good condition, Stapleton', 'Jungle cleared to make watering place for stock', or 'New School, Pine Creek', indicating a positive agricultural economy. The images and captions present a place of plentiful water, lush grass plains, thriving crops, scenic surrounds and a settled white society. A picture of the parliamentary visitors

13 Note, Secretary of Department of External Affairs to JP Campbell, 15 Febuary 1912, in NAA: A1, 1913/14458. As we have seen, at least two of these albums have survived.
14 Introduction, *Views* of the Northern Territory of Australia.

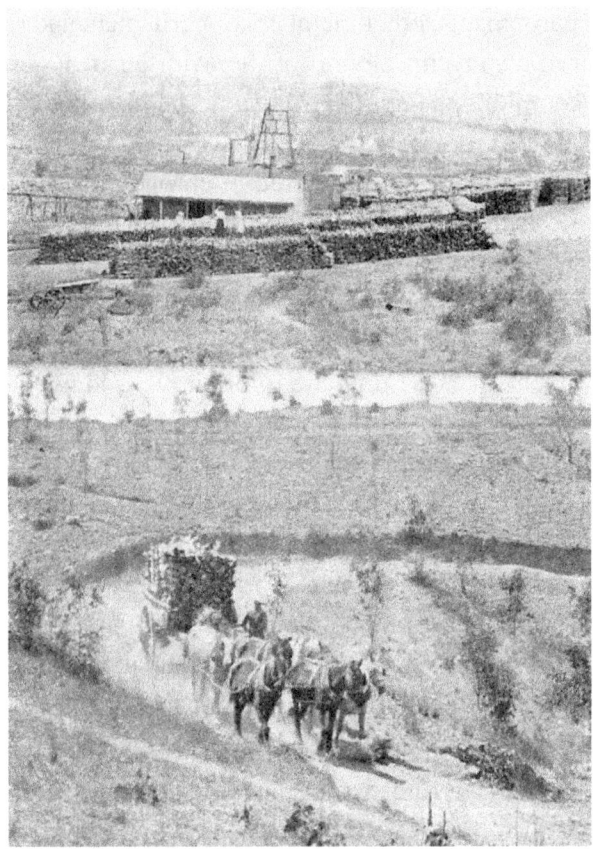

Fig.49. 'Pine Creek Gold Mine – CartingTimber'.
Getting a balance: a utilitarian and pictorialist scene
from the *Views* booklet.

inspecting a garden on the Daly River has alternative captions. In the *Souvenir* album it is captioned 'Scenes on Thomas and Roberts' Plantation on the Daly River 2 miles above the Landing – Tobacco'.[15]

In the *Views* booklet the caption is: 'Tobacco, bananas, lucerne, maize, &c., successfully grown'. The crop was not merely there, but was successful, proof of the fecundity of the land, and suggesting prospective settlers could achieve the same results. Further pictures in *Views* optimistically displayed wool growing, even though this industry was a dismal failure in the North from the start.[16]

15 This caption refers to two photographs with the subject tobacco on the same leaf or page, along with two other images of other crops on the same leaf.
16 Bruce Davidson, *The Northern Myth*, p. 68.

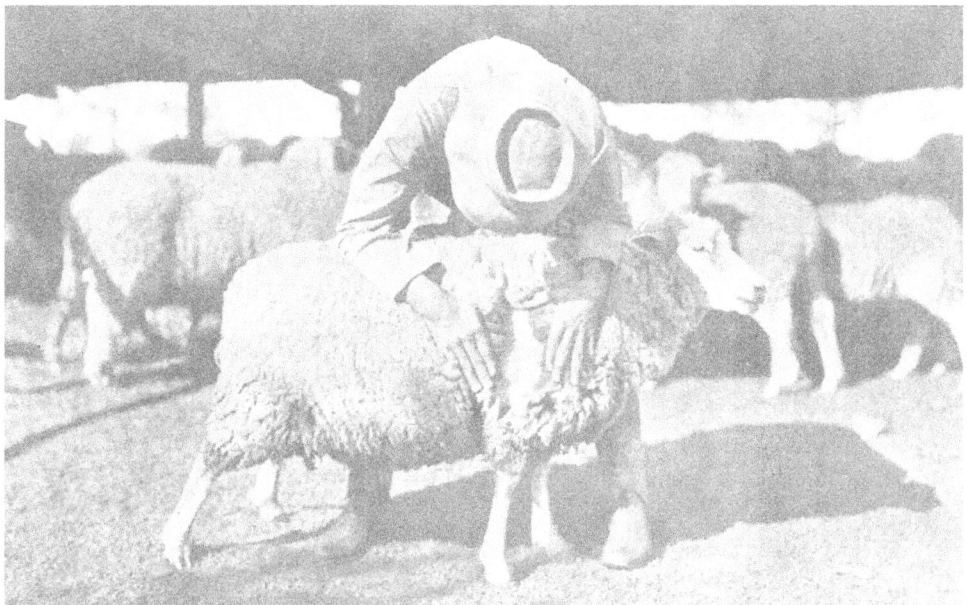

Fig. 50. 'Good fleece'. Campbell was adept at making agricultural show images come alive. *Views* booklet.

Here Campbell demonstrated photography skills acquired at country agricultural shows down south (Fig. 50).[17]

To ensure the message spread to a wider audience, the Commonwealth Government produced from the images in *Views* a series of postcards which still circulate among postcard collectors (Fig. 51).

He produced composite postcards under his own copyright, made up of photographs of images which appeared in *Views* and the *Souvenir* album.

Campbell also produced postcards under his own copyright and for his own private gain from official External Affairs images he took as Commonwealth photographer in the Northern Territory. For example, on a Vallan Studio composite postcard titled 'Port Darwin With Merry Wishes', there are six small scenes, two of which appeared in *Views* and the other four in the *Souvenir* album. The postcards are signed 'J.P. Campbell', with the address '12 Hunter St., Malvern,

---

17 Campbell's official images were also used to illustrate official reports. The Commonwealth report on operations in the Northern Territory for the year 1912 contained six of his photographs in its forty-eight pages, scenes of farmland, forest, rivers, horses and coconut groves. They are benign images showing a picturesque and productive place in line with the advertising objectives. *Northern Territory of Australia, Report of the Administrator for the Year 1912*, Parliament of the Commonwealth of Australia, 1913.

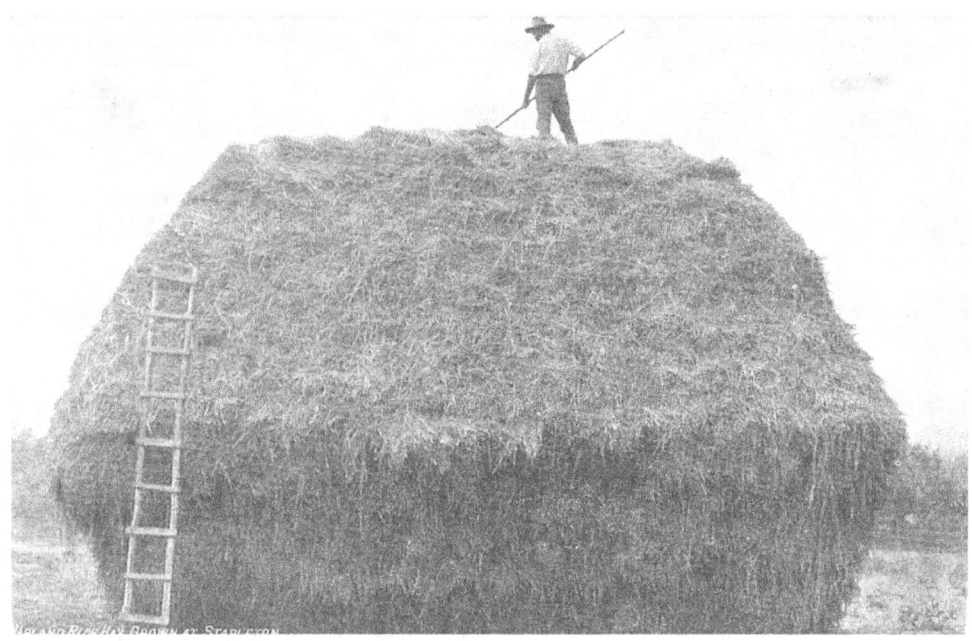

Fig. 51. An example of a Commonwealth of Australia Northern Territory Series of postcards, captioned 'Upland Rice Hay Grown at Stapleton'. (Author's collection)

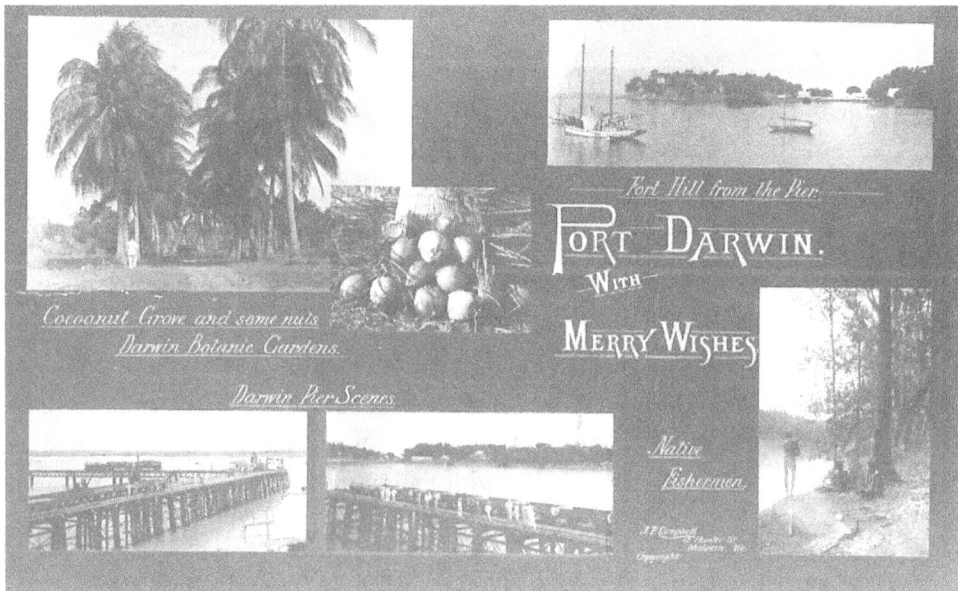

Fig. 52. A Vallan Studio commercial postcard produced from Campbell's External Affairs Department photographs. (Author's collection)

Vic.', and 'Copyright', in very small white-ink writing (Fig. 52). In addition, a number of his Northern Territory photographs were published in the Melbourne *Leader*.[18]

Campbell believed he had poured a lot of his own resources into the Territory job, but these postcards go some way to proving the veiled assertion of his employer that Campbell was using Department of External Affairs resources for his, and possibly Herbert Vallance's, gain.[19] A blurred boundary existed between private and official photographer. Campbell was not a permanent public servant and not subject to the Public Service Act, and was not the first photographer to use 'official' images for private purposes, as documented by photography historians Anne Maree Willis and Jane Lydon in their discussion of official and commissioned photographers. Willis relates how photographer Charles Bayliss was appointed official photographer to a Royal Commission on the conservation of water, examining the Darling River system in the 1880s. His images were used to illustrate the commission's report, but few seemed to be directly related to the specifics of the project. Instead, Bayliss had taken the opportunity 'to build up his [private] stock of saleable views'.[20]

Lydon, in her study of photography at the Coranderrk Aboriginal Reserve in Victoria, points out that a succession of professional photographers for the reserve, including Nicholas Caire, profited from their official commission by producing postcards for public sale from the images produced.[21] This entrepreneurial behaviour may have been an unwritten part of commission agreements, or the officials involved may have turned a blind eye to it. After all, it did mean the official images reached a wider market, and for the photographers it was a bonus in the competitive world of professional photography.

Many of Campbell's Northern Territory photographs, and his movie film, ended up overseas, the majority sent to the Australian High Commissioner in London. From there the photographs were widely distributed in publications, and the film was shown in movie houses, with the hope that some Britons might

---

18 This will be discussed in more detail later in this chapter.

19 This discussion is based on three composite postcards in the author's collection obtained from a postcard collector. The other two are titled 'Pine Creek Township, Northern Territory' and 'Darwin, N.T.'. It may well be that the glass plates Campbell used in taking these images were also his own, as well as the camera.

20 Willis, Anne Marie, *Picturing Australia: A History of Photography*, Angus and Robertson, North Ryde, NSW, 1988, p. 95.

21 Jane Lydon, 'Regarding Coranderrk', p. 213.

immigrate. When Joanna Sassoon tried to trace the photographs of Campbell's contemporary, Western Australian state photographer EL Mitchell, from the time of taking to the present, she found that the large collection of up to 30,000 items of 'photographs, lantern slides and associated documentation' once held at Australia House in London no longer existed. It was the same situation at the Australian embassy in Washington.[22] Some of this collection was probably destroyed due to storage space reasons. Away from the 'archival eye in Australia' the material simply disappeared. Sassoon concludes that perhaps this is what the collection was designed for, to be distributed, serving its intended purpose, and so becoming a 'phantom'.[23] Many of Campbell's promotional photographs of Australia presumably suffered the same fate, along with his movie film, which had the added disadvantage of a tendency to decay quickly, especially after exposure to the Northern Territory climate. As publications the *Views* booklet has survived, while the *Souvenir* album remains, preserved in our public archives. Campbell's images of Aboriginal people have also survived in the *Souvenir* album, in bequests to his family, in the *Leader* newspaper, and in postcards in private collections. Some of his Northern Territory photographs were reproduced in the highly successful book, *Australia Unlimited*, a survey of Australia's resources and economic potential written by E.J. Brady.[24]

Campbell's knowledge exposure to Aboriginal culture prior to his visit to the Northern Territory is unknown; I have been unable to find any photographs of Aboriginal people taken by Campbell in Victoria. He knew JW Lindt, a photographer renowned for his ethnographic work, and visited his home 'The Hermitage' near the Coranderrk Aboriginal Station.[25] Lindt's good friend Nicholas Caire, predominantly a landscape photographer like Campbell, was commissioned in 1904 to take photographs of Coranderrk. In her study of photography at Coranderrk, the historian Jane Lydon described these images as stereotypes, that is, records of what many people at that time perceived was a dying race. Caire was famous for showing the bush as a romantic setting with

---

22 Joanna Sassoon, 'Chasing Phantoms in the Archives: The Australia House Photograph Collection', *Archivaria*, Number 50, Fall 2000, p. 119.

23 Ibid., pp. 121-2.

24 Brady, Edwin James, *Australia Unlimited*, George Robertson and Co., Melbourne, 1918, pp. 519, 525, 534, 536, 549, 566, 584. Also, in the Appendix on how to acquire land in the Northern Territory: pp. xxix, xxx.

25 Interview with Noel Fethers, 20 April 2005. Campbell took his daughter, Ada, with him on these visits. He may have visited this station in his capacity as a traveller with Henry Berry and Company, or out of interest, perhaps with his photographer friends.

the settler's hut nestled neatly in the forest. This did not, it seems, transfer to his Aboriginal subjects at Coranderrk: 'Caire', Lydon declares, 'seems to have saved his sentiment for the trees'.[26] Lindt and Caire set an example for other photographers to follow in this field.

Campbell would have no doubt viewed the ethnographic images of Lindt and Caire, and also the work of biologist and anthropologist Professor Baldwin Spencer, whose photographs, movie film and audio recordings of the Aboriginal people of central Australia were given public exposure in the early 1900s, along with his written anthropological publications of expeditions into the interior. Lindt became Spencer's photography consultant, suggesting another possible link to Campbell.[27] Presumably Campbell held similar attitudes towards indigenous people as Caire and Spencer, as is made clear in his comments on Northern Territory people already quoted. While Spencer was kind and considerate towards Aboriginal people, as documented by the archaeologist John Mulvaney, his 'fieldwork and analysis of data were filtered . . . through the preconceptions and value systems of both Evolution and Empire'. As Mulvaney argues:

> Spencer believed that biological evolution went along with mental development and material progress. He conceived of Aborigines as surviving fossil remnants from the remote past, whose social and belief systems reflected this pristine condition. The implicit racial superiority of such assumptions is unacceptable today.[28]

As valuable as Spencer's ethnographic photographs are, they were influenced by his underlying Darwinian beliefs.

There is a probability that Spencer influenced Campbell's photographic approach to Aboriginal people whilst in the Northern Territory in 1912, as the two came into contact with one another a number of times. Campbell gave Spencer 3,000 feet of Commonwealth supplied movie film, presumably because Spencer had run out of film due to the harsh climatic conditions.[29] Spencer and Campbell

---

26 Jane Lydon, 'Regarding Coranderrk', pp. 208-9, 219-21, 235-7.

27 See Baldwin Spencer, *The Aboriginal Photographs of Baldwin Spencer*, Introduction by John Mulvaney, Photographs selected and annotated by Geoffrey Walker, Ron Vanderwal, John Currey (Eds), O'Neil Pty Ltd, South Yarra, 1982, p. viii.

28 Ibid., p. x.

29 Memorandum, DB Edward to Atlee Hunt, 8 March 1913, in NAA: A1, 1913/14458. John Mulvaney gives a good account of the problems Spencer had with both movie and still photography in the unforgiving Northern Territory climate in his introduction to *The Aboriginal Photographs of Baldwin Spencer*, p. ix.

had plenty of time to 'swap notes' on the technicalities of photography in such difficult conditions, as they had both participated in a weeklong excursion to the Daly River in May 1912, as already mentioned.[30] Overall it is in the context of Campbell's experience (or lack of) with Aboriginal photography, the influence of contemporaries like Spencer, and the social attitudes of colonialism, that the creation of his images of Aborigines in the Northern Territory should be assessed. The images, contained in his booklet, album and postcards, reached a range of audiences.

Looking at the promotional *Views*, one might think Aboriginal people did not exist in the Northern Territory, for none appear in it. In the *Souvenir* album there are fourteen pictures of Aboriginal people. Some are close studies, while others are distant. The Northern Territory photographs in the Falconer collection include nine uncaptioned images of Aborigines out of a total thirty-five photographs, a random extant sample of what must have been scores of prints. Five of these are also in the *Souvenir* album, two appeared in the *Leader*, while six are unique to the Falconer collection. Interestingly, in the 'Kirkbride collection' album of JP Campbell's 1912 Northern Territory images held by the State Library of Victoria, there are approximately ninety-seven photographs containing Aboriginal people, nineteen percent of the total number of 500 images in the album.[31] Pictures of Aboriginal people were clearly available for use in Commonwealth Government publications. Perhaps Aborigines were not included in the *Views* booklet as photographic subjects because this might deter settlers; creating an image of an Anglo-Saxon dominated agrarian arcadia in the Northern Territory was preferred. The introduction to the *Views* booklet makes this pretty clear: 'Australian people have resolved that this land [in the Northern Territory] shall be occupied by white men'.[32] Thus Aboriginal people were rendered invisible in material promoting the Territory.

When Aboriginal people did appear in a scenic picture they were sometimes obliterated from it for promotional purposes. One scene of the Daly River containing an Aborigine was deemed generally suitable to include in *Views*, but he was simply blanked out. In the original image, included in the *Souvenir* album with the caption 'The Daly River above the Landing, A fine waterway 100 yards

30 DJ Mulvaney and JH Calaby, *So Much That Is New*, p. 295.
31 State Library of Victoria, Kirkbride collection, Accession no. H27744.
32 From introduction to *Views of the Northern Territory of Australia*, External Affairs department, 1913.

wide, tidal influence four feet', he is seen sitting on a log on the riverbank in the foreground fishing by a tree, with the expanse of the river beyond, and a boat load of white-clad parliamentary members ploughing through the water in the background (Fig. 53). The same photograph, published in the *Views* booklet, was captioned 'A beautiful reach on the Daly River'. The Aboriginal fisherman has gone, expunged from the landscape. The fishing pole he was holding is still there, suspended in mid air (Fig. 54).

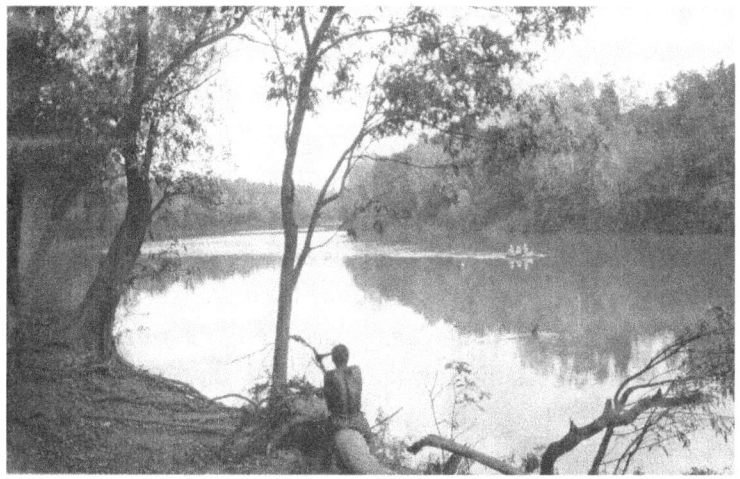

Fig. 53. Campbell's original photograph 'On the Daly River above the Landing', from the *Souvenir* album. (Northern Territory Library, <http://hdl.handle.net/10070/3833>)

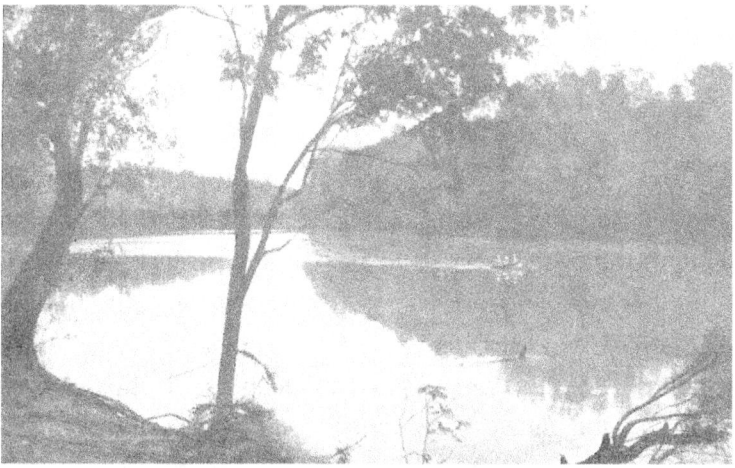

Fig. 54 (below) shows the *Views* version, captioned 'A beautiful reach on the Daly River'. The fishing pole is suspended in mid-air.

Campbell would have deliberately included the Aboriginal fisherman in the foreground as a point of interest, and an integral part of his photographic composition. Why the fishing pole was left in the *Views* booklet image is a mystery.

Although they were obliterated from the official *Views* publication, Campbell chose to send photographs containing Aboriginal people to the *Leader*, where they were exposed to a more general, mainly Victorian, readership. Campbell's attitude towards Aborigines reflected the general view of the time – he saw them as primitive and inferior to Europeans, but fascinating and photogenic. The example of the incident at Katherine, when he was angry at being prevented from photographing a 'blacks camp', demonstrates his interest.

Of the thirty-seven photographs of the Northern Territory trip he had published in the Melbourne *Leader*, at least nine contained Aborigines. In two issues they were the primary subject. One of these is a large, pictorialist image of four Aborigines fishing by the Daly River, captioned 'View on the Daly River, Northern Territory'. One man is standing, legs apart, back to camera and silhouetted against the river, two are sitting at the base of a tree, the other standing and leaning against the tree. In the foreground the smoke from a fire drifts sideways in front of the figure fishing, giving him an even more mystical appearance (Fig. 55).[33] The photograph was placed in the middle of the newspaper's page, taking up most of it, with a wide, decorative border. It conveys a feeling of the primeval, the 'noble savage' in a timeless environment, and yet at the same time is an everyday scene on the river.

Another group of images Campbell contributed to the *Leader* was headed 'Melville Islanders', three photographs with the following captions: 'Melville Island Natives showing the Markings cut in flesh'; 'Melville Island Bark Canoe. The Melville Islanders are Much More Primitive than the Mainlanders'; and 'Melville Island Woman'. Underneath this group of photographs is a separate series of five Campbell images on the buffalo hide industry in the Northern Territory.[34]

The nine Aboriginal images that survive in the Falconer collection include five boys lined up along a wire mesh fence (Fig.56), showing Campbell's liking for the linear. Like all the Aboriginal images in the Falconer collection it is uncaptioned, but it appears in the *Leader*, captioned 'Bathurst Islanders'. The Falconer

33 *Leader*, 27 July 1912, p. 25.
34 *Leader*, 17 May 1913.

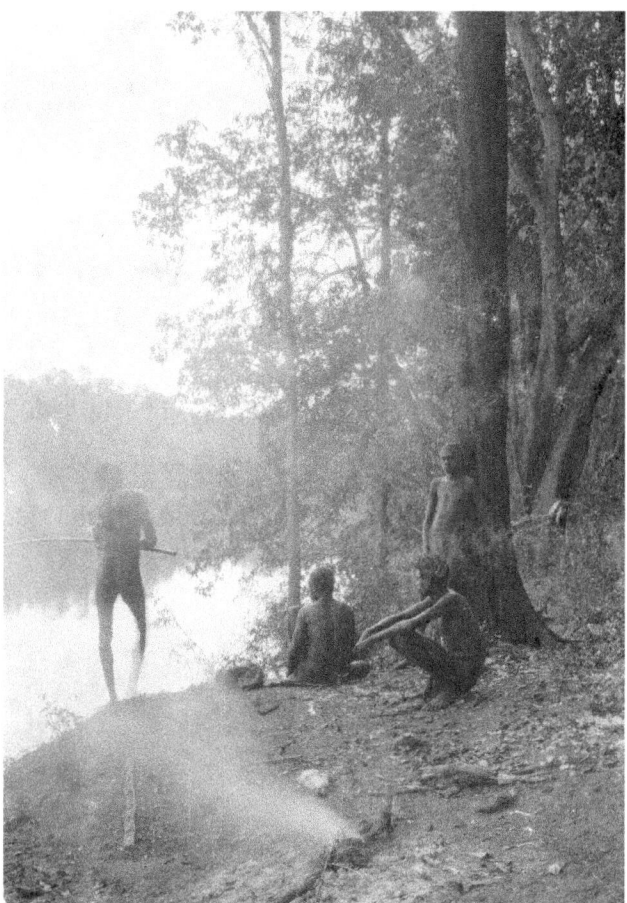

Fig. 55. Captioned 'View on the Daly River, Northern Territory', in
the *Leader*, 27 July 1912, this image also appears in the *Souvenir*
album, captioned 'Daly River Natives Fishing for Barramundi'
(Northern Territory Library, <http://hdl.handle.net/10070/1401>)

collection series of Aboriginal photographs shows a typical choreographed
Campbell image of three children and a gunyah (Fig. 57); two pictures of young
men carrying and eating what looks like melons; children washing clothes in
a creek; women and a pile of rice grass; and men standing around grave posts
during a mourning ceremony, probably on Bathhurst Island (Fig. 58). A very
similar picture appears in a book of Baldwin Spencer photographs, published in
2007.[35]

---

35 Phillip Batty, Lindy Allen and John Morton (eds.), *The Photographs of Baldwin Spencer*, The
Miegunyah Press and Museum Victoria, Carlton, Victoria, 2007, p. 188.

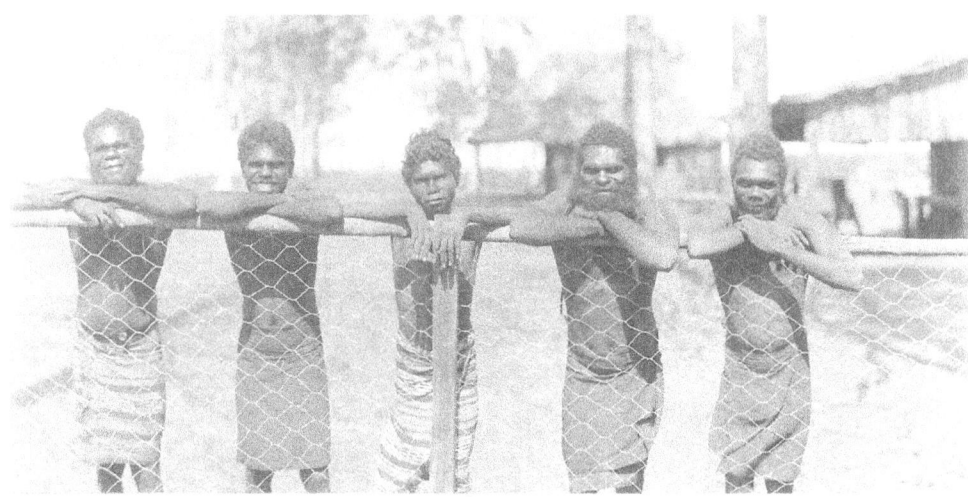

Fig. 56. 'Bathurst Islanders', the *Leader*, 22 March 1913.
(Courtesy of Falconer collection)

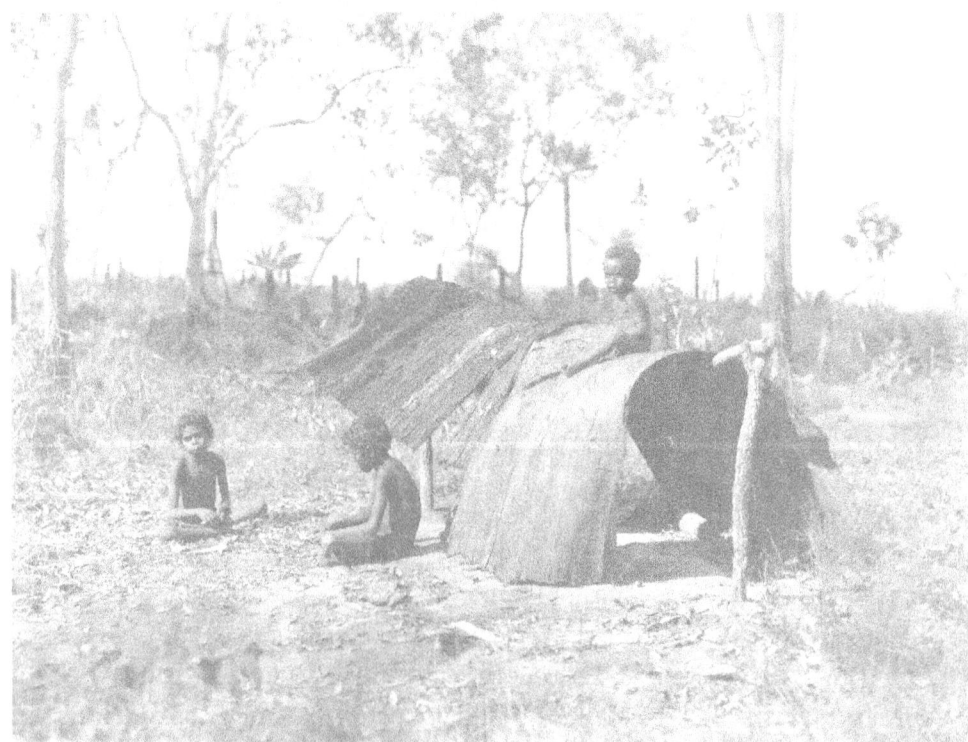

Fig. 57. Aboriginal children and gunyah. Uncaptioned by Campbell. He may have put the
child on top of the structure for pictorial interest, as he had often choreographed scenes
involving children, particularly relatives. (Courtesy of Falconer collection)

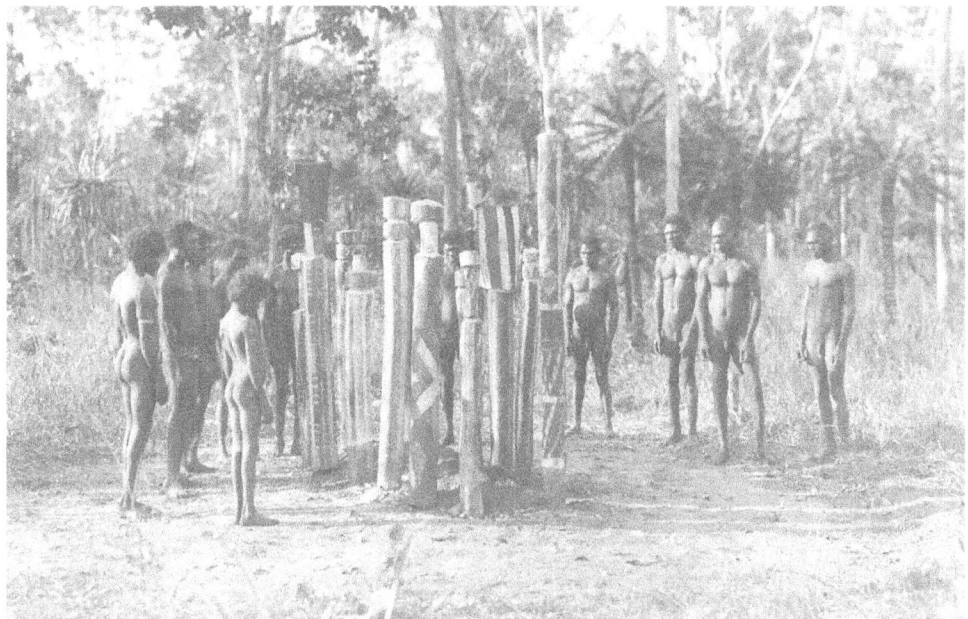

Fig. 58. Mourning ceremony. Uncaptioned by Campbell. Aboriginal men and boys gathered around grave posts, probably on Bathurst Island. (Courtesy of the Falconer collection)

Campbell's images of Aborigines were not commissioned, and he had them published in the *Leader* for popular consumption. He was using the opportunity whilst on his official assignment to take photographs to satisfy his own creative impulses and to market them in order to derive income. As he took a lot of his own photographic equipment and materials to the Northern Territory, he probably felt justified in amassing private images. Campbell's photographs appeared in the *Leader* in July 1912, eleven photographs under his name and the heading 'The Northern Territory Visit of the Ministerial Party'.[36] Another eight photographs were published in May 1913, including 'Melville Islanders', already discussed, and five pictures of the 'Buffalo Hide Industry in the North'.[37] It was another way of advertising the Territory to a mass market, but the inclusion of Aborigines contradicted the approach taken in *Views*, giving mixed signals. *Views* was aimed primarily at the overseas market, advertising to attract settlers from the United Kingdom, Europe in general, and America, where there was less knowledge of the Northern Territory. In Australia, the population would be generally aware of

36 *Leader*, 6 July 1912. These photographs covered the arrival in Darwin, aspects of the town, Daly River 'Blacks' and the trip to Brocks and Pine Creek.
37 *Leader*, 17 May 1913.

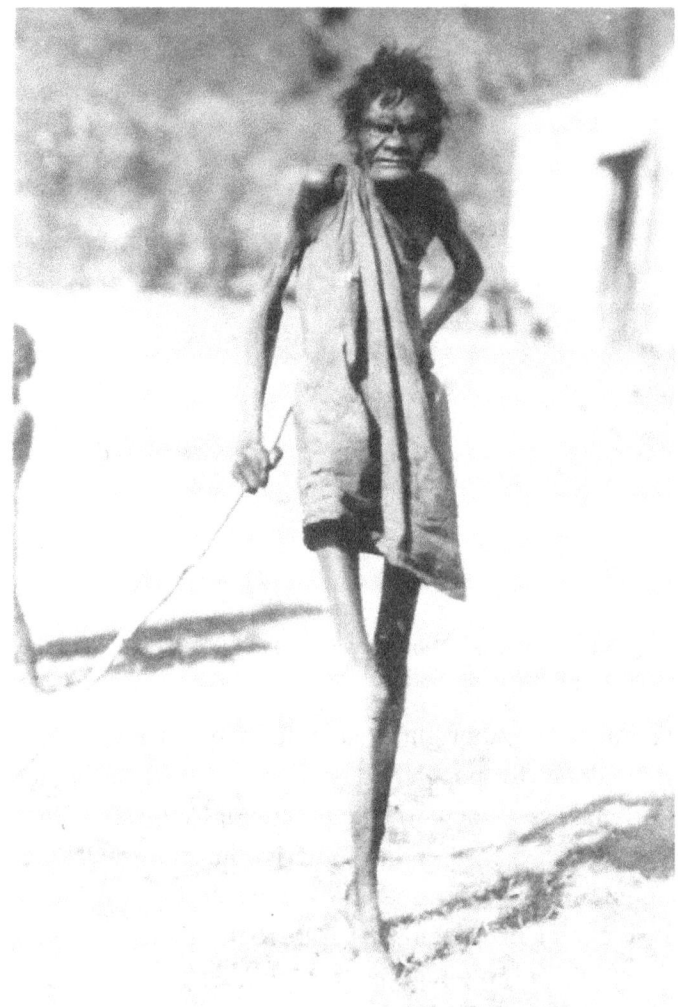

Fig 59. 'Skeleton Annie, Northern Territory'.
(Copy of original Vallan Studio postcard, Author's collection)

the presence of Aboriginal people in the wild north, and thus concealing their presence would be futile.

Campbell also included Aborigines in the postcards he produced of the Northern Territory. Of the handful I have been able to find, the photograph of an emaciated Aboriginal woman captioned 'Skeleton Annie, Northern Territory' is both memorable and disturbing (Fig. 59). That Campbell could exploit her condition for use in a commercial postcard seems remarkable, given that he was a Mason and regarded himself as a Christian gentleman. Did she cooperate? Was she paid to pose? She appears defiant, hand on hip, staring straight into the lens. Was her European nickname 'Skeleton Annie'? Was Campbell trying to show the state of some of the Aborigines in the Territory, or was she presented as a grotesque curio, her image appropriated to titillate the consumers of postcards? Campbell, it seems, could not resist photographing her.

Joanna Sassoon writes about a contemporary of Campbell, EL Mitchell of Perth.[38] Mitchell took pictures of Aboriginal people in active contexts such as fishing, and, like Campbell, he had them published in pictorial weekly newspapers. His photographs showed 'his desire to represent a pre-contact and pristine notion of Aboriginality', whereas Campbell was willing to include European influences.[39] Mitchell turned ethnographic photographs into popular postcards, and while these are now a good source of ethnographic information, they were not created to provide anthropological information, but were taken speculatively or under contract for economic gain.[40] The original captions could be changed to become stereotypical, or as Sassoon terms it 'a generic national symbol in the hands of the Commonwealth'.[41] Lydon also documents a similar use of Nicholas Caire's postcards of Aborigines.[42] They became part of burgeoning Australian nationalism, as promoted by the Heidelberg School of impressionist painters, with the appropriation by whites of symbols like the boomerang, emblems easily understood and consumed, replacing the complexities of personal contact with Aboriginal people.[43]

The images of Aboriginal people taken by photographers such as Caire, Mitchell, Spencer and Campbell have changed in meaning over time, becoming particularly valuable a source of information about traditional Aboriginal life. As Jane Lydon writes, the 'process which produced the photographs within colonisation, has become the means through which descendants may reclaim their Aboriginality'.[44] Campbell's known photographs of Aborigines have contributed

---

38 Joanna Sassoon, 'Becoming Anthropological: a Cultural Biography of EL Mitchell's photographs of Aboriginal People', [online], *Aboriginal History*, Volume 28; 2004, pp. 59-86, viewed 12 May 08, <http//search.informit.com.au/documentSummary;dn=905511597172384;res=E-LIBRARY>ISSN: 0314-8769.

39 Ibid., pp. 61-2.

40 Ibid.

41 Ibid., p. 71.

42 Jane Lydon, 'Regarding Coranderrk', pp. 235-6.

43 Ibid., p. 221.

44 Ibid., p. 268.

to this knowledge. John Mulvaney points out that Spencer's ethnographic photographs have attracted 'renewed interest, particularly by Indigenous people preserving their heritage'.[45]

Campbell's Northern Territory photographs, taken while he was the inaugural Commonwealth photographer/cinematographer, are a valuable record of various aspects of the Northern Territory in 1912, and an important contribution to Australian photography. His propensity to let his private aspirations as a photographer sit alongside his paid work, and his adherence to his own photographic philosophies, jeopardized his position. He was not willing to conform to departmental procedures. In this he was like his father who, failing to cope with the demands of the Victorian Education Department, lost his teaching position at Seaton.

So confident was Campbell in his abilities as the Commonwealth Photographer that, after his term of employment had been extended for another twelve months by the Department, he asked for a rise in salary, from £200 per annum to £310, bringing him closer to the earnings of comparable photographers in private industry. He was looking forward to getting his '[new departmental] indoor outfit in full swing' and hoped then he would 'be considered in every way equal to rank with the best men in the trade and well worthy of my hire'. The request was made in early January 1913, to be backdated to December 1912, the date of his extension of service.[46] This may have been the beginning of Campbell's undoing as a contracted departmental employee.

In early March 1913 the newly appointed bureaucrat in charge of the Department of External Affairs photography department, DB Edward, wrote a damning report on Campbell for the departmental secretary. Edward accused Campbell of wasting photographic material, mainly film, glass plates and slides, during the indoor phase of his work, and of poor quality in still picture output. In his opinion Campbell:

> exhibited too great a tendency to strive after "artistic" effects whereas the Department simply requires prints of useful advertising value of good technical quality, sharp and clear. To meet the demand of the High Commissioner's Office [in London] . . . "artistic" quality must, to a large extent, be sacrificed to quantity.[47]

---

45 Mulvaney in Batty, Allen and Morton, *The Photographs of Baldwin Spencer*, p. 19.
46 Letter, JP Campbell to Minister for External Affairs, 11 January 1913.
47 Memorandum, DB Edward to Atlee Hunt, 8 March 1913, in NAA: A1, 1913/14458.

He found some of the Northern Territory pictures 'technically good but many are flat, wanting in incident and of little use for advertising purposes'. Campbell had taken a series of photographs and movie film at Burrinjuck Dam near Yass in NSW, which Edward criticised as being 'uneven' in quality and lacking in sharpness.[48]

Quoting from Campbell's work diaries, Edward accused him of a poor rate of return for his developmental work at Vallan Studio where he had an arrangement with Vallance to use the photographic equipment at the Department's expense. The unwritten accusation in Edward's report was that Campbell was stretching out the duration of his work in order to benefit his business partner and himself financially. Edward had no concerns with Campbell's cinematographic work at this time, either in regard to quality or materials, or of his purchase of 'non-consumable articles' such as cameras, lenses and tripods. There was even faint praise for Campbell's approach to field work. Edward found Campbell 'willing, energetic and [a person who] does not spare himself in attempting to get the best'. His concern was with hundreds of missing or stale glass plates, and again there was a between-the-lines suspicion that some were being stored by Campbell and Vallance for their own use. Edward concluded that the loss of plates and film 'from all sources [breakages, lost, stale]' was 'over 44% . . .an exceedingly high percentage of loss and is at least three or four times as great as it should be'.[49]

Edward was also concerned about the difficulty in supervising Campbell's work methods, so he took control, deferring Campbell's request for an increased wage and tightening stock ordering procedures.[50] The Secretary of the External Affairs Department, Atlee Hunt, approved these recommendations and ordered the report be shown to Campbell for explanation of the high percentage of loss in plates and lantern slides. Hunt's observation that 'when Mr Campbell is properly installed in this building there will be no further cause for comment', suggests he attributed the lack of departmental facilities provided to Campbell as the cause of the photographer's inability to perform his job adequately.[51]

In his spirited letter of defence, Campbell made no apology for his quest for quality, artistic images. He emphasised that when he joined the Department it was 'impressed upon me that the photographic work required was all the time

48 Ibid.
49 Ibid.
50 Ibid.
51 Ibid., internal departmental note by Atlee Hunt, 10 March 1913.

to be of exhibition quality', and he had pursued that goal. He cited Professor Baldwin Spencer on how glass plates deteriorated rapidly in the tropics, claiming this explained the high percentage of stale plates. Campbell claimed there was a clerical error in the quantity of film received. Other waste was due to a warped part of his reflex camera which allowed light in, spoiling the images taken. Campbell reiterated his preference for using plates because of their quality, saying the only inducement to use film was that it was light in weight. The dry plate process used by Campbell resulted in wastage.[52] Edward admitted that Campbell informed him 'that in his opinion a waste of 50% in lantern [slide] plates to get good slides is fair and reasonable'.[53]

The end came for Campbell when Edward wrote to Atlee Hunt a month later severely criticising Campbell's films of the christening of Canberra in March 1913, the Sydney Agricultural Show, and the launching of HMS *Stuart*. He described most of the Canberra film and agricultural show as 'useless', and the 'Stuart' effort only as 'fair'. After receiving the letter, Hunt consulted with the minister and scrawled a note on the bottom of Edward's letter: 'Minister has concurred in Mr Campbell's service being dispensed with'.[54] Hunt advised Campbell face-to-face that his services were terminated, and asked him to finish his work at hand, including albums of Northern Territory views. He gave him a month's notice from 14 April 1913.[55]

Campbell responded almost immediately with a letter to the Minister, enraged that he had been sacked for incompetence without being able to give his side of the story. There was more to it than Edward had presented:

> the secret of the whole affair being my hearty dislike to the man who
> has insulted me more than once, has used profane and filthy language in

---

52 Ibid., memorandum, JP Campbell to Atlee Hunt, 31 March 1913. Campbell's contact with Professor Baldwin Spencer is discussed in section two of this chapter.

53 Ibid and Edward to Atlee Hunt, 8 March 1913. Campbell pointed out that the work done at Mansfield was done on premises where there was no rent and other costs were very low: the Department was getting the work done cheaply. He felt that Edward had 'gone out of his way to demerit my work', when he was well aware that Campbell had obtained free rent of Vallan Studio premises for the Department. He emphasised that he had no business interest in Vallan Studio, but was happy to obtain Departmental work for Vallance in exchange for the use of the studio facilities. According to Campbell Vallance took offence when told Edward had criticised the time taken over developmental work and had withdrawn permission to use his facilities. Campbell had then offered his bathroom in Malvern, but withdrew this when his terms were not agreed to.

54 Ibid., letter, Edward to Secretary, 8 April 1913.

55 Ibid., memorandum by Atlee Hunt, Secretary, 9 April 1913, and letter to JP Campbell, 11 April 1913.

office and public places that I have felt ashamed of his presence, and I
have openly resented his style, one that I don't intend to get used to.

Campbell cited the Canberra assignment as an example of a comedy of errors,
resembling the Parliamentary visit to the Northern Territory. Campbell was
instructed by Edward to attend the ceremony to name the Australian National
Capital and celebrate its commencement. Edward organised Campbell's visit,
leaving the photographer little time to get organised himself, particularly at the
site of the ceremony. There was no accommodation for him at Queanbeyan so
he had to sleep on a railway station bench. He was lucky to find transport to the
Camp Hill site but once there the authorities said they had no prior knowledge
of his attendance, having not been advised of his role by the External Affairs
Department (that is, Edward). When Campbell returned the next day he found
the photography organisation, Spencers, had been commissioned to film the
ceremony, and the Government Printer to take the still pictures.[56] Frustrated
and annoyed, Campbell was forced to telegraph Attlee Hunt, asking him to
telegraph the authorities and introduce him to Colonel Miller, the man in charge
of organising the media, and Hunt quickly complied.[57]

Eventually Campbell was allotted a position on the stand with the guests.
Observing the operations of the five Government Printer photographers and
assistants on the big day, Campbell became bitter: 'Comparisons between their
methods and Mr Edward's are odious, as I am expected to be a beast of burden
and get film and still pictures as well'. He left the bulk of the work to them, but
the movie film he did take turned out to be overexposed. The other photographers
had the same problem because of a batch of over-sensitive film, but were in a
position to make a fresh exposure whilst Campbell was not.

Campbell's hatred of officialdom emerges in his account of attending the
Sydney Agricultural Show, where he used 400 feet of movie film. His nemesis,
Edward, who was also present, did not help Campbell. Rather, he interfered by
stopping Campbell filming horse teams, because of the advertisements on the
vehicles. Campbell, a very experienced show photographer, was incensed: 'I
cannot see any difference in advertising Tom Bonus, Butcher, to the many huge
hoardings of whiskies etc necessarily taken in a panorama of the stock parade. It

---

56 Ibid., letter on Departmental letterhead, JP Campbell to Josiah Thomas, Minister for External Affairs,
14 April 1913.
57 Ibid., telegram from JP Campbell to Secretary, A Hunt, 10 March 1913, and telegram from Secretary,
A Hunt, to Colonel Miller, 10 March 1913.

is very little show stuff one can get without showing advertisements'. To him it was 'merely officiousness' on Edward's part, something he had come to expect from his archetypal public servant superior.[58]

Campbell continued to argue, with some merit, that he had not been given a darkroom or any facilities by the Department to process film and glass plates, and had done his best under the circumstances to do indoor work at Vallan studio or at his home in Malvern. But saying 'he had no wish to go to Mansfield as my family is at Malvern, and I prefer to be nearer home than 130 miles away' was a bit deceptive, given he had spent two years working and living in Mansfield before becoming the Commonwealth photographer, as well as years on the road with Henry Berry and Co.[59]

When he could not access Vallance's facilities, he had 'inconvenienced [his] house [at 12 Hunter Street, Malvern] by temporarily converting the bathroom into a dark room'. He had done:

> his best in a hot stuffy place in the summer heat because Mr Edward wanted stuff out quick, and he has the ill manners to growl at the time taken. Probably he reckons the household should go unbathed to please him.[60]

All this may have been avoided, according to Campbell, if the External Affairs Department had taken up his recommendation to buy the Victorian Railway Department's indoor photographic equipment premises which they were relinquishing, but this opportunity 'was lost through procrastination'.

Campbell had expended a lot of time designing new photographic facilities for the Department. They were almost complete, and he found it 'a burlesque that when I have almost a chance to work under favourable circumstances I am told I am not wanted'. Further, he wrote to the Minister:

> I have done nothing wrongfully, and I fear no-one. I have always worked and lived amongst gentlemen, and I have never had but the "white" man's treatment till now, and I am trusting to you to see that I get fair play. There is more behind the scenes, but I have said as little as possible to put my case before you.

---

58 Ibid., internal Departmental letter, JP Campbell to Minister Josiah Thomas, 14 April 1913.
59 Ibid.
60 Ibid.

On this note Campbell finished his plea for clemency. He looked forward to confronting Edward 'amongst gentlemen who understand my side of affairs'.[61]

The accusations flew backwards and forwards. Campbell unsuccessfully requested his case go before a tribunal. Edward denied insulting Campbell, and of using profane or filthy language, but he 'may have used strong words when seeing Mr Campbell's lack of appreciation of what the Department required of him'.[62] The entrenched public servant was always going to be believed ahead of the individualist Campbell, who could not be told how to go about his artistic work as a photographer. Campbell's period of notice quickly ran out and he ceased work with the Department of External Affairs on 13 May 1913.[63]

Indignant at the way he was sacked, Campbell never lost hope of reinstatement. He made his last appeal in July 1913 to a new Minister for External Affairs, Patrick Glynn, in a recently elected liberal government. He raked over old ground, familiarising the new Minister with the background of his case.[64] Glynn replied that he could not see the point in opening up the question again.[65] Campbell did not reply to this until a month later, as he had been absent 'abroad', though where he did not say. This is perplexing, given he would not have been present if an enquiry was suddenly launched into his dismissal.[66] Glynn's final word came in early September 1913: he had looked at the files and did not think a review of the original decision was justified.[67] Here the war of words ended. Campbell's foray into the public service had definitely finished. Campbell's successor, Bert Ive, was appointed at £5 a week, compared with £4 Campbell received.[68] He also benefited from the new in-door facilities Campbell had designed, starting off on a much better footing after Campbell's pioneering work.

As with all cultural artifacts, Campbell's work has changed in meaning over time, while still providing insight into the difficult early years of developing the

---

61 Ibid.

62 Ibid., internal memo, first part by Atlee Hunt asking Edward to advise Campbell that the Minister had perused his comments and that Edward's answer Campbell's accusations, 16 April 1913, and the second part Edward responding to the Secretary's request, 17 April 1913.

63 Ibid., letter, Atlee Hunt to Commonwealth Public Service Commissioner advising of Campbell's dismissal, 21 June 1913.

64 Ibid., letter, JP Campbell to Patrick Glynn, Minister for External Affairs, 11 July 1913.

65 Ibid., letter, Glynn to Campbell, 24 July 1913.

66 Ibid., letter, Campbell to Glynn, 21 August 1913.

67 Ibid., letter, Glynn to Campbell, 10 September 1913.

68 Dougal Macdonald, 'A Vision of National Film-Making', *Canberra Times*, 8 June 1991, p. 85.

Northern Territory. His photographs are now historical items to be dissected, or to be enjoyed for their aesthetic beauty. The Northern Territory Library's *Souvenir* album of the 1912 parliamentary visit is highly valued. The library displayed photographs from the album, along with other Territory 'gems', in a complementary exhibition to the National Library of Australia's National Treasures exhibition when it visited Darwin in 2007.[69] The *Souvenir* album is also listed by UNESCO as being of significance.[70]

Campbell's Northern Territory photographs still circulate privately today as postcards, and they are reproduced in numerous history books and articles on the Territory's past. Campbell is also regarded as a pioneer of Film Australia. In late 1991 Film Australia toured the country with films partly to commemorate the eightieth anniversary of JP Campbell's letter of appointment to the External Affairs Department, a fitting tribute to him.[71] As Dougal Macdonald, writing in the comfortable world of 1990s Australia, pointed out: 'One can hardly imagine the experience of the travel that [Campbell] must have undertaken in that pre-aviation era, toting cumbersome equipment into parts of the continent that even today are not easy to reach'.[72] Greater challenges were to confront him during the First World War.

69 Elliot McAdam (Minister for Local Government, Northern Territory Government), 2007, *National Treasures Coming To The Territory*, media release, 13 March, Department of Local Government, Darwin, viewed 21 August 2009, <http://newsroom.nt.gov.au/index.cfm?fuseaction=printRelease& ID=2212>

70 UNESCO, Annex 8, *List of Nationally and Internationally Significant Collections: Held in each Institution*; '19. Northern Territory Library – Australia; Name of Collections: Photo Album – Parliamentary Visit to Northern Territory of 1912; Reason for Significance: Snap shot of the Northern Territory at the time of the Commonwealth taking control. Very few sets of this have survived'. Viewed 21 August 2009, <www.unesco.org/webworld/mdm/administ/en/annex8.htm>

71 Dougal MacDonald, 'A Vision of National Film-Making', *Canberra Times*, 8 June 1991, p. 85.

72 Ibid.

6

'ON ACTIVE SERVICE WITH A CAMERA'

*The 8th Light Horse – Soldier-Tourist – In the Shadow of the Pyramids –
Heliopolis – Gallipoli*

JP Campbell found himself back in Mansfield after his roving days as the official
Commonwealth photographer ceased. He resumed work as a professional
photographer in the north-east district, returning to some of his old haunts like
Walwa on the Upper Murray. Newspaper advertisements appeared in Corryong
offering his photographic services.[1] But this wasn't enough after his adventures as
Commonwealth photographer. The opportunity to further satisfy his wanderlust
came quickly in the shape of the First World War, during which he embraced the
chance to combine photography with soldiering by enlisting in the AIF.

There are four known surviving albums of Campbell's First World War
photographs, compiled by his son, Aubrey.[2] Through the lens of Campbell's
camera, these albums chart, in chronological order, the journey of the 8th Light
Horse, from Broadmeadows in February 1915, to the aftermath of the Nek
disaster in August 1915. Just how many albums were produced is unknown.
Campbell forwarded photographic prints to Aubrey with descriptions of their
contents written in pencil on the back. Aubrey used this information to compile
captions for the albums. Two of the albums were originally owned by members
of the Ritchie family, pastoralists in the Mansfield district. One of these Ritchie
family albums is now held by the National Library of Australia, the other by the
Mansfield RSL. The third album is held privately by the Gillespie family of the
Western District, Victoria. The fourth album, almost identical to the Mansfield
RSL album, is in the 8th/13th Victorian Mounted Rifles Regimental Collection,
North Bandiana, Victoria.

---

1 ' J.P. Campbell (late Commonwealth Photographer) will visit Corryong during this week. Anyone
desiring to engage the services of this high class photographer may leave orders with Mr Playle'.
Corryong Courier, 18 March 1914.

2 Ada Campbell (Ada Falconer from 1917), Aubrey's sister, assisted him in the compilation of least
one of the albums, as the National Library of Australia lists her as one of the 'authors' of the 8th Light
Horse Album held by them. Call Number PIC PIC/6109/1-184 LOC Album 1009, National Library of
Australia.

Campbell enlisted in the army at Mansfield on 12 September 1914, only a few weeks after Australians learned the Empire was at war with Germany. As with his application for the Commonwealth photographer position, he lied about his age, saying he was forty-five instead of forty-nine. Lean and relatively short in stature (5 feet 6½ inches tall) with 'scanty' (receding) brown hair, Campbell talked his way in.[3] The average age of those enlisting from the north east of Victoria was twenty-four.[4] His children were now adults and he was spending little time at 'home' in Malvern.[5] The disappointment of his sacking from the External Affairs Department still haunted him and his prospects with Vallan Studio were limited. Guns and horses in the army were no problem: he had been shooting and riding since he was a child. As a conservative, a member of the Presbyterian Church, and as a Mason, his whole value system revolved round a strong work ethic. Besides a strong commitment to serving the Empire, a motivation for enlisting may have been commercial: to record his own and his comrades' war experiences and sell the photographs while being paid as a serving soldier.[6]

Whatever the reasons, he went into camp at Broadmeadows about ten miles north of Melbourne where his suitability to join the Light Horse was tested, a task which involved jumping a horse over a 3ft. 6in. hurdle. In his own words, 'he cleared it like a bird'.[7] His physical fitness saw him through. Campbell was eventually assigned to the 8th Light Horse, one of three regiments making up the 3rd Light Horse Brigade.[8] He had joined an elite section of the army (Fig. 60).

---

3 NAA: B2455, Campbell JP.

4 John McQuilton, *Rural Australia and the Great War – from Tarrawingee to Tangabalanga*, Melbourne University Press, 2001, p. 173. Mansfield is on the edge of the southern border of the area defined by McQuilton as the North East.

5 Indeed he was a grandfather, his eldest daughter Vera having married Percy Pike in 1913 and given birth to a son, Lance Campbell Pike, in early 1914.

6 In early March 1914 Campbell took a series of photographs (later turned into Vallan Studio postcards) of the Australian Light Horse in camp and on manoeuvres near Broadford. Whilst doing this he may have been inspired to join the Light Horse. Interestingly, the troops were inspected by Sir Ian Hamilton who was out from England touring Australian military facilities. *Kilmore Advertiser*, 7 March 1914. Later, Hamilton, as commander of the Allied forces in the Dardanelles campaign, was to command many of these men, including Campbell, on Gallipoli.

7 *Mansfield Courier*, 8 March 1919.

8 John Hamilton, *Goodbye Cobber, God Bless You: The Fatal Charge of the Light Horse, Gallipoli, August 7th 1915*, Pan Macmillan Australia, Sydney, 2004, pp. 22-3. The 3rd Light Horse Brigade consisted of between 1500 and 1700 men. The other two regiments making up the brigade, the 9th and 10th Light Horse, were formed in Adelaide and Perth respectively. The 9th Light Horse, made up of two squadrons from South Australia and one from Victoria, joined the 8th Light Horse in training at Broadmeadows. All were part of the second contingent.

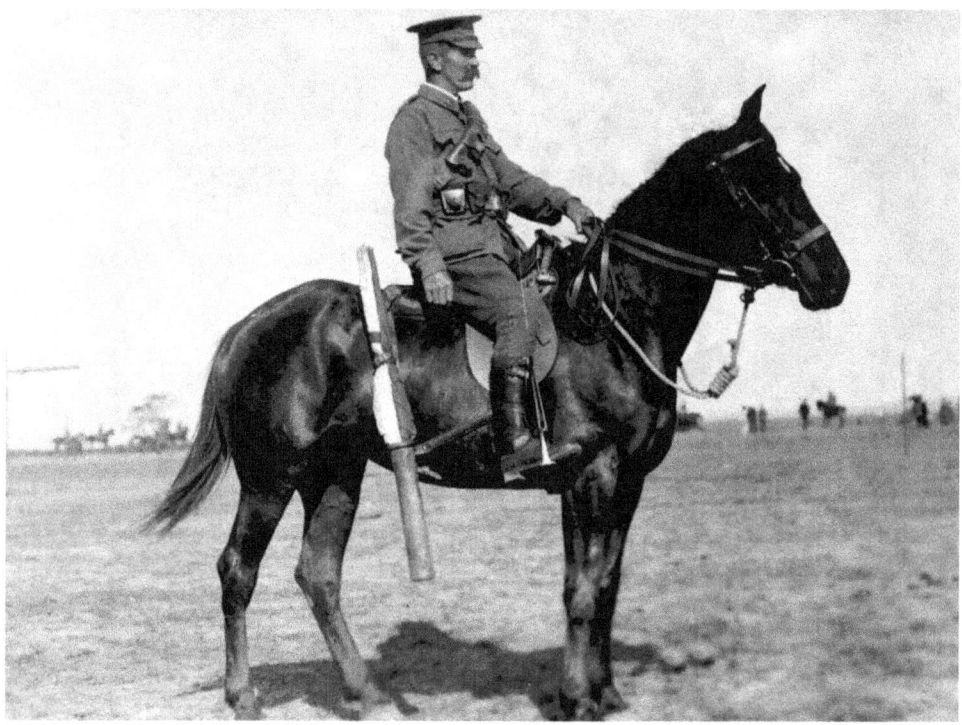

Fig. 60. Signaller JP Campbell of the 8th Light Horse. Photographer unknown.
(Courtesy of Falconer collection)

One trooper commented that 'the Light Horse are a very decent lot, especially the 8th Regiment, but the infantry are very rough & there seems to be millions of them here now'.[9] Although the 8th Light Horse soldiers were recruited from across Victoria, many of its members came from the Western District with its solid history of Scottish settlement. This resulted in 26% of the regiment being Presbyterian, which would have been of comfort to Campbell as he settled into life in the bustling camp.[10]

9 Jeff Pickerd, 'More Majorum: Chronological History of the 8th Light Horse Regiment, 3rd Light Horse Brigade, A.I.F., 1914-1919', unpublished manuscript and work in progress, p. 17. My copy was obtained in 2005 and the pages were numbered by me.

10 Peter Burness, *The Nek*, Kangaroo Press, Kenthurst, NSW, 1996, pp. 49-51. The 3rd Light Horse Brigade overall had a higher proportion of men who claimed adherence to the Church of England than the national average, so the 8th Light Horse was an aberration. The commanding officer of A troop, B squadron in which Campbell was placed was Edward 'Ted' Henty, grandson of Victorian pioneer Stephen Henty. Henty was killed in action at the charge of the Nek, Gallipoli, 7 August 1915, aged 27. Peter Burness, *The Nek*, p. 51 and Cameron Simpson, *Maygar's Boys: A Biographical History of the 8th Light Horse Regiment, AIF, 1914-1919*, Just Soldiers, Military Research & Publications, Moorooduc, Vic., 1998, p. 45.

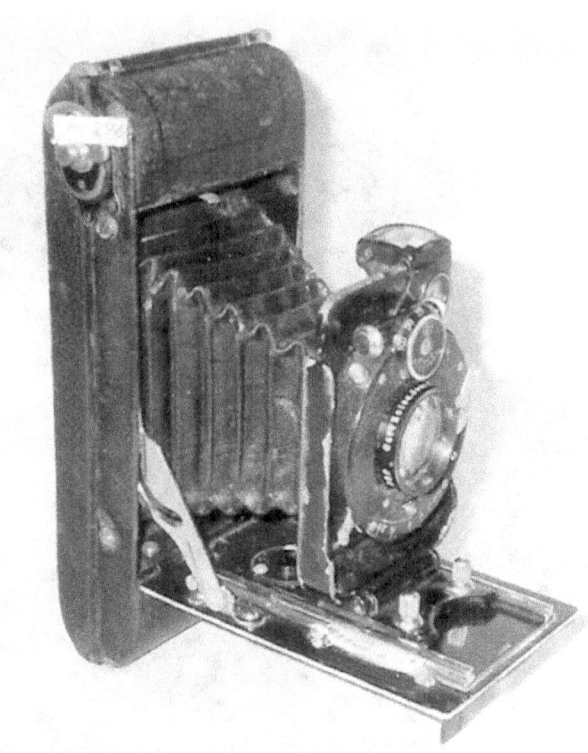

Fig. 61. The camera JP Campbell used on Gallipoli.
(Courtesy Ian Affleck, Australian War Memorial)

Broadmeadows Concentration Camp, as it was initially called, was spread out over 200 acres and 'surrounded by rolling country, little farmhouses and golden haystacks'.[11] Lines of bell tents stretched across the landscape. The crowded camp was given more space when the first contingent left for overseas service in late September 1914. Many of these new, excited soldiers wanted to record the moment, and small, hand held cameras were becoming popular. The camera company Kodak soon advertised 'The Soldier's Kodak', a vest pocket model for those wanting 'to keep a lasting record of the brave part that he and his own Company is playing in the Great War'.[12] Small, light, strong, simple and convenient were the catchwords used to describe these cameras.

Campbell, the professional, award winning photographer, chose more sophisticated camera equipment. He took into camp a new hand-held folding

[11] *The Herald*, 17 August 1914.
[12] Weston Bate, Euan McGillivray, & Matthew Nickson, *Private Lives – Public Heritage: Family Snapshots as History*, Hutchinson, Melbourne, 1986, pp. 11-12.

camera, a compact German model with its quality Carl Zeiss lens mounted on a metal plate connected to paper bellows which contracted back into the camera body when not in use (Fig.61). A swivelling glass prismatic viewfinder allowed photographs to be taken in landscape or portrait form; dials situated around the lens enabled adjustment of aperture and shutter speed. When folded up this steel bodied, black leatherette-finished camera fitted neatly into a case strapped to the user's waist belt.[13] It was to serve Campbell well on Gallipoli.

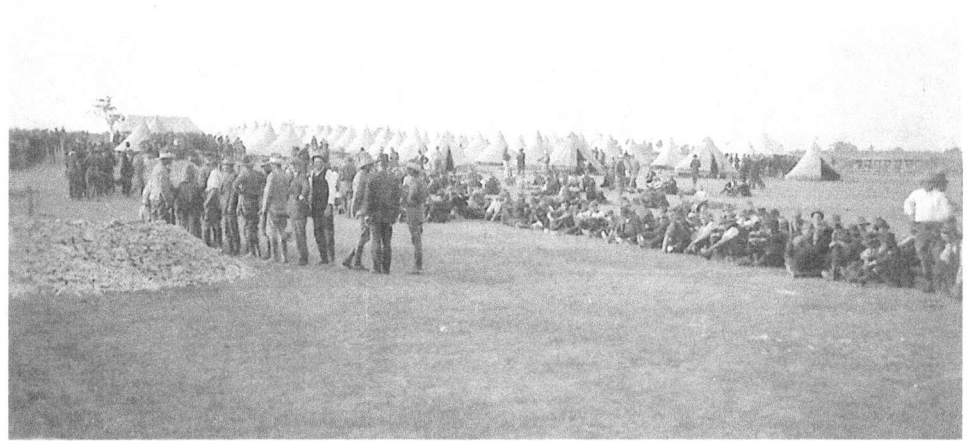

Fig. 62. '8th Light Horse 1st Pay day. Broadmeadows'. (Courtesy Nance Tyson collection)

In November 1914 Campbell, deemed suitable to be a signaller, moved to the Signals School of Instruction at the Broadmeadows camp along with eight others of the 3rd Brigade.[14] Between exercise drills and signalling practice Campbell took photographs. None of his Broadmeadows letters survive, but fifteen briefly captioned postcards sent to Lilian Pitts do. Some of these depict camp life, for example: the '8th Light Horses' 1st Pay day. Broadmeadows' (Fig. 62), with men sitting and lined up with a sea of bell tents in the background and a bare foreground, and '2nd Camp. 1st Church Parade, Broadmeadows', a mass of men lined up in an open paddock forming three sides of a rectangle with the minister at the open end. This was taken from a distant, elevated position.

---

13 Campbell's camera and case are held by the Australian War Memorial, ID No. REL32968.001 & REL32968.002 respectively.

14 Jeff Pickerd, 'More Majorum', p. 12.

According to his granddaughter, Campbell loved lines as a photographic subject, so he was fortunate to have joined an organisation obsessed with them.[15] He also photographed the surrounding countryside and the military training ground, where his artistry as a landscape photographer came to the fore.[16] Campbell began what became one of his trademark photographic habits whilst in military service, capturing the mundane activities of soldiers in camp or at the 'front', like the charabanc at the Broadmeadows camp piled high with the bedding of the 4th Light Horse 'off to be washed' (Fig. 63).[17]

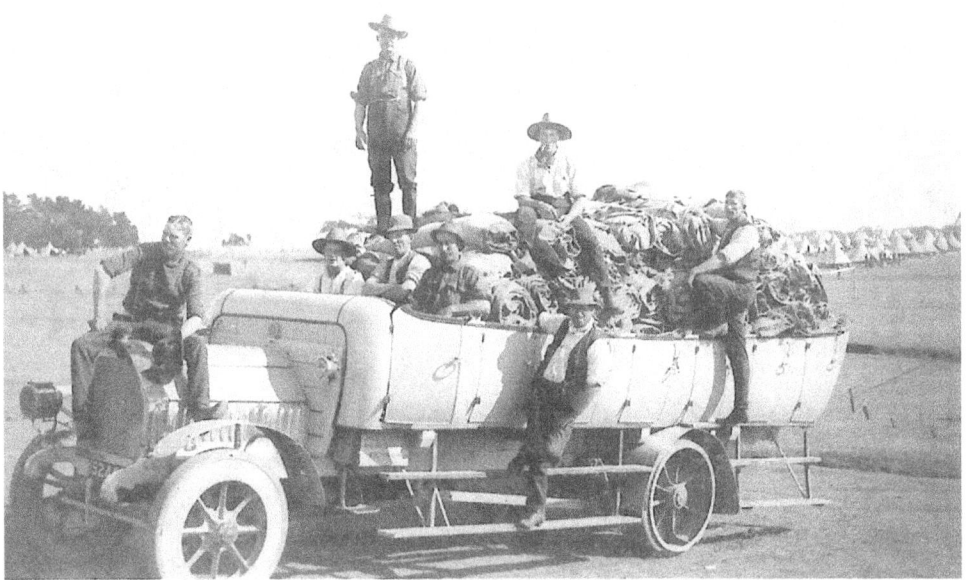

Fig. 63. 'Bedding of the 4th Light Horse off to be washed'.
(Courtesy Nance Tyson collection)

In early January 1915 the signallers completed their training and were absorbed back into normal regimental activities to await embarkation to the front.[18] On 20

---

15 Interview with Noel Fethers, 20 April 2005. A series of five numbered photographs shows a swarm of khaki making up the 5th Battalion leaving the camp 'Off to honor (sic) Australia'. The last two depict a huge line of soldiers, four or five abreast, stretching into the distance, marching across the plain towards Broadmeadows Railway Station and their destiny overseas. Photograph number five is captioned 'The 5th [Battalion] nearing Broadmeadows Station'. Another is simply captioned 'Leaving the camp behind'.

16 There are JP Campbell pictures held by the Australian War Memorial of the 8th Light Horse signallers training in the vicinity of Broadmeadows.

17 Postcard held by the Tyson family.

18 Jeff Pickerd, 'More Majorum', p. 16.

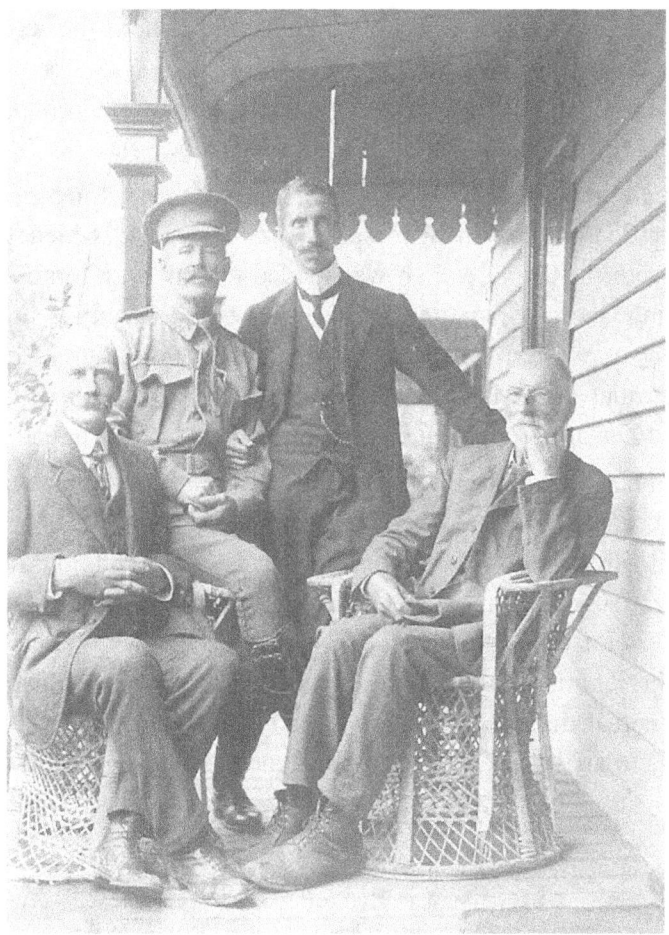

Fig. 64. Left to Right: William Campbell, JP Campbell, Emil Grotjan and Archibald
Campbell. (Courtesy of Falconer collection)

January, the 8th and 9th Regiments of the 3rd Light Horse Brigade participated
in a march through Melbourne. They were a spectacular sight to the patriotic,
admiring crowds: beautifully groomed horses, uniformed soldiers erect in the
saddle, rifles protruding at their sides, their slouch hats decorated with flowing
emu-feather plumes. The long column of 2000 men rode down King Street, into
Collins and around into Spring Street, where they took the salute of the Governor
General outside Parliament House.[19] Aubrey Campbell took a photograph of his
father in the ranks from a window high in the Danish Club, as the parading
soldiers swung round a corner. He marked the picture with a cross in front of his

19 *Age,* 22 January 1915, and Jeff Pickerd, 'More Majorum', pp. 17-18.

father's horse: 'it is possible to just distinguish Pa . . . he is the second figure in the [four horse] section,' he wrote proudly.[20] Before leaving for war Campbell farewelled his brother William, cousin Archibald, and Emil Grotjan, the German born husband of Archibald's daughter, Catherine (Fig. 64).[21]

JP Campbell embarked for service overseas with other members of the 8th Light Horse on 25 February on the troopship *Star of Victoria*, which was travelling in company with the *Runic*, which was loaded mainly with infantry.[22] They set course for King George Sound, on the shore of which Albany is situated, on the southern coast of Western Australia.[23] After four days the troopships departed Western Australia on 6 March 1915 *en route* for Egypt. No shore leave was allowed: New Zealand troops had visited earlier and created havoc in Albany.[24]

That Campbell regarded himself as the unofficial photographer for the 8th Light Horse became apparent when he assembled twenty officers on deck for a group portrait. He showed his affection for Mansfield by photographing sixteen soldiers collectively known as the 'Rutledge Group', a group centred around Mansfield grazier, twenty-nine year old Noel Rutledge, who was a very popular member of the regiment.[25] On-board lectures were given, including one by the doctor on venereal disease, a scourge already rampant amongst the first wave of Australians to arrive in Cairo. Campbell captured these earnest occasions on film, the men sitting on the deck, crowded together in shirtsleeves and sun hats.

---

20 Postcard and photograph held by Noel Fethers.

21 Grotjan, a merchant, arrived in Australia in 1903. In 1907 he was naturalised and married Catherine Campbell. He was not interned as an enemy alien during the First World War. But, under an act of parliament which stated enemy aliens could not hold shares in a company incorporated in Australia, he was forced to sell his shares in his company, Grotjan & Co Pty Ltd, and 'give up his business' as an importer, resuming trade in 1919. JP Campbell and Grotjan have linked arms, perhaps to show they are friends, and that Emil is loyal to his adopted country. Application for Certificate of Naturalisation, 13 October 1907, and Oath of Allegiance, 26 November 1907, in NAA: A1, 1915/14251, Interview with Noel Fethers, 20 April 2005, and Emil Grotjan to Minister of Defence, 4 April 1919, in NAA:A3201, TE660.

22 John Hamilton, *Goodbye Cobber, God Bless You*, pp. 102-4 and NAA: B2455, Campbell JP.

23 Ibid., p. 107. Albany harbour was the assembly point for Australian and New Zealand convoys before the long haul across the Indian Ocean.

24 John Hamilton, *Goodbye Cobber, God Bless You*, p. 110. Campbell's photographs in this period are all from the deck of the *Star of Victoria*. They are given little in the way of captions, simply 'Albany' or 'Albany Harbour'. One, reproduced in the Christmas Number of the 1915 Melbourne *Leader*, shows the headland seen off the bow of the *Star of Victoria*, the railing of the bow in the foreground, sea and land in middle ground. Again there is a linear perspective to it. Another linear creation is a tugboat towing eight cutters in a row from the *Runic* across the harbour parallel to the shoreline.

25 Cameron Simpson, *Maygar's Boys*, p. 42.

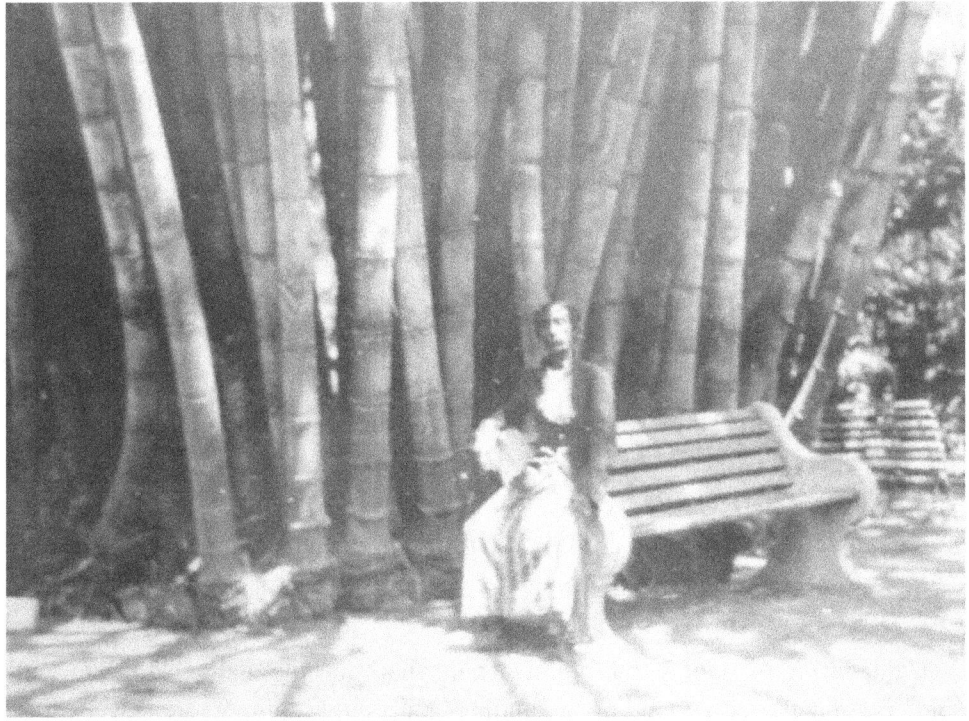

Fig. 65. 'Jam Bamboos', Colombo. One of Campbell's 'tourist' photographs.
(Courtesy of Mansfield RSL)

As they crossed the Equator he photographed the traditional Father Neptune ceremony, a shaving and dunking in water ritual for the newcomers (Pollywogs) to the Equator.[26]

The two ships arrived at Colombo, Ceylon, on 18 March 1915 and the land-deprived passengers on the *Star of Victoria* were allowed shore leave. In Colombo we get Campbell's first brief written reaction to this new, exotic environment: 'The color scheme of the Tropical Spring defies detailed description – just magnificent', he wrote on a local postcard to Lilian. Like other wide-eyed soldiers Campbell compared this alien world to his known world in Australia: 'A bullock team in a Gippsland forest is a big contrast to this', he wrote, referring to a commercial postcard picture which showed two white bullocks pulling a cart through jungle.[27]

---

26 John Hamilton, *Goodbye Cobber, God Bless You*, pp. 117-18 & Jeff Pickerd, 'Majorum', p. 29.

27 Ceylon postcard sent to Lilian L Pitts, posted in Aden, probably on the 28 March 1915. It should be noted that Campbell was probably a much more seasoned traveller than many of his comrades.

His fourteen photographs in the Colombo region were varied.[28] Military and tourist photographs were intertwined: the taker could not forget why he was there, but the observer and artist in him was stimulated by what he saw. The professional photographer-as-tourist was in his element (Fig. 65).

The contingent left Colombo on 20 March, arriving at the Port of Aden, Yemen, eight days later. Here Campbell took three photographs of the harbour, including one of an armoured merchant ship converted for combat – the war was edging closer. The two Australian troopships slipped into the Red Sea *en route* to Suez, where recent Turkish attacks on the Suez Canal caused them to take protective action on the *Star of Victoria*, filling bags with ash and barricading the starboard side of the ship in anticipation of their move into the Canal.[29] Campbell took a snap of this barricade as excitement mounted. The thought of impending action after a relatively uneventful trip galvanised those on board. The *Star of Victoria* and the *Runic* arrived in Suez harbour on Easter Saturday, 4 April 1915, and in the early hours of the morning men and horses boarded three trains for the trip west to Cairo.

Campbell took many photographs of Suez harbour, the 'natives' trading with soldiers, and the latter landing, including one of the commanding officers of the 8th Light Horse, Major Arthur Deeble, striding on to Egyptian soil for the first time. Campbell was coping with his small camera, but he longed for the equipment he used in landscape photography. On 5 April 1915 he wrote briefly to Lilian Pitts saying he missed his 'Reflex and long focus lenses and if fortunes favour me I'll have one for my return journey'.[30] One photograph in particular, of soldiers unloading bags of saddle gear, gives us some insight into how Campbell conveyed the meaning of his photographic work to his son Aubrey in Melbourne. He wrote a note to Aubrey (undated and perhaps accompanying a print or proof) stating the following: 'Suez. Passing bags of saddle gear down to truck – C Squadron – B Squadron [of which Campbell was a member] carried theirs down

---

28 The obligatory sunset over Colombo Harbour; three of 'coaling' the *Star of Victoria* (barges alongside providing coal to the steamer); entrance to the harbour; a Tamil family (mother, father and child in arms); a 'Budda' temple; Cingalese children in the streets; covered wagons lining up outside the Railway Goods Yards; the *Star of Victoria* at anchor in the harbour; a scene of the dock; Villas and a Rickshaw in a quiet street; a local sitting on a bench in front of towering Jam Bamboo, and the regiment's horses lined up feeding from troughs in a local stable.

29 John Hamilton, *Goodbye Cobbers, God Bless You*, pp. 127-8, and Jeff Pickerd, 'Majorum', p. 34.

30 Postcard, JP Campbell to Lilian Pitts, 5 April 1915.

in very much less time'.[31] It also demonstrates how the competitive Campbell had adapted to Army life, and even revelled in the rivalry between squadrons.

The train trip to Cairo dazzled Campbell with its images.[32] He described his feelings to Lilian: 'Arrived at Suez last Friday and left for Cairo 5 a.m. next morning and had a delightful trip through beautiful irrigated fertile Egypt till 11 a.m. Camel, Ass, Mule, plough oxen, goats, sheep, & robed inhabitants pictures in multitude – Haven't recovered breath yet'.[33] Unfortunately this was his last surviving piece of correspondence to Lilian Pitts until 8 September 1915.

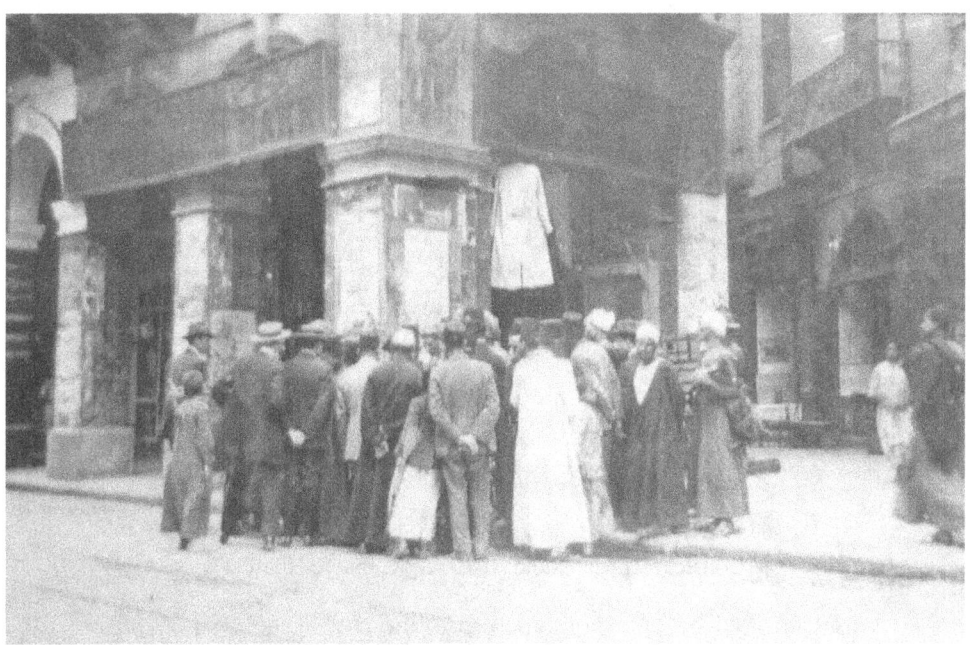

Fig. 66. 'Street squabble. Cairo' (Courtesy of Mansfield RSL)

Cairo fascinated him. He 'snapped' a tightly bunched group of people embroiled in a 'street squabble' in front of a large columned building (Fig. 66). Later that day the regiment, their horses leading, marched out to Mena camp eight miles out of Cairo. As they got closer to Mena the Pyramids loomed up out

---

31 Note held by Noel Fethers.

32 He photographed the railway stations (one at a large town called, theatrically, Zig Zag Station); the 'horse scarer', a camel loaded with foliage; soldiers sitting on top of a railway carriage as the train travelled through an area of high bulrushes; the first and second views of Cairo past Palm Trees and going through a Railway Crossing; the entry into Cairo through the Railway Goods Yards.

33 Postcard to Lilian Pitts dated, mistakenly (or on purpose for censorship reasons) 9 May 1915 (should be 9 April 1915).

of the desert (Fig. 67).[34] They were to spend over three weeks in this location on the edge of the Sahara Desert, described by one soldier as 'one great circus' with the bustle of military equipment and soldiers, 'native' drivers of camels and donkeys delivering fodder around the camp, and 'native' shops scattered about like 'little townships', all material for Campbell's camera.[35]

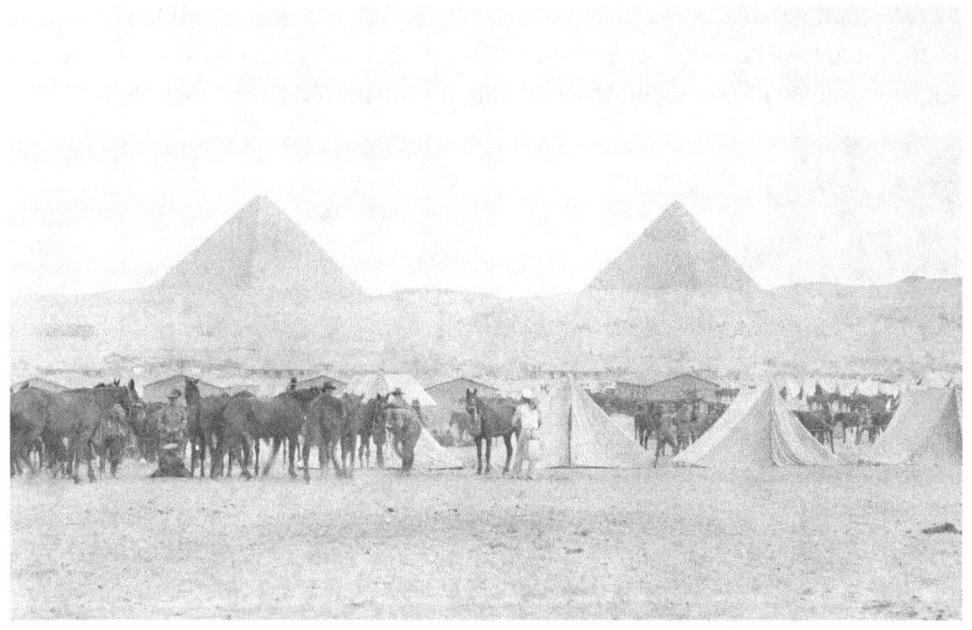

Fig. 67. 'Arrival at Squadrons Lines Mena Camp 4 P.M. 4-4-15'.
(Courtesy of Mansfield RSL, AWM image H03084)

As with Campbell's correspondence from the Northern Territory in 1912, the *Heyfield Herald* published extracts of his letters to his sister Margaret Chester from Egypt and Gallipoli in 1915 and 1916. One of his favourite photographic subjects was the beast of burden, whether person or animal. 'Water Carriers' is a study of two people carrying goatskin water containers on a wide road leading to the Pyramids, their backs to the camera (Fig. 68). The head of the carrier on the right seems to have morphed into a water container, slanting sideways. In the distance the tip of one of the Pyramids peaks over the hills. It is a bizarre, absorbing, almost grotesque image.

---

34 He photographed them at five miles and three miles, framed by trees and in the closer picture with a tram track drawing you into the picture. It became a cliché, the Australian soldiers training in the 'shadow of the pyramids'.
35 Jeff Pickerd, 'More Majorum', p. 36.

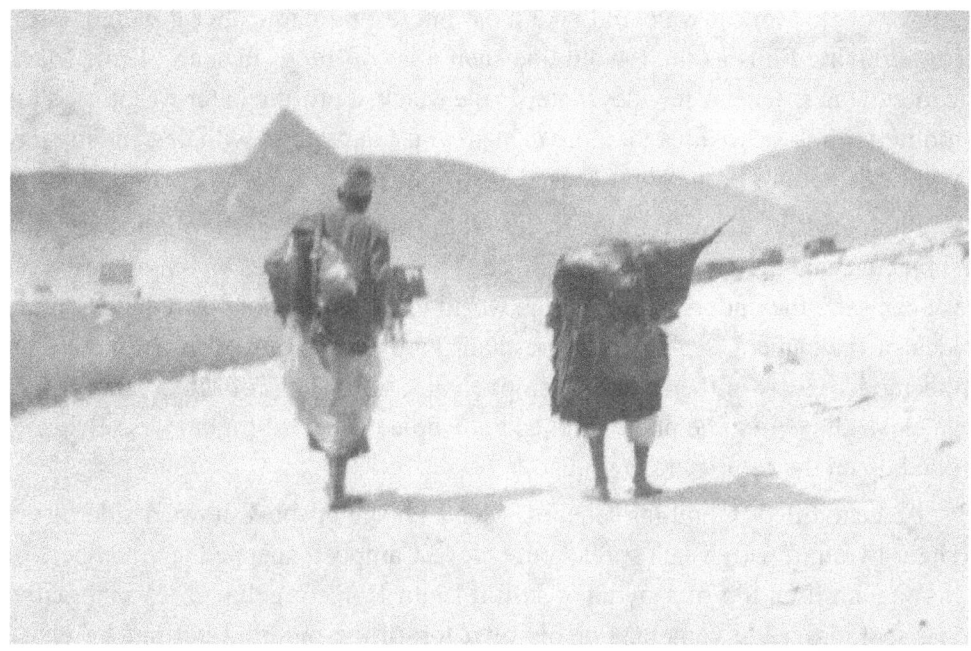

Fig. 68. 'Water Carriers', April 1915. They looked like 'they were hawking dead animals blown up with a bicycle pump', Campbell told his sister.[36]
(Courtesy of Mansfield RSL)

Daily routine in camp revolved around feeding and exercising the horses, which could not be ridden for twelve days after arrival, as they were still recovering from the confinement aboard ship. Rifle drill and 'foot slogging' through the hated sand took up the rest of their working day, with the occasional route march.[37] Other members of the 8th Light Horse were also enthusiastic users of their cameras during the leisure time they had. Electric trams serviced the camp, allowing quick access to Cairo. Tom Austin sent his pocket camera film negatives home to Australia along with a proof of each and a description of the image, much as JP Campbell was to do over the course of the war.[38] Some bemoaned the fact they did not have a camera: 'If we only had a camera and

36 Letter, JP Campbell to Margaret Chester, 1 May 1915, extracts published in the *Heyfield Herald*, 22 July 1915.
37 Jeff Pickerd, 'More Majorum', pp. 35-39. Campbell, presumably, had his share of these activities, as well as being involved in signal practice. Leisure time was spent in Cairo or exploring the vicinity of Mena: virtually every inch of the pyramids were climbed and rummaged over. The Sphinx with the Great Pyramid Cheops in the background became a much-photographed scene. Campbell captured it with a party of Egyptians in front. He also sought out more obscure subjects.
38 Letter, Ernie Mack to his sister Mary, 8 May 1915. Austin was a friend of Ernie Mack's.

knew how to work it we could take most interesting photos but it would cost a lot in buying films as there would be such a lot of things to snap', Ernie Mack wrote to his sister.[39] A few days later Ernie Mack, a prolific letter writer, told his mother: 'Photos explain a lot more than all you can write so with that end in view we [Ernie and his brother] purchased a No. 1 Brownie Kodak yesterday'.[40]

Photography theorist Don Slater sees photography as eliminating the subjective and the magic from the world. The notion of 'we can only know what we can see', the understanding of the world via scientific fact, is reflected in the idea of the camera explaining more than words.[41] Ernie Mack was expressing this modern view of the camera. Campbell also took views of Mena camp. From an elevated position he photographed the whole of the 3rd Light Horse Brigade, lined up on the camp parade ground.[42]

A scene titled 'Climbing Cheops. Mena village at foot' shows a side of the Great Pyramid with Mena spread out below. Campbell snapped ten members of his squadron on top of a pyramid in full Light Horse regalia, grouped together and looking at the camera. For his own top-of-the-pyramid portrait he chose to be captured in profile, in full uniform, legs braced apart, hands behind his back looking contemplatively down on the desert below (Fig.69). Helen Ennis, a commentator on twentieth century photography, believes this pose is significant given other soldiers chose to be seen at the base of the pyramid with its recognisable, iconic structure behind them.[43]

Campbell revealed a much bleaker side to their stay in the Mena camp. In mid April the 3rd Light Horse Brigade was sent on a fast foot march around the pyramids on a blazing hot day 'whilst the coots responsible for the joke [the officers] rode on horseback'.[44] As a consequence a number of the men succumbed to the heat and exertion. It did not worry Campbell as he was fit, despite being much older than most of his fellow soldiers, but many of the men were not used

---

39 Ibid., 18 April 1915.

40 Letter by Ernie Mack to his mother, 25 April 1915. Many soldiers took their cameras with them to Gallipoli.

41 Don Slater, 'Photography and Modern Vision', in *Visual Culture*, Chris Jenks (Ed.), Routledge, London, 1995, pp. 220-3.

42 The 8th Light Horse had reunited with the 9th and 10th regiments, who had arrived earlier at Mena camp.

43 Helen Ennis, *Intersection*, p. 138.

44 *Heyfield Herald*, 3 February 1916. AD Callow noted in his diary that on 15 April 1915: 'The whole 3rd Brigade went on a dismounted route march of about seven miles around the Great Pyramids'. Quoted in Jeff Pickerd, 'More Majorum', p. 39.

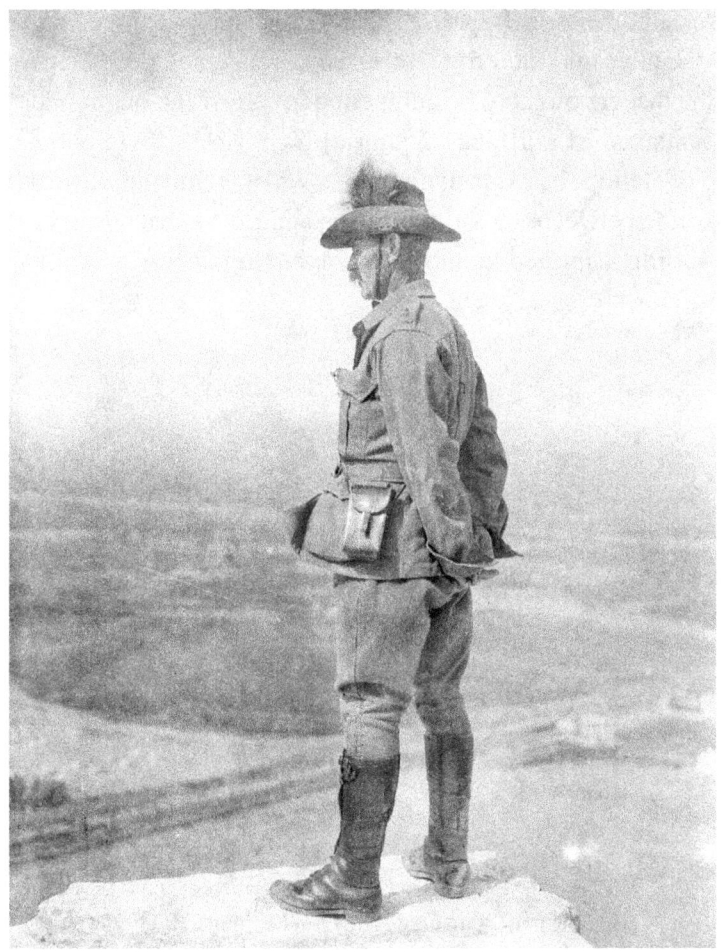

Fig. 69. 'Signaller J.P. Campbell of 8th L.H. on top of pyramid'.
Photographer unknown. Note the camera case on his hip.
(Courtesy of Mansfield RSL, AWM image H03068)

to rigorous exercise. Campbell was bitter about this incident, and writing about it in late 1915 described it as an 'absurd caper'. Of the perpetrators he wrote: 'Their souls are now resting on Turkish soil'.[45]

In late April 1915 the 8th Light Horse moved from Mena, along with the rest of the 3rd Light Horse Brigade, to a comfortable new campsite at a racecourse

---

45 *Heyfield Herald*, 3 February 1916. It is interesting that Campbell revealed this in a letter after returning from Gallipoli. Perhaps he thought he was free to speak as those who supervised the march were now dead and he was no longer a member of the 8th Light Horse. His experiences on Gallipoli and the loss of so many comrades would have also influenced his reflection on this incident.

in the Cairo suburb of Heliopolis.[46] Campbell and two other signallers rode bicycles to the new site, 'and rotten brummy things they are', he complained to his sister, 'the makers ought to be compelled to follow me on my old "scrapiron" over the mountains [of north-east Victoria] for a week'.[47] He photographed the architecture of Heliopolis extensively. The tents of B Squadron, with their horses hobbled in a line between, look out of place against the backdrop of extravagant buildings carefully captured in his photographs (Fig. 70).

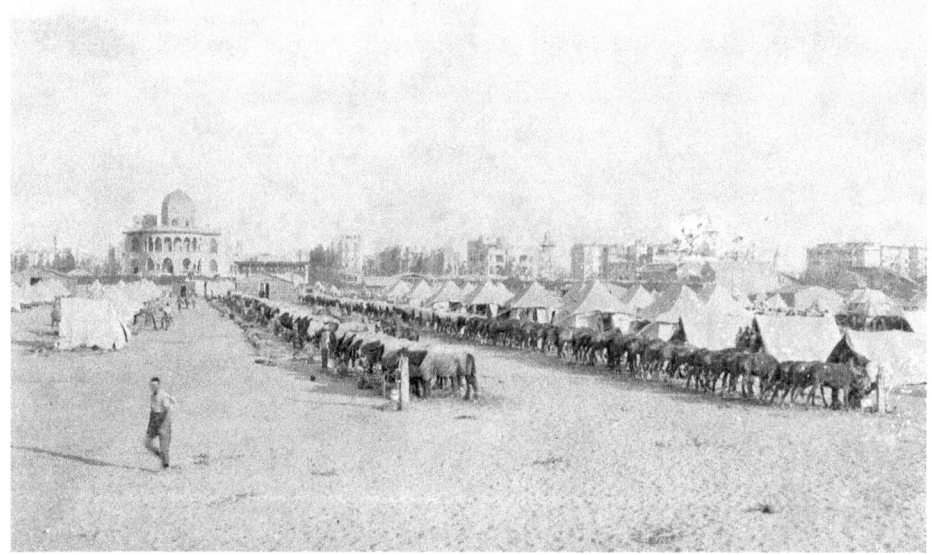

Fig. 70. 'Heliopolis Camp. B Squadron Lines'
(Courtesy of Mansfield RSL, AWM image HO3098)

Here the 8th Light Horse awaited orders, many of its members impatient to get into action. They watched the wounded arriving in their hundreds from the Gallipoli peninsula and listened to the false rumours of the evil deeds of torture and mutilation committed on Allied troops by the Turks, rumours encouraged for propaganda purposes.[48] Campbell told his sister that he did not think they would 'go amongst the bullets for quite a while yet', but he 'was not in any hurry, as

46 Heliopolis had been created as a gambling location to rival Monte Carlo but the creators failed to obtain an operating licence. Its plush hotel/casino (converted into a hospital), the Sultan's equally extravagant racecourse grandstand plus a Luna Park (like its namesake in St Kilda) added to its attractiveness. Even the private houses were three or four stories high.
47 Letter, JP Campbell to Margaret Chester, 1 May 1915, *Heyfield Herald*, 22 July 1915.
48 John F Williams, *Anzacs, The Media and The Great War*, p. 86, and Hamilton, *Goodbye Cobber, God Bless You*, p. 151.

there's lots I haven't seen yet'.[49] Life as a soldier-tourist seemed much more attractive, particularly when there was such a rich source of 'scenes' to capture. Not everybody had an activity like photography to immerse themselves in when not on duty.

The commanding officer of the 8th Light Horse, Lt Col AH White, expressed the frustration of his men in early May when he wrote: 'They do not want us in Turkey, no place for the Light Horse, in the meantime we get burned by the sun, cussed by the Old Man [Commanding Officer of the 3rd Brigade, Colonel F.G. Hughes], and eaten by flies, our tempers are being destroyed. Egypt is a rotten place, only fit for natives'.[50] Events, however, moved quickly as the Anzacs became bogged down on Gallipoli. Because of the difficult terrain, there was to be a role for the Light Horse after all, without their horses.

On 9 May 1915 the 8th Light Horse Machine Gun section and the 1st Light Horse Brigade were farewelled at church parade before they left Heliopolis for Gallipoli with the New Zealand Mounted Rifles. As at Broadmeadows, Campbell photographed the farewell to the troops departing for the front, in this case the men assembled on the parade ground, giving encouraging cheers for the departing soldiers. Campbell did not have long to wait for embarkation to Gallipoli himself. After a burst of intensive training to prepare them for their role as infantry involved in trench warefare, and a chaotic period of packing, the 3rd Light Horse Brigade left by train for Alexandria on 16 May 1915 where they were to board the troopships for Gallipoli. Five days later the men of the 8th Light Horse were woken early as they rested on the troopship *Menominee* in the inner harbour of Mudros off the island of Lemnos in the Aegean Sea. The 8th and 9th Light Horse, brigade staff and signallers, transferred to three fast destroyers. Campbell went aboard HMS *Foxhound* along with most of his regiment, and the rest of the 8th Light Horse went on HMS *Scourge*.[51] Campbell took a dramatic photo from the back half of the *Foxhound* looking forward as it sped towards Anzac Cove (Fig. 71). The troops landed at Anzac Cove that afternoon, virtually without mishap, and dug in at Reserve Gully at the foot of Plugge's Plateau to the left of the Cove.[52] One snap by Campbell with his German camera, possibly taken around the time of his first landing, shows the whole sweep of ANZAC

---

49 Letter, JP Campbell, to Margaret Chester, 1 May 1915, *Heyfield Herald*, 22 July 1915.

50 Jeff Pickerd, 'More Majorum', pp. 45-6.

51 John Hamilton, *Goodbye Cobber, God Bless*, p. 180.

52 Ibid., pp. 181-3.

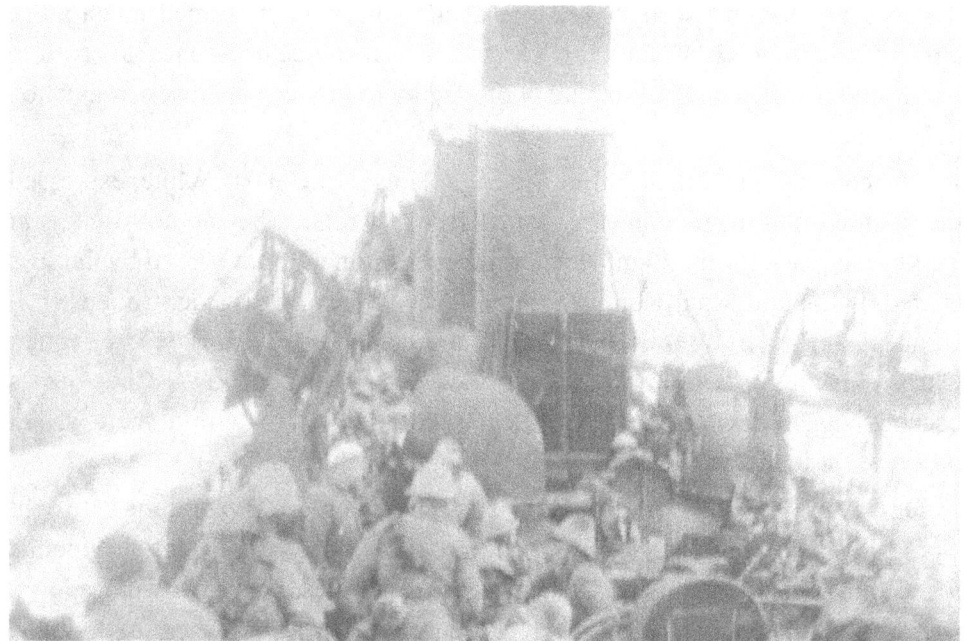

Fig. 71. 'Approaching Turkey on the Destroyer Foxhound'. (Courtesy of Mansfield RSL)

cove looking north, littered with the paraphernalia of war: men pushing a cart in the foreground, boats drawn in close to shore, the land looming up on the right of the picture. It is now the archetypal Gallipoli scene. This image appeared in the 'Christmas Special' of the Melbourne *Leader* in December 1915, illustrating (along with other Campbell photographs) a long article on the exploits of the Anzacs on Gallipoli (Fig. 72).[53]

After racing ashore amongst the bustle of a crowded Anzac Cove, the rugged landscape of the peninsula towering before him, Campbell recorded his first impressions on film. He was immediately alert to the photogenic appeal of the landscape:

> When landing on the beach I thought the cliffs and slopes and shore the most interesting picture of my rambles to date. The hills are steep to

---

53 *The Melbourne Leader*, Christmas Number 1915, Australia at War, Special Issue 25 December 1915, p. 28. Aubrey Campbell captioned this photograph (using JP Campbell's notes) variously in the three albums he produced: 'Beach Scene', 'Beach Scene. Anzac', and 'The Base looking N. The 8th L.H. Cemetery is round the point'. The latter caption was possibly written much later than the others, with a more considered approach. Campbell's submissions of Gallipoli photographs to the *Leader* are discussed later.

perpendicular in places, the easier slopes being covered by a short bush as troublesome as gooseberries – no good for kilts.[54]

He photographed the 8th Light Horse's first camp on Gallipoli, men scrambling to dig in on the hillside to shelter from the Turkish guns. He also snapped, no doubt with some trepidation, the scrub-covered hill behind them leading up to the ridge and the waiting Turks. A notorious Turkish gun called 'Anafatta Annie' shelled them whilst they dug, fortunately without casualty.[55] The regiment had arrived just after the Allies repelled a major offensive by the Turks, who suffered heavy casualties. Their bodies lay strewn in no man's land, reeking in the sun, in front of the trenches all along the rugged front between the two combatants. A one-day armistice to bury the dead was held, whether by design or accident, on Empire Day 24 May 1915.[56]

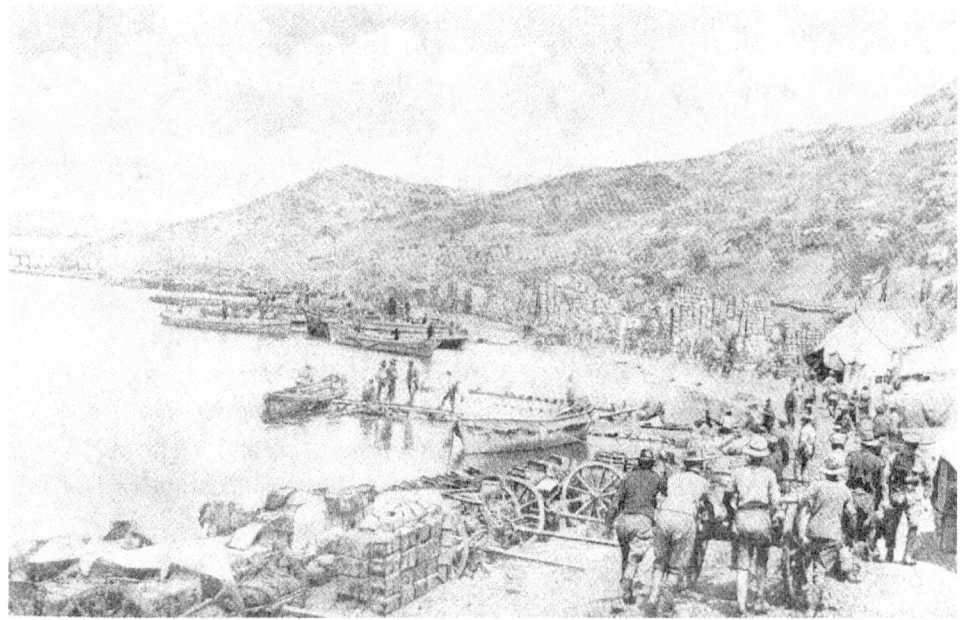

Fig. 72. 'ANZAC BAY'. Campbell's photograph of Anzac Cove as it appeared in the *Leader* of 25 December 1915.

One of the conditions of the armistice stipulated no photographs, a point ignored by some, including Campbell, but complied with by the Australian war

---

54 Letter, JP Campbell to Margaret Chester, 15 June 1915, *Heyfield Herald*, 19 August 1915.
55 Hamilton, *Goodbye Cobber, God Bless You*, pp.183-5.
56 Ibid., pp. 197-9.

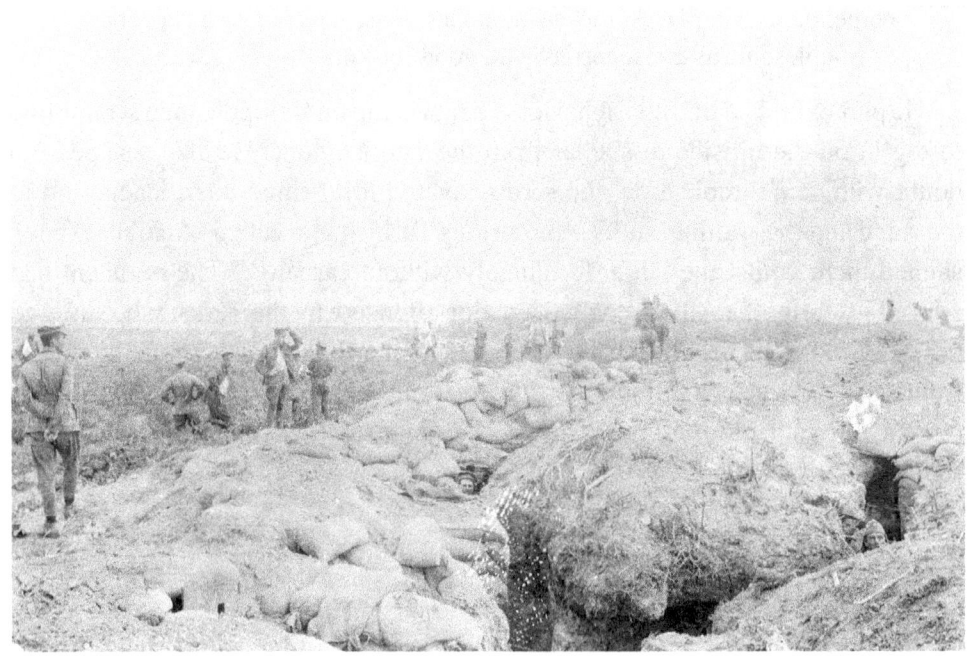

Fig. 73. 'Armistice Day. Our trenches and those of the Turks a short way off'.
(Courtesy of Mansfield RSL, AWM image HO3187)

correspondent, C.E.W. Bean.[57] Campbell explained the armistice to his sister Margaret:

> During war conflicts it is usual, as you know, to have "barley" for a period for burial purposes. Well there was "time off" the other day and I was inquisitive enough to wander between the firing lines, and the flowers I sent you were plucked there, so they will be of geographical interest as well as a souvenir of a grim item.[58]

As well as gathering flowers, Campbell took two pictures, still extant, of the gruesome task of burying the dead, one showing the Australian trenches in the foreground, the Turks' trenches 'a short way off', with soldiers from both sides in between conducting the burials. On the edge of the picture a Turk can be seen with a white flag of truce (Fig. 73). The other more obscure, faded photograph (not reproduced here) shows two barely visible figures and

---

57 CEW Bean, *Frontline Gallipoli: CEW Bean's Diary from the Trenches*, Selected and annotated by Kevin Fewster, Allen and Unwin, Sydney, 1990. p. 115.
58 Letter, JP Campbell to Margaret Chester, 15 June 1915, *Heyfield Herald*, 19 August 1915.

white flags protruding from the scrub. This photograph is not captioned in the National Library and Gillespie albums. The National Library, beside its digitised copy of the picture on its Internet site, has this annotation: 'View of adjoining topography to the Anzac camp'. The author of the annotation had missed the flags entirely in the faded image. Without the caption to anchor and explain the image it becomes just another topographical scene to the uninformed viewer. Thankfully the Mansfield album does have a caption for this picture, written (as they all are) by Aubrey Campbell from his father's notes, giving it a whole new meaning: 'Turk on left, Australian on right [with a] Turkish burial party down the valley'. These are poignant, solemn images, etched on the minds of those who were there. After the armistice life in the trenches quickly returned to normal, as Campbell was about to experience.

The day after the armistice the 8th Light Horse moved up to Walker's Ridge from their initial camp to occupy the trenches on Russell's Top, replacing New Zealanders.[59] Here they took up position in the firing line for the first time, protected from frontal attack by a parapet of sandbags with loopholes for observation and sniping, and facing the Turkish positions higher on the ridge on the side of a hill called Baby 700 (Fig. 74). Between them was a narrow saddle called the Nek, with cliffs on both sides.[60]

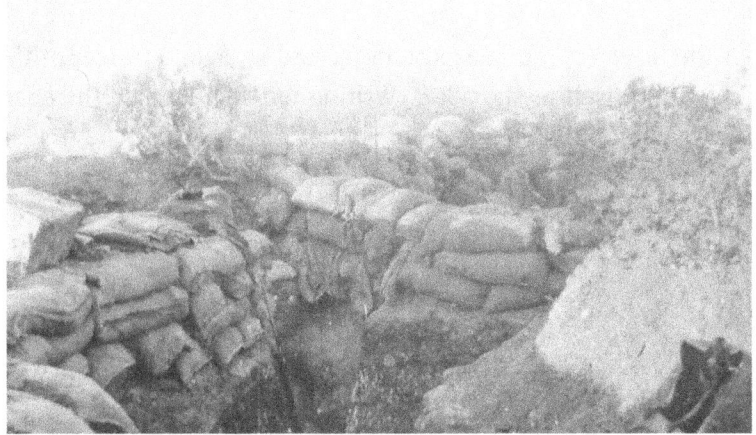

Fig. 74. 'Our first position in the firing line looking towards Achi Baba'.
(Courtesy of Mansfield RSL)

---

59 Walker's Ridge is a spur running from Russell's Top to the sea not far inland and north-east of Anzac Cove.

60 John Hamilton claims The Nek, named by Boer War veterans, means 'mountain pass' in Afrikaans. Hamilton, *Goodbye Cobber, God Bless You*, p. 188.

Their camp, in the trenches on the side of Walker's Ridge 'facing the crumbly sheer sides of the Sphinx' and not far from Russell's Top and the Nek, was 'home' to the 8th Light Horse whilst on Gallipoli, and the place where JP Campbell operated as a signaller.[61]

After the Anzac landing of 25 April the Gallipoli campaign had quickly developed into a siege situation with the Turkish and Allied armies dug in to the rugged terrain and facing one another across no-man's land, with the Turks holding the advantage of higher ground.[62] Lt Col White described the trenches as 'wonderful . . . we are living in burrows like rabbits . . . in some places they are only 20 yards from the Turks. They are a maze, a network, and quite easy to get lost in'.[63] Troops rotated through the firing line, forty-eight hours on, and then forty-eight hours in the rest trenches doing the fatigue work for those on the line.

The signallers soon found that visual signalling was out of the question due to the steep terrain and sniper fire, and so resorted to field telephones and the use of runners.[64] Campbell was part of the 3rd Squadron Signallers, in a section with two other signallers and a stretcher bearer.[65] They occupied a wide, deep trench on Walker's Ridge called Broadway, situated at the back of a maze of other trenches, leading up to the main firing line. A photograph of Campbell was taken in this trench, sitting in a dugout sleeping area, bare headed, writing a letter (Fig. 75).

Forever the observer, he had possibly asked someone to record the activity of writing, with himself as the actor. Writing letters occupied the spare time of most soldiers, making this image emblematic of daily life in the trenches. It is a peaceful scene, blocking out the ever-present horror of war beyond the confines of the trench walls. Three other signallers sit further up the trench. In the three albums that Campbell and his son produced of the 8th Light Horse's experiences on Gallipoli, this same image is captioned 'Writing in the trenches'; 'Scene in the Broadway Trench' and 'In my bedroom in the main communication trench by the telephone box'.[66] Another view of this trench, taken by Campbell, shows

---

61 Ibid., p. 191.

62 Stanley, *Quinn's Post*, p. 31.

63 Jeff Pickerd, 'More Majorum', p. 57.

64 Jeff Pickerd, 'More Majorum', pp. 57-8.

65 Letter, JP Campbell to Margaret Chester, 16 June 1915. *Heyfield Herald* 19 August 1915.

66 The 8th Light Horse albums produced by JP Campbell and his son Aubrey, and their varying captions on identical images, will be discussed later in the chapter.

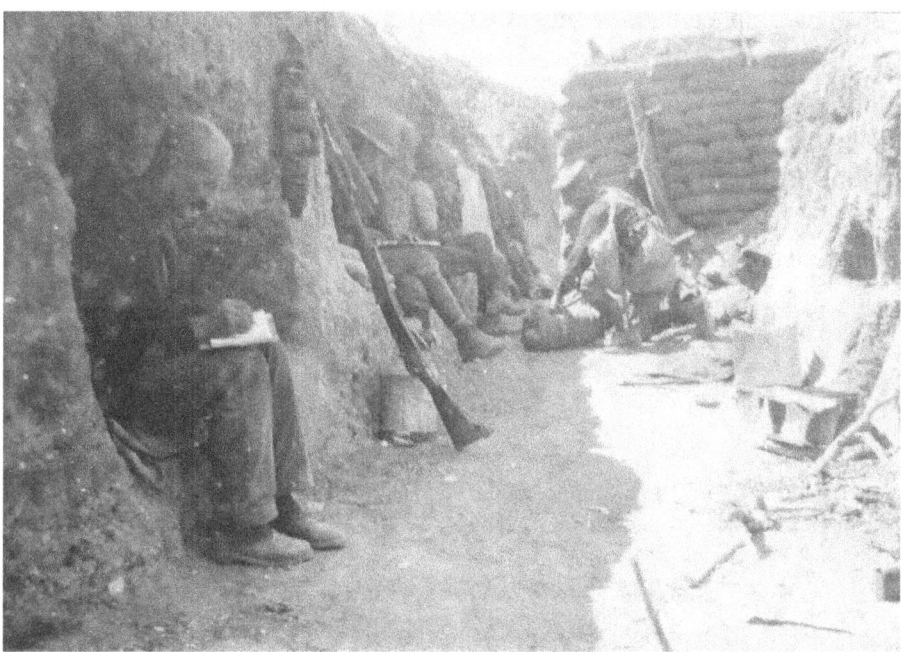

Fig. 75. 'In my bedroom in the main communication trench, by the telephone "box".'
Photographer unknown. (Courtesy of Mansfield RSL)

it as a sandbagged firing place and is captioned 'Signallers about the telephone 'box' (rabbit hole)'.

Humour was a feature of Campbell's writing in his postcards and letters. It may have been cultivated during his days as a knockabout traveller-cum-photographer in eastern Victoria. In a letter to his sister Margaret, written on the Gallipoli peninsula, he gave his address as 'Wombat Pimple, Dug-out-ville (by the sea)'.[67] Campbell reassured his sister that he had enough good, plain food to eat, albeit biscuits 'hard enough to satisfy the work of any dentist' but digestible if 'soaked for a quarter of an hour and fried in fat', and denounced those complaining about food as 'grumblers and inefficients'. 'My fire tried to scare me a couple of mornings ago while I was standing over it', he wrote.

> The thing scattered itself over the landscape, and I had visions of an enemy bomb, wings and halo, and other good things, but when I mustered up pluck to open my eyes I found there had been a live cartridge in the ashes. The darned thing cost me another match, and they are not as plentiful as cartridges.[68]

67 Letter, JP Campbell to Margaret Chester, 3 June 1915, *Heyfield Herald*, 19 August 1915.
68 Ibid.

He photographed bathing scenes, nude men diving from pinnaces and rickety piers into the waters of the cove, a seemingly carefree recklessness in the face of danger. Some died doing it, including the beloved Dr. SJ Campbell of the 8th Light Horse, who was hit by shrapnel from the intermittent shelling that raked the beach.[69] One of Campbell's bathing images appeared in the *Leader* in September 1915 (Fig.76).[70] It projected an image of the children of the Empire playing, unconcerned about enemy fire.

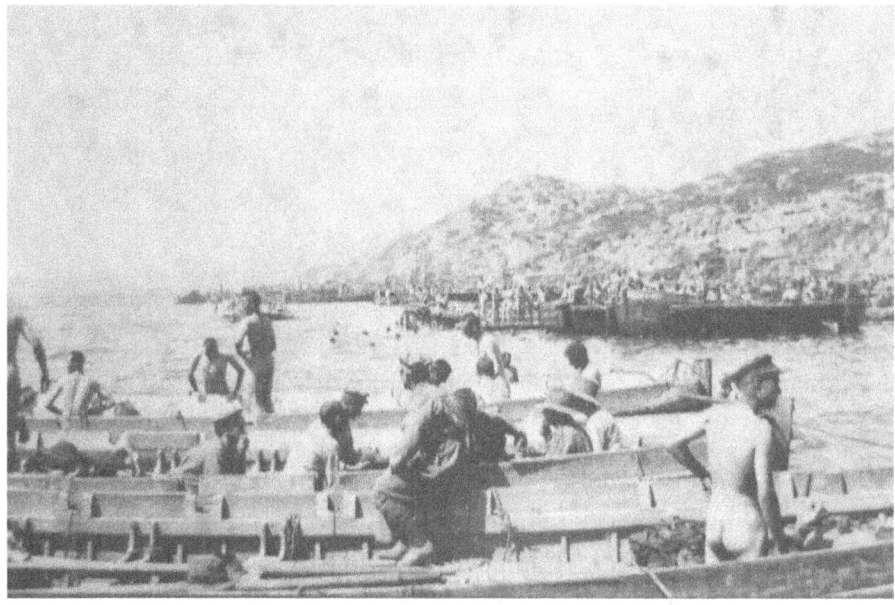

Fig. 76. 'Enjoying a Bath'. *Leader*, 25 September 1915.

The English journalist Ellis Ashmead-Bartlett reported a similar scene with the first dispatch on the Gallipoli campaign published in England and Australia in early May 1915, stating that the 'Colonials are extraordinary cool under fire … often exposing themselves rather than to keep [*sic*] in under the shelter of a cliff … bathing in the sea with shrapnel bursting all around them'.[71] CEW Bean made

---

69 Hamilton, *Goodbye Cobber, God Bless You*, pp. 249-53.

70 This image, reproduced in Fig. 76 from the Mansfield RSL album because of the poor quality of the *Leader* picture, was captioned in that album 'Bathing scene. Anzac Cove'.

71 Quoted in John F Williams, *Anzacs, The Media and The Great War*, UNSW, Sydney, 1999, p. 79. Bartlett produced 'high-profile imperial propaganda' for the first two years of the war and then repudiated it and wrote a secret letter to Prime Minister Asquith exposing how the Dardanelles campaign was bungled. See also: LL Robson, *The First A.I.F.: A Study of its Recruitment 1914-1918*, Melbourne University Press, Melbourne, 1982, p. 43.

similar observations with his first dispatch, published in the Sydney *Telegraph* 15 May 1915, writing that the 'beach in the midst of the fiercest battle ever fought in the Dardanelles looked more like Manly on a public holiday'.[72]

Campbell wrote letters 'sitting in the shade of an artillery gun' after having his daily swim in the sea at 'a splendid beach for the purpose'. He described the scene:

> Crowds [of Anzacs] are in swimming. Shells are flying around looking for targets at the same time. Have seen fully a dozen just now land about 150 yards away in the water, and performing geysers – to amuse the New Zealanders, maybe.[73]

Fancying himself as a writer, Campbell continued the pattern he had established in his letters when he was Commonwealth photographer, describing his work and travels. It complemented his work as a photographer. He had the ability to lead the reader from peace to war, as this extract from another Gallipoli letter to his sister shows:

> At present it is midnight Sunday with you, so if you have kept the hours that youth and beauty should, I can imagine you as an unsymmetrical heap of counterpane, puffing steam out through a blanket tunnel, as I was doing this time last year on the verandah at Mansfield with the thermometer down in the lower 20's. Am busy trying to keep the pipe alight while I talk to you, and big guns boom in by way of accompaniment to the cracking of bullets overhead. The cracks are just like whips, at which I am sure bullocks would wonder muchly, not hearing any swear words.[74]

In his memoir, Harold Hinckfuss, a signaller on Gallipoli from September 1915 to the evacuation in December 1915, gives an insight into the signaller's duties. His first job was to set up an 'antique' switchboard. Communication was conducted via the field telephone or sometimes by morse code using a primitive signalling lamp.[75] It was not all 'work'. Campbell wrote that a signaller 'has just

---

72 John F Williams, *Anzacs, The Media and The Great War*, p. 83.

73 JP Campbell to Margaret Chester, 15 June 1915, *Heyfield Herald*, 19 August 1915.

74 *Heyfield Herald*, 16 June 1915. He often sent photographs with the letters, complementing them. Just how he had the film developed on Gallipoli is unknown.

75 Harold Hinckfuss, *Memories of a Signaller: The First World War, 1914-1919*, UQP, 1982, p. 10. Hinckfuss also ended up on Russell's Top, possibly in the same trench occupied by JP Campbell only a couple of months before. The signallers 'office was situated in the last trench, not far from the latrine'. He initially enjoyed the position: 'The view looking out to the Aegean Sea was fantastic and the sunsets were glorious', pp. 13-14.

semaphored across the ravine asking if I had an "Australasian" [weekly pictorial newspaper], so I'm able to oblige him'.[76]

In a landscape virtually devoid of trees Campbell managed to take a spectacular shot looking down on signallers working at a telegraph station under a scraggy tree on 'One Tree Hill, Shrapnel Gully' with a back drop of towering hills (Fig. 77).[77] These pictures of signallers at work are a valuable contribution to understanding the overall Anzac operations on Gallipoli.

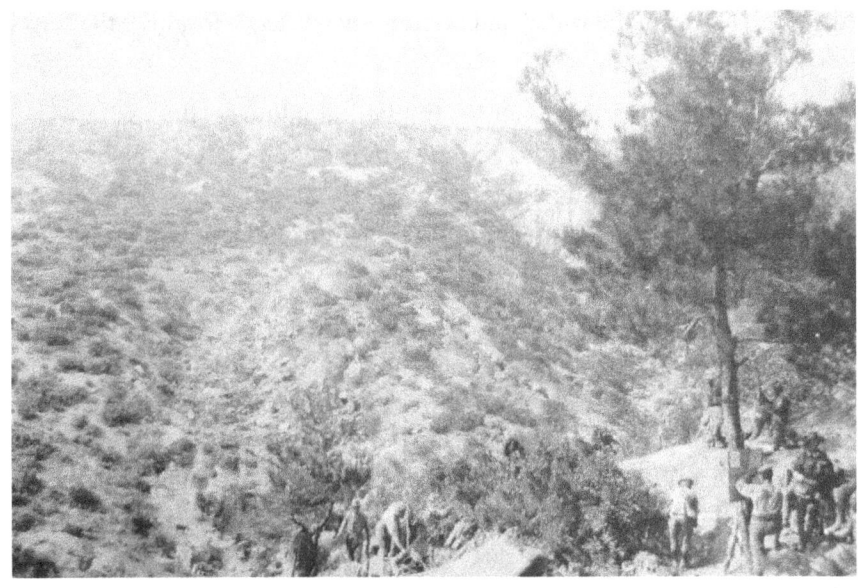

Fig. 77. 'One Tree Hill, Shrapnel Gully. Signallers at Telegraph Station'. This image from the Mansfield RSL album appeared in the *Leader*, 25 September 1915, as the 'Telegraph Station'.

The 8th Light Horse suffered the first of many men killed on 29 May 1915 when Trooper CB Coe was shot in the head during a major Turkish attack. On 5 June, two days before the regiment was relieved from the front line, Campbell found time for humour amidst the horror of war, photographing fellow signaller Dick Healey looking down the steep slope he had accidentally fallen down at 1.00 a.m. in the morning. Healey was wounded in action on Walker's Ridge some three weeks later, taken off Gallipoli and sent home.[78] Campbell continued to rove about with his camera capturing the precarious state of the Allies as they clung to the peninsula.

---

76 Letter, JP Campbell to Margaret Chester, 16 June 1915, *Heyfield Herald*, 19 August 1915.

77 This image appeared in all three 8th Light Horse albums.

78 Cameron Simpson, *Maygar's Boys*, p. 71.

7

THE NEK

*Hanging on by your Eyebrows – Back on the Firing Line – Charge at the
Nek – Leaving the Peninsula – The 8th Light Horse Albums – Caption
Complexities – The* Leader *– The Army Pay Corps*

When relieved by New Zealanders on 7 June 1915 the 8th Light Horse
went down to bivouac in a rest camp sheltered under the Sphinx at Mule
Gully, a deep ravine separating the Sphinx from Walker's Ridge. Campbell's
photograph of this camp shows the Sphinx looming in the background with
scrub-covered undulating land in the foreground scattered with tent-covered
dugouts. They stayed there for two weeks. It was anything but restful as the
soldiers were sent out to make roads and trenches, work that caused fatigue.
In addition they were regularly under fire from the Turks, sustaining frequent
casualties as a result. Whether Campbell participated in this gruelling work is
not known. The important job of communication may have exempted signallers
from such activities, although three months later Signaller Harold Hinckfuss,
also on duty at Russell's Top, found 'something happening every day' and 'one
was either on signalling duty, on fatigues or on duty as a runner', suggesting the
work was shared by all.[1]

Campbell most probably took many of his photographs during these rests.[2] His
picture of dugouts near Courtney's Post at the head of Shrapnel Gully, aptly and
ironically captioned in one album "Hanging on by your eyebrows", shows soldiers
perched precariously on the side of a precipitous, barren slope by their sandbagged
dugouts, going about their everyday activities away from the firing line (Fig. 78).
There is a feeling of shared deprivation, of a comradeship born out of suffering.[3]

---

1 Hinckfuss, *Memories of a Signaller*, p. 13. Hinckfuss was also a much younger man (aged about 22)
than Campbell when he was on Gallipoli.

2 There are at least ten photographs of camps showing clearly the conditions soldiers existed under
in such unforgiving terrain even in the warmer part of the year, as it was during Campbell's time on
Gallipoli.

3 This was not an area of 8th Light Horse operation; Campbell may have been in the vicinity in his
leisure time seeking suitable scenes to photograph, or been sent there on signaller duties, perhaps to
deliver a message.

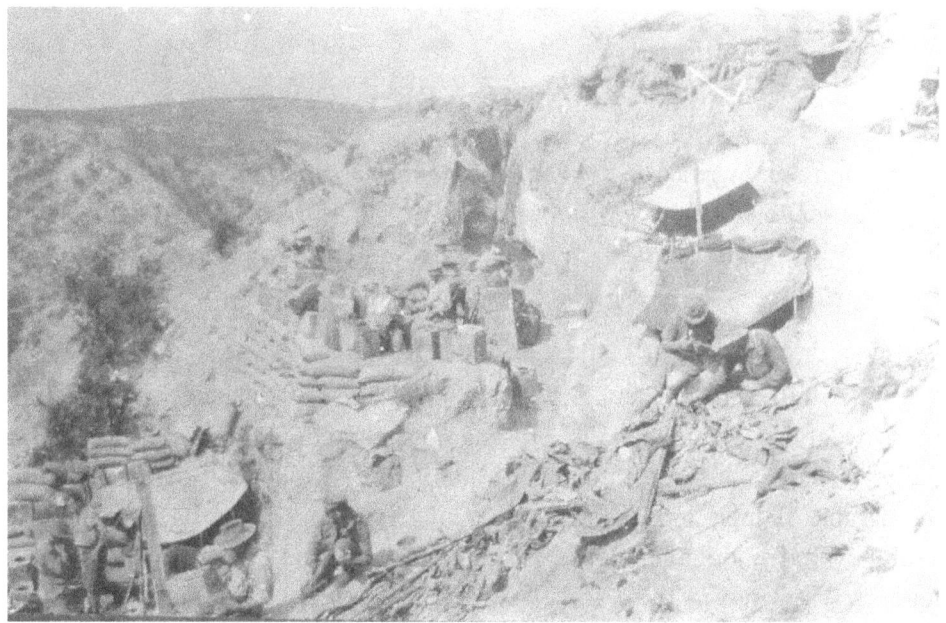

Fig. 78. '"Hanging on by your eyebrows". Near Courtney's Post – head of Shrapnel Gully –
Infantry situation – snipers on distant hill – the Chessboard – Quinns Post at head of gully'.
(Courtesy of Mansfield RSL)

It is an image which captures the nature of the Gallipoli campaign, for it
was up on the escarpment where the epic events of Gallipoli unfolded, not on
the beach, the curved icon which haunts our minds, where the first landing had
occurred on 25 April. The real epic was hanging on for months, rather than
being driven back into the sea.[4] On 25 April some Anzacs had briefly gained the
heights, but as the Turks counter-attacked they were driven back. For example,
Baby 700 kept changing hands until the Australians fell back to lower ground on
Russell's Top – a place later to become so familiar to Campbell and the 8th Light
Horse – leaving Baby 700 to an enemy determined to expel them from Turkish
soil. The Turks dug in on the high ground, and the siege began.[5]

Campbell's only photograph of corpses was taken away from the Walker's
Ridge 'home' of his regiment (Fig. 79). Reproduced in his three 8th Light Horse
albums, the photograph has various captions: 'Dead Turks', 'Dead Turks close
to our trenches' and 'Dead Turks lying in front of our trenches at Quinn's Post'.

---

4 Les Carlyon, *Gallipoli*, Pan Macmillan, Sydney, 2001, p. 169.
5 Ibid., pp 167-9. In chapters 8 & 9 Carlyon explains the achievements of 25 April and 'the loss of
the heights'.

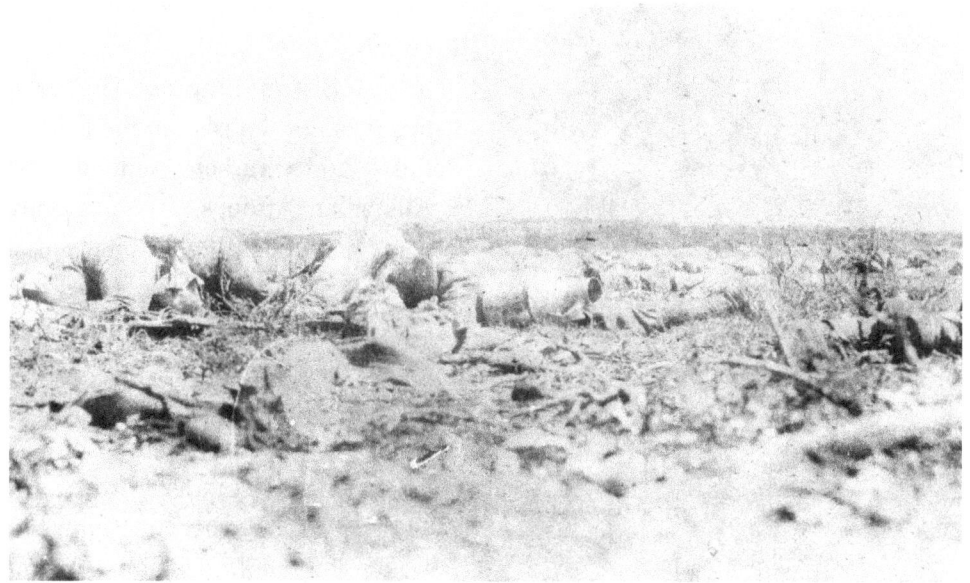

Fig. 79. 'Dead Turks close to our trenches'.
(Courtesy of Mansfield RSL, AWM image HO3117)

His camera was held up overhead during rifle fire to get this picture, risking the lens being shattered'.[6] The northern extremity of Quinn's Post was only 450 yards south from Baby 700, from which vantage point the Turkish machine guns could fire into the Australian trenches.[7] Campbell may have felt the need to record the results of war, or to show that the Allies were producing casualties amongst the Turks.

Like other soldiers on Gallipoli, Campbell was allowed to use a camera but under a degree of censorship restraint. In his thesis on military censorship in Australia during the Great War, Kevin Fewster concludes censorship was widely used at home in Australia, causing 'considerable social and political ructions'.[8]

6 National Library of Australia, Mansfield and Gillespie albums respectively.

7 Stanley, *Quinn's Post*, p. 41, 47. As with the Courtney's picture, Campbell may have been on signalling duty when he took this photo, or he may have been simply searching for photographic subjects during a rest period. The distances between these major trench positions were not great. It shows the risks Campbell took to obtain a photograph.

8 Kevin J. Fewster, 'Expression and Suppression: Aspects of Military Censorship in Australia during the Great War', PhD Thesis, University of NSW, 1980. In the various theatres of war Australian troops came under the British Field Censorship Regulations, the object being 'to intercept military dangerous information sent, whether deliberately or in ignorance, from the war theatre to people at home or abroad, and secondly to discourage troops from writing facts which, if found on captured or dead soldiers would reveal the situation and strength of the Allied armies'. Kevin Fewster, 'Expression and Suppression', p. 61.

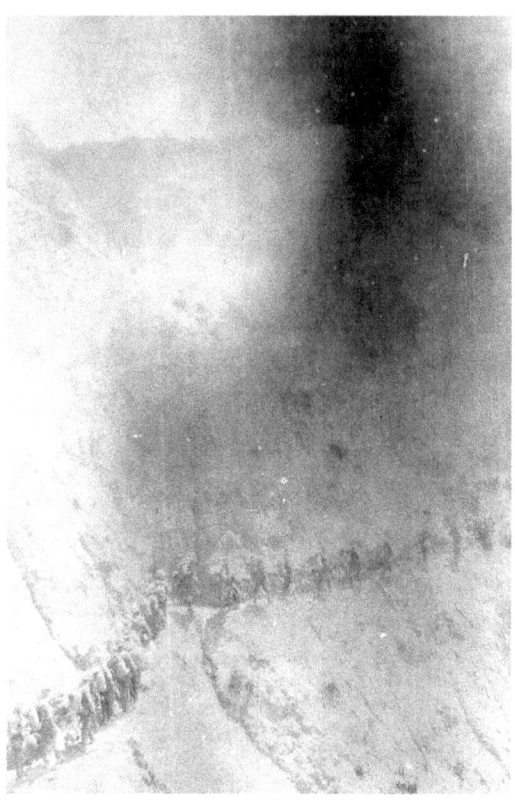

Fig. 80. 'Eighth L.H. filing down the Goat track from the firing line. Smoke & dust from a shell bursting on crest of hill'. (Courtesy of Mansfield RSL)

Indeed, he argues, Australia had possibly the harshest censorship in the British Empire.[9] However, this was not the case in the Middle East and Turkey among the Australian troops. Photography was theoretically prohibited in a theatre of war, but was tolerated on Gallipoli and later in the Sinai and Palestine. As a consequence a valuable photographic record produced by ordinary soldiers exists. This contrasts with the Western Front, where the embargo was rigidly enforced, all cameras being confiscated on the voyage from Egypt to France.[10] Campbell took full advantage of the lax approach to censorship on Gallipoli, photographing his regiment at its daily chores at every opportunity.

Two other 'combat' pictures are worthy of mention. One is an eerie, faded picture with a dark, patchy area obscuring one third of the image (Fig. 80). Its description is: '8th L.H. filing down the great track from the firing line [probably on 4 July 1915]. Smoke and dust from a shell bursting on crest of hill', which gives it a dramatic edge. In the bottom part of the picture a line of soldiers can be discerned winding wearily along the narrow track cut into the bare precipice. Smoke and dust rises above them on the right, partly obscuring half the line of tramping men, with the mountainous terrain towering above them. Like many of Campbell's shots, the

---

9 Ibid., p. 317.

10 Peter Liddle, *Gallipoli 1915: Pens, Pencils and Cameras at War*, Brassey's Defence, London, 1985, p. x, and Kevin Fewster, 'Expression and Suppression', p. 64. However, cameras did get through the net and were used on the Western Front, as the story of the Grinton brothers, soldiers and amateur photographers, attests. See Corinne Perkin, with essays by Les Carlyon and Colin Harding, *A Camera on the Somme*, Bendigo Art Gallery, Bendigo, 2009.

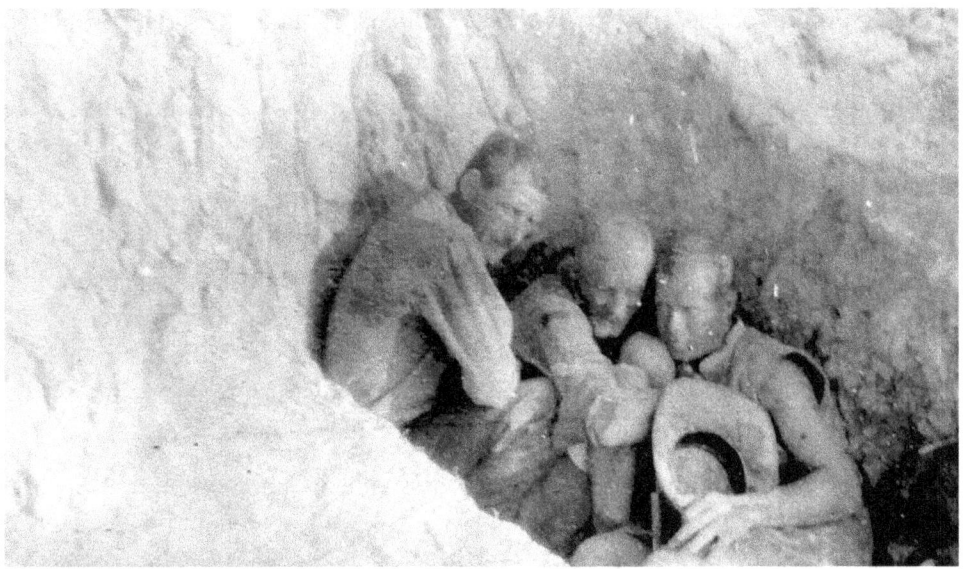

Fig. 81. 'Ducking for shelter from a coming shell. Sgt. Mjr. Barr in middle, Laidlaw who sent the Herald envelope on right'. (Courtesy of Mansfield RSL)

figures are distant and small, but they seem oblivious to the shelling, and too tired to care. This is an example of his unique landscape photography, emphasising the subject (the soldiers) with the smoke and dust from the exploding shell providing a hazy effect. Here art and documentation work in conjunction. The tension between these two aspects in Campbell's photography must have tested him in the dangerous environment of Gallipoli.

Rarely did he have time to exercise his artistic skills, nor did he have the equipment to do so.[11] Occasionally, however, Campbell managed to capture a dramatic moment brilliantly, as he did in this and the following photograph.

This other 'combat' picture is of three soldiers huddled together in a shallow dugout, unarmed and bareheaded, enduring shelling by the Turks (Fig. 81). In an album it is captioned: 'Ducking for shelter from a coming shell. Sgt Mjr Barr in middle. Laidlaw who sent the Herald envelope on right'. The image shows shared vulnerability and fear; Campbell may have risked his life in snapping it.

---

11 *The Age* photojournalist Phillip Schuler, by contrast, appeared to photograph his soldier subjects close-up showing clear facial features. His images are sharper; he appears to have taken fewer landscape scenes. As a professional on assignment for *The Age* he would have had, presumably, the best available photographic equipment whereas Campbell, a working signaller, had to make do with his German folding camera in his spare time.

As Helen Ennis points out, 'they are like animals, functioning at an instinctive level where the most urgent desperate requirement is shelter'.[12]

Soldiers got used to the whizzing bullets but they feared shrapnel. Lance Corporal Cyril Lawrence wrote that when they heard the sound of an incoming artillery shell:

> every one ducks for shelter. You can't help it and sometimes it is the most ridiculous shelter too. A small bush, a waterproof sheet, a blanket – anything at all – and most of it could not stop a pussy. Yet everyone ducks and, on the other hand, let them burst ever such a little distance away and no one takes much notice except to enjoy the joke of watching others duck into cover in all sorts of undignified positions.[13]

Campbell captured one of these moments with his photograph of the three soldiers cowering in a hole. He made light of artillery bombardments when writing to his sister Margaret:

> [The] fact [remains] that if a shell hit me it would be difficult to find my hat. But these "marbles" give you as much warning to get out of their road as an excited tram conductor. First you hear the gun and then the shriek of the projectile, and if you are expecting visitors and are not too inquisitive you hide as safely as from a debt collector. Of course if you can't hide – well, if you will play football you've got to chance a bump.[14]

The 8th Light Horse served the next stretch of duty on Walker's Ridge and Russell's Top from 20 June to 4 July. Campbell had his fiftieth birthday on 4 July, sharing the distinction of turning fifty on Gallipoli with others higher in rank such as John Monash and Harry Chauvel. That he coped well with scrambling up and down steep slopes, often under fire, keeping up with men half his age, is a tribute to his determination. 'I'd like to be about 20 years younger', he wrote to his sister Margaret before landing on Gallipoli, 'but then I mightn't have as

---

12 Ennis, *Intersections: Photography, History and the National Library of Australia*, p. 140. The naming of two of the soldiers does not seem to matter, although just what the 'Herald envelope' is is unclear. They appear to be James Walker Barr, ex-traveller from Toorak, Victoria, and Victor Rupert Laidlaw, previously a tailor from South Melbourne. Both were in the 2nd Field Ambulance. Laidlaw ended up in hospital on Mudros in September 1915 and was sent to France in March 1916 where he was severely wounded in the face in July 1916. He was sent back to Australia in April 1917 and invalided out of the Army. NAA: B2455, Barr JW and NAA: B2455, Laidlaw Victor Rupert.

13 Jeff Pickerd, 'More Majorum', p. 68. Quote from a letter by L/Cpl Cyril Lawrence.

14 Letter, JP Campbell to Margaret Chester, 15 June 1915, *Heyfield Herald*, 19 August 1915.

much sense, so, perhaps, that about balances things'.[15] When others succumbed to illness he survived, as he did the Turkish attack on their trenches at the end of June, although he eventually sustained a minor wound.[16] The regiment was relieved of duty in the morning and moved down to their rest camp at the foot of Walker's Ridge, providing Campbell with some degree of relief on his birthday.

Casualties mounted. Dysentery, enteritis, diarrhoea and septic sores were also playing havoc with the regiment, and many were sent off Gallipoli to either Lemnos or Malta.[17] Campbell's luck ran out the day after the regiment moved back into the trenches on Russell's Top. He received a shrapnel wound in the right knee on 30 July when a bomb burst overhead while he was lying awake in his bunk late at night. The pellet was gouged out of a perspiring Campbell by a doctor who gave him a cocaine injection. The wound, 'right in the ham of the knee', was two inches long by two thirds of an inch deep.[18]

According to his son Aubrey, Campbell was wounded at the battle of Lone Pine, but the date, Campbell's written account and photographic evidence indicate otherwise.[19] There are two photographs of Campbell's dugout on a steep slope behind the trenches with the following captions: 'The hole I was bombed in' which shows Campbell sitting in the dugout with a bandaged right knee (Fig. 82), and 'In front of my dugout in which I was bombed. Signaller O'Mullane who was killed is the figure'.[20] Campbell told his sister that he 'voluntarily went

---

15 Letter, JP Campbell to Margaret Chester, 1 May 1915, *Heyfield Herald*, 22 July 1915

16 The average age of Campbell's fellow 8th Light Horse Signallers who served on Gallipoli was 24, compared to the average age overall of the 'other ranks' in the regiment of 25.5 years (Peter Burness, *The Nek*, p.49). Out of fourteen of the 8th Light Horse Signallers (including Campbell) surveyed as listed in *Maygar's Boys*, six were evacuated to hospital, five were wounded, one was killed in action, and two appeared to escape unscathed, notwithstanding the possibility of psychological damage.

17 Jeff Pickerd, 'More Majorum', p. 89. They were to stay in the rest camp most of July where they were pushed to the limit carrying supplies, digging trenches and performing all manner of other support jobs, including piquet duty (backing up other soldiers on duty in the trenches). In between this frantic activity they bathed in the sea when they could in a bid to get rid of the lice, or wrote letters on anything suitable they could find, such was the scarcity of paper. It would have been during this time that Campbell took many of his photographs.

18 NAA: B2455, Campbell JP, and JP Campbell to Margaret Chester, 2 August 1915, *Heyfield Herald*, 14 October 1915.

19 NAA: B2455, Campbell JP. The battle of Lone Pine went from 6 August 1915 to 10 August 1915, a week or more after the official record states Campbell was wounded.

20 Cameron Simpson, *Maygar's Boys*, p. 43. This book has Campbell wounded at the charge at the Nek on 7 August 1915, but it makes the assumption that if you were in the 8th Light Horse and shipped off Gallipoli after the charge you must have been wounded during it. Bernard L. O'Mullane, an athlete in private life and probably selected as a signaller/runner because of this, was killed in action at the Nek a week later.

back to telephone duties, though the Colonel reckons I should be resting, but I don't feel mean enough to trade on a trifling incident to get away to hospital'. As it turned out he was lucky to be wounded when he was, before the August offensive and the slaughter at the Nek.

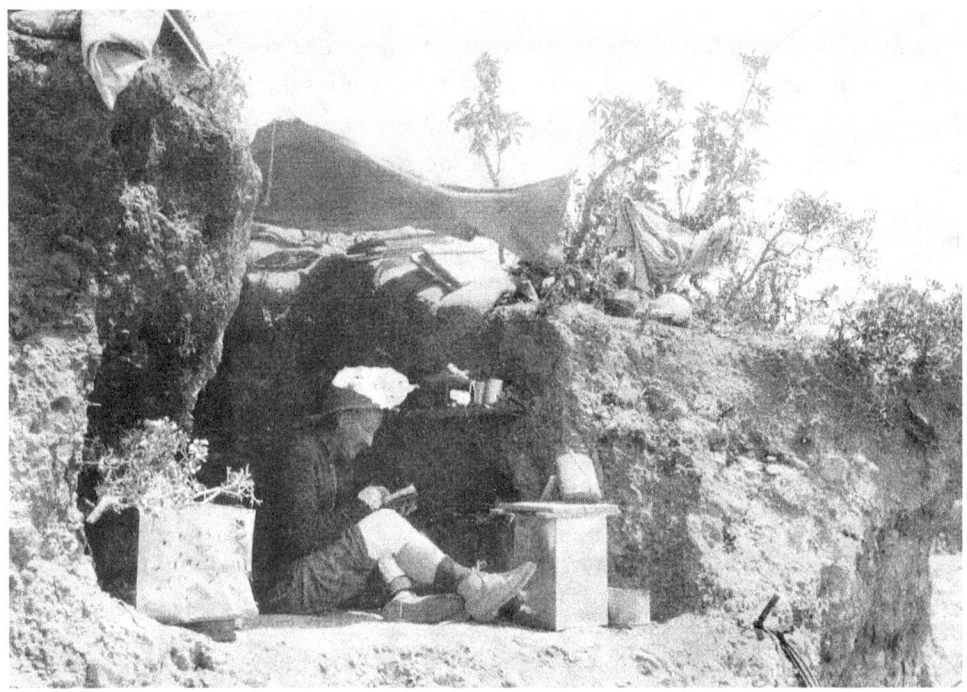

Fig. 82. 'The hole I was bombed in'. Photographer unknown.
(Courtesy of Mansfield RSL, AWM image HO3197)

On his return to Australia in early 1919 Campbell was reported as saying that he was wounded at Lone Pine, a battle his regiment was not involved in.[21] There was certainly a lot of kudos to be gained from associating yourself with Lone Pine, but not with the 8th Light Horse's bayonet charge at the Nek, a failure and massacre on 7 August 1915, in which the regiment suffered 154 soldiers killed and 80 wounded out of the 300 members who participated. The Nek charge, which was part of a major Allied August offensive against the Turks, involved the

21 *Mansfield Courier*, 8 March 1919. This contradicts his letter published in the *Mansfield Courier* of 25 September 1915, which stated he was wounded prior to the Nek charge and which does not mention Lone Pine. There is the possibility that the *Mansfield Courier* made an error in reporting Campbell's story.

Australians storming the Turkish trenches at the base of Baby 700.[22] Campbell observed this terrible action, but did not participate because of his leg wound. The Nek, a tiny saddle area the size of only three tennis courts between the Anzac and Turkish trenches, was bathed in blood and heaped with bodies. Four lines of Light Horse troops went over the top at intervals, two from the 8th Light Horse and two from the 10th Light Horse, who had at least 80 men killed and 58 wounded.[23] All were mown down by withering Turkish machine gun and rifle fire. Bombs finished off what the bullets did not. Many of the wounded crawled back to the Australian trenches.[24]

Two days before the charge Campbell wrote to his sister from the 'Phone Box, Walker's Ridge':

> Sitting on my rolled up blanket on the floor [of the trench]; receiver on head, buzzer on lamp box, and speaker gear lying thereon; aeroplane humming around like you at the sewing machine. There is every sign of a big dust up in the next few days. Sorry I'm a bit in the road with a gammy leg, but I want to see the scrum after waiting so long on one perch. Fresh blood will do the heavy work as we are all jolly stale and unhinged with the monotony and incessant shell and rifle fire.[25]

Campbell's account of the Nek debacle has survived in a letter reprinted in the pages of the *Mansfield Courier*. It is a frank account written only six days after the event, and not one that would have made the pages of the major metropolitan

---

22 John Hamilton, *Goodbye Cobber, God Bless You*, p. 323, Peter Burness, *The Nek*, p. 123, and Cameron Simpson, *Maygar's Boys*, p. 12, which states 170 were killed and 85 wounded. The figures vary from source to source. This disaster was attributed to poor decision making by commanding officers of the 3rd Light Horse Brigade.

23 John Hamilton, *Goodbye Cobber, God Bless You*, p. 323, and Peter Burness, *The Nek*, p. 123. There was only a two minute interval between the first line of 150 8th Light Horse soldiers and the second line of 150 (Hamilton, p. 294). The next two successive lines of 10th Light Horse were fewer in number, and just how many soldiers there were, and who made up the numbers, appears unclear (Burness, p. 116).

24 The Turkish forces had lost a similar number of dead (if not more) in their charge over the same short distance of rough ground between the opposing trenches (about 40 yards) on 29 July The Australians charged over their decaying bodies. The courage and self-sacrifice of those involved has become a significant part of the Anzac legend. The Nek charge has been depicted in film (most famously in Peter Weir's 1981 film *Gallipoli*, focusing on the 10th Light Horse from Western Australia), paintings and literature. Peter Burness concluded his book, *The Nek*, with the following: 'The Nek remains an enduring Australian legend. It possesses a grand heroic quality, while being a testament to the tragedy of war, and a reminder of the terrible cost in human lives upon which military legends are built' (p. 157).

25 Letter, JP Campbell to Margaret Chester, 'Anniversary of the War' (5 August 1915?), *Heyfield Herald*, 14 October 1915.

daily newspapers, given the censorship climate of the time. Casualty information started filtering back to Australia almost two weeks after the charge, but no official details of the action were given. The Melbourne *Herald* published a brief piece on its front page on 25 August under the bold heading 'LIGHT HORSE SUFFERS', using as a source 'wounded officers from the Dardanelles' and stating that the 8th and 10th Light Horse Regiments 'were practically wiped out in the heavy fighting on August 7'.[26]

By late September the official correspondence cables arrived outlining the disaster that had befallen the 3rd Light Horse Brigade.[27] Campbell's account, published in the *Mansfield Courier*, 25 September 1915, appeared therefore before those in the major Melbourne metropolitan dailies. Another less detailed description of the charge was included in a letter to his sister Margaret, extracts of which were reprinted in the *Heyfield Herald* of 14 October 1915. In this letter he told how he had prepared a curry stew on the evening of the charge 'for Rev. Hughes and party of four, as they had no time or material', then 'said good-bye in the twilight, and back they went to their position in the trenches'. George Hughes was a Presbyterian minister from Balranald in New South Wales. Campbell had given him his last meal, for he died in the charge the next morning.[28]

As he was not on signaller on the morning of the charge because of his leg wound, Campbell was able observe the carnage as it unfolded. His account as witness to the Nek charge, as written to HJ Vallance, went to a much wider audience when it was published in the *Mansfield Courier*:

Alexandria Pier, 13/8/'15

From the above you will see that I am back again in Egypt, and the reason [for] that is I got a junk of bomb in my leg at the back of the knee; 'tis a mere minor affair, and I kept telephone duty most of the time, as I did not want to go away, as we were on the eve of doing something in the way of an advance, and the 8th and 10th Light Horse having the task of attacking the enemy trenches in front of our position. The general battle started on Friday [6 August 1915] night, when the enemy was routed from his

26 Melbourne *Herald*, Final Edition, 25 August 1915.

27 Peter Burness, *The Nek*, p. 133.

28 Cameron Simpson, *Maygar's Boys*, p. 49, and John Hamilton, *Goodbye Cobber, God Bless You*, pp. 325-6. Lance Corporal Hughes was a section leader in the 8th Light Horse and no doubt a friend of Campbell's. Campbell gravitated towards educated people, in this case a minister of Campbell's own religion, Presbyterianism, and a person with outdoor interests like shooting (Hughes was a 'first class shot'), an activity Campbell had enjoyed from a young age, so they had much in common.

outpost trenches on our left. The searchlights of our gunboats, flares on the battle ground, bombs bursting, likewise shells, made a memorable scene in the night, to say nothing of the noise. This died down after an hour or so, and the next violence was before dawn [of Saturday 7 August], when the bang of the biggest cannon yet fired from down below on the water startled me, and the shell tearing the crest of the hill away some 200 yards above me. This was a preliminary bombarding of the enemy trenches where we were to attack. The bombarding ceased, when the enemy at once opened up a furious rifle and machine-gun fire on our position. They were fully conversant with our move, and for all the tomfool capers, our fellows got out over our parapet into this hailstorm, and now there are very few left to tell the tale. Half the regiment went as chargers, and the other half as supports, the latter having a good deal of natural shelter, but the supports were never needed, the other was simply wiped out, and not many got far from our own trenches, some being wounded on its edge and got away. A few got out, and, seeing everyone plugged, lay down in depressions; a few got back wounded, and a very few without a scratch, and four lay out all day (it was well into daylight before the scrum was over), and wriggled in the next night, one without wounds. The whole of B Squadron's officers [were] killed, as was also the Commanding Officer [Lt. Col. Alexander H. White], the Adjutant and Major. I don't know how the other squadrons fared exactly, but there is only one officer [Lt. Mervyn Higgins] to answer the roll; also the second in command, Major ---------- [censored – it was Major Arthur V. Deeble], who led the second line, and got back with an ankle graze only. Only one got back from B troop, and three from another troop – D, I think. A number of the supports were killed, too, and I understand the final strength of the Squadron, including men whose duties did not take them out, such as stretcher-bearers, ammunition carriers, etc., was 47 out of 150; thus in a few minutes, I've lost a number of good fellows, and the officers were a grand lot of chaps; However I've a good pal in Major ----------[Deeble], who will now be C.O., I suppose, and he got me away for a spell, so as to rest my leg – a gammy one is of no use at all in case of an advance, and as I am due a lot of sleep I hope to be in good trim in a month, anyhow.[29]

29 *Mansfield Courier*, 25 September 1915. Three of his letters were published in this issue, written on successive days and all addressed to his old friend and former business partner, HJ Vallance, who handed them on to the *Courier*. Campbell gave an account of his trip from Gallipoli to Alexandria and vivid descriptions of the hospitals he was sent to, along with news of survivors of the Nek charge, particularly Mansfield soldiers.

John Hamilton wrote in his book that Lieutenant Mervyn Higgins and Major Arthur Deeble were the 'only two officers of the 8th to emerge unscathed from the charge'.[30] Campbell took a photograph of the two officers sitting with Dr Francis Beamish, the regiment's medical officer, in a rudimentary dugout-cum-shelter on the side of a precipice, the officers no doubt still in shock (Fig. 83).[31]

In a further letter published two weeks later in the *Mansfield Courier*, he expressed his feelings on the whole affair:

> I am sure I don't know how the Regiment will reorganise. The shock of losing all my comrades in a few minutes has been great, also to all who remained out of the scrum, so I don't care if we are sent home to our womenfolk at once. Anyhow, I expect I will be free from the battle line for three or four weeks yet, and my word! I am enjoying the "loaf."[32]

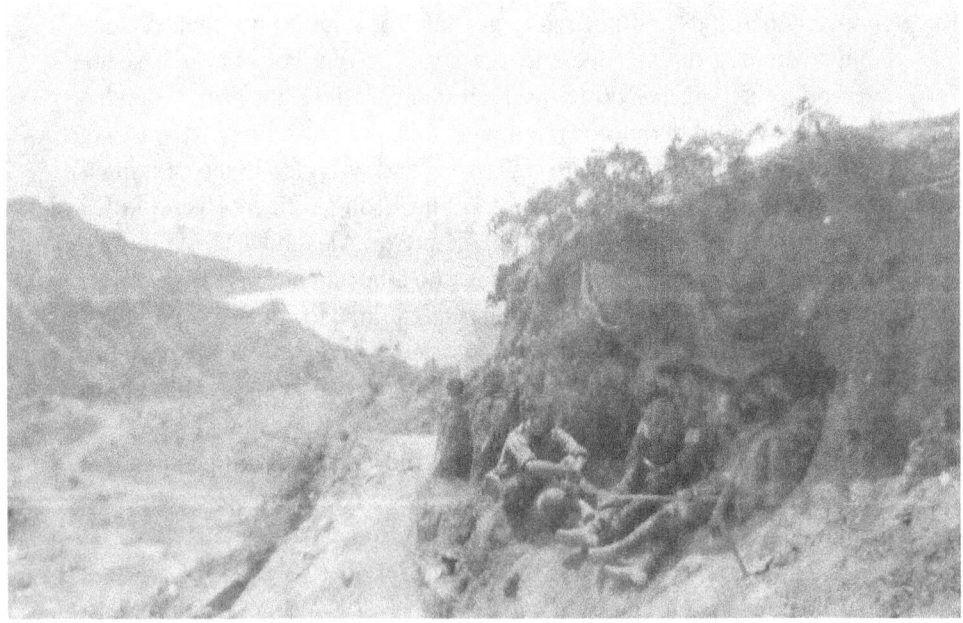

Fig. 83. 'The only 2 officers left in the 8th L. Horse after the Charge. Lt. Higgins, Mjr Deeble and Dr. Beamish'. (Courtesy of Mansfield RSL)

---

30 Hamilton, *Goodbye Cobber, God Bless You*, p. 299.
31 Cameron Simpson, *Maygar's Boys*, p. 231. Lt. Mervyn Higgins was the only child of Justice Henry Higgins of Harvester judgement (establishment of the basic wage in Australia) fame. Mervyn survived the Nek charge, but was killed at the battle of Magdhaba in 1916. Cameron Simpson, *Maygar's Boys*, p. 65.
32 *Mansfield Courier*, 9 October 1915.

Despite this trauma he seemed to bear no animosity to the Turks. He told his sister Margaret:

> From all sides reports are that the Turks fight fairly – doesn't fire on Red Cross and hospital ships. Any yarns you hear about maltreatment are all bunkum. Our wounded have even been found bandaged and water left for them, and as a trench fighter he is our superior in methods, but in the open he's done.[33]

Campbell's granddaughter says she never heard her grandfather talk of his Gallipoli experiences, nor did she hear any of the extended family mention it. It was common, apparently, for those surviving the Nek charge to associate themselves with Lone Pine. Nettie Palmer, biographer of Justice Henry Higgins, referred to his son Mervyn as being involved in 'the charge at Lone Pine'.[34] Les Carlyon wrote that the affair 'at the Nek was like incest: no-one in the family much wanted to talk about it'.[35] Members of the 8th Light Horse had watched the 1st Infantry Brigade's successful assault on Lone Pine from their vantage point on Russell's Top 'with enthusiasm', and had hoped to emulate it at the Nek.[36] It was not to be. Campbell's written account of the Nek charge, combined with his photographs before and after, help us gain some understanding of the disaster.

The day after the Nek charge Campbell was sent to the Australian Clearing Hospital on the beach where he witnessed scores of wounded being treated and 'some shocking stretcher cases'.[37] The next day he left Gallipoli bound for hospital in Egypt. His knee wound had deteriorated, requiring medical attention, although he could still hobble about. His last photograph on Turkish soil was of

---

33 Letter, JP Campbell to Margaret Chester, 12 August 1915, *Heyfield Herald*, 14 October 1915.

34 Nettie Palmer, *Henry Bourne Higgins: A Memoir*, George G. Harrap & Co., Sydney, 1931, p. 233. Sometimes it may have been mere confusion as to the name of the place. Alan McColl of Mansfield wrote a letter dated 18 September 1915 which was published in the *Mansfield Courier*, 13 November 1915. He was on the way to England for a 'good spell' after his stint on Gallipoli: 'I would not mind in the least going back to the front again if Sam [his brother who was killed at the charge of the Nek] and all my mates were alive, but they all went under in the charge of the 8th Light Horse at *Lonesome Pine* [my emphasis]. It breaks a fellow up to see his own brother and all his pals go under. I don't know how I escaped in that charge; it was dreadful while it lasted. The Light Horse Brigade have made a great name for themselves, but at a great cost of life. There are not many of the original 8th left now, and there is not much to look forward to in going back to the front, as I suppose the 8th will be reinforcements – all strangers to me'.

35 Les Carlyon, *Gallipoli*, p. 410.

36 CEW Bean, *Anzac to Amiens*, Australian War Memorial, Second edition, 1947, p. 154.

37 Letter, JP Campbell to Margaret Chester, 12 August 1915, *Heyfield Herald*, 14 October 1915.

a barge full of Turkish prisoners about to embark from Anzac Cove (Fig. 84). On the back of a flimsy print of the scene he wrote a note in pencil to Aubrey, describing the contents of the photograph and the dangers in taking it:[38]

> 7/ Turk Prisoners embarking at the base – caught on the 7th – just as I was arranging the camera a shell fragment whizzed over my head and pinged into the bow of the barge – the shell had burst a very long way off – fragments of all sizes have the unhealthy knack of flying in any direction after they burst by impact – I embarked from another pier immediately after this snap.   9/8/1915

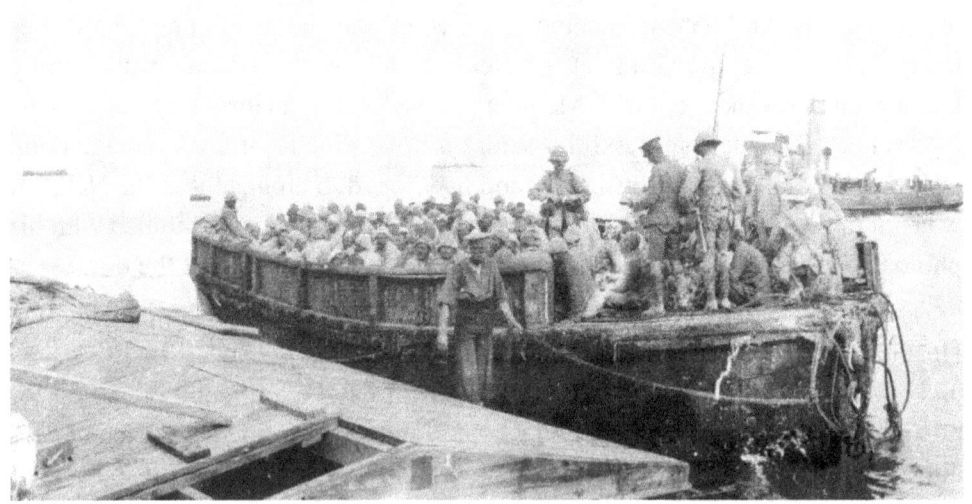

Fig. 84. 'Turks captured on the 8 Aug being shipped on the 10th Aug'. Campbell's last photograph on Gallipoli. (Courtesy of Mansfield RSL, AWM image HO3121)

Campbell was transported off Gallipoli on the hospital ship *Canada*. He had depicted his arrival at the Dardanelles with a three-print panorama of Gallipoli viewed from the sea, captioned 'ANZAC'.[39] His photographs on leaving reveal his elevated mood in a joyous series starting with 'Leaving Turkey', although,

---

38 Photograph in the collection of Noel Fethers. Greg Gillespie has a non-album photograph the same as this with a note on the back similar to the Mansfield album image caption: 'Turks captured on 8/8/15 being shipped on 10/8/15', i.e. the dates given are each different by a day. The Australian War Memorial also has this photo attributed to JP Campbell, numbered H03121. In a letter to his sister Margaret he described this incident 'as a sort of "tig" to the Turks on leaving their native heath'. Letter, JP Campbell to M Chester, 12 August 1915, *Heyfield Herald*, 14 October 1914.

39 This panorama appears in the Mansfield album.

true to form, there is one sombre picture of bodies trussed up on deck ready to be jettisoned from the ship, and captioned 'Sea Burial'. Campbell described the burial in a letter to HJ Vallance:

> Some [of the wounded] have died aboard, and I have seen my first burial at sea; the corpse is sewn up in a blanket, placed on a stretcher, and covered with a Union Jack. The service is read, the stretcher tilted over the stern, and the body slides from under the flag to the best of all final coverings – clean water.[40]

He remained detached from all this, telling his sister Margaret that he had become 'as callous as a doctor'.[41] Included in this 'leaving Gallipoli' series were pictures of Imbros Island, views along the side of the ship, 'Gurkhas playing cards', the 'Wounded on board the Canada', and a portrait of himself in a deck chair displaying his wound. He seems to have maintained a healthy ego at all times (Fig.85).

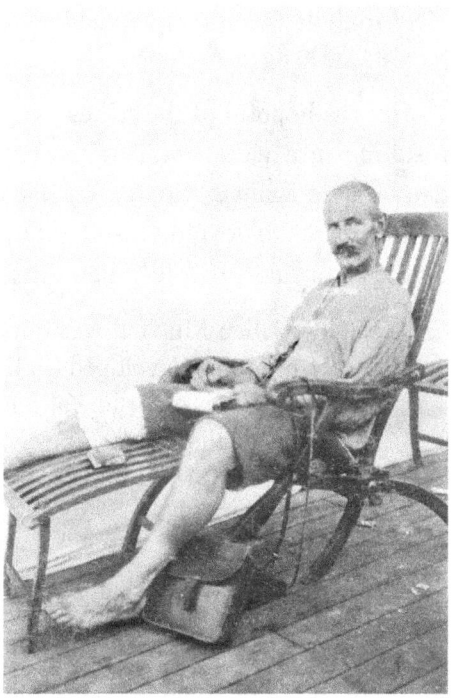

Fig. 85. 'Signaller J.P. Campbell on board the "Canada".' Photographer unknown. Note the bandaged right knee, writing material and camera case. (Courtesy of Mansfield RSL, AWM image HO3173)

No doubt he echoed the sentiments of most soldiers departing Gallipoli when he wrote:

> Glory, it is lovely to be away from the sound of strife, after three months incessant risk of being shot any moment. The first night of sudden awakening [on the hospital ship] I thought I was in a new dug out, and feeling the roof (bunk above) I said this is a nice, safe corrugated iron roof, anyhow; and nice kerosene tin walls (smooth white boards). Wonder what telephone dug out I'm in, and kept on wondering till the

---

40 Letter, JP Campbell to HJ Vallance, 13 August 1915, in *Mansfield Courier*, 25 September 1915.
41 Letter, JP Campbell to M Chester, 12 August 1915, *Heyfield Herald*, 14 October 1915.

truth dawned on my befuddled brain. So I giggled, and went thankfully to sleep again.[42]

He was hopeful of the Allies' August offensive on Gallipoli being a success, resulting in a withdrawal of the Light Horse, 'and maybe I'll never see that demon hole again'.[43] Soon after his arrival at a hospital in Heliopolis, he made arrangements to develop his Gallipoli film taken during his nearly three months on the peninsula. He told Lilian Pitts in a postcard:

> Nephew Allan Mitchell was out [at the hospital] again and brought me one of my films developed – all right – so I'll get the rest done – Am not sending any more to Val but to Aubrey instead – I fancy I can rig up a page for the Leader from what I have on hand – I expect to have a complete set of prints to enclose.[44]

His son Aubrey had completed a photography course at the Working Men's College, Melbourne, in 1908, when only eighteen years of age.[45] Aubrey produced the 8th Light Horse albums we see today. JP Campbell was quick to get a selection of Gallipoli prints away to the Melbourne *Leader*, suggesting this may have been planned before leaving Australia or arranged by letter whilst he was on campaign.[46] Campbell's photographic contribution during his service with the 8th Light Horse is contained in the four albums compiled by Aubrey, plus the photographs JP Campbell submitted to the *Leader*.

While in hospital in Heliopolis Campbell was nursed by Marjorie Ritchie of Mansfield, with whom he was presumably already acquainted. Immediately after the war Marjorie was given an album by JP and Aubrey Campbell, containing 184 of JP Campbell's Great War photographic prints. It may have been presented to Marjorie in appreciation of her nursing Campbell in Egypt. Marjorie's daughter,

---

42 Letter, JP Campbell to M Chester, 14 October 1915, *Heyfield Herald*, 14 October 1915.

43 Ibid.

44 From an undated postcard to Lilian Pitts, written soon after his arrival at Heliopolis and upon returning from Gallipoli.

45 Student Attendance Registers 1887-1935, details for Aubrey Campbell, Accession No. 99/80/11, Years 1907, 1908, RMIT Archives.

46 Campbell would have had to submit his photos to a censor. The photos passed in Egypt would have no doubt run the gauntlet of the censor in Melbourne. Some of his more censorable pictures (those showing army operations) may have survived: a collection of photographs donated to the Australian War Memorial by a Mr S Sayers look strikingly like Campbell photos, some of them showing machine-gunners and other more sensitive subjects.

Jean Lester, and her son, RW Lester, donated the album to the National Library of Australia in 2001.[47] The inscription in this album attributes the photographs to 'Signaller J.P. Campbell whilst on Active Service with The Glorious 3rd Brigade of Light Horse (whose Heroic Deeds will long be remembered.)'.[48]

The other Ritchie family 8th Light Horse album was either given to or commissioned by Geoffrey Ritchie of 'Delatite Station', a relative of Mansfield grazier and Light Horseman Noel Rutledge, who was killed in action in Belgium in 1916. Geoffrey Ritchie, the original recipient's grandson, donated this album to the Mansfield RSL in 2005.[49] It is a large, decorative album, with 225 photographs, all with captions. Unlike the National Library of Australia album it is a 'reproduction' album. An individual leaf was produced by mounting prints on a board, decorating around them, adding captions and then photographing the finished product, much the same as a composite postcard was created. This was presumably a cheaper and quicker way of producing albums.

The privately owned album, held by the Gillespie family, is the smallest and the least complete, containing 135 photographic prints. It was owned by Mary Mack who had three brothers, John, Ernest and Stanley, in the 8th Light Horse. Letters written by the Mack brothers during their war service, along with the album, were discovered tucked away in a chest of drawers after their sister Mary died at an advanced age. They had been there for decades, without the knowledge of the family. Two of the Mack boys returned home. Ernest, after surviving the Nek charge, was shot dead in Palestine in 1916.[50]

In June 1916 John Mack, still on active service in the Middle East, wrote to his sister Mary at home in the Western District on the property 'Berry Bank', replying to a letter from her, and mentioning that he would 'like to see that photo book of Campbell's, it must be interesting especially if it contains the snaps he took on 24th May last year.'[51] He was referring to the armistice on Gallipoli to

---

47 Marjorie Ritchie joined a Volunteer Aid Detachment in Melbourne and sailed for England in 1915 via the Suez Canal. The ship stopped off in Egypt where there was a need for nurses because of the Gallipoli campaign. Allan Rice, Volunteer Gallery Guide, 'James Pinkerton Campbell: Album of First World War Photographs (nla.pic-an 23297150)', National Library of Australia, background paper, 7 November 2003, pp. 2-3, and a telephone conversation with Jean Lester, 16 October 2003.

48 Call Number PIC PIC/6109/1-184 LOC Album 1009, National Library of Australia

49 Telephone conversation with Geoffrey Ritchie, 9 September 2009. Also: *Mansfield Courier*, 20 April 2005, and Cameron Simpson, *Maygar's Boys*, p. 42.

50 Hamilton, *Goodbye Cobber, God Bless You*, pp. 331-2, 362, and an interview with Greg Gillespie, Mary's son, 11 February 2005.

51 Letter, John Mack to his sister Mary, 12 June 1916.

bury the dead, which he had witnessed, and which Campbell photographed. This demonstrates how quickly Campbell acted in sending photographic prints home to Aubrey after he had returned to Egypt from Gallipoli. Aubrey had assembled an album and somehow it was in the hands of Mary Mack in approximately April 1916. That it was compiled in a hurry is evident in its small number of photographs relative to the other albums, the lack of captions on some photographs, and the absence of a number of the images Campbell had taken when leaving Gallipoli.[52] The inscription in this album, written by Aubrey, is revealing:

On Active Service with a Camera

A remarkable set of photographs taken with a hand camera by Private J.P. Campbell of Malvern, Victoria, under all kinds of circumstances whilst on service as a signaller with A Troop, B Squadron, 8th L. Horse Reg. 3rd L.H. Brigade. This Album will serve as a History of The Glorious 8th L. Horse whose memory will ever bring feelings of pride to the hearts of all British Australians.

Compiled by Aubrey J. Campbell

These would have been JP Campbell's sentiments as conveyed to his son. Not only was the album a photographic record, but a memorial to the 8th Light Horse, all but wiped out on Gallipoli. The events at the Nek weighed heavily on Campbell. What started out as a record of the regiment on active service, an almost adventure jaunt, had quickly become a memorial to its fallen. This had happened before the war showed any signs of ending. The album was a salute to imperial sacrifice, as displayed in the mention of 'British Australians'.

The fourth album is also a reproduction album. Aubrey Campbell had given an 8th Light Horse album to Justice Henry Higgins prior to the end of the war in memory of his son, Mervyn Higgins, who had survived the charge at the Nek only to be killed later in the Middle East.[53]

Justice Higgins presented this album to the newly created Australian War

---

52 For example, on the last leaf of the album there are six photographs, but only two have very brief captions. There were loose Campbell photographs amongst the many letters written by the three boys, along with the album.

53 Campbell's granddaughter, Noel Fethers, said her grandfather and his daughter Ada (Noel's mother) lunched with Justice Higgins after the war, one of a number of families of 8th Light Horse soldiers Campbell visited on returning from Egypt. Conversation with Noel Fethers, 7 February 2006.

Museum (later Memorial) in December 1918.[54] The Australian War Memorial does not appear to have it in its collection today. However, in September 1921 Higgins presented a duplicate of it to the 8th Light Horse Association.[55] This found its way into the 8th/13th Victorian Mounted Rifles Regimental Collection at North Bandiana, where it is today. It differs from the Mansfield RSL reproduction album only in that it is a tribute to Mervyn Higgins, with his letters home typed and pasted in opposite the images of the Gallipoli campaign, and the addition of a number of larger images at the end.[56]

The more elaborate Mansfield and North Bandiana reproduction albums have a very basic inscription. Both are titled 'The Eighth Light Horse Book', and are described as 'A collection of Photographs taken by Signaller J.P. Campbell whilst on Active Service with the Regiment in Egypt and Turkey'. There is no mention of the albums being compiled by Aubrey, but the inscription and captions are in the same handwriting as the other two albums. The photographs in the albums are essentially the same until towards the end of each, where they differ because of the addition of images, depending on the time of compilation. The JP Campbell 8th Light Horse/Gallipoli photographs held by the Australian War Memorial, and obtained from Campbell after the war, are much the same as those held in the four albums, but are not arranged in album form.[57]

Helen Ennis comments on the tonal flatness of Campbell's Gallipoli photographs in the National Library album, attributing the indistinct detail to his small, roll-film 'snapshot camera' and the poor quality prints it produced. This, she believes, 'explains the power of the image'; they are authentic because of the 'technical modesty and informality' and can be accepted as 'un-manipulated, un-posed and therefore as emphatically real'.[58] It seems Ennis was unaware of

---

54 *Argus*, 16 December 1918. The reporter noted the comments by the Minister of Defence, Senator Pearce, on receiving the album: 'the record was particularly valuable – probably one of the most valuable of the whole war. Years would add to its interest and value'. Also: notes by Director, Australian War Museum, John Treloar, 17 January 1923 and 2 August 1923, to Assistant Director, in Commonwealth of Australia, Home and Territories Department file, 'Mr Campbell re – photo's of Gallipoli', 93 17/3/294, Australian War Memorial.

55 *Argus*, 21 September 1921.

56 Lt Col Doug Hunter of the 8th/13th Victorian Mounted Rifles Museum kindly showed me the album when I met him in Wodonga on 25 August 2011. The album was donated to the VMR museum in 1992 by Mrs Bailey, sister of Trooper Matthew Maynes who was in the 8th Light Horse (see Cameron Simpson, *Maygar's Boys*, p. 117.)

57 Campbell's dealings with what was then the War Museum are discussed in chapter eight.

58 Ennis, *Intersections*, p. 139.

Campbell's award-winning background in pictorialism photography. He sought out the misty, the unclear, the informal and the authentic: it was his stock-in-trade. If his pictures lacked clarity it was not entirely due to his camera's shortcomings, it was intentional.

The sense of authenticity was also influenced by the way Aubrey Campbell assembled the albums from photographs forwarded to him by his father. The National Library and Gillespie albums were assembled quickly: certainly the Gillespie album was in the hands of its owner in late 1915 or early 1916. In these albums the photographic prints were stuck in on various angles in their original state, with no lines involved. JP Campbell was front and centre on the first leaf (Fig. 86). The Mansfield reproduction album is the later 'deluxe' model. The images were linked by two parallel lines across the page, relating them to one another (Fig. 87).

All the Mansfield album photographs are captioned, usually with more detail

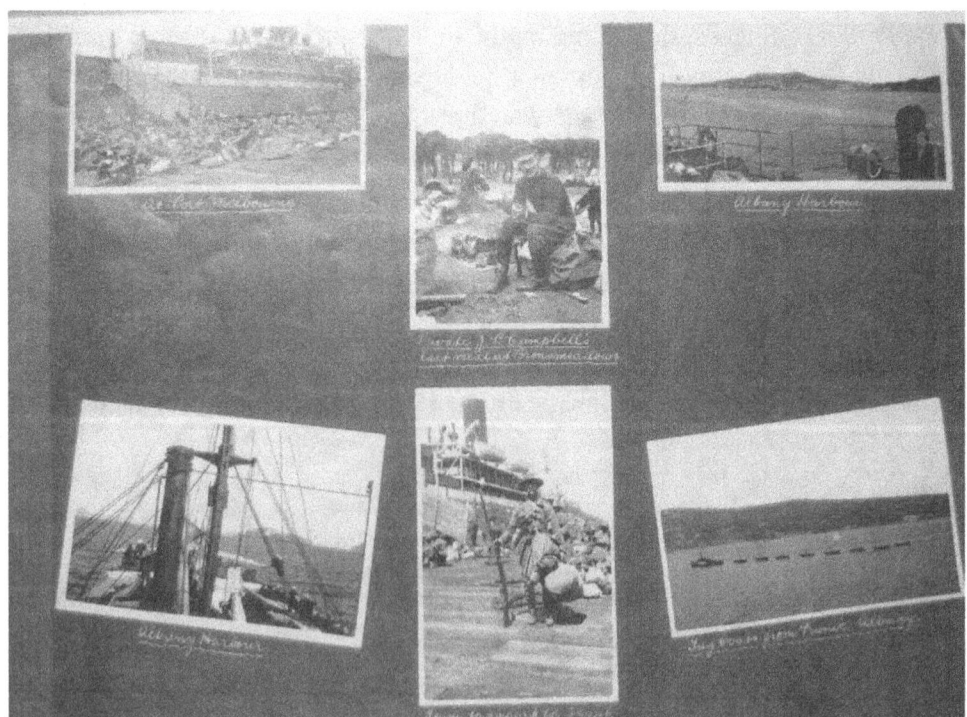

Fig. 86. The first leaf of the Gillespie album, showing Campbell posing at Broadmeadows (see title page of this book), about to board the 'Star of Victoria' with others of the 8th Light Horse, and the ship *en route* to Egypt via Albany, Western Australia.
(Courtesy of Greg Gillespie)

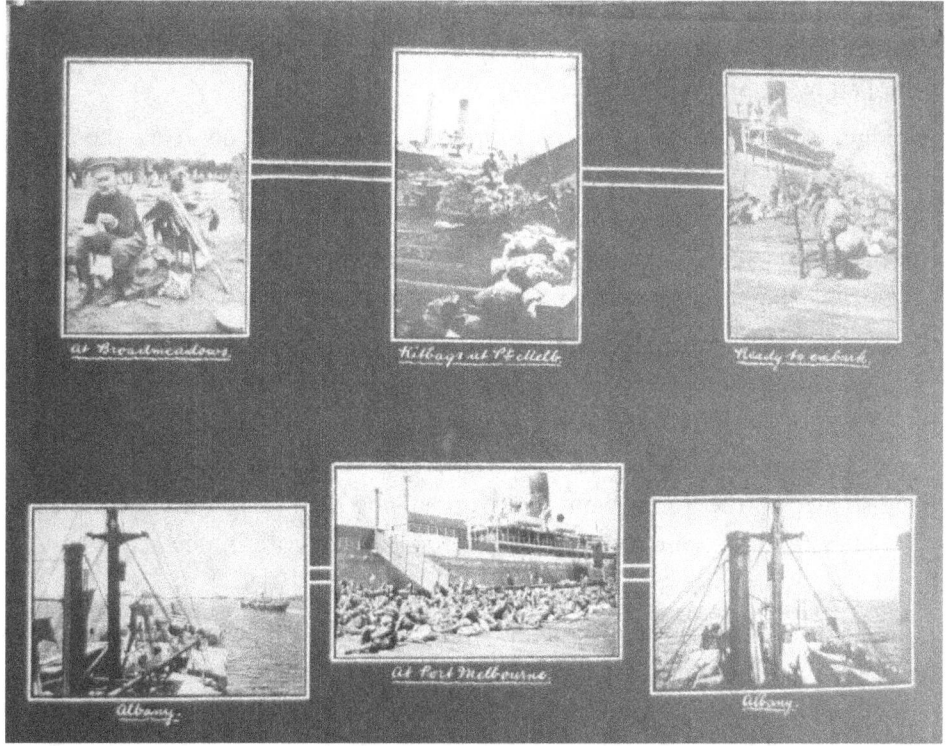

Fig. 87. The first leaf of the Mansfield reproduction album, with four of the same or similar images as those on the first leaf of the Gillespie album, but with decorative presentation. (Courtesy of Mansfield RSL)

than the other albums. Aubrey may have had more time to reflect on his father's accompanying notes and to take more care in their application to the individual photographs. This filtering process through his son distorts, but perhaps even enhances, JP Campbell's work. Different meanings are conveyed of Gallipoli and the 8th Light Horse's place in history, depending on which album you view and the captions you read.

Helen Ennis attributes the assembling of the National Library album to JP Campbell, believing he probably did so in the Heliopolis hospital after he was wounded. Indeed 'the care he lavished on his album demonstrates [that] photography was enormously important to him', as of course it was.[59] Further, she wrote: 'Taking the photographs and later arranging them into coherent narratives seems to have provided these soldiers with a means of structuring their

59 Helen Ennis, *Intersections*, p. 140.

experiences and, one suspects, of making sense of them'.[60] As we have seen, the National Library album and the Gillespie and Mansfield albums were physically compiled by Aubrey Campbell.

Ennis was not to know who Aubrey Campbell was, nor was she able to recognise the handwriting of father and son. JP Campbell did put together his photographs into a coherent narrative, but it was through his son, whom he was close to, and whom he wanted to involve. Aubrey did not go to war, so he may have been experiencing something he missed out on through his father.[61]

Another important aspect of the albums, particularly of the Gallipoli photographs, is their historical content, as Helen Ennis observed in the National Library of Australia album. Many of the images show the hauling of guns and water tanks up steep slopes, as well as the everyday domestic tasks of survival. They show how the troops went about organising themselves, their supplies and equipment, and the animals they used.[62] Such images are important to us today in helping understand what transpired on Gallipoli in 1915.

The captions appended to Campbell's Gallipoli images often differ in the three albums. Photography critic Mary Price believes that the description of a photograph influences how a person views it, directing the viewer's observation. The use of the photograph also determines its meaning.[63] In the case of Campbell's 8th Light Horse albums different captions on the same photograph add descriptive information and enrich the narrative. One of the reasons Campbell took photographs whilst on active service was to provide mementos for regiment members and their families. Their use has changed: they have gone from personal memorabilia to objects of analysis by historians, and are in demand by a Gallipoli-hungry public.

One Campbell landscape photograph of the rugged Gallipoli ranges peeling away into the distance is captioned in two of the albums, 'This picture speaks for itself' and 'A picture that needs no title' (Fig. 88). The meaning is left up to the viewer's imagination. The landscape looks rough but benign; there is no sign

---

60 Ibid.

61 Aubrey worked in the printing industry, in a firm run by JP Campbell's old friend, ER Peacock, who may have asked that Aubrey be exempted from armed service because his skills were needed at home. Interview with Noel Fethers, 20 April 2005.

62 Helen Ennis, *Intersections*, p. 139.

63 Mary Price, *The Photograph: A Strange Confined Space*, Stanford University Press, Stanford, California, 1994, p. 1.

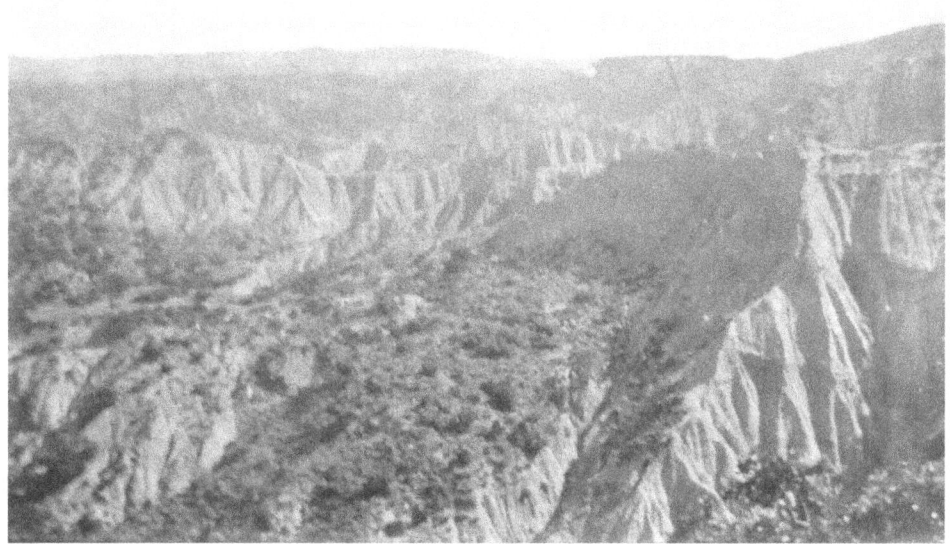

Fig. 88. 'Country beyond our left flank – occupied by snipers. Ana Farta Hills in distance'.
(Courtesy of Mansfield RSL)

of soldiers from either side. The Mansfield album's caption to the same photo reads: 'Country beyond our left flank – occupied by snipers. Ana Farta Hills in distance', immediately investing it with a more sinister aspect.[64] This caption generates more questions about it. Susan Sontag's observation that the 'camera's rendering of reality must always hide more than it discloses' comes to mind here.[65]

Another of these geographical illusions is a view of the Sphinx at Gallipoli, on the face of it a spectacular landscape photograph: no caption in the National Library album, and a bland descriptive caption in the Mansfield album; 'Overlooking Mule Gully. Sphynx on left. The Base (Anzac Cove) is other side the big hill to the right' (Fig. 89).

64 This northern part of the peninsula, the Anafarta Hills, with their rugged, twisting gullies and tortuous ridges, cliffs and tangled vegetation was to be one of the major reasons why the Allies' August 1915 offensive failed.

65 Susan Sontag, *On Photography*, p. 23.

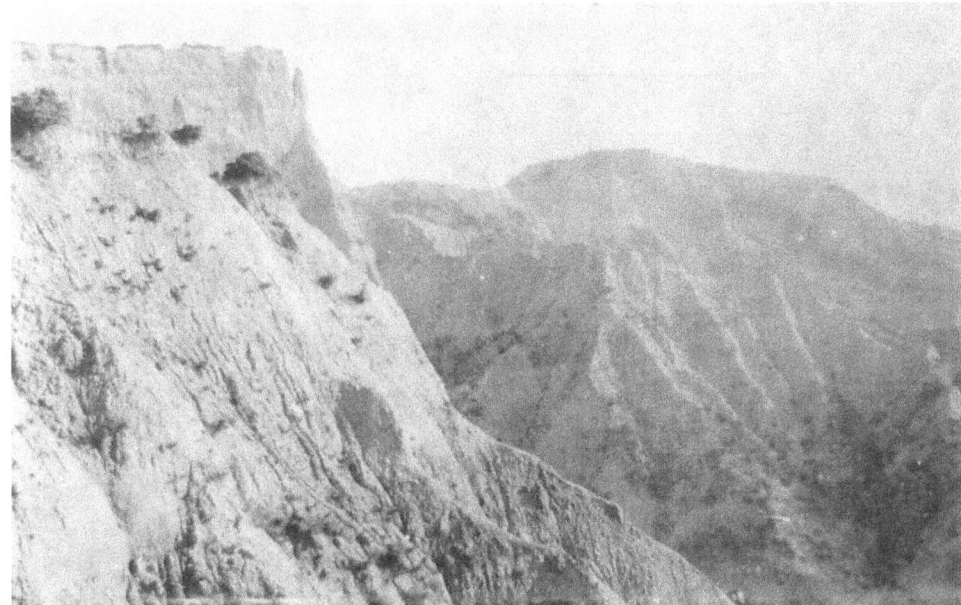

Fig. 89. 'Overlooking Mule Gully. Sphynx on left. The Base (Anzac Cove) is other side [of] the big hill to the right'. (Courtesy of Mansfield RSL)

The Gillespie album caption is arresting:

> X [a white ink cross on the photograph marks the cleft at the point of the Sphinx] A Turkish Sniper was hidden in this crevice for a long time and shot many of our engineers. At last he was discovered & a machine gun brought him down. He was found to have three months provisions & ammunition.

Why did Aubrey Campbell choose not to use this dramatic caption in the other albums? Did he doubt its authenticity, or did he simply like to vary the use of his father's notes at his own whim? The sniper in the Sphinx cleft is recorded elsewhere as rumour, so Aubrey may have picked up this story from his father and used it as fact.[66]

The images and captions display Campbell's interest in the mundane and the momentous. Campbell used photography on Gallipoli to contrast the everyday tasks of existence with scenes of the catastrophic, 'showing the awful aftermath of battle', as Helen Ennis perceptively observed.[67] There are snaps of men around

---

66 Jonathan King and Michael Bowers, *Gallipoli*, p. 225.
67 Helen Ennis, *Intersections*, p. 139.

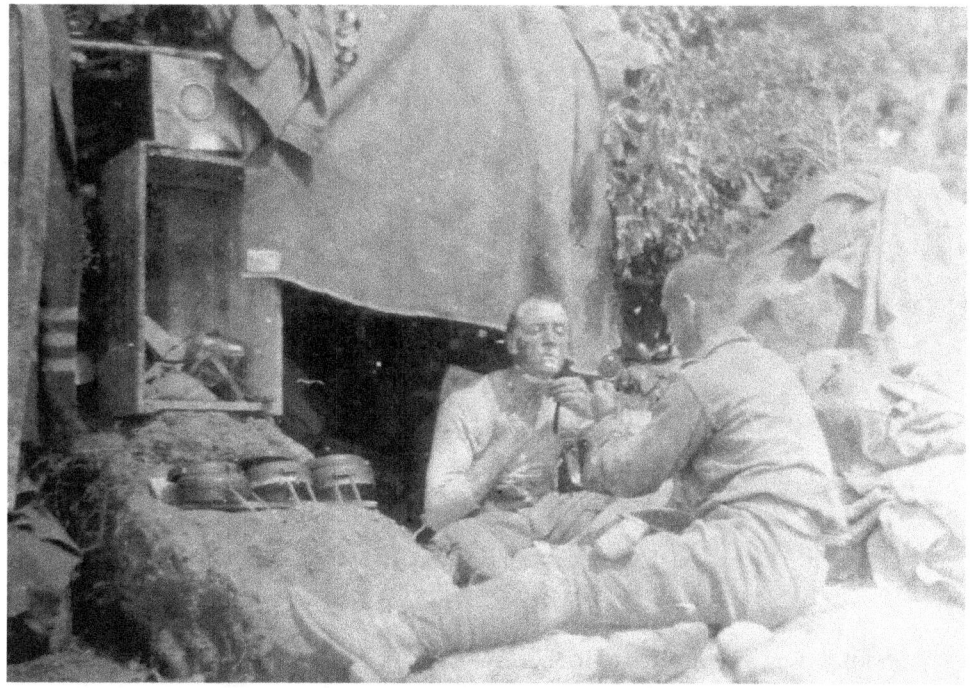

Fig. 90. 'At our first camp. Q.M.S. Maloney has a shave'.
(Courtesy of Mansfield RSL)

the water tank, Indians carrying stores on their heads along the beach, soldiers eating and Anzacs pulling a water tank up Walker's Ridge. They give the viewer an idea of the daily activities of people in a war zone. Campbell's snap of 'Squadron Quarter Master Sergeant Maloney [Molony]' shaving, while another soldier holds the mirror, is the picture of domesticity; Anzacs performing everyday tasks under extraordinary circumstances (Fig. 90). In the National Library album he is 'Q.M. Maloney shaving', in the Gillespie album 'Q.M.S. Maloney shaving. (Killed [unclear])', and in the Mansfield album 'At our first camp. Q.M.S. Maloney has a shave'. In the Mansfield album it becomes apparent that he was indeed killed when we read a caption three photographs later on a picture of a stationary ship, prominent in the foreground among three others, which records 'Hospital Ship "Gascon". Burial spot of Q.M.S. Maloney' (Fig. 91). This image has no caption in the National Library album, so we are not informed about what happened to him, or how to make the link between photographs. The general viewer of the National Library image sees four troop transports, a mundane picture, nothing more. The Gillespie album does not contain this photograph, but we know it was Molony who was killed from the information contained in the shaving picture caption.

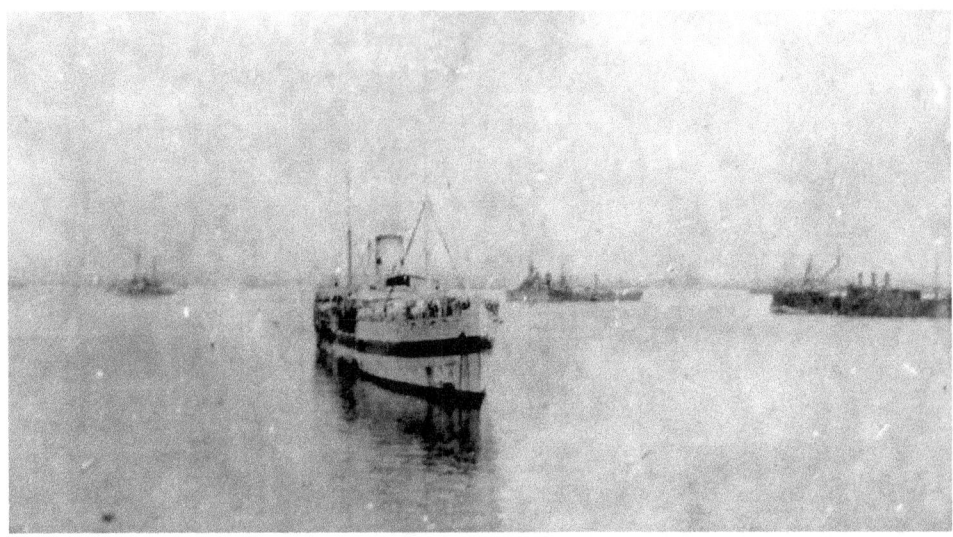

Fig. 91. 'Hospital Ship "Gascon". Burial spot of Q.M.S. Maloney'.
(Courtesy of Mansfield RSL)

Leopold 'Leo' Molony, a Boer War veteran, was wounded by shrapnel in the communication trench on Walker's Ridge on 26 June, evacuated to the hospital ship but died later in the day. He was buried at sea where the ship was anchored.[68] Campbell may have been in the communication trench when Molony was hit; they could well have been close friends. He lived in the trenches with men like Molony, his photographic subjects, through ordinary and extraordinary moments on Gallipoli, and so was intimately connected to them. Campbell was moved to record Molony's watery grave, one among the many grave sites surrounding him. Molony's story is just one of the smaller narratives within the larger album narrative.[69]

Altogether, twenty-two of JP Campbell's photographs were published in the Melbourne *Leader*, between September and Christmas 1915. For an image-starved public they would have had great impact, particularly for the many

---

68 Jeff Pickerd, 'More Majorum', pp. 79-82, and Cameron Simpson, *Maygar's Boys*, p. 47.

69 There are, however, contradictions between captions on other photographs. In a photograph of two soldiers on the firing line – one using a periscope, the other binoculars – the men are called Major Redford & Leiut. (sic) Mitchell in one album, Major Redford and Capt. Mitchell in another, and Major Redford and Lt Baker in the third. Again, as discussed above, is this a case of poor memory on the part of JP Campbell or a mistake or memory lapse by his son? We are told in two of the albums that two soldiers standing to attention in front of a dugout in full combat regalia are on guard duty, in the third they are 'Sgts Crawford and Synnot in front of dugout ready for off to the firing line for the first time', a different scenario.

families of those serving on Gallipoli. The war disrupted the rural idyll of Australian life as depicted in the *Leader*, which had traditionally concentrated on country photographs and stories. In early 1915 photographs of slaughtered prisoners and peasants in Europe under the overall caption 'Incidents Of The War' were sandwiched between pictures of a wild bee hive and boy scouts camping peacefully on Diamond Creek at Eltham.[70] Scenes of country shows were interspersed with pictures of troopships departing from Port Melbourne, views of the Broadmeadows military camp, the horrors of war in Belgium, and the Australian Expeditionary Forces in Egypt.

The first photographs under the main caption 'The Dardanelles Campaign' did not appear until late May 1915.[71] From 8 May 1915 onward at least one page was taken up in each issue by mini portraits of the dead and wounded, eighty to the page, lined up beside a rural scene on the opposite page.[72] Despite the disruption caused by the war, life continued on as normal as possible in country Australia. In early July 1915 images appeared of the wounded in Egypt, and on 24 July a drawing of the Allies landing on Gallipoli was published, along with vague photographs of the peninsula. The first clear landscape pictures appeared in early September, four photographs with the overall caption 'Scenes of Gallipoli', one showing a gun being hauled into position.[73] When Campbell's nine images appeared on 25 September 1915 they were the first comprehensive photographs of Gallipoli to appear in the *Leader*, showing the rugged landscape and soldiers at work and play.[74]

---

70 *Leader*, 2 January 1915

71 *Leader*, 29 May 1915. They related vaguely to Gallipoli and could have been taken anywhere. A map of 'Gaba Tepe [the Anzac Cove area] On The Gallipoli Peninsula, Dardanelles, Where The Australians Distinguished Themselves Greatly' appeared in the same issue, then on 19 June 1915 the first photographs of soldiers on Gallipoli appeared, fourteen pictures 'taken on the spot', including images of wounded men and soldiers 'going up to the firing line'.

72 *Leader*, 10 July 1915.

73 *Leader*, 4 September 1915. The *Leader* used the overall heading 'Forcing the Dardanelles' for all its news articles on Gallipoli and often as a main caption for a group of Gallipoli photographs.

74 The *Australasian* was quicker in showing the Gallipoli landscape to its readers. In its edition of 17 July 1915 the weekly off shoot of the *Argus* published ten photographs of 'The Australians and New Zealanders at Gaba Tepe' showing the terrain and Anzac Cove. The paper continued to publish Gallipoli photographs until the end of the campaign under the main caption 'Scenes and Incidents at Gallipoli'. The *Australasian* also had an equivalent soldier-photographer to JP Campbell, Private WA Gornall, who, like Campbell, was a photographer in civilian life. He had at least eighteen of his photographs published in November and December 1915. More research is necessary to compare both papers presentation of World War One photographs to that of other weekly newspapers in Australia.

The newspapers sometimes wrongly transcribed captions, whether accidentally or intentionally, altering the meaning of the image concerned. Among the nine JP Campbell pictures in the September 1915 issue of the *Leader*, one showed soldiers in full gear assembled in camp against a mountainous backdrop. The *Leader's* caption read 'Red Cross Helpers on the March'.[75] The National Library album has no caption for this image, the Gillespie album states simply 'Ready for the advance' and in the Mansfield album they are 'New Zealanders ready to go on the day's duty sapping. Firing line on top of hill'.[76]

The same thing occurred with the 1915 Christmas Number of the *Leader*. The caption to a Campbell Gallipoli image, 'Road Construction', was incorrect, as Campbell pointed out to his friend, John Bramley at home in Australia:

> This year's [*Leader*] annual is to hand and I've a good number of scenes in it as well but they are not of such a peaceable nature [photographs Campbell took of the Upper Murray district appeared in the Christmas Number of the *Leader* in 1914]. Anzac Bay and the Road making scenes are mine also though my illustrious JPC is not appended. The Road making is an imagination of the printer as the chaps are hauling a 6 inch gun on a sledge [up Walker's Ridge].[77]

The accompanying text to this image in the *Leader* reviewed the Gallipoli campaign and described the charge at the Nek. The actual term 'the Nek' is not mentioned, although this is not unusual in early accounts of the charge:

> Of all the many incidents in that fighting [during the August offensive] there is nothing which stands out so conspicuously as the supreme devotion and self sacrifice of the Third Light Horse Brigade in their

---

75 *Leader*, 25 September 1915.

76 Ibid. Another of this group of nine photographs is of refugees proceeding up a mountainous road and captioned 'First Refugees' in two of the albums, but named as 'Armenian Refugees' in the *Leader*. The same image in the Mansfield album is more specific with its caption: 'Greek refugees coming in with our men from the outpost on the ridge across the valley – the ridge with no trees on'. There is also the possibility that captions were changed because of censorship rules.

77 Letter, JP Campbell to John Bramley, 20 December 1915, reproduced in Susie Zada, *Memories of the Bramley & Goghill Families*, p. 244. This image appears in all four 8th Light Horse albums and again the captions differ, each adding a telling piece of information: 'Heavy work', 'The hill where the first big fight took place' and 'Hauling a 6" gun up Walker's Ridge. It was placed in position at foot of steps. The position is shown in the bursting shell snap further over'. Combining them you get a full, informative account of what is going on in the image, where and why, conveying the meaning of the scene as taken by the photographer at the time.

attack on what were called the chess board trenches on the afternoon of 7 August.[78]

The *Leader* continued: 'It was the second charge of the Light Brigade and it was carried out as unquestionably and as unflinchingly'.[79] As Peter Burness points out: 'Comparisons with the charge of the Light Brigade, a cavalry action during the Crimean War, an inspiring story of Victorian valour, known to all the First World War generation since childhood, were inevitable'.[80] By evoking such a legendary battle, in comparison with the actions on Gallipoli, and combining it with Campbell's Gallipoli photographs, the *Leader* presented a powerful mix of imagery and prose designed to create feelings of national pride and a sense of worthy sacrifice. By reaching a wider audience with his photographs, Campbell was contributing to the legend that was to become Anzac. Campbell's photographs of diggers nonchalantly swimming whilst under fire, manually hauling water tanks and artillery up steep slopes and performing everyday tasks like shaving under extraordinary conditions all contributed at the time to the emerging concept of the Anzac legend. Compelling as they were then, they have taken on an almost mythical form as time has progressed. With the 'renaissance' of Gallipoli in recent years, these images with their accessibility enhanced by ever-developing technology, sparked a new curiosity and have found a new mass audience, an audience that can no longer speak to the Gallipoli veterans themselves.

Soldier-photographers such as Campbell on Gallipoli were constrained by their roles as working soldiers, but nevertheless made their own contribution over and above their tenacious fighting reputations. Campbell was no amateur with a camera, which gave him a good start over the many soldiers around him. He even had something to say on the emerging digger image, commenting to Lilian Pitts on how Australian soldiers hid their feelings: 'a lot of the sentiment they may think but not talk about – except in a breezy style'.[81]

---

78 *Leader*, Christmas Number, 25 December 1915. The text accompanying Campbell's photograph contained errors. The Turkish trenches charged by the Australians are wrongly referred to as the Chessboard, a maze of trenches on a ridge slightly further to the south, rather than those situated at the base of the hill Baby 700 and facing the Australians. And the Nek charge occurred on the morning of 7 August, not the afternoon.

79 Ibid., p. 30.

80 Peter Burness, *The Nek*, p. 14.

81 Postcard, JP Campbell to LL Pitts, 22 December 1917. Campbell was commenting on a book they had both read, and was of the opinion that the author had not been amongst soldiers and thus did not understand them. This extravert image, of course, is part of the digger legend, the brash and loud, anti top-brass Australian soldier swaggering around Cairo coping with the more serious aspects of life by laughing them off.

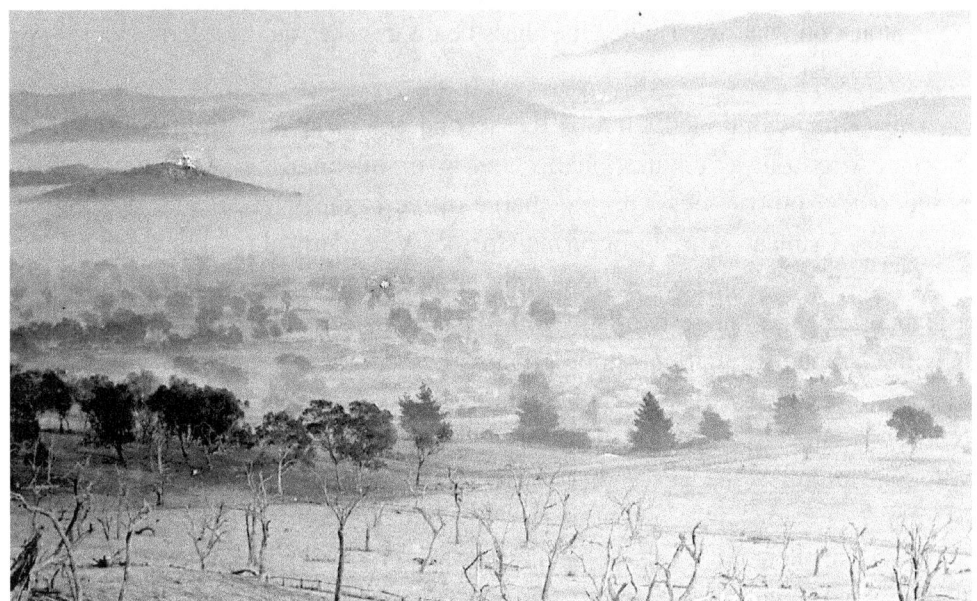

Fig. 92. 'Corryong under a misty blanket'. A typical JP Campbell 'fog card', possibly the image carried by the soldier in Cairo. (Author's collection)

As he recovered from his wound Campbell moved around Heliopolis and Cairo, readjusting to a more relaxed life. He left the 8th Light Horse and on 9 September started work at the Staff Pay Office with the AIF Army Pay Corps, although he was still at the hospital. He told Lilian Pitts that he 'had a very pleasant days initiation – hours 9 to 1 & 4 to 7 – Have been on a march behind ledger all day – funny sitting quietly at figures after the previous violent surroundings'.[82] The events during his time on Gallipoli were still playing on his mind, particularly when he had to deal with the affairs of the dead, many of whom were his comrades. He told John Bramley he was:

> busy typing lists of soldiers killed or died or returned to Australia, their dates of service, rank, rates of pay, amounts received and amounts due with balance, which lists go to Melbourne to enable the Office there to square accounts finally. It was a melancholy job doing the 8th Light Horse.[83]

Towards the end of 1915 Campbell met an Australian soldier in Cairo who

82 Postcard, JP Campbell to Lilian Pitts, 8 September 1915.
83 Letter, JP Campbell to John Bramley, Melbourne Cup Day, 1915, in Susie Zada, *Memories of the Bramley & Goghill Families*, pp. 243-4.

came from the Upper Murray district of Victoria. As they talked, the soldier pulled out a Vallan Studio postcard, a photograph of a fog-shrouded valley taken by Campbell from the top of Hanna's Hill near Corryong (Fig. 92). Campbell was overcome with nostalgia: 'The memory of that morning floated through me as I looked at it'.[84] Those days were gone forever: he still had three years of war to experience and many photographs to take. After a period of marking time in the Pay Corps he was to be anointed in 1918 by the illustrious Frank Hurley as his successor to the position of official photographer for the AIF in Egypt.

---

84 Letter, JP Campbell to John Bramley, 20 December 1915, in Susie Zada, *Memories of the Bramley & Goghill Families*, p. 244. Campbell referred to this style of postcard as a 'fog card'.

8

OFFICIAL WAR PHOTOGRAPHER

Settling Down to Military Life in Egypt – CEW Bean, The Australian War
Records Section and Frank Hurley – Hurley and Campbell – Official
Photographer to the AIF – Es Salt – Heat, Dust, Flies and Mosquitoes in the
Jordan Valley – The Camel Corps – The Kia Ora Coo-ee

In 1915 Lilian Pitts wrote to JP Campbell in Egypt, telling him she believed he would achieve great things during the war. He wrote back: 'notion as to my crowning exploit has not come to pass yet – but the war isn't over yet is it?'[1] The faith Lilian had in Campbell reflected her affection for him – her vision of his successful deeds as a soldier/photographer was a premonition of things to come.[2]

Back in Cairo, Campbell's social life expanded, despite the war time restrictions. Late in 1915 staff at the Army Pay Corps, including Campbell, met up with nurses from a Cairo hospital, crammed into a convoy of ten cars and motored to Mena to attend a moonlight concert of singers accompanied by organ music at the foot of the Sphynx. As they sped towards Mena, Campbell and fellow Pay Corps worker, Frederick Tuohy, also ex-8th Light Horse and wounded on Gallipoli, reflected on their foot march around the pyramids in April 1915 and the toll it had inflicted on their ranks. Campbell told his sister Frances that 'here we were safe after our many escapades doing the lazy, in the best of company, [driving] over the same track we laboured so perspiringly on, and we felt that Fate was kind to us'.[3]

When they got to the Sphynx Campbell described the occasion to his other sister Margaret as

> a novel one and weird . . . in a huge sandy basin, half in deep shade, the

---

1 Postcard, JP Campbell to LL Pitts, 2 October 1915.

2 See the beginning of the Bibliography for an explanation of the images used in this chapter and chapter nine, including the numbering system and how the captions are organised.

3 Cameron Simpson, *Maygar's Boys: A Biographical History of the 8th Light Horse Regiment, AIF, 1914-1919*, p. 53, and letter, JP Campbell to his sister Frances Trimble, undated, *Gippsland Times*, 22 May 1916.

towering above us [of a] lump of carved world in weak light and heavy gloom, some figures in the moonlight up under the chin, a straggling audience in front of the basin edge, Arabs with their camels and donkeys, [and] fortune tellers.[4]

After the concert they roared back into Cairo, only to find it virtually closed down under the curfew applied to the capital at the time.[5] It was hardly a wild evening, genteel compared to the early months of 1915 when bored Australian soldiers rioted in the market places and brothels of Cairo.[6]

Campbell was never bored. He took 'before breakfast strolls' with his camera, capturing scenes like goats and cows being milked by footpaths, but complained to one of his sisters 'that the sun is getting up too late for snapshots in the shade, and I can't afford a faster lens for the job'.[7] If he was not roving about taking photographs he was producing a prodigious number of letters to send home to relatives and friends. These were often handed on to the *Heyfield Herald* or *Gippsland Times*, who published extracts. With a photographer's eye Campbell observed the locals:

> The poor here are dreadfully so. Workmen get busy as soon as they can see, and it is a usual sight in the middle of the day to see them asleep on the footpath, and maybe the street cart horse is standing half way across the path asleep also, with his empty nosebag dangling over the driver. One does not dream of 'shooing' them out of the way, for it is just as easy to walk round, and nothing like that seems a nuisance.[8]

He saw 'the well bred Egyptian [as] a magnificent creature, dressed in the very best English tailor-made, adorned with a red fez'. The elite patronised a restaurant called Groppi's, and Campbell marvelled at the cheerful atmosphere as diners sat at tables set outside on the footpath, in contrast to the indoor eating habits in Australia. Always a dapper dresser himself, the clothing displays in the higher-class shops overawed him, and he told his sister that they were 'in no way of a retiring nature'.[9]

---

4 Letter, JP Campbell to his sister, Margaret Chester, undated, *Heyfield Herald*, 20 January 1916.
5 Ibid.
6 Bill Gammage, *The Broken Years: Australian Soldiers in the Great War*, Penguin Books, Ringwood, 1975, pp. 37-41.
7 Letter, JP Campbell to Frances Trimble, undated, *Gippsland Times*, 22 May 1916.
8 Letter, JP Campbell to Margaret Chester, undated, *Heyfield Herald*, 20 January 1916.
9 Ibid.

He was writing as much as he was taking photographs. During January-February 1916 the *Heyfield Herald* published two long articles by Campbell, titled 'Something about the Nile', and attributed to 'J.P. Campbell, on Active Service', rather than the usual 'extract of letter to sister' explanation. He combined his own observations with a history of the river and its use by humans.[10]

By February 1916, Campbell was looking forward to promotion to sergeant in the Pay Corps. He was receiving visitors, usually acquaintances in the forces, or those caught up in the war for other purposes, like Ernest Peacock, an old friend and businessman from Melbourne, in Cairo as a representative of the Young Men's Christian Association.[11] Campbell was sending photographs to Lilian Pitts, knowing she would appreciate them, imploring her not to tell 'anyone of [their] circle' of friends as they might be jealous.[12]

In early 1916 he managed to find 'a decent photo man' in Cairo, a Frenchman, to develop his film at a cheap rate, and consequently was considering placing more photographs in the press.[13] He was touring voraciously in his spare time, 'doing' sites like any manic tourist, driven by the desire to capture images. More than once he went south from Cairo by train, squatting in the crowded corridors, travelling far up the Nile Valley to capture views of the weirs at Assuit and Esna, the antiquities at Luxor, and to visit a friend at Aswan.[14] After the war he explained his rather indulgent behaviour to an audience back home:

> That it may seem strange that an office soldier could get away on such excursions, it may be well to intimate that they were mostly Christmas and week-end ones, and the night train services allow[ed] one full use of any daylight leave granted. Of course, there were many [soldiers] discontented with life in Egypt, but they were the ones that could see no charm in the stones of the desert, etc., ruins of ancient temples of the Pharaohs, and the agricultural scenes similar to those days of 4000 years ago.[15]

---

10 *Heyfield Herald*, 27 January 1916 & 3 February 1916. The contents and style appear to have been directed to a wider audience, but this is hard to ascertain with certainty.

11 Postcard, JP Campbell to Lilian Pitts, 3 February 1916. Peacock had written a glowing reference for Campbell when he applied for the External Affairs job in 1911.

12 Postcard, JP Campbell to Lilian Pitts, 7 April 1916.

13 Postcard, JP Campbell to LL Pitts, 12 April 1916.

14 Ibid., 19 April 1916.

15 *Gippsland Mercury*, 18 March 1919. Campbell addressed a 'Welcome to Returned Soldiers' function in Seaspray, Gippsland.

Campbell particularly enjoyed photographing buildings, including churches, using half glass plates.[16]

Campbell kept in contact with his old regiment, the 8th Light Horse, bonded by the terrible experiences on Gallipoli, even though it was now made up primarily of new faces, reserves rushed over from Australia. In August 1916 he had a weekend with them on the Sinai Peninsula. At other times he roamed the streets of Cairo photographing anything of interest, such as prisoners arriving at the local barracks, or the funeral of the sultan's mother. He had to wait a while for elevation above the rank of corporal, achieving promotion to sergeant on 1 September 1916.[17]

In November 1916, on one of his trips to Port Said to socialise with his former comrades from the 8th Light Horse, Campbell and a number of friends took a yacht along the Suez Canal to visit an Armenian refugee camp containing 5000 people, survivors of the massacre of hundreds of thousands of Armenian Christians by the Turks beginning in April 1915.[18] Although they were spread throughout the Turkish Empire, the Armenians were concentrated in particular regions, particularly on the north-east border with Russia. The ruling faction of the Ottoman government, known as the Young Turks, had considered the Armenians an internal threat to the Ottoman Empire, particularly as many were allied with the Russians.[19] Armed with his Kodak camera, Campbell was shocked at what he saw at the camp, and showed great empathy for the refugees. He had followed accounts of the atrocities in the newspapers, reading what he supposed were exaggerated stories, accounts of the killing which did not reveal to him the human tragedy unfolding. But, as he wrote in an account published in the *Heyfield Herald*:

> seeing this camp brought the item home to me very forcibly, when I saw children, of whom there are 1600 in all, with identity discs on, showing

16 Postcard, JP Campbell to LL Pitts, 14 July 1916.

17 NAA: B2455, Campbell JP.

18 Letter to the *Heyfield Herald*, November 1916, published 21 December 1916. This letter was titled 'A Week End at Port Said: And a Few Remarks Thereon', and attributed to 'Signaller J.P. Campbell', even though he had been in the Pay Corps for a year, i.e. it was not designated as a an extract from a letter to his sister Margaret, suggesting it may been written specifically for the *Heyfield Herald*.

19 David Stevenson, *1914-1918: The History of the First World War*, Penguin Books, London, 2005, pp.115-6, and Donald Bloxam, *The Great Game of Genocide: Imperialism, Nationalism, and the Destruction of the Ottoman Armenians*, Oxford University Press, New York, 2005, pp. 1-4.

that their parents had been murdered, and ever so many adults had a similar fate happen [to] them in regard to their closest relations.[20]

He used this example of Turkish brutality to try to rally the 'slackers at home' to enlist, boost the war effort and take revenge against the Turks for committing such atrocities, at a time when conscription had just been rejected in an Australian referendum.[21] Social and political commentator Robert Manne has questioned why historians of the Gallipoli campaign, most prominently Charles Bean, had virtually ignored the Armenian genocide while praising the Turks as basically decent enemies. Manne links the Anglo-French Dardanelles campaign with the decision of the Turks to massacre the Armenians.[22] Campbell, who, as we have seen had great respect for the Turks, was under no illusion as to how 'Johnny Turk' had behaved in regard to the Armenians:

> Of course we do not know the Armenians, but they are Christians, and that in itself is sufficient [reason to seek retribution against the Turks]. Though as far as Gallipoli was concerned the Turk's fighting was British in its cleanliness, but that does not forgive his killing helpless civilians . . . and he will have to pay for his misdeeds.[23]

He concluded his letter with a rallying call to all those at home, or at least those in Heyfield and district:

> I think you will understand from this small story that it is very necessary for us to be on the winning side. I think the decision is a very long way off yet, and the more shirkers there are the longer it will be, and the greater will be our proportionate losses.[24]

Meanwhile, photography was growing as a sideline business, and he told Lilian Pitts that he had:

---

20 *Heyfield Herald*, 21 December 1916.

21 Ibid and LL Robson, *The First AIF: A Study of its Recruitment 1914-1918*, Melbourne University Press, Carlton, 1982, p. 116.

22 Robert Manne, 'A Turkish Tale: Gallipoli and the Armenian Genocide' in *The Monthly: Australian Politics, Society & Culture*, February 2007, pp. 20-28. Manne concludes that the Turks are remembered with respect for merely being present 'when the Australian nation was born and when Australians discovered who they were [on the shores of Gallipoli]', p. 28.

23 *Heyfield Herald*, 21 December 1916. From his comments it would seem that the refugees in the camp were members of the Armenian Christian minority.

24 Ibid. Campbell took at least one photograph at the refugee camp, a 'group . . . at the doorway around a loaded cot of youngsters', but I have been unable to find a copy within private or archival collections.

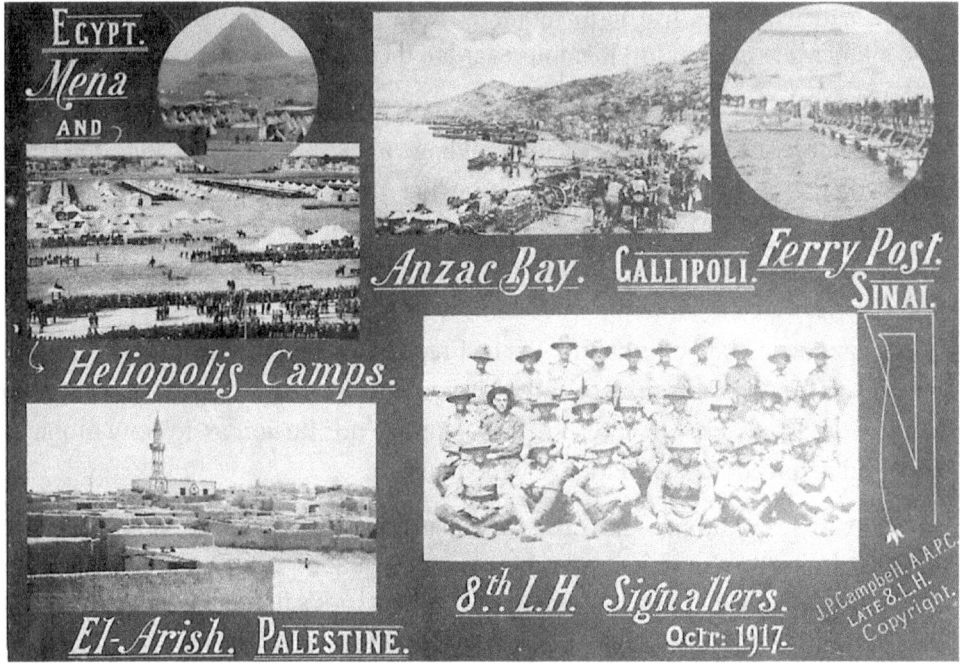

Fig. 93. One of Campbell's private compilations, the middle section of an 8th Light Horse
Signallers greeting card. (Courtesy of Falconer collection)

been very busy in my own time on a lot of printing lately, and am making
3 sets of 100 (about) different card scenes – about half done – can do
100 of an evening and take the curl out next morning without losing any
needed sleep. I expect orders for a few thousand but am dubious as to
supplies of cards.[25]

On another occasion he told her he had 1500 prints on order and expected half
a piastre profit on each, which would help pay for films. He also profited from
the 8th Light Horse, photographing groups of soldiers, clearing one third profit
from the sale of prints. In this way Campbell was able to pursue his photography
under austere war conditions (Fig. 93).

His relationship with Lilian Pitts had photography at its centre. Lilian sent
him photographs and, as he was her original teacher, he gave his opinion: 'Your
fruity card to hand today. Yes, the composition is right but the effect chalky –
try 3 or 4 times as much exposure and diluted developer, you will then get the

25 Postcard, JP Campbell to Lilian Pitts, 12 March 1917.

details in the shadows before the high lights are too dense'.[26] This was written on a card of his own making, showing a group of officers and himself partying on a houseboat. He also commented on his own work, in this case one of the houseboat images: 'This was our party after lunch. The light all around flatters everything'.[27] Campbell was fascinated by light, perspective, antiquity, and the Christianity he had been immersed in from childhood. Gallipoli was now behind him and he seemed to be enjoying the war and life in Egypt. The campaign by the Allies against the Turkish forces, however, was gathering strength, and Campbell's involvement in the war was about to increase in intensity once more.

On 28 June 1917 General Edmund Allenby replaced General Archibald Murray as commander of the British/Allied forces in the Middle East. This occurred after the failure to take the town of Gaza, moving journalist and historian Henry Gullett to describe it as a 'second Gallipoli' in the official war history to which he contributed.[28] After it was eventually captured in early November 1917, via an inspired attack on Beersheba, the Turkish army was driven north, and the allies advanced towards Esdud.[29] Capturing Jerusalem was the 'the great sentimental and moral, if not the religious, goal of every man in the British army', according to Gullett.[30]

Ludd (or Lydda) was captured on 15 November 1917.[31] The campaign now moved into the hills, 'a rough, stony skeleton of a country', particularly the hills of Judea between Jaffa and Jerusalem.[32] The Seventh Turkish Army could not successfully defend Jerusalem against Allenby's forces: the mayor of Jerusalem surrendered the town to the British on 9 December 1917.[33] Close proximity to places significant to Christianity amazed those soldiers with a religious inclination. Bibles and Holy Land guide books were read aloud round every camp-fire by soldiers as they fought over a landscape dotted with holy sites.[34]

---

26 Postcard, JP Campbell to Lilian Pitts, 22 May 1917.

27 Ibid.

28 Henry Somer Gullett, *The Official History of Australia in the War of 1914-1918: The Australian Imperial Force in Sinai and Palestine*, Volume VII, Angus and Robertson, Sydney, Fourth Edition, 1937, pp. 335, 338, 354.

29 Ibid., p. 444.

30 Ibid., p. 450.

31 Ibid., p. 480.

32 Ibid., pp. 486-8.

33 Ibid., p. 516.

34 Ibid., p. 493.

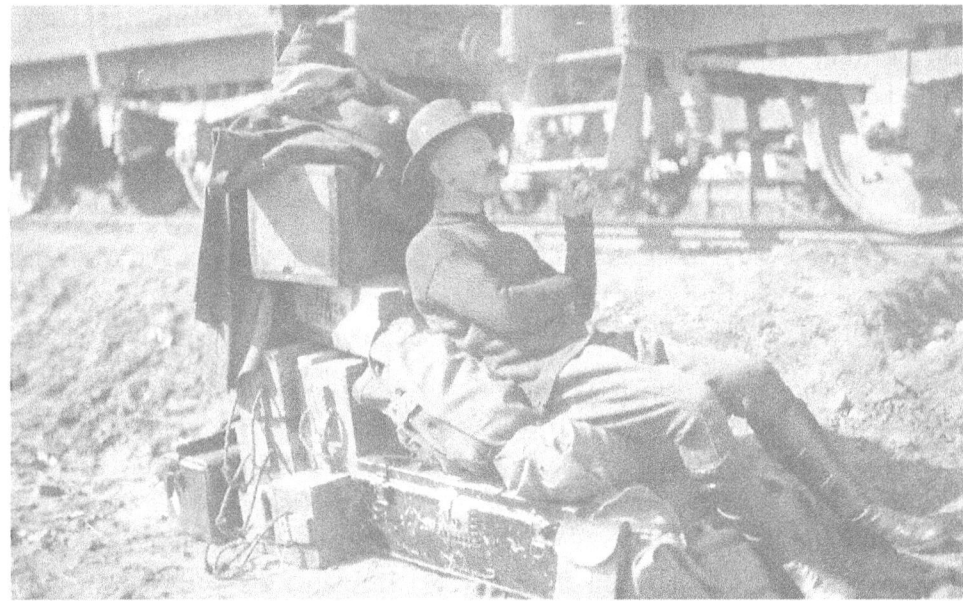

Fig. 94. Campbell in Palestine on Pay Corps business, December 1917, sitting and smoking on 'a most expensive sofa', £25,000 in a tin box, presumably pay for the soldiers.[35]
(Courtesy of Falconer collection)

Many of these men explored Jerusalem, guided by army chaplains, who worked hard to explain its significance in the history of Christianity.[36]

In early December 1917 Campbell travelled into Palestine on pay business, a 'flying visit', having been 'detached to Head Quarters Desert Mounted Corps' (Fig. 94).[37] At last he was in the Holy Land, midway between Gaza and Ascalon at the 'head of the road camp'. The Allies were constructing a railway line, pushing it further towards Turkish held territory. The place hummed with trains, thousands of camels and motor lorries, all transporting supplies. Three days of rain had caused chaos on the loamy flats. Campbell described the blue, treeless hills and the high sand dunes stretching two or more miles to the Mediterranean Sea. Shell fragments and craters dotted the earth. Equipped, as usual, with his camera, he took 'a dozen typical scenes'. He was looking forward to hitching a ride on a motor lorry to Ramleh and Jaffa in order to sightsee.[38]

In mid December 1917 Campbell began working with the newly-formed

---

35 Postcard, JP Campbell to William Campbell, 22 December 1917.
36 HS Gullett, *The Official History of Australia in the War of 1914-1918*, Volume VII, pp. 551-2.
37 NAA: B2455, Campbell JP.
38 Postcard, JP Campbell to Lilian Pitts, 12 December 1917.

Australian War Records Section, an organisation created in May 1917, mainly at the instigation of CEW Bean, with the aim of collating and controlling Australia's war records 'in the interests of the national history' of the country.[39] Campbell's war record does not state how he was recruited to the AWRS, but it coincided with his transfer to the Head Quarters of the Desert Mounted Corps. He told his brother William that 'Hurley the A.I.F. Photoman for France is here and I understand I am having a fortnights outing with him early in the New Year. Maybe I'll be able to send you a snap of myself in Jerusalem – hope so anyhow'.[40] He told Lilian Pitts the same thing, adding [that] 'if I can get say 50 scenes for myself I'll be ready to "get a move on" overseas – backwards or forwards', an indication of ambitions to become a photographer in Britain or Europe. He had been tramping round Ascalon and Gaza, covering thirty miles over two days, so his knee must have well and truly healed.[41] On 13 January 1918 he was formally attached to the Desert Mounted Corps for war records duty.[42]

The Australian War Records Section started life with the methodical John Linton Treloar as officer-in-charge.[43] It was modelled on the Canadian War Records Office, at the urging of the Canadian Colonel Sir William Maxwell Aitken (later Lord Beaverbrook) in 1916. From 1915 the British used photography for wartime propaganda.[44] CEW Bean, in his capacity as a war correspondent and influenced by his observations of soldiers collecting mementoes on Gallipoli, lobbied hard for some form of memorial for the Australian soldiers of whom he stood in awe.[45] Bean stressed that photographs would provide historical evidence of how battles were conducted, as well as becoming museum exhibits.[46] His attitude to war records bordered on the spiritual: he saw photographs as 'sacred records – standing for future generations to see forever the plain, simple truth'.[47]

Initially the Australian War Records Section confined itself to the collection of written materials, mainly war diaries. War relics were included in September

39 Michael McKernan, *Here is their Spirit: A History of the Australian War Memorial 1917-1900*, University of Queensland Press with the Australian War Memorial, 1991, p. 37.
40 Postcard, JP Campbell to William Campbell, 22 December 1917.
41 Postcard, JP Campbell to Lilian Pitts, December 1917. 'Ascalon' is spelt 'Askalon' in H.S. Gullett, *The Official History of Australia in the War of 1914-1918*, Volume VII, p. 439 & p. 456.
42 NAA: B2455, Campbell JP.
43 Michael McKernan, *Here is their Spirit*, p. 37.
44 Ibid., pp. 34-35.
45 Ibid., p. 32.
46 Ibid., p. 35.
47 Quoted in Michael McKernan, *Here is their Spirit*, p. 42.

1917, and, finally, photographs. The collectors of relics in the field were told to tell the story of items they sent to London as 'a good description transforms a piece of salvage into an interesting relic'.[48] This could also apply to a caption on a photograph.

Although devoted to war photographs as records, as the war drew agonisingly on Bean emphasized their importance as propaganda in a letter to Henry Gullett in early 1918: 'I think that propaganda in Australia has been hopelessly neglected. I mean the putting fair and square of the soldiers and of the Allied case to people out there'. The Allied case should be put to our own people in 'the fairest possible way', and it was necessary 'to keep before them . . . the real things for which they are fighting'.[49] Henry Somer Gullett (1878-1940), an Australian with a farming and journalistic background, had been an official correspondent earlier in the war, and in 1917 Bean selected him to head the Australian War Records Section branch in Egypt.[50]

Bean wished to engage dedicated official war photographers for the newly formed Australian War Records Section, photographers who had 'proper regard for the great sacrifices, and the sacred memory of the great men', the Australian soldiers, who were fighting and dying. The photographs were to be a monument to them.[51] Bean wanted Australian official photographers to be under his direction in France, but initially had to settle with two British photographers who did not last long.[52] Their successors, Frank Hurley and George Hubert Wilkins, went on to be the major figures of Australian First World War photography. Hurley was already a household name across the Empire because of his polar exploits. As a photographer he had been part of Douglas Mawson's Australasian Antarctic Expedition from December 1911 to March 1913, much the same period that Campbell, a man twenty years Hurley's senior, was travelling Australia for the Department of External Affairs as photographer and cinematographer.

Hurley's biographer, Alasdair McGregor, described Hurley's photographic

---

48 Ibid., pp. 44, 47.

49 Letter, CEW Bean to HS Gullett, 6 February 1918, AWM25 1013/36.

50 AJ Hill, Entry for Sir Henry Somer Gullett, in Bede Nairn and Geoffrey Serle, (General Eds.), *Australian Dictionary of Biography*, Volume 9, 1891-1939, Gil-Las, MUP, Carlton, 1983, pp. 137-8. After the war Gullett wrote the seventh volume of Bean's monumental official history and became a Federal politician and minister in the Menzies government. He died tragically in a Canberra plane crash in 1940.

51 Quoted in Michael McKernan, *Here is their Spirit*, p. 50.

52 Ibid., pp. 53-5.

style as 'caught somewhere between the urgencies of the postcard trade, with its appetite for the novel, the showy and the daring, and a desire to be taken seriously as a camera artist in the spirit of pictorialism'.[53] Photography historian Gael Newton maintains that Hurley was not a pictorialist, but was influenced by the pictorial movement because of its prominence in his youth.[54] Like Campbell, Hurley had also been a partner in a photography business, and involved in the postcard trade.[55] By 1910, however, demand for postcards had begun to wane, so the Antarctic venture must have looked enticing, as the job with the Department of External Affairs did for Campbell in 1911.[56]

Hurley went on his second trip to the Antarctic in October 1914, joining Ernest Shackleton's expedition. It was on this trip that he produced his famous photographs of their ship, the *Endurance*, stranded in pack-ice. He also documented the men's heroic battle for survival. This photographic work established his reputation. It was Mawson who recommended Hurley to Bean in August 1917.[57] He became Captain Frank Hurley, Official Photographer, AIF. His assistant was George Wilkins, also a seasoned, much travelled photographer. A South Australian, he also had a polar background, having been on the Canadian Arctic expedition from 1913 to 1916.[58] This partnership set a high standard in war photography.

After only a few weeks on the Western Front in 1917 valiantly trying to get action shots, Hurley decided he could not capture the reality of warfare without constructing composite prints, a process he was familiar with before the war. He inevitably clashed with Bean over this. Bean saw such images as inherently untruthful and not an accurate war record.[59] Large photographic exhibitions were held by the Canadians, British and Australians, including Hurley, from 1916 to 1918. At their centre were explicit 'fakes', photographs of action either staged or done in training for the camera, manipulated by having smoke or aeroplanes

---

53 Alasdair McGregor, *Frank Hurley: A photographer's life*, Viking, Camberwell, 2004, p. 24.

54 Gael Newton, *Silver and Grey: Fifty Years of Australian Photography 1900-1950*, Angus and Robertson, Sydney, 1980, 'Biographies of the Photographers', p.7.

55 Alasdair McGregor, *Frank Hurley*, p. 21.

56 Ibid., p. 24.

57 Michael McKernan, *Here is their Spirit*, p. 54, and AF Pike, 'Hurley, James Francis (Frank) (1885-1962)', *Australian Dictionary of Biography*, Volume 9, Melbourne University Press, 1983, pp. 411-12.

58 R.A. Swan, 'Wilkins, Sir George Hubert (1888-1958)', *Australian Dictionary of Biography*, Volume 12, Melbourne University Press, 1990.

59 Martyn Jolly, 'Composite Propaganda Photographs during the First World War', p. 162.

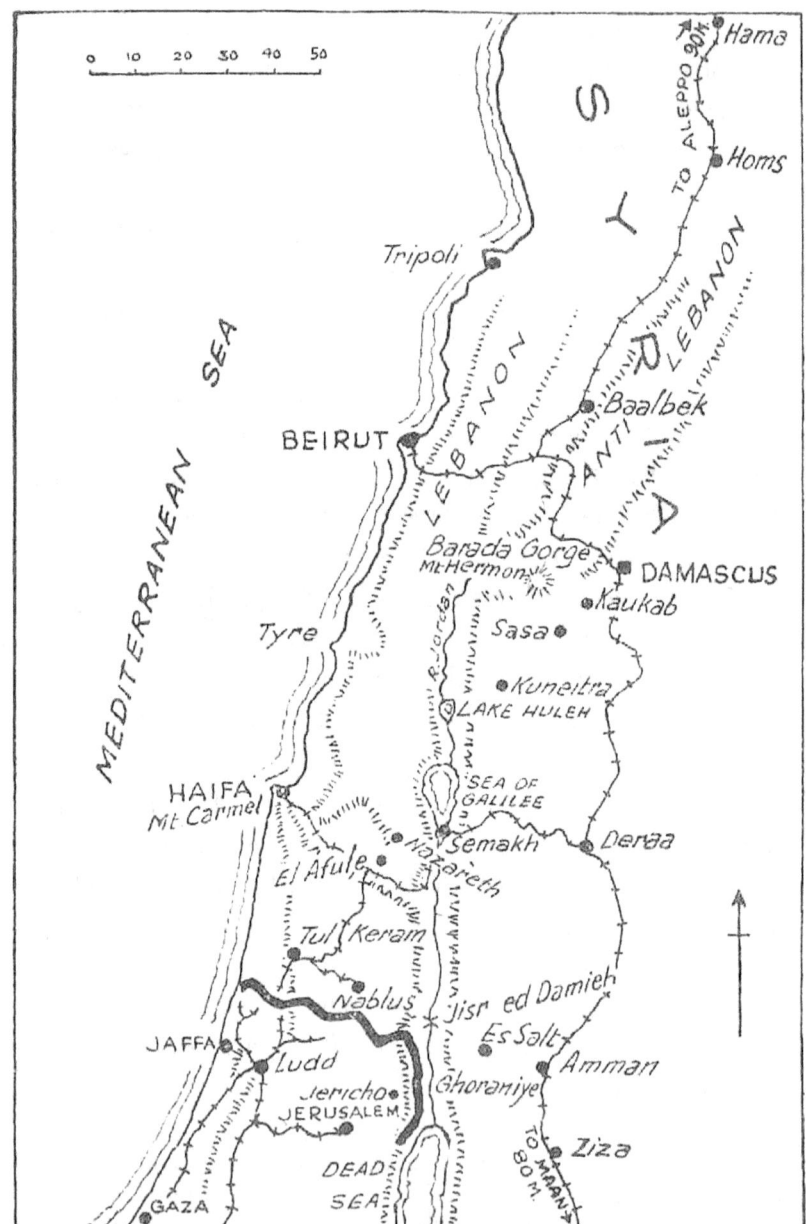

*PALESTINE AND SYRIA, SHOWING THE BRITISH LINE
(BLACK) IN FEBRUARY 1918, BEFORE THE RAIDS ON
AMMAN AND ES SALT*

Fig. 95. Map of Palestine and Syria showing the main places mentioned in this chapter.
(From HS Gullett, *The Official History of Australia in the War of 1914-1918*,
Volume VII, p. 496)

184

montaged into the picture, or constructed into a composite form by the use of a number of negatives.[60] Shaune Lakin, former curator of photographs at the Australian War Memorial, believes Hurley's use of composites has been over-emphasised given they make up only a small percentage of his First World War work, being produced for exhibitions held in London in 1918 as part of 'contemporary trends in visual entertainment'. They were a threat to Bean's focus on realism.[61]

As a result of the conflict with Bean, Hurley threatened to resign, and eventually a compromise was reached.[62] Hurley was virtually banished to cool his heels in the Middle East, filming the activities of the Australian Light Horse. It was in Palestine that he linked up with JP Campbell, who was at the Desert Mounted Corps headquarters in the Jewish village of Deiran, just south of Ludd, where Hurley was to be based (Fig. 95).[63] Hurley had arrived at Port Said on 20 December 1917 and worked his way north, meeting up with Henry Gullett who had recently established a branch of the Australian War Records Section in Cairo.[64] A few days later Hurley was travelling with General Wilson of the 3rd Light Horse Brigade to Latron in the Judea Hills. Assistants hauled his heavy photographic and cinematography equipment.[65] In early January the entire 3rd Light Horse Brigade paraded for his cinematographic camera, forming a column more than two miles long and setting a pattern for the way Hurley was to obtain many of his images in the Middle East. On 26 January he was at the Crusaders' Tower, Ramleh. Although Campbell is not mentioned in Hurley's diary entry for that day, the photographic evidence points to his presence, suggesting he had commenced his 'fortnights outing' with Hurley. Campbell sent Hurley's official photograph of the tower to Lilian Pitts in the form of a postcard. He may have

---

60 Ibid., pp. 156-7.

61 Shaune Lakin, *Contact: Photographs from the Australian War Memorial Collection*, Australian War Memorial, Canberra, 2006, p. 71.

62 Martyn Jolly, 'Composite Propaganda Photographs during the First World War', p.163.

63 NAA: B2455, Campbell JP.

64 Ann Millar, 'Gallipoli to Melbourne: The Australian War Memorial, 1915-19', *Journal of the Australian War Memorial*, Number 10, April 1987, p. 37.

65 Frank Hurley, 'My diary official War Photographer Commonwealth Military Forces, from 21 August 1917 to 31 August 1918, (220 parts)', entries for 29-31 December 1917, Parts 128-130, Digital Collections Manuscripts On Line, MS 883 Papers of Frank Hurley, Series 1: Diaries, 1912-1961, Item 5, National Library of Australia, Canberra, viewed 27 November 2004 and 20 July 2006, <http://nla.gov.au/nla.ms-ms883-1-5>

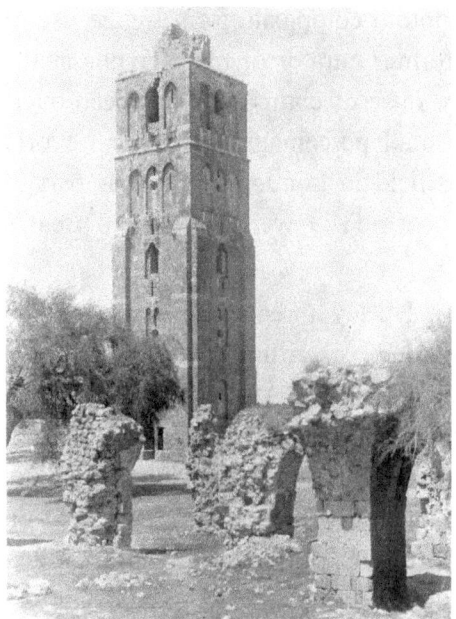

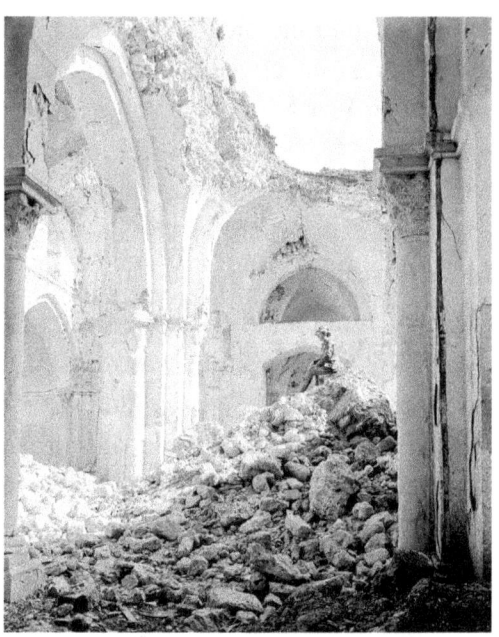

Fig. 96. 'No. 4. Tower Ramleh. Crusaders'. A private photograph of Campbell's, or an official image taken by Hurley? (Courtesy of Falconer collection)

Fig. 97. 'No. 3. Mosque at Gaza shelled by Navy'. This is regarded as one of Hurley's best photographs. (Courtesy of Falconer collection, AWM image B01613)

taken his own photograph of the tower, or developed one taken by Hurley as part of his duties as Hurley's assistant, (Fig. 96).[66]

In early February Hurley moved between Deiran, Jerusalem and Bethlehem, then went south to Dire El Beulah to work with the 4th Brigade. Two squadrons were sent to Gaza for him to film, a place where one sight impressed him greatly, the ruins of Gaza's Grand Mosque. Gaza had been relentlessly shelled by the British, and Hurley commented that 'nowhere did [he] see an intact building, not

66 Ibid., entry date 26 January 1918, part 153; postcard, JP Campbell to Lilian Pitts, 1 February 1918, and *Kia Ora Coo-ee* 15 July 1918, in which the official photograph of the tower appeared. Campbell wrote a short outline of the history of the Ramleh tower for Lilian Pitts but, as in many of his postcards, gave no indication of what he was doing there, probably for censorship reasons. His photograph of the tower (Fig. 96, if it is indeed his) differs from Hurley's official version in it appears to have been taken slightly closer to the subject. Just why Hurley's official photograph was on a postcard less than a week after it was taken is of interest. Perhaps such images were used on postcards *en masse* as part of Australian War Records Section policy, or had Campbell, as he had developed the picture for Hurley, decided to utilise the image for his own purposes? Had he taken the official photograph himself with Hurley's blessing? He always carried his own camera, as he did in the Northern Territory, or had he used Hurley's camera?

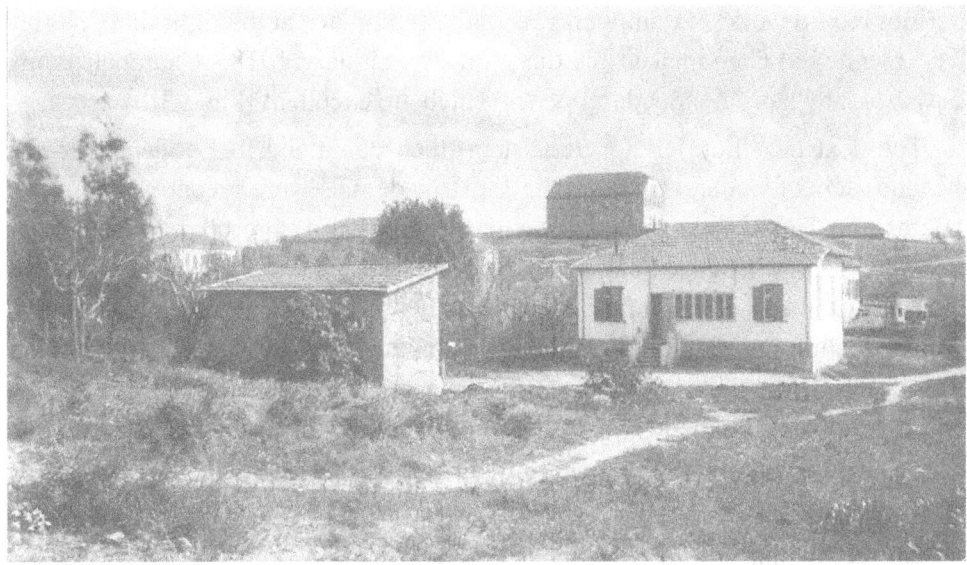

Fig. 98. Unnumbered. 'My Darkroom at Deiran [Jewish village, Palestine], the right hand window of the white house – west side'. Campbell had to improvise when developing photographs in the field. This photograph was probably taken in January 1918 when he was assisting Hurley. (Courtesy of Falconer collection)

even a room'. One of Hurley's most famous photographs is of a Light Horseman sitting on rubble in the mosque shell (Fig. 97).

This photograph is in the Falconer collection in the form of a contact print, and on the back written in pencil is the caption 'Mosque at Gaza shelled by Navy' in Campbell's handwriting. The photograph is numbered three in Campbell's usual methodical way. Campbell had developed this image for Hurley and kept a contact print for himself.[67] Hurley had the battle of Beersheba, a significant victory by the Light Horse when they charged Turkish lines on horseback, re-enacted for his camera. A few days later, travelling with Gullett, he arrived at the headquarters of the Imperial Camel Corps led by General Smith, and proceeded to have the battle of Rafa re-enacted for filming purposes.[68]

As Hurley's stay in the Middle East drew towards a close he discussed his successor with Gullett. He was having difficulty finding a suitable candidate to carry on his work and commented: 'The Kodak appeared to be part of the equipment of the Light Horse, but all are raw amateurs, and unsuited to carry on

67 Campbell sent a postcard of his own distant photograph of the damaged mosque to Lilian Pitts.
68 Hurley diary, Parts 163-166, Digital Collections Manuscripts On Line, MS 883 Papers of Frank Hurley, National Library of Australia, viewed 27 November 2004.

serious record work'.[69] Campbell was in the right place at the right time. Hurley first mentioned Campbell in his diary on 17 February 1918: 'Campbell is my assistant, and has developed my plates which are excellent [Fig. 98]'.[70]

The next day they left for Jerusalem, then continued to Bethlehem to the headquarters of General Cox and the 1st Brigade who were preparing for action against the Turks. Over the next few days Hurley (and presumably Campbell) accompanied the brigade in an attack on Nebi Musa and the advance on Jericho, which was taken without a fight. This would have been Campbell's first taste of military action since Gallipoli, albeit as an observer. Towards the end of February Hurley went to Julis to photograph an inspection by General Harry Chauvel, the Australian commander of the Desert Mounted Corps, and on 1 March he completed the filming of Jerusalem by air, two of his last duties in the Middle East.[71]

On the of morning of 2 March 1918 Hurley and Campbell left the Desert Corps headquarters in Deiran in the Box Ford car to take pictures and movies along the road from Jerusalem to Jericho.[72] They went off the new road onto the old Jericho road, winding along the Wady Kelt. The descent into the Jordan Valley was steep and rough, nearly throwing them out of the car. It was Hurley's last day in the field before returning to Cairo, and leaving for England in early May.[73] On 5 March Hurley wrote in his diary: 'Have arranged that Sgnt Campbell should take over'.[74] Henry Gullett, Hurley's boss, wanted a Sergeant Coulson from the Flying Squadron in the job, but Hurley insisted Campbell should succeed him.[75] Campbell's succession was probably discussed on this last trip through the hills, with tips from Hurley on how Campbell should proceed in his new job. JP Campbell was appointed Honorary Lieutenant, Official Photographer to the AIF and Egyptian Expeditionary Forces, on 11 March 1918. He was attached to the ANZAC Mounted Division in Jericho in April 1918 and the HQ Desert Mounted Corps soon after.[76]

---

69 Hurley diary, entry date 30 January 1918, Part 155, Digital Collections Manuscripts On Line, MS 883 Papers of Frank Hurley, National Library of Australia, viewed 27 November 2004.

70 Ibid., Part 174.

71 Ibid., Parts 175-89.

72 Ibid., Part 189.

73 Ibid., Parts 190-3. A Wady is a creek or water course.

74 Ibid., Part 192.

75 HS Gullett to J Treloar, 2 September 1918, AWM 16 4379/5/21.

76 NAA: B2455, Campbell JP.

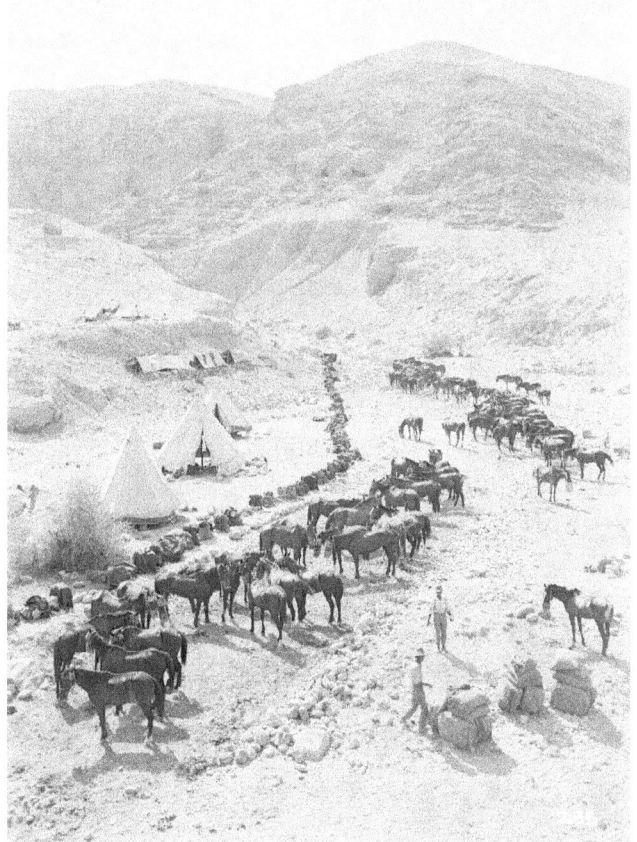

Fig. 99. 'No 59. Jordan Valley Camp. 7th L.H. Camp Ain Duk'.[77]
(Courtesy of Falconer collection, AWM image B00235)

The instructions issued to official photographers detailed strict record keeping, for example listing the number of negatives to be dispatched for record and publicity purposes to Cairo, London and Melbourne. It also made

> explicit the policy of the section regarding the general nature of official photographs. As a rule the desire is to get pictures of movements. Views of the environment of the troops are not, in general required unless the troops appear in them.[78]

---

77 This image is also in the Melbourne *Leader* of 30 November 1918 with the caption 'Australian Light Horse Camp Close to Front Line in Jordan Valley'. It also appears in the *Kia Ora Coo-ee* of 15 December 1918, a full page spread with a thick decorative border, including Light Horse motifs. Both photograph and *Leader* captions conformed to Australian War Records Section guidelines.
78 HW Dinning, 'Instructions for Official Photographer, A.I.F. in Egypt', AWM 16 4379/5/4 Part 1, Australian War Memorial.

This last requirement was always going to be difficult for Campbell, who almost instinctively looked for a scenic view, given his background in landscape photography. However, as we have seen, he was quite capable of taking stunning streetscape photographs and scenes incorporating the human form. The author of the instructions, HW Dinning, used Campbell's Jordan Valley photograph as an example of where Australian Light Horse camps, horse lines 'and the like' should be shown in official photographs (Fig. 99).[79]

Towns were to have occupying troops evident in them. The general landscape included religious antiquities, which emphasized the crusading aspect of the war against the Turks and their German ally. The newspaper captions attached to official war photographs conveyed some of the general cultural aspects of the region in which the Australians were fighting (Fig. 100).[80]

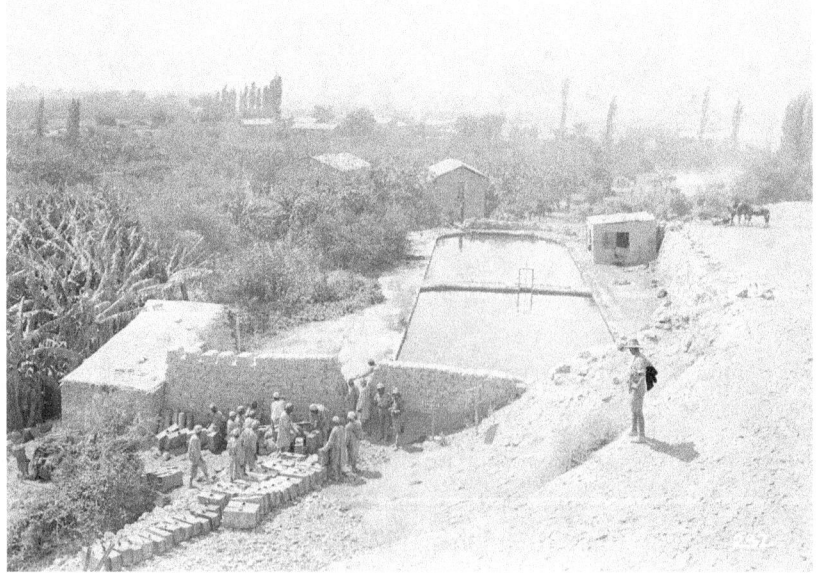

Fig. 100. 'No 52. Ain Sultan Jericho. Elishas Spring – Jericho'.[81]
(Courtesy of Falconer collection, AWM image B00232)

79 Ibid.

80 Ibid. I found one set of Campbell's official photographs in an Australian newspaper, the 30 November 1918 edition of the Melbourne *Leader*, after the war ended, a set of three photographs taken early in Campbell's time as official photographer.

81 This picture was also in the *Leader* of 30 November 1918 with the caption: 'Elisha's Spring Ain Sultan (Sultan's Spring), Jericho. The Spring is on the Site of the Old Jericho of the Bible. The Reservoir is Walled up to About Twelve Feet at the Further End, and the Overflow Drives a Corn Mill'.

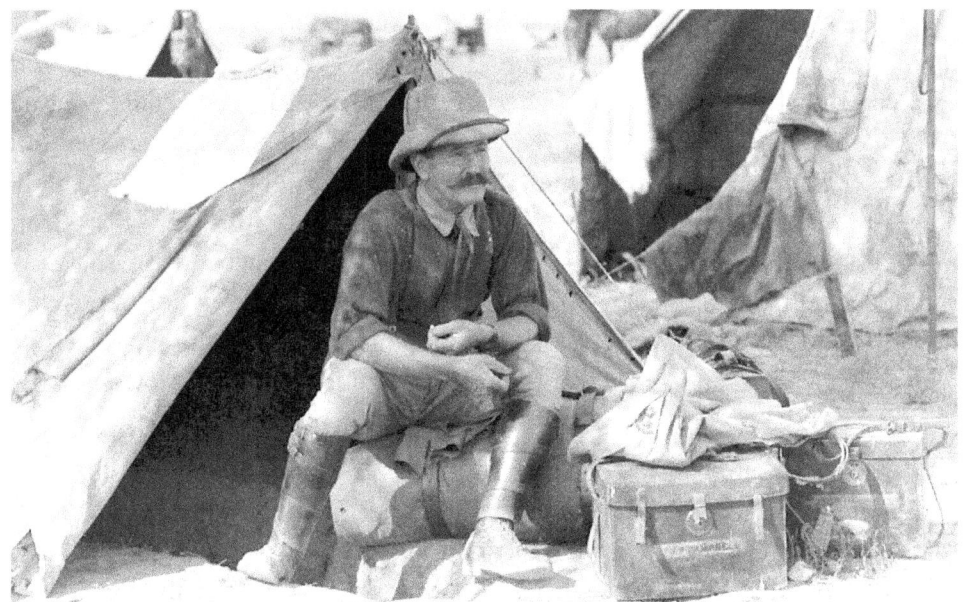

Fig. 101. Postcard. JP Campbell, the newly appointed official photographer, at General Ryrie's 2nd Light Horse Brigade camp on the plains of Jericho, 9 April 1918.
(Courtesy of Nance Tyson and Falconer collections)

As the Australian War Records Section also provided photographs for use in recruitment campaigns in Australia, the images needed to convey soldiering as a desirable occupation.[82] Campbell largely adhered to these requirements, but ultimately attracted criticism, partly due to his stubborn nature and the fact that his war weary body gradually caught up with him.

In his first two and a half months in the job Campbell exercised his newly found freedom to practice his profession, although within the parameters of the Australian War Records Section. He sent a postcard to Lilian Pitts of himself wearing a pith helmet, sitting next to his camera gear at the opening to a tent on the plains of Jericho in Granville Ryrie's camp. Ryrie was one of the politicians he had travelled with on the Northern Territory parliamentary visit six long years ago, and had been an ardent critic of the tour (Fig. 101).[83] Campbell looks relaxed and every bit the professional photographer, with his photographic equipment bags, appropriately adorned with his name, at his side.

---

82 In late August Campbell was directed to give Capt HV Throssell VC, of the 10th Light Horse, any photographs that may be of use to him for recruitment purposes. Throssell called, according to a JP Campbell note, and collected 50 prints on 26 August 1918. AWM 25 1013/38A.
83 Postcard, JP Campbell to Lilian Pitts, 17 April 1918.

On Gallipoli Campbell's photography was limited by his role as a signaller, the stagnant, confined trench warfare, the steep, rugged terrain and the fear created from being constantly under fire. Now he was being paid to be a full-time photographer in a vast, equally harsh landscape, where the warfare evolved around regular movement across large distances. Everywhere he went – photographing the Australian Light Horse in the Jordan Valley, from el Auja in the north to the Dead Sea – he was surrounded by antiquities of religious significance, which added to his private portfolio of images. While he conformed to the AWRS criteria of including troops in this landscape, it was often the land and water that dominated, which satisfied his own creative needs.

It was in the Jordan Valley that Campbell fine-tuned the dust theme in his photographs (Fig.102). In another twist on this dust/mist theme he photographed a soldier enjoying a shower, with light and water creating a glowing effect. It is a celebration of the human body, the Light Horseman as God-like figure. Another soldier awaits his turn (Fig. 103).

In this way he took Australian pictorialism to war. Perhaps parts of the Middle

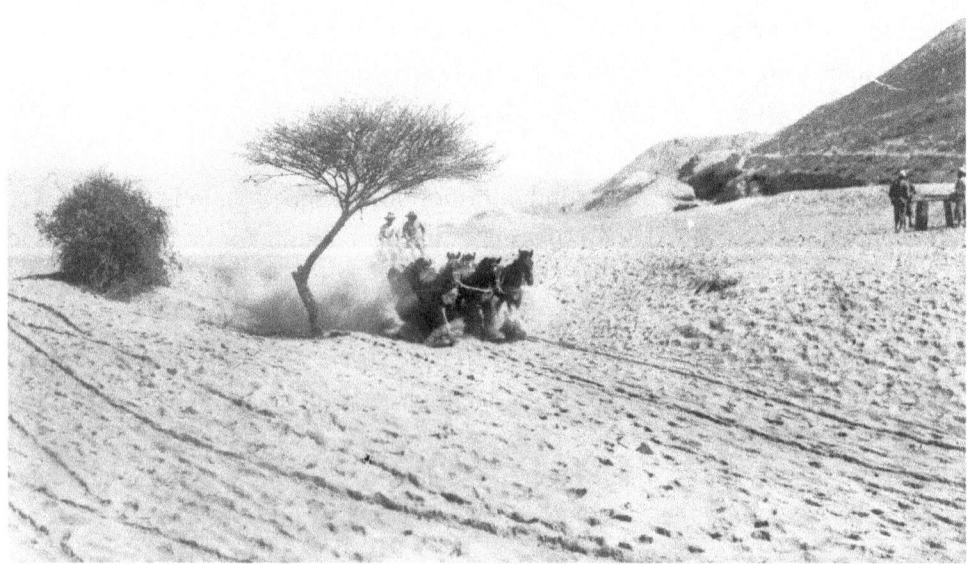

Fig. 102. 'No. 47. Jericho Dust'. Campbell at his pictorialist best. He may have arranged for the wagon to track under the tree. It satisfied the Australian War Records Section criteria of troops moving. (Courtesy of Falconer collection, AWM image B00230)

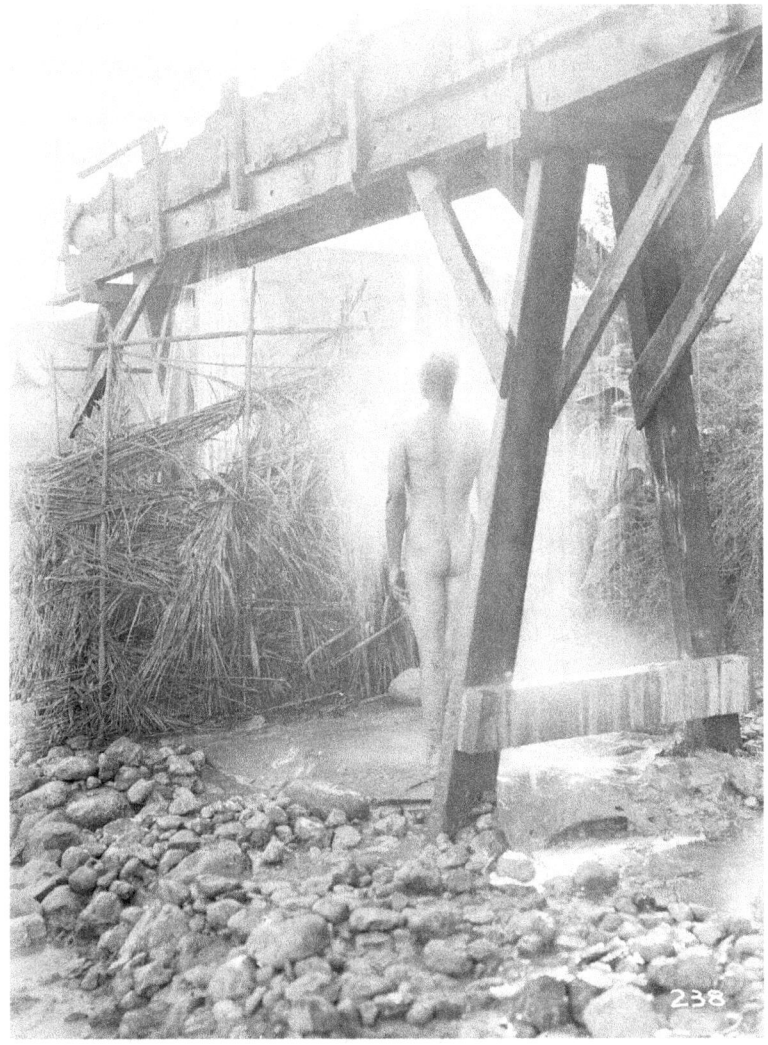

Fig. 103. 'No. 51. After a dusty day. Ain (Spring) Duk near Jericho'.
(Courtesy of Falconer collection, AWM image B00238)

East reminded him of summer landscapes in his home country. In some of the official photographs of the el Auja/Auja crossing/Ghoraniye areas on the Jordan River, the human figures are miniscule amidst the grandeur of the landscape. Some, like the rear view of the 5th Light Horse outpost in the clay hills of Ghoraniye (Fig. 104) have the urgent military aspect of holding a strategic position, with soldiers at the ready.

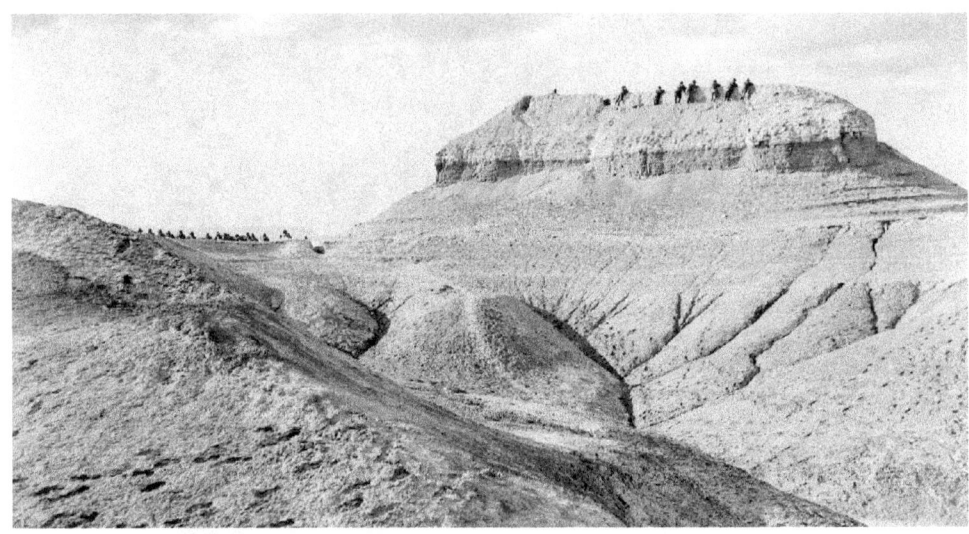

Fig. 104. Unnumbered. 'Outpost – Jordan River'.
(Courtesy of Falconer collection, AWM image B00009).[84]

Other images, like the sweeping view of the bridgehead at Auja with the Light Horse camp in the far distance near the flats, and people carrying brush on the side of a hill in the right foreground (a Campbell 'beast-of-burden' pictorial favourite) are of more scenic value (Fig. 105). In another image of remarkable clarity and depth members of the Australian Light Horse trek down the hills in a long winding column, with packhorses crossing fast flowing water on a pontoon bridge at Auja Ford. The figures on the bank in the foreground add interest and perspective. In this engaging photograph Campbell achieves balance between military record and landscape (Fig. 106).

In early May Campbell was at Es Salt east of the Jordan River, having accompanied the 3rd Light Horse Brigade as the Allies made their second assault on the town. In March 1918 Allenby's forces moved east of the Jordan, and later that month captured Es Salt high on the mountain plateau, but further east the assault on Amman failed, with heavy losses inflicted on the Allies.[85]

---

84 There is a rather more dramatic side view of this outpost showing the soldiers on the lower ground on the left of this picture with their rifles resting on the top of their trench-like position (Australian War Memorial image B00010). As previously mentioned, the Australian War Memorial uses a 'B' prefix to indicate its official war photographs for the Middle East in World War 1, and 'H' to indicate those privately taken and donated to the memorial.

85 HS Gullett, *The Official History of Australia in the War of 1914-1918*, Volume VII p. 567. Campbell was attached to the ANZAC Mounted Division in Jericho in April 1918, so he may have missed the first raid on Es Salt and Amman which ranged over the period 21 March 1918 to 2 April 1918.

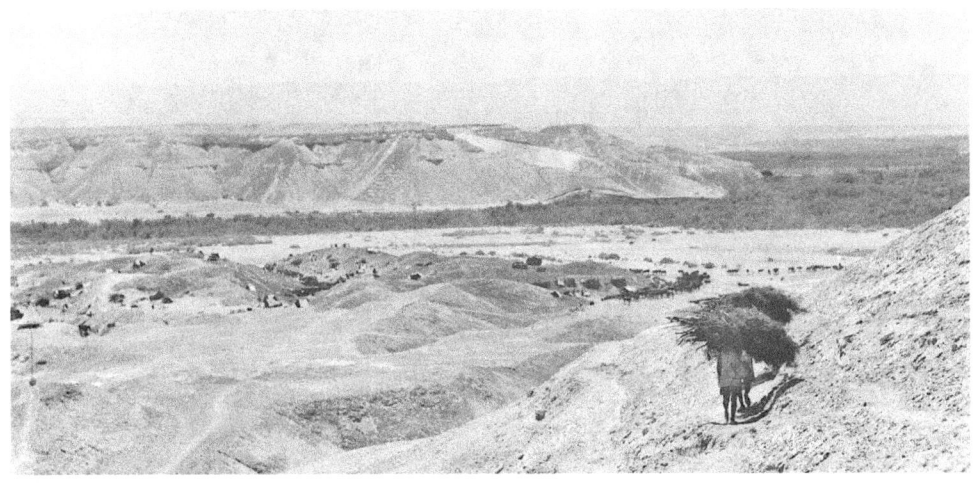

Fig. 105. The bridgehead at Auja. (Courtesy of Falconer collection, AWM image B00017)

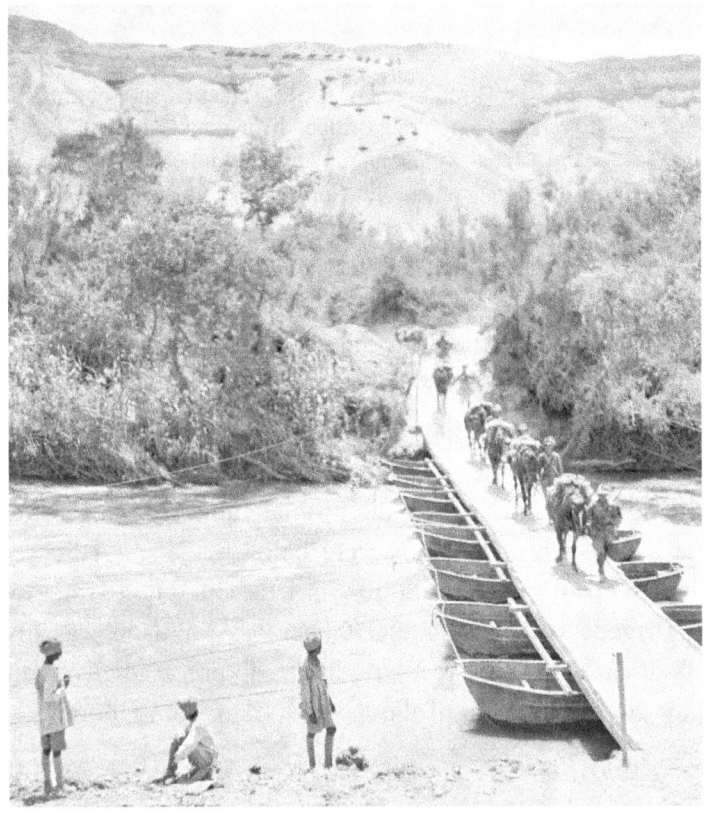

Fig. 106. 'No 34. Jordan River. Auja Ford'.
(Courtesy of Falconer collection, AWM image B00029)

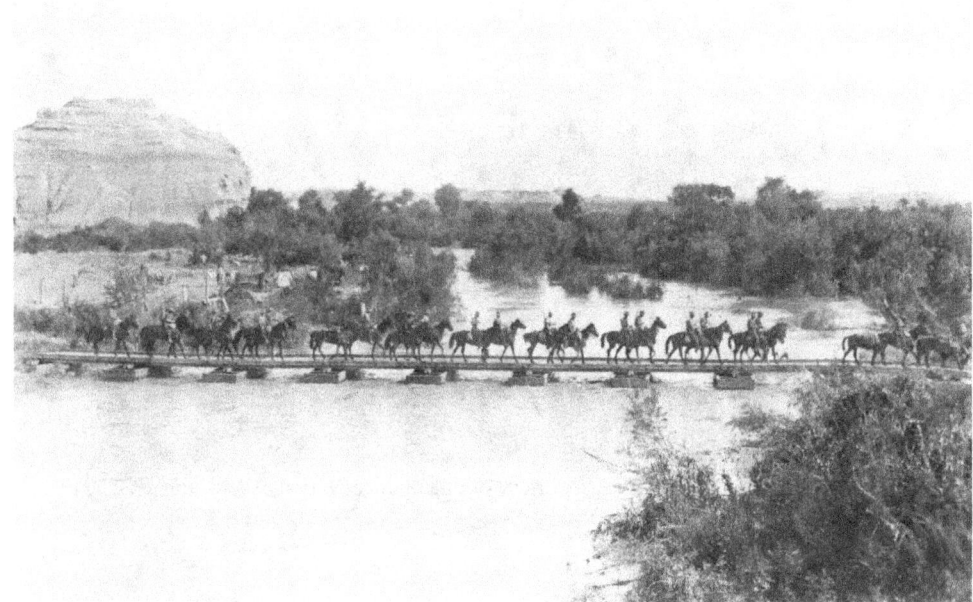

Fig. 107. 'No. 32. Jordan River. Ghoraniye Ford'. A spectacular shot of the 5th Light Horse crossing the fast flowing river on a pontoon bridge, displaying Campbell's ability to use the landscape to create an overall pictorial effect.
(Courtesy of Falconer collection, AWM image B00007)

As a result troops had to withdraw from Es Salt on 1 April 1918, fleeing down the road to the Jordan Valley. The first raid east of the Jordan had been a failure.[86] The Turks attacked the bridgehead on the Jordan at Ghoraniye and also Musallbeh on 11 April 1918, but were driven back (Fig. 107).[87]

On 25 April 1918 General Harry Chauvel established Desert Mounted Corps Head Quarters on the wilderness country east of Talat el Dum.[88] Allenby planned another raid east of the Jordan with the ultimate aim of taking Deraa far to the north east, at a time when demands were being made for Allied troops to be withdrawn and sent to France.[89] On 30 April the 8th Light Horse with the 3rd Light Horse Brigade led by Brigadier General LC Wilson was involved in a second attack on Es Salt, again resulting in its capture. It involved a fifteen mile dash north, up the eastern side of the River Jordan from Ghoraniye to Damieh

---

86 Ibid., p. 582.
87 Ibid., p. 588.
88 Ibid., pp. 594-5.
89 Ibid., p. 599.

by the 4th and 3rd Light Horse Brigades, some of it under Turkish artillery fire, and then a steep climb eastward by the 3rd Light Horse Brigade up a rugged track into the hills where Es Salt was located. Campbell's old regiment was the first into the town and quickly quelled resistance. It was gradually joined by other Light Horse regiments and British troops. But, on 3 May 1918 they again withdrew, exhausted, back to the Jordan Valley, after the 4th Light Horse Brigade was defeated in the Red Hill/Damieh region to the west, and Turkish troops advanced on Es Salt from Amman in the east.[90]

Trooper William Griffiths of the 8th Light Horse, a soldier from the Mansfield district, participated in this second raid on Es Salt. He described how he 'noticed a man with a big camera taking photos whenever he got a chance. That man was Lieut. Campbell, who used to be in Mansfield with Mr. Vallance. I didn't get a chance to speak to him'.[91] Campbell, riding with the 3rd Light Horse Brigade or close on their heels, took a series of official photographs of Es Salt and environs on this raid, (for example see Fig. 108).[92] He, like many others, was lucky to survive it. He also took private photographs in Es Salt, and produced postcards from at least two of these. One resembles closely an Australian War Memorial official image, again a rather benign, scenic photograph (Fig. 109).[93] He was continuing his habit, commenced while an official photographer with the External Affairs Department, of compiling a parallel private photographic collection.

Casualties were relatively light during this second Es Salt raid. For Allenby and Chauvel it was a strategic disaster, but with a silver lining. The Allies gave the impression they were still determined to advance towards Damascus on the eastern flank via Es Salt and Amman, while in reality they were preparing to

---

90 Ibid., p. 615-33. This is a very basic account of complicated military action and does not, for example, explain the important role of British troops. For details of this second Es Salt raid see Lindsay Baly, *Horseman, Pass By: The Australian Light Horse in World War 1*, Kangaroo Press, Sydney, 2003, pp. 201-20.

91 *Mansfield Courier*, 20 July 1918, and Cameron Simpson, *Maygar's Boys*, p. 214.

92 Australian War Memorial images from approximately B00061 through to B00077 are Campbell photographs concerning the second Es Salt raid.

93 These two pictures were sent as postcards to Lilian Pitts. The official photograph containing the minaret appears to have been taken further back than the private image, showing more of the chimney-like structure. The other postcard is a beautiful image of a quiet, ancient street showing an archway and the almost indistinguishable figure of what looks to be a Muslim woman at the end of the street carrying something on her head (a favourite Campbell subject). Campbell had sought out a peaceful, ancient, domestic scene away from the turmoil of war, something he was to do later in Damascus. I have been unable to find an equivalent in the Australian War Memorial digitised photography collection, suggesting this was a private photograph not donated to the Australian War Museum after the war.

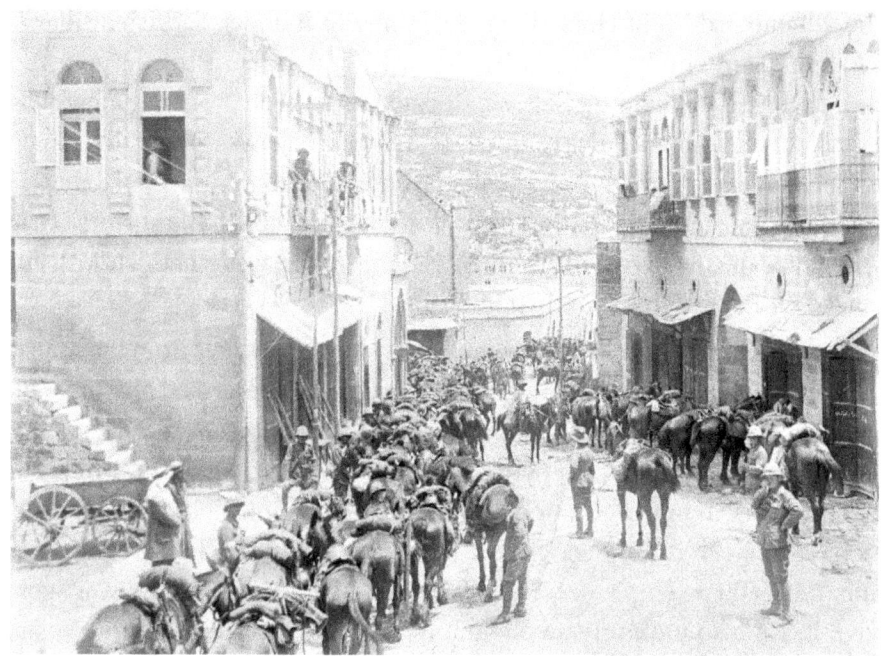

Fig. 108. Australian and British troops occupying Es Salt for the second time, 2 May 1918
(AWM image B00064)

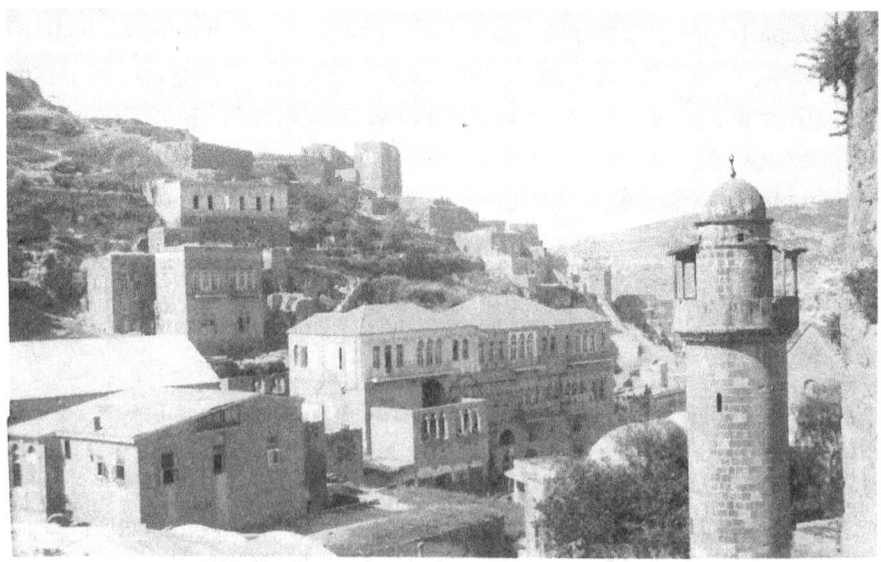

Fig. 109. No date or text on back. An image of part of Es Salt featuring a minaret in
the foreground, right, and a Turkish Hospital in the centre.
(Courtesy Nance Tyson collection, see also AWM image B00068)

move up the west coast. Campbell was also to be involved in recording this 'big push', or 'Great Ride' to Damascus.[94]

Gullett, as the head of the Australian War Records Section in Egypt, was scrutinising Campbell's efforts, and reporting to Treloar, the head of the Australian War Records Section in London: 'Campbell is not a Hurley but he will no doubt improve as he finds himself'.[95] In June 1918, Lieutenant Archer, press officer, returned four sets of six prints of photographs to Campbell. They were suppressed because of their subject, bridges, 'the nature of whose construction is unknown to the enemy, and it is not possible to allow such photographs to appear at present'.[96] Bridges had been a favourite subject of Campbell's in civilian life, but he could not resist photographing them under construction for military purposes by the British, despite his awareness of the censorship rules.

Campbell wrote to Lilian Pitts in mid May, describing the ruggedness of the country bordering the Jordan Valley: the 'Lights in the Holy Land are beyond my expectations but the main thrills are motoring in much more dangerous looking corkscrew mountain glades than any wheel roads I've ever been on'.[97] The role of official war photographer also involved aerial photography, and Campbell was packed up for a flight to the Jordan Valley at 6.30 am the next day, revealing that, like Hurley, he used the services of pilots like Ross Smith (Fig. 110). He commented on Frank Hurley – his one and only descriptive assessment of the revered photographer I could find – presumably at the request of a curious Lilian in a letter, wondering what Hurley had been like during his time with Campbell: 'Hurley is from Sydney and no Ballaratite', which possibly means, according to historian Weston Bate, that Hurley was not very democratic and inclined to do things his way (a reference to the Eureka Stockade of 1854).[98]

In May 1918 a decision was made for a large force of Allied troops to remain in the Jordan Valley during the summer, despite warnings from the locals about the extreme heat and disease they were likely to experience (Fig. 111).[99] Campbell

---

94 HS Gullett, *The Official History of Australia in the War of 1914-1918*, Volume VII, p. 639, and Lindsay Baly, *Horseman Pass By*, p. 220.
95 HS Gullett to J Treloar, 19 May 1918, AWM 16 4379/5/21.
96 Lieut. Archer to JP Campbell, 10 June 1918, AWM 25 1013/38A.
97 Postcard, JP Campbell to LL Pitts, 18 May 1918.
98 Ibid., and a conversation with historian Weston Bate, 29 June 2006.
99 HS Gullett, *The Official History of Australia in the War of 1914-1918*, Volume VII, p. 639.

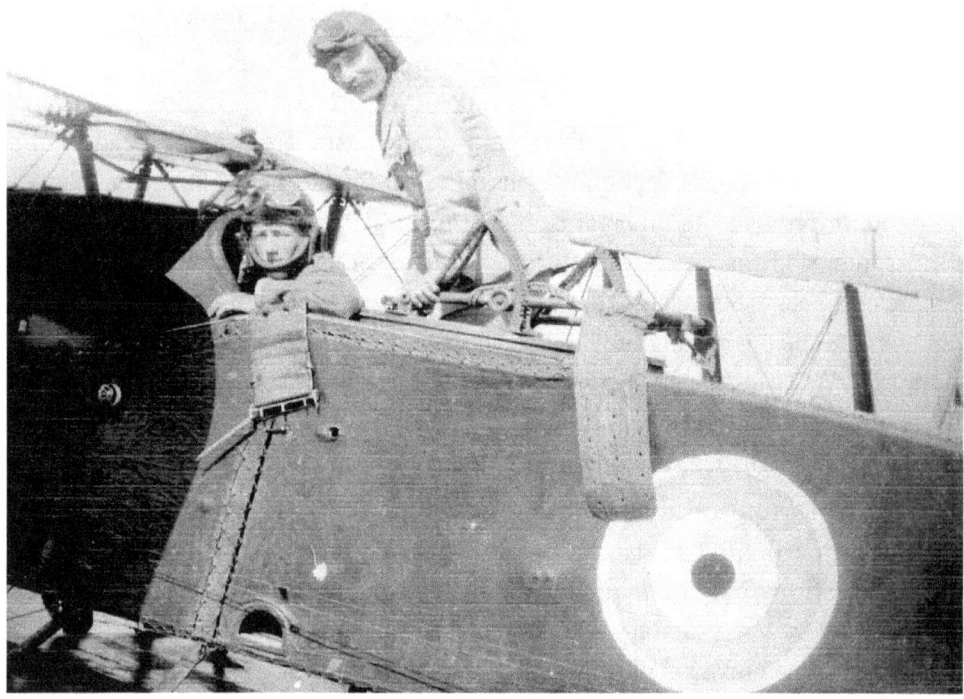

Fig. 110. An uncaptioned image of JP Campbell (standing) in an aeroplane somewhere in the Middle East. Photographer unknown. (Courtesy of Falconer collection)

took a number of photographs in the dust bowl of this valley. As Gullett reported to Treloar:

> Campbell is working keenly, but has been restricted for photographic material. However it is now about due. Jordan Valley where the temperature reaches 120° [F] in the shade is causing a good deal of sick wastage. Campbell has just wired to say he has malaria.[100]

The official photographer spent eight days in a Jerusalem hospital, from 21 to 29 June 1918.[101]

The troops were suffering intolerable dust, heat, flies and mosquitoes as summer progressed. It was hard labour for the Allies to establish solid defences and prevent disease, particularly malaria, whereas the Turks took no such precautions in their camps yet suffered little from the sicknesses that plagued British troops because, wrote HS Gullett, of 'their remarkable powers of resisting

---

100 HS Gullett to J Treloar, 20 June 1918, AWM 16 4379/5/21
101 NAA: B2455, Campbell JP.

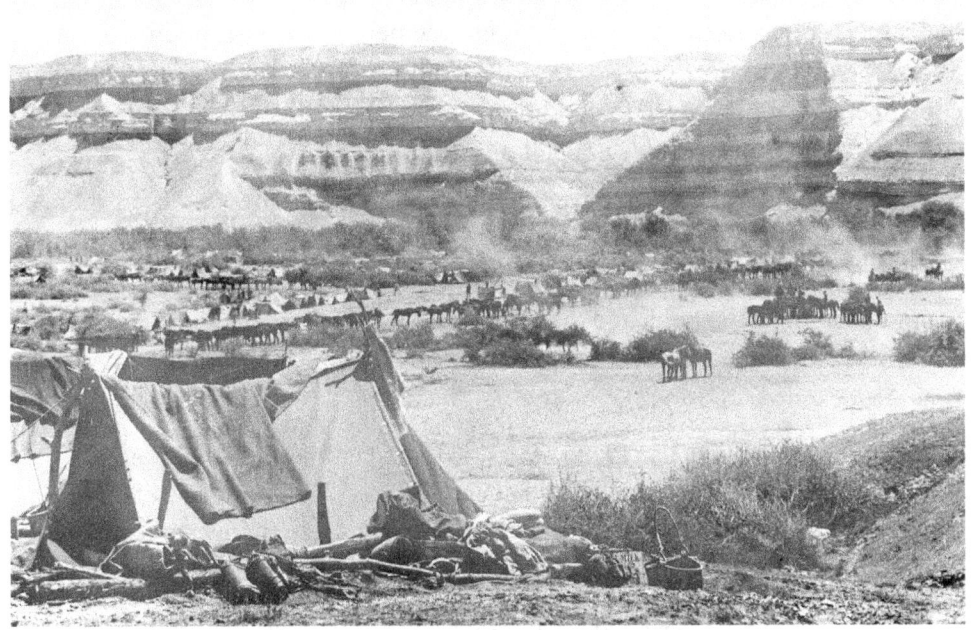

Fig. 111. 'No. 55. 9th L.H. Camp on Jordan. Auja Ford'.
(Courtesy of Falconer collection, AWM image B00021)

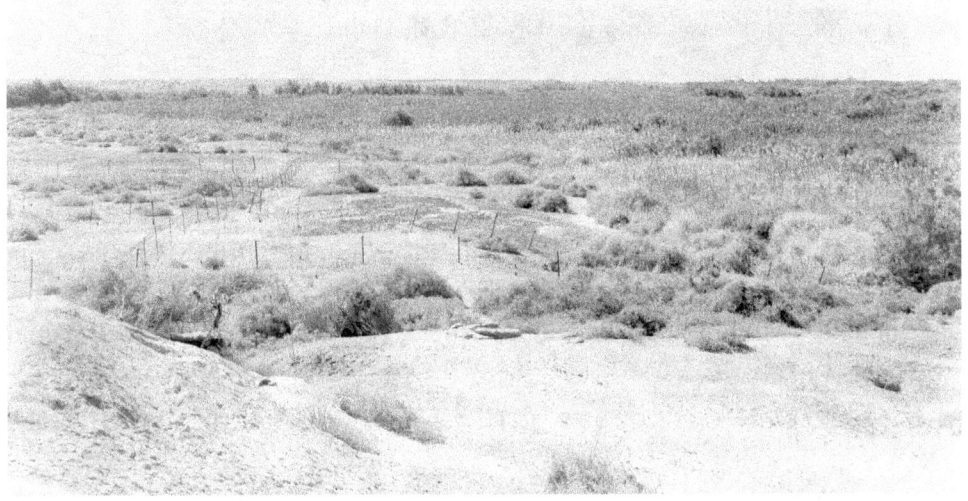

Fig 112. 'No. 42. Malarial Swamps Jordan Valley. Hills of Moab in distance. Dead Sea
just showing'. (Courtesy of Falconer collection, AWM image B00226)

disease' (Fig. 112).[102] Illness drained the Allied ranks of fit men, but if disease had struck *en masse* there were few reinforcements available, due partly to the failure of conscription in Australia. Generally the older men, like Campbell, coped better with the terrible conditions in June and July in the Jordan Valley, although, as we have seen, Campbell did succumb, but not severely.[103]

As Campbell gradually recovered from his bout of illness he corresponded with a Mr Murphy, presumably a staff member of the Australian War Records Section in Cairo. The correspondence gives some idea of how Campbell was communicating in the field, and the difficulties he faced in obtaining supplies. On 12 July 1918 he wrote to Murphy from the Mandarah Railway Station, Aboukir Line, requesting

> 7 prints from the Italian Photo Stores [in Cairo] from each of 13 negatives of Jerusalem which should be suitable for press illustrations – if the prints are not up to usual appearance please hold them for my approval – I could not get the use of the darkroom to do them myself.

He was 'feeling [himself] again after a lovely loaf', but lamented that he had 'not a plate or film left'.[104] He wrote to Murphy again the next day:

> I'll be along about Thursday – I forgot you have not got the titles of the prints I mentioned in last memo. Please tell Editor Barrett [of the soldier's newspaper *Kia Ora Coo-ee*] that I'll be along as I think he wants more illustrations for August. Presume no news has arrived of plates from London yet. Please forward enclosed to Mr Gullett.[105]

The lack of glass plates and adequate photographic equipment were to cause Campbell many problems as the war progressed.

Part of Campbell's photography involved group portraiture of Australian military personnel for record purposes, as his work with the Imperial Camel Corps shows. In mid June he found himself swimming in the Mediterranean near Jaffa, enjoying a break away from the Jordan Valley, and renewing his acquaintance with his 'roommate at Mansfield, Lt. Col. Langley of the Imperial

---

102 HS Gullett, *The Official History of Australia in the War of 1914-1918*, Volume VII, pp. 641-4, 660. Turkish soldiers did not escape disease and were to suffer terribly from it at the end of the war, as will be discussed later.
103 Ibid., pp. 662, 674.
104 JP Campbell to Murphy, 12 July 1918, AWM 25 1013/38A.
105 JP Campbell to Murphy, 13 July 1918, AWM 25 1013/38A.

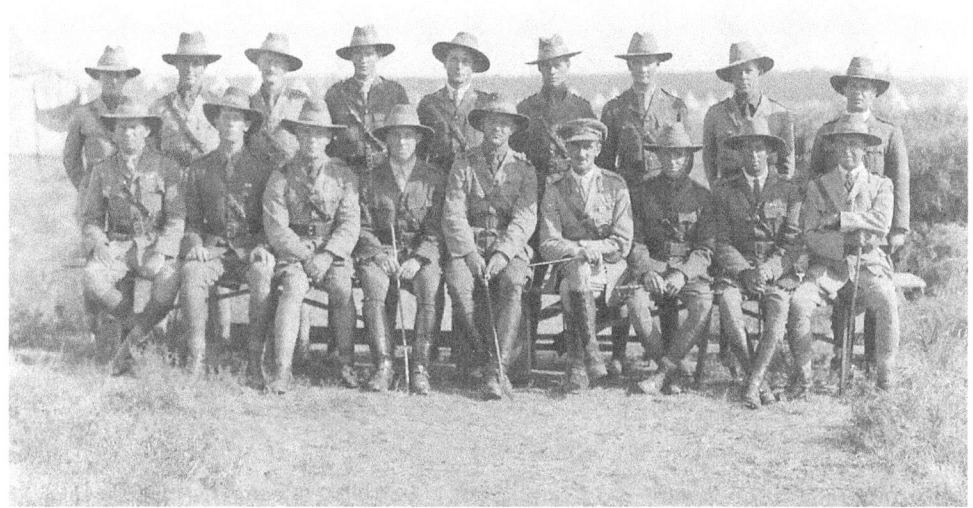

Fig. 113. 'No. 3. I.C.C. Lt Colonel Langley with Brig Gen CL Smith & officers of 7th Battn'. Campbell disliked portraiture work. (Courtesy of Falconer collection)

Camel Corps.[106] George Langley was a much-decorated soldier who was working as a teacher at the Mansfield Agricultural High School when war broke out. [107]

In June 1918 the Camel Corps was in its last days, Langley having joined the Corps in January 1916. Campbell was at the Jaffa camp to obtain group portraits of Langley's unit prior to the Camel Corps dismantling in favour of the faster, more versatile horses. He complained to Lilian Pitts of having to 'do groups in sunlight' (Fig. 113).[108] He had never liked portraiture work and had avoided it in his Vallan Studio days. Portraiture was an important part of the Australian War Records Section assemblage of records, and Campbell's disdain for it would not have endeared him to his superiors. He gave Langley photography lessons during the visit and took eighteen photographs of Jaffa and the Camel Corps camp.[109]

106 JP Campbell to Lilian Pitts, 13 June 1918.
107 George F and Edmee M Langley, *Sand, Sweat & Camels: The Australian Companies of the Imperial Camel Corps*, Lowden Publishing Co., Kilmore, 1976, p. xv, and *Mansfield Courier*, 15 August 1915.
108 Postcard, JP Campbell to Lilian Pitts, 13 June 1918. Campbell's granddaughter, Noel Fethers, maintained 'he didn't like inside work', which includes portraiture. Interview with Noel Fethers, 20 April 2005.
109 Papers of GF Langley, PR00096, Australian War Memorial. Langley did not mention Campbell by name in his letters, referring only to the official photographer, nor did he mention him in his book, *Sand, Sweat & Camels*, published after his death by his wife. Campbell was twenty-six years older than Langley. Langley was also a close friend of HS Gullett.

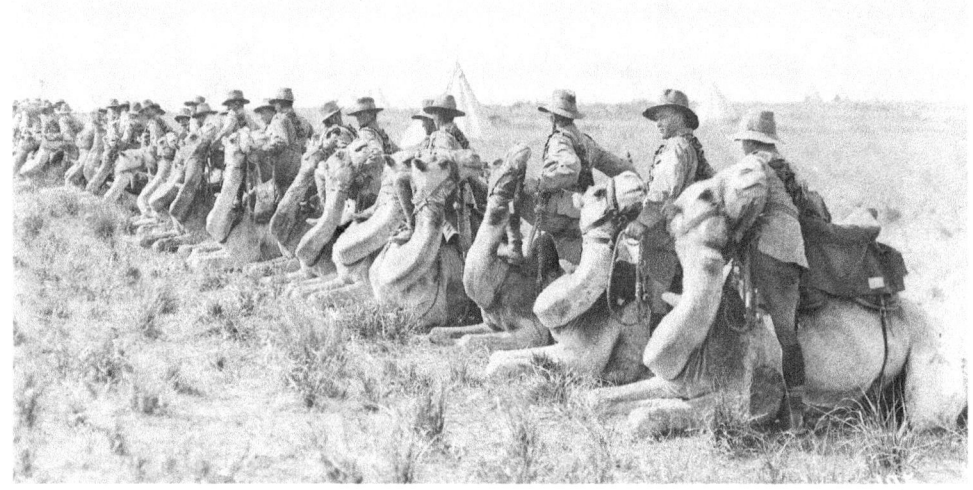

Fig. 114. Members of the Imperial Camel Corps, preparing to mount their camels. One of Campbell's 'snaps' at the Jaffa camp showing his enthusiasm for the linear.
(AWM image B00195)

These photographs of the camp at Jaffa and the final days of the Camel Corps, along with the group portraits, are held by the Australian War Memorial (Fig 114). Campbell photographed Langley sitting sewing on a rug at Daman in 1918, a picture also in the Falconer collection (Fig. 115).[110] It is a typical Campbell portrait of a person performing a mundane task amidst the chaos of war', as on Gallipoli.

Campbell arrived at the seaside, the Mediterranean, on 3 July 1918, presumably to convalesce from his bout of malaria. From here he sent a copy of the *Kia-ora Coo-ee* to Lilian Pitts, telling her: 'The "Kia ora Cooee" much improved will go along to you regularly in future, I sent the first issue but 2nd & 3rd were "no class". I'll be the chief pictorial contributor with occasional descriptions'.[111] The *Kia Ora Coo-ee* was produced by Australian and New Zealand troops serving in the Middle East. It was printed in Cairo and appeared in monthly issues between March and December 1918. The editor, Sergeant Charles Barrett, was an experienced journalist and author, having worked on the staff of the Melbourne *Herald*.[112] The paper consisted mainly of imaginative verse and prose

---

110 George F and Edmee M Langley, *Sand, Sweat and Camels*, opposite p. 16.
111 Postcard, JP Campbell to LL Pitts, 4 July 1918.
112 David Kent (Introduction), *The Kia Ora Coo-ee*, Cornstalk Publishing (A & R Publishers), 1981, p. viii. JP Campbell is not mentioned in David Kent's introduction.

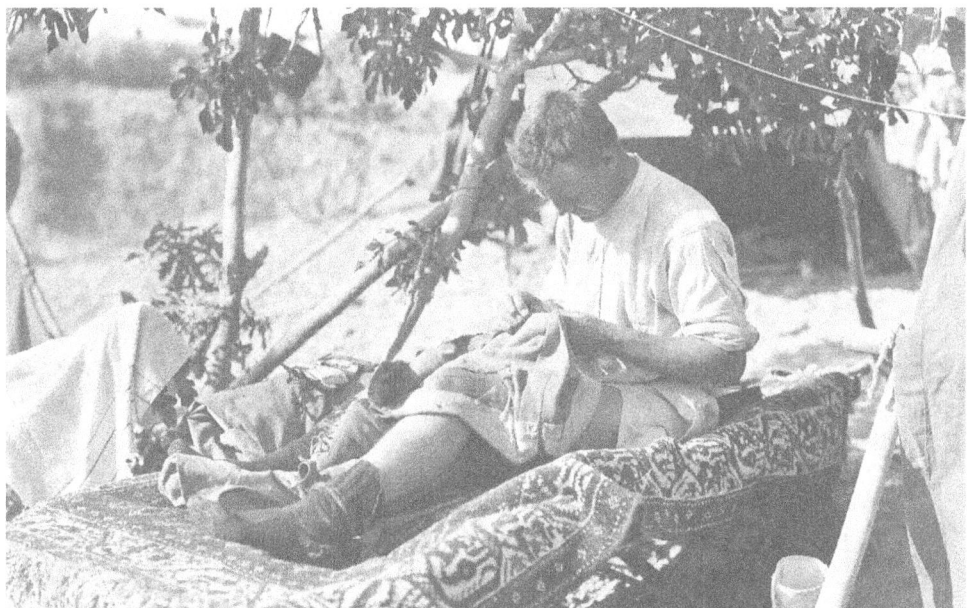

Fig. 115. No caption and unnumbered. This picture of GF Langley appears in the book
Sand, Sweat & Camels with the caption: 'George Furner Langley 1891-1971. Shown here
mending his only breeches at Daman, about six miles from Damascus, in 1918'.
(Courtesy of Falconer collection)

contributed by service personnel, but there were also feature articles and nature
notes. Campbell contributed three substantial feature articles to *Kia Ora Coo-ee*:
'The Pilgrimage to Nebi Musa', illustrated with his own photograph of the tomb;
'The Holy Sepulchre', nearly a complete double page spread illustrated with six
of his own official war photographs, and 'The Walled City', a double page spread
on Jerusalem including a sizable map and a page of six photographs, some his,
others by Frank Hurley, all of them official photographs.[113]

In the 'Walled City' article Campbell described the new, Europeanised
town surrounding the old Eastern City inside the wall, suggesting the visitor
approaching from outside 'with a mental idea of Jerusalem drawn from Sunday
school pictures of the "invincible wall" will more than likely be greatly
disappointed'.[114] The article was accompanied by a beautifully drawn map of Old
Jerusalem created by Campbell, displaying the cartography skills developed in his
schooldays in Seaton. His article on the annual pilgrimage to Nebi Musa (Tomb

---

113 *Kia Ora Coo-ee* , 15 July 1918, p. 15, 15 August 1918, pp. 10-11, and 15 September 1918, pp. 10-11.
114 Ibid., 15 September 1918, p. 11.

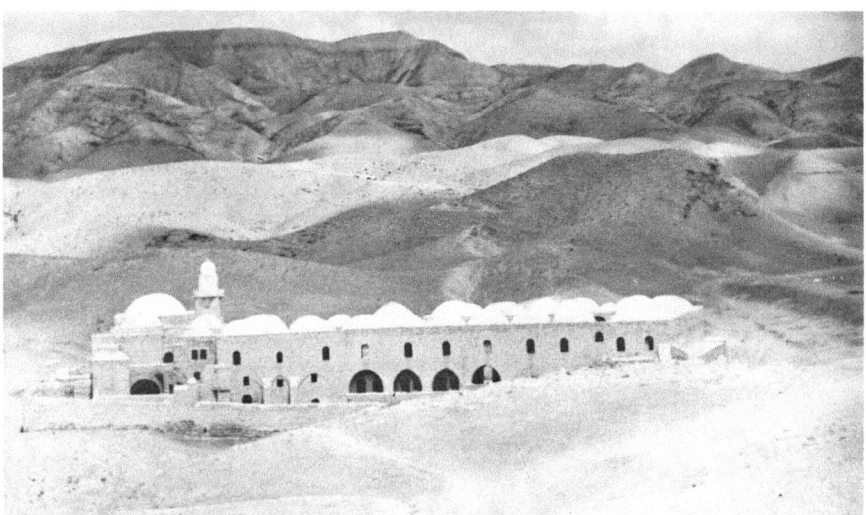

Fig. 116. 'No. 28. Tomb of Moses'. This photograph illustrated Campbell's *Kia Ora Coo-ee* article 'The Pilgrimage to Nebi Musa'.
(Courtesy of Falconer collection, AWM image B00059)

of Moses) by the Moslems of Jerusalem was a piece of descriptive reportage.[115] His postcards to Lilian Pitts were full of descriptions of such events and she, a devoted Methodist, fed off his Holy Land rambles, encouraging his exploits as a soldier-tourist. Campbell used an official photograph he took of Nebi Musa to illustrate his article on the pilgrimage. A strategic advance by the Allies took place in the rugged hills beyond it, an operation in which he and Hurley were involved when they accompanied the 1st Light Horse Brigade in February 1918 (Fig. 116).[116] By using this image to illustrate his article, he showed the soldier readers of the paper an ancient holy building, as well as a strategic battle site they could strongly identify with. According to David Kent the type of feature articles Campbell contributed on 'historical, archaeological and Biblical items', which regularly appeared in the paper, 'provided a backcloth to the events of the war, and they presumably helped the readers in the war zone, and at home, to appreciate the antiquity of the land over which they were fighting'.[117]

---

115 Ibid., 15 July 1918, p. 15.

116 In a postcard to Lilian Pitts dated 17 April 1918 Campbell describes 'Ton nebi Musa (Tomb of Moses) where Muhammedan pilgrims and Dervishes congregate on Good Friday – the other places are Greek Orthodox'. The Australian War Memorial also has a private Campbell photograph (AWM H02998) of this tomb taken from the opposite side to the official picture above. It was donated by Aubrey Campbell and is attributed to JP Campbell, who had visited the tomb on the morning of 17 April 1918.

117 David Kent, *Kia Ora Coo-ee*, p. xi.

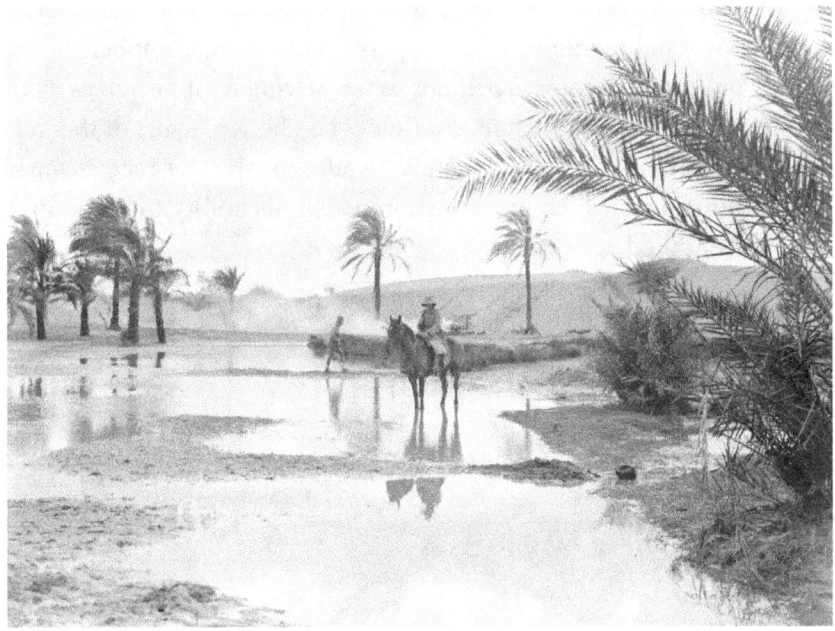

Fig. 117. This is a Hurley photograph developed and printed by JP Campbell, and is
variously titled 'Winter – Mediterranean Coast' or 'A Palestine Pool'
(AWM image BO1610)

The August edition of *Kia Ora Coo-ee* carried a photograph captioned 'A
Palestine Pool' showing a horseman riding through a pool surrounded by palm
trees with his reflection and that of a person on foot behind him clearly visible in
the water (Fig. 117).[118] The image was taken by Hurley and developed and printed
by Campbell, and is a good example of the collaboration between them.[119] If he
indeed was picture editor of *Kia Ora Coo-ee*, as he told Lilian Pitts, Campbell

---

118 *Kia Ora Coo-ee*, 15 August 1918, p. 2.

119 There are three original prints of different subjects with the initials *FH* (Frank Hurley) on them
(on the bottom and inside the picture), but with the initials *JPC* at the end of the caption, held by a
Melbourne photographer and dealer. Presumably these are photographs taken in the first three months of
1918 by Hurley and developed/printed by Campbell. The prints are captioned: 'Ludd (Lydda) Palestine
– *JPC*'; 'Winter – Mediterranean Coast – *JPC*' (the same image as 'A Palestine Pool' described above),
and 'Jerusalem from the South – *JPC*'. Information supplied courtesy of Joyce Evans, 28 October
2004. The Australian War Memorial has copies of all three, with the series numbers as follows (in
same order as listed in the text above): B0174P/P03631.242, B01610 and B01609. There is another
photograph in the Falconer collection attributed to Hurley elsewhere and taken about the same time as
the 'Crusader Tower, Ramleh' (Fig. 96), and the 'Palestine Pool', i.e. late January early February 1918.
This photograph is labelled on the back 'No. 5. Beach Camp, Palestine. 8 LH at Belah' by Campbell.
Another photo, No. 6, with no caption, is clearly of the same camp.

was able to use the position to exhibit a number of his own images. He was, after all, the official war photographer over the paper's life span. Campbell expended a lot of energy on *Kia Ora Coo-ee*, perhaps to the detriment of his job as an official photographer, although it did come at a time when he was short of the materials necessary to perform his duties adequately. In addition, he was recovering slowly from a bout of malaria, which must have impeded his ability to work, given the rigours he had endured.

9

ON THE ROAD TO DAMASCUS

Campbell is Judged in Need of Assistance – The 'Great Ride' to Damascus – Barada Gorge – Demise as Official War Photographer – Back to Australia – Campbell's War Photographs in the Archives

At the end of July 1918 Gullett reported to Treloar, summing up the role of the Australian War Records Section in the Middle East and the task it faced in obtaining records. He estimated there were up to 1000 cameras used by operational Light Horse soldiers, producing 'a wonderful pictorial record', but they were amateur photographers who did not supply the AWRS with prints. Gullett concluded that record gathering was much harder in the Middle East than in France because of the large distances and rough terrain. The men were isolated from civilisation and 'people of their own race'. But, he conceded, 'they fight superbly'.[1]

He was understanding towards Campbell's predicament, stating:

> much can be done if the Official Photographer takes a keen personal interest in the matter, seeks out the men with cameras and visits them regularly. Unfortunately as I have told you Campbell has been some weeks out of action with Malaria. But in any case he is and has been for several weeks clean out of material.[2]

Desperate to get glass plates to Campbell, he suggested that Treloar divide material up into parcels and entrust them to AIF officers going Campbell's way.[3]

In early August Treloar told Gullett that he was 'glad to hear that Campbell is getting on well. We have received some copies of his photographs, and they have been very interesting . . . I will send out to you a complete set of Hurley's photographs. One is rather afraid that a big number are posed and his titles, from a record point of view, are not all they might be'.[4] This was a compliment to

---

1 HS Gullett to J Treloar, 29 July 1918, AWM 25 1013/38A.
2 Ibid.
3 Ibid.
4 J Treloar to HS Gullett, 8 August 1918, AWM 16 4379/5/21.

Campbell, lightly praised in the same paragraph as Hurley was soundly criticised by a person devoted to Bean's philosophy of obtaining genuine records. On 21 August 1918, Sergeant Duncan McPherson was recruited by the Australian War Records Section to help Campbell. McPherson, a master grocer from Canterbury, Victoria, had enlisted in July 1915. In September 1918 he was attached to the Anzac Mounted Division Headquarters near Amman as an Australian War Records Section operative.[5]

But one month after reporting that Campbell had the excuses of illness and lack of supplies for his meagre output, Gullett changed his opinion:

> I am sorry to say that the photographic outlook is not satisfactory. Campbell was not a wise selection. Personally I would not have taken him, but recommended as he was on technical grounds by Hurley and strongly suggested from your end I had I think no option. [He] is too old, being about 50 [in reality he was 53]; he lacks initiative and a sense of live pictures and is not an easy man to handle. However he is an exceedingly good old chap and a sound photographer in a humdrum way. We shall do the best we can. Personally I do not think it is much use loading him with cinema and color plates. The work should be done, and we would be justified I think in making a special appointment for it. There is a very good man indeed, a Sergt. Coulson, at the Flying Squadron. He was my fancy originally but Hurley voted against him.[6]

In his job as Commonwealth photographer in Australia, Campbell had demonstrated an unwillingness to take direction, particularly if he thought their knowledge of photography was poor, or if they behaved in an aggressive manner towards him. Gullett had a reputation as being rather fiery and a difficult person to work with.[7] With similar personalities, the two were likely to clash. Gullett's role in the Middle East had changed. In August he had handed the running of the AWRS in Cairo over to HW Dinning and taken up the appointment of

---

5 NAA: B2455, McPherson D. Good examples of his official war photography are the Australian War Memorial pictures B00090 and B00091. The latter has a coloured version, P01130.003. They were taken on 29 September 1918 near Amman, and show Turkish prisoners captured by the 2nd Australian Light Horse Brigade. McPherson left Egypt for London on 2 August 1919 and appears to have worked in War Records, London, in September 1919. He returned to Australia in November 1919.

6 HS Gullett to J Treloar, 2 September 1918, AWM 16 4379/5/21.

7 AJ Hill, entry for Sir Henry Somer Gullett, *Australian Dictionary of Biography*, Volume 9, 1891-1939, p. 138.

official war correspondent in Egypt.[8] He was also contributing to *Kia Ora Coo-ee*, writing descriptive articles on the progress of the Middle East campaign.

In early September 1918 Dinning advised Treloar that a dark room in Cairo was being arranged for Campbell, adding to 'the somewhat slap-dash place' he was using in Jerusalem. In a submission Campbell had fought for better facilities, saying his current facility in Jerusalem was 'unsuited to delicate and critical work'.[9] On 8 September 1918, only eleven days before the commencement of the 'Great Ride' to Damascus, Campbell scrawled a note to his superiors complaining about stale glass plates, which he regarded as 'fatal to best results', sent from London 'older than what Capt. Hurley brought with him' back in late 1917.[10] Campbell's cries for quality materials often fell on deaf ears.

Allenby decided to advance up the Plain of Sharon in the west rather than persist in going east. He set out to deceive the Turks that he was again going to attack east of the Jordan, but at night he started moving troops west out of the Jordan Valley. To lull the Turks into a false sense of security 15,000 dummy horses were set up in the Jordan Valley to make it look like it was business as usual to enemy spy planes. The air-force dominance by the British helped greatly in keeping the troop movements secret.[11] Chauvel left his Desert Mounted Corps headquarters at Talat ed Dumm on 16 September 1918 and that afternoon opened his new headquarters at Sarona, a few miles north of Jaffa. The offensive up the west coast commenced on 19 September and the drive north by the Allied force was swift, but not so for Campbell, whose participation in the campaign was delayed by poor travel arrangements.[12] He rode some of the way with the 4th Light Horse Brigade, 'a very unsuitable method [of transport] with a heavy whole plate camera outfit'.[13] The driver of his car had gone to hospital before the advance began, and his replacement did not arrive in Jerusalem until after the 'Great Ride' started. He then had to collect a supply of glass plates dropped off

8 HS Gullett to J Treloar, 2 September 1918, AWM 16 4379/5/21.

9 HW Dinning to J Treloar, 5 September 1918, AWM 16 4379/5/4 Pt 1.

10 JP Campbell to Australian War Records Section Headquarters, Cairo, 8 September 1918, AWM 16 4379/5/4 Pt 1.

11 HS Gullett, *The Official History of Australia in the War of 1914-1918*, Volume VII, pp. 682-8.

12 Ibid., p. 688, 692, and Campbell to Commandant, Australian Headquarters, Cairo, 14 November 1918, AWM 16 4375/2/2.

13 JP Campbell to Commandant, Australian Headquarters, Cairo, 14 November 1918, AWM16 4375/2/2.

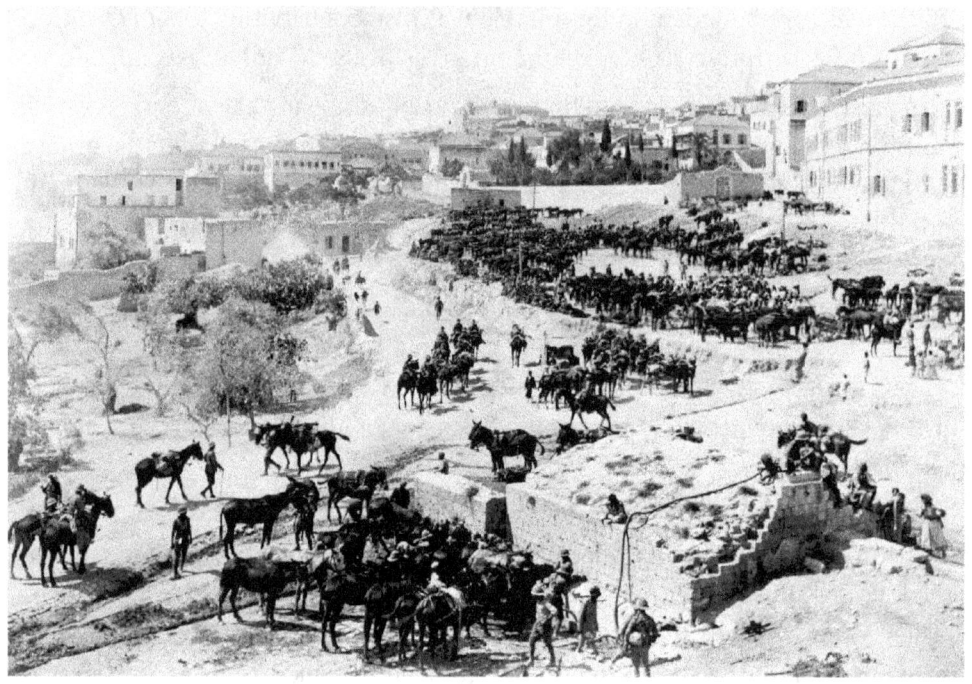

Fig. 118. 'No. 71. Nazareth' (Caption courtesy of Falconer collection, AWM image B00273)

by Dinning, his new boss, in the vicinity of Ludd, but could not find them, and lost valuable time searching.[14] It was a poor start to an important photographic mission for Campbell.

On 20 September Nazareth was captured and Chauvel went on to establish his head quarters at Megiddo (Lejjun) on the southern edge of the Plain of Esdraelon.[15] When Campbell finally caught up to the advancing Allied forces by car, he used all his photography skills to cleverly capture the occupation of Nazareth (Fig. 118), the vastness of the military operation and the spectacular geographical setting, as the Australian Mounted Division assembled at Megiddo (Fig. 119).

At the same time he conformed to the strict Australian War Records Section guidelines of getting 'pictures of movements'. In the Megiddo image the mass of people in the centre of the picture (to the right and at the edge of the billowing dust) are prisoners, remnants of a Turkish Garrison Battalion of El Afule, who

14 Ibid.

15 HS Gullett, *The Official History of Australia in the War of 1914-1918*, Volume VII, pp. 696-7.

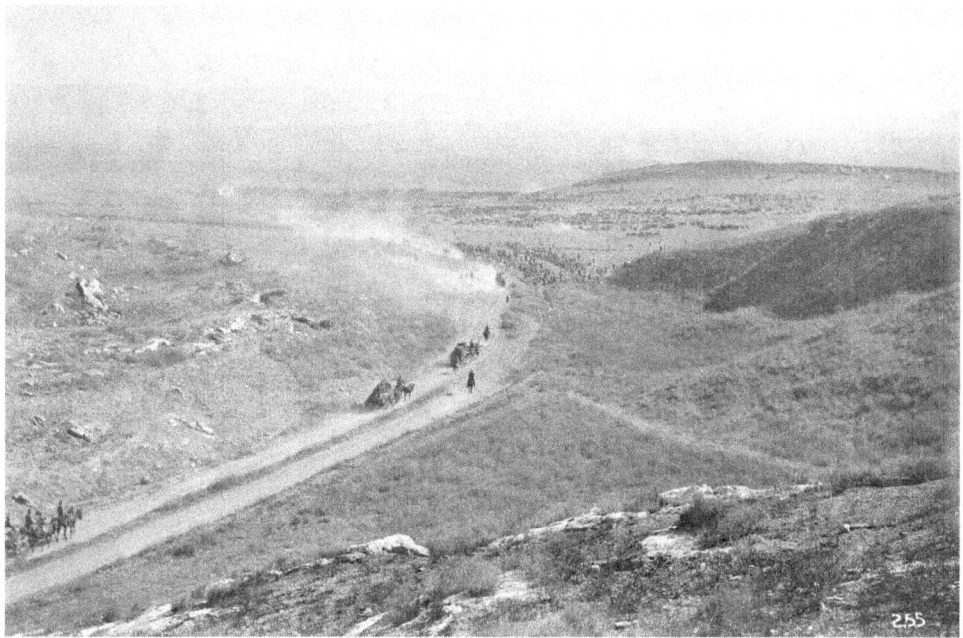

Fig. 119. The Australian Mounted Division assembling at Megiddo. This image displays all the elements Campbell loved: the hills, the plain, the dust, moving wagons, horses and riders, the linear aspect of the road leading the viewer in to the scene, and a good vantage point from which to capture it all.
(AWM image B00255)

were charged on the plain by the 2nd Lancers of the Indian army, and beyond is the Mounted Division assembling. Division supply wagons trundle past Campbell's vantage point.[16] The Turkish forces were quickly demoralised. An infantry force of 10,000 Turks tried to escape up to the road from Samaria to Jenin, a large village standing on a hillside at the south eastern edge of the Esdraelon plain. The 3rd Light Horse Brigade was sent from Megiddo by Chauvel to intercept them, capturing hundreds of prisoners on the way. The 10th and 9th Light Horse blocked the escape of the enemy already in Jenin and faced fierce resistance in the streets (Fig. 120).

A column approaching the town from the south was also captured, and altogether a small number of Light Horsemen managed to bluff their way into holding upwards of 3,000 prisoners in and around Jenin on 20-21 September

---

16 *Australasian*, 23 January 1926 and HS Gullett, *The Official History of Australia in the War of 1914-1918*, Volume VII, p. 695. Sir Harry Chauvel donated a print of this image to the Army and Navy Club, Melbourne, in 1926. The *Australasian* published the picture plus a key to its various features.

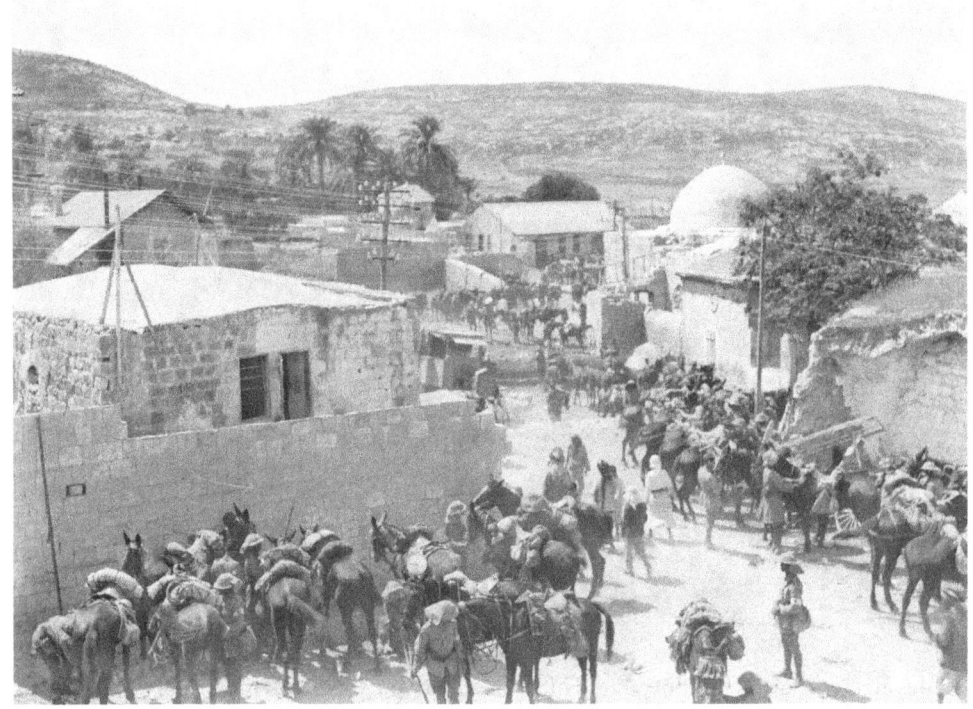

Fig. 120. 'No. 68. Jenin Village. 7000 prisoners [this contradicts the figure below] here ran
into the arms of the 8th L.H.'. (Courtesy of Falconer collection, AWM image B00261)

1918. The Turks set fire to a large dump of ammunition and other material at
the Jenin Railway Station as the Australians arrived on the night of the 20th.[17]
Campbell photographed Arabs sifting through the embers.

The 8th Light Horse marched the prisoners to Megiddo on 21 September.[18]
Again Campbell captured the atmospheric grandeur at Megiddo with a view of
the Light Horsemen riding past a mass of prisoners, everything shrouded in dust
(Fig. 121). These pictures captured all that the Australian War Records Section

17 HS Gullett, *The Official History of Australia in the War of 1914-1918*, Volume VII, pp. 707-8. The
figure of 3000 prisoners in the Official History contradicts Campbell's figure of 7000 in his pencilled
note on the back of the contact print (Fig. 137), which may have been a rough estimate by him and his
superiors at the time.

18 Ibid., pp. 706-9. On 22 September 1918 Campbell took a private photograph (AWM H02981)
of the main street of the town of Jenin, Palestine, the morning after the Australian Light Horse had
captured it. It is attributed to him, the donor being 'J. Campbell'. An AustralianWar Memorial official
photo (B00259) of the Light Horse on the outskirts of Jenin the morning after it was captured (22
September 1918) is attributed to an 'unknown' photographer, when clearly it must have been Campbell,
as McPherson was east of the Jordan (see Dinning to Treloar below, 11 October 1918).

wanted: a vanquished enemy, the victors strutting majestically on their horses, the bushman-soldier in a rugged, dry environment, riding forward towards further glory, swathed mystically in dust. It was a record, it was propaganda. It expanded the Anzac legend created on Gallipoli at places like the Nek, where the Australian Light Horse regiments had fought valiantly without their horses.[19] And it satisfied Campbell's artistic nature.

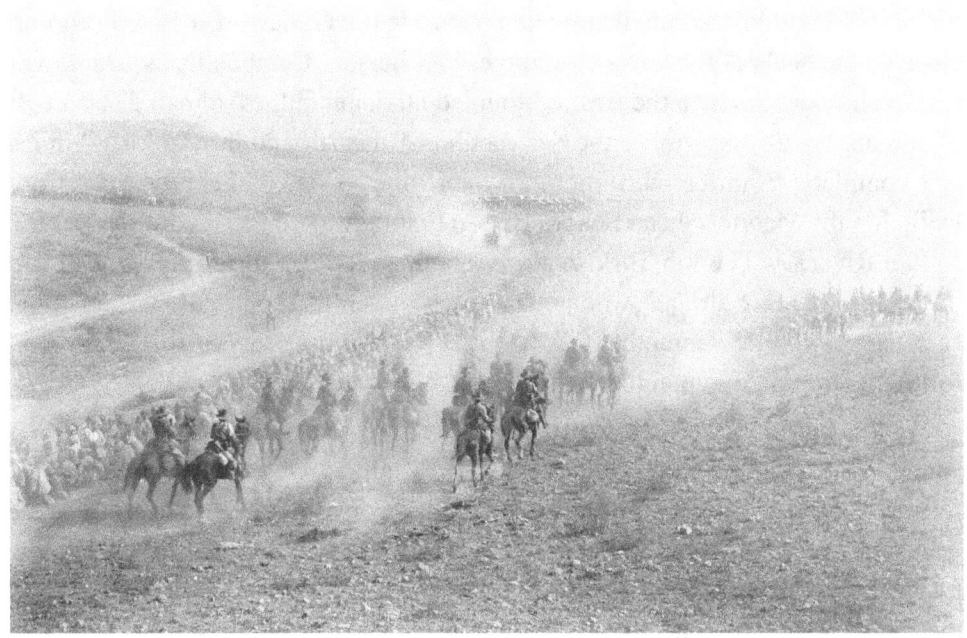

Fig. 121. 'No. 65. Prisoners waiting in the dust at Desert Corps H.Q. [Megiddo]', 22 September 1918. (Courtesy of Falconer collection, AWM image B00256)

When Campbell caught up to the advancing Light Horse at Megiddo he found Gullett there, and Dinning had arrived the next day. Much to his dismay Campbell found his fragile plates on a 4th Brigade packhorse. To make things worse Dinning took Campbell's car, with the disgruntled Campbell instructed to share Gullett's.[20] Dinning had good reasons for putting Campbell and Gullett together on such an important mission as the drive to Damascus. He was following official Australian War Records Section instructions on who official

19 Joan Beaumont, 'Australia's War, 1914-18', pp. 1-34, in Joan Beaumont (ed.), *Australia's War, 1914-18*, Allen & Unwin, St Leonards, NSW, 1995, p. 27.
20 JP Campbell to Commandant, Australian Headquarters, Cairo, 14 November 1918, AWM 16 4375/2/2.

photographers should be responsible to in the field.[21] The official correspondent, Gullett, was to be in charge, advising the official photographer, Campbell, on what subjects to photograph, as the correspondent had to be on the scene quickly after the Light Horse captured a town. Thus the official photographer should get 'almost a first look at everything new', if he accompanied the correspondent.[22] This was good in theory, but did not take into account the personalities of the two men.

From Megiddo Campbell travelled with Henry Gullett in a Box Ford car, close on the heels of the advancing force. McPherson, Campbell's assistant, was taking photographs with the Anzac Mounted Division in the Amman district east of Jordan. By 24 September the destruction of the 7th and 8th Turkish Armies was complete; from the morning of 23 September 'Chauvel held the plain from Haifa [on the Mediterranean Sea] to Beisan [a long way to the south east near the Jordan River]'.[23] The 4th Turkish Army commander east of the Jordan decided to fall back to Es Salt and Amman, and then march to Damascus.[24] The British seized Es Salt on 22 September for the third time, this time successfully.[25] Amman followed suit on 25 September, captured by Chaytor's forces.[26]

At the time these towns were being taken, to the north at Semakh on the southern end of the Sea of Galilee, the 11th Light Horse was fighting amongst railway carriages and buildings, losing men and horses before they overcame the Turks and took the village.[27] Campbell took a photograph of the graves of fallen Light Horsemen after this action at Semakh.[28]. Gullett could not help but compare the Light Horse regiments to the Crusaders of 700 years earlier, writing that:

> no sworn and fiery Crusader of old carried a more terrible sword against
> the foe, and none rode nearer to the Christian precept to do justice, love

21 'Notes in connection with War Record work in Egypt and Palestine 1917-18', AWM 25 1013/36. On a chart regarding the 'Distribution of Duties in the Australian War Records Section', in the 'No 3 Photographic Sub Section', it read the 'Official Photographers will, as regards their work be under the Official Correspondent'.

22 HW Dinning to J Treloar, 'Weekly Report 2', 4 October 1918, AWM 16 4379/5/4 Pt 1.

23 HS Gullett, *The Official History of Australia in the War of 1914-1918*, Volume VII, pp. 711-12.

24 Ibid., p. 713.

25 Ibid., p. 719.

26 Ibid., p. 722.

27 Ibid., pp. 730-3. See Falconer collection photograph number 79 and Australian War Memorial official photograph B00288.

28 Photograph 'No. 79. 11th Cemetery at Semakh south shore Sea of Galilee' in the Falconer collection.

mercy, and walk humbly before his God than these seemingly careless young light horsemen.[29]

Tiberias, on the western shore of the Sea of Galilee, fell to these 'careless young light horsemen' on 25 September 1918.[30] Campbell created some memorable images here, including a panorama of a long column of the Light Horse travelling along the shore, part of which is shown in Fig.122, and signallers from his beloved 8th Light Horse on a pier at Tiberias (Fig 123). This was the sort of small group portraiture he enjoyed, rather than the wooden line up of subjects looking at the camera with a bland backdrop.

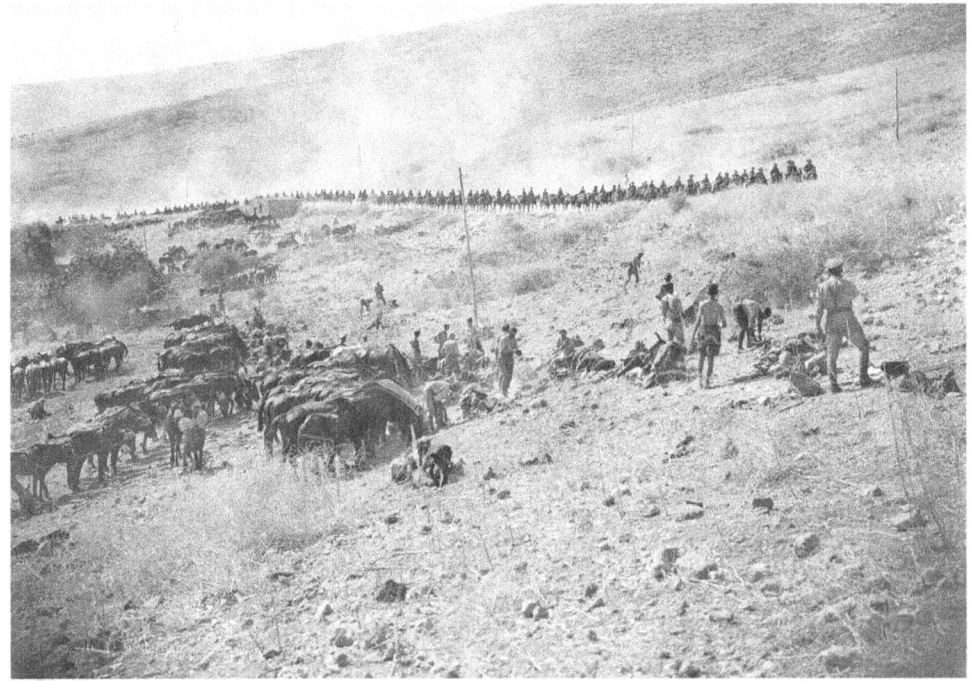

Fig. 122. 'No 82 (B). 3rd L.H. Bde on march from Tiberias to Damascus along shore road of Sea of Galilee. Indian Mounted Cavalry resting for breakfast'. Part of a panorama. (Courtesy of Falconer collection, AWM image B00281B)

Campbell and Gullett drove to Haifa on the coast of the Mediterranean Sea, where the front part of Campbell's camera fell off when he attached a heavy lens. The camera's woodwork was already warped by the Jordan Valley heat, and Campbell blamed Gullett for its further deterioration, saying he 'had no respect

29 Ibid., p. 735.
30 Ibid., p. 736.

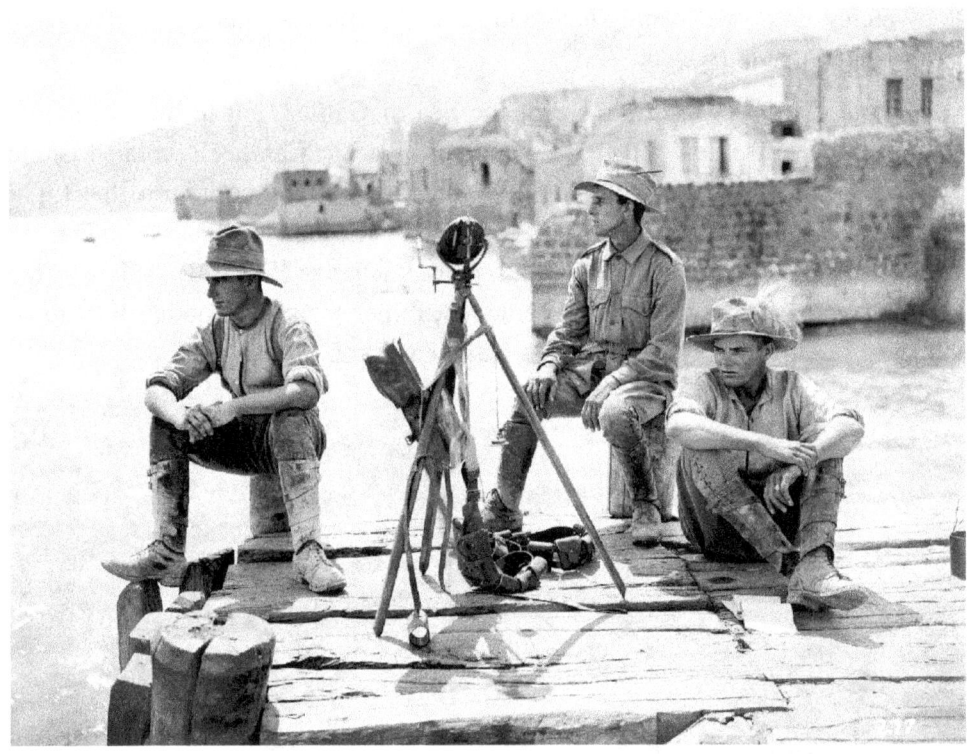

Fig. 123. 'No. 80. 8th L.H. Signallers on wharf at Tiberius – Sea of Galilee'.
(Courtesy of Falconer collection, AWM image B00277)

for camera or glass when motoring over rough country'.[31] According to Ian Affleck, former curator of photography at the Australian War Memorial, Campbell would have been using a Thornton Pickard glass plate camera. It was made out of a light wood; the glass plates and the tripod were heavier than the camera itself. Campbell claimed there were limited opportunities to take photographs when they were on the road, dependent as he was on Gullett deciding to linger in the one place or move on. He was often limited to taking 'roadside scenes', as fighting usually took place at night at a distance from the car.[32]

Commanders Allenby, Chauvel, Chetwode and Bulfin met in conference at Jenin, and Allenby, unsurprisingly, announced his intention to advance to Damascus.[33] On 27 September the Australian Mounted Division *en route* to Damascus headed for the ancient stone bridge at Benat Yakub (the Bridge of

31 JP Campbell to Commandant, Australian HQ's, Cairo 14 November 1918.
32 Ibid.
33 HS Gullett, *The Official History*, Volume VII, pp. 738.

Jacob's Daughters) across the Jordan between the Sea of Galilee and Lake Huleh, finding it partly destroyed by the retreating Turks as they fled northwards.[34] As the Allies gained control, the bridge was quickly repaired by engineers, allowing support traffic to cross the river. Campbell was there, with Gullett in the Box Ford, photographing the repair work (Fig. 124).[35]

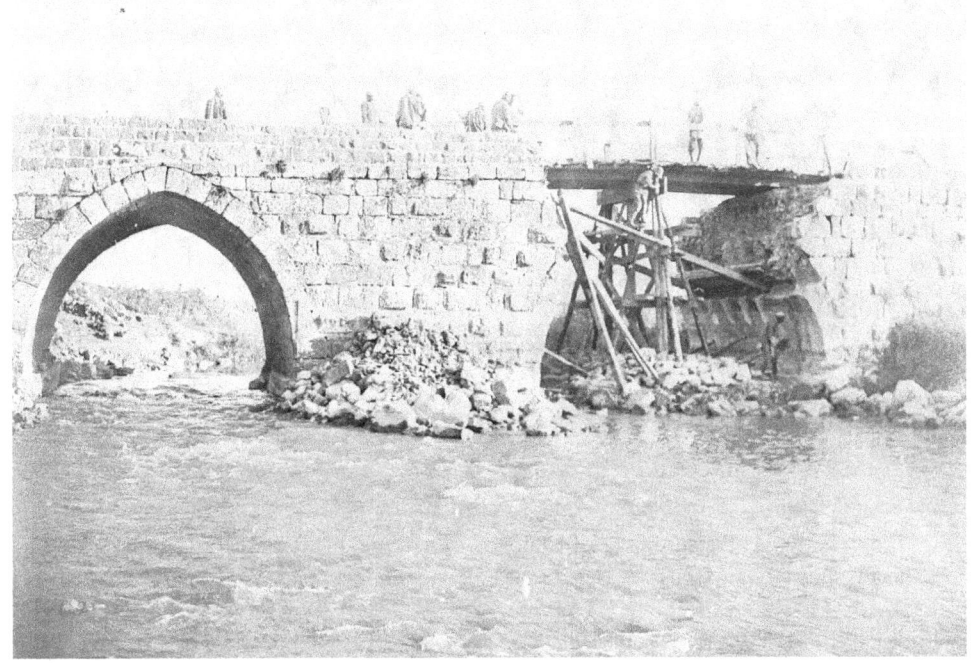

Fig. 124. 'No. 93. Traffic went over the bridge 4 hours after commencement of repairs'.
(Courtesy of Falconer collection, AWM image B00296)

Members of the 3rd Light Horse Brigade on the road to Damascus entered and claimed the Circassian town of Kuneitra, 'a hungry little bluestone village on the edge of the Hauran' on 28 September (Fig. 125).[36] Further south, remnants of the Turkish army were struggling north from Deraa, harassed by TE Lawrence ('Lawrence of Arabia') and the Arabs, and the British Air Force.[37]

After breaking through resistance at Sasa, the 10th Light Horse took the

---

34 Ibid., pp. 740-3.
35 See Falconer collection photographs No. 92, 93, & 93A, and Australian War Memorial Official Photographs B00295, B00296 & B00297.
36 HS Gullett, *The Official History*, Volume VII, pp. 743-4. See also Falconer collection photograph Number 94, and Australian War Memorial official photograph B00300.
37 Ibid., p. 744.

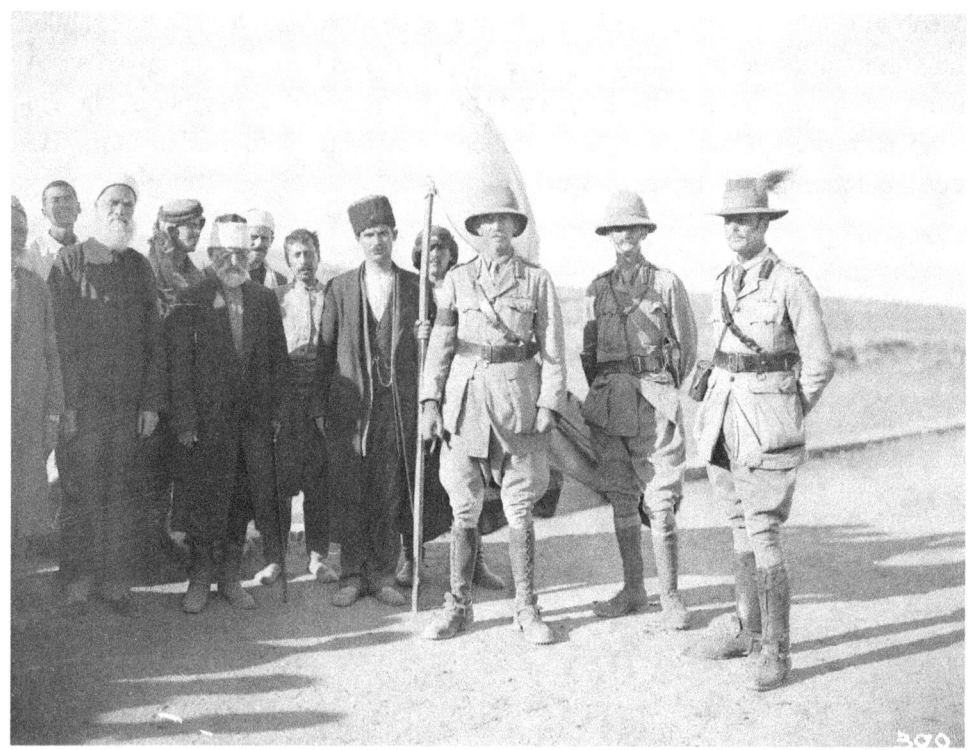

Fig. 125. 'No. 94. At the surrender of Kuneitra – First village after crossing Jordan [during the advance to Damascus]'.(Courtesy of Falconer collection, AWM image B00300)

lead and fanned out across the plain leading to Damascus.[38] The Turks dug in at Kaukab, but the 4th and 12th Light Horse charged their position, swords drawn. The Turks and Germans, terrified by the oncoming horsemen and the French on their right flank, fled towards Damascus.[39] Campbell and Gullett were at times at the edge of such skirmishes as the Allies pushed towards their final goal; the enthusiastic Campbell 'was a number of times under fire' as he strove to take photographs.[40]

Four major roads led out of Damascus, one along the Barada Gorge westwards through the hills and plains to coast at Beirut. The role of Chauvel's Australian Mounted Division was to isolate Damascus by capturing Barada Gorge and the northern route to Homs. Wilson's 3rd Light Horse Brigade was ordered to cross the Barada Gorge and cross the foothills north-west of Damascus and block the

38 Ibid., p. 746.
39 Ibid., pp. 748-9.
40 HS Gullett to Lt Col Fulton, 29 October 1918, AWM 25 1013/38A.

road at Homs.[41] They reached the gorge and on 30 September were positioned one mile south-west of Duma high above its roaring waters. Not more than one hundred yards in width, the gorge contained the snaking, roaring Barada River with a road and railway crammed beside it. When the Light Horsemen looked down they saw the gorge packed to capacity with a massive column of confused enemy troops, railway trains and horse drawn vehicles fleeing from Damascus towards them, attempting to escape out of the hills to the Baalbek plain and the road to Beirut. Onslow's brigade was in a similar dominating position further west.[42] The German machine gunners refused to surrender 'and all along the gorge the unequal issue was joined. The result was sheer slaughter. The Light Horsemen, firing with fearful accuracy, shot the column to a standstill and then to silence'.[43] George Auchterlonie of the 8th Light Horse wrote in his diary:

> Our MG's [machine guns] had done deadly work & there was dead & dying Turks & Germans, horses, mules, sheep everywhere & there were wagons, carts, motor lorries, limbers, guns, MG's & heavens knows what not, littered for at least two miles, at places so thick we could hardly get along the road. It was an awful sight.[44]

Campbell and Gullett arrived in Damascus close on the heels of the Light Horse, and Campbell created two remarkable and contrasting images of the aftermath of the Barada Gorge incident, one a scene of the residue after the carnage in the gorge, with a Light Horseman posing, stationary on his horse, facing the camera (Fig. 126). There is a dinner plate in the foreground, possibly placed there by Campbell for effect like some bizarre symbol of domesticity. The other is a peaceful scene in a quiet village street nearby with a woman and child strolling along and a Light Horseman washing his sleek horse in the foreground (Fig. 127).[45] It is as if Campbell needed to seek out some form of normality

---

41 HS Gullett, *The Official History*, Volume VII, p. 752.

42 Ibid., pp. 753-4.

43 Ibid., p. 754.

44 Gloria Auchterlonie (ed.), *'Dad's War Stuff' – The Diaries: The Complete Personal Diary Entries and Selected Photographs of George Auchterlonie, an Australian Lighthorseman, who served in the 8th Lighthorse Regiment in Egypt, Sinai and Palestine during World War 1*, Advance Morwell Inc. and Gloria Auchterlonie, Morwell, 2001, diary entry for 1 October 1918, p. 88.

45 By including the Light Horseman and his mount, Campbell was conforming to Australian War Records Section instructions. In another photograph of the debris in Barada Gorge a Light Horseman is riding laconically past the abandoned wagons, away from the camera. Clothes can be seen scattered on the ground.

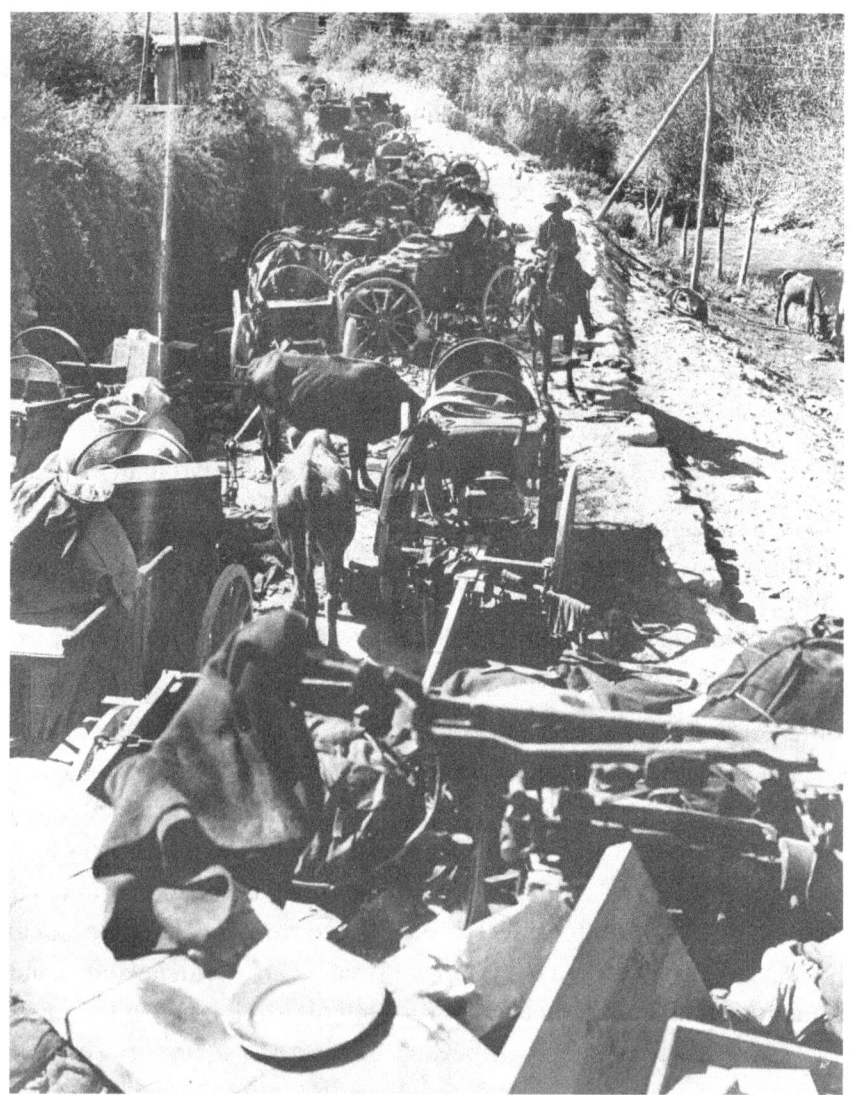

Fig. 126. 'No. 129 Barada Gorge – morning after capture'.
(Courtesy of Falconer collection, AWM image B00331)

after viewing the aftermath of the one-sided Barada Gorge engagement. It also illustrates his tendency to take photographs of more artistic value, something Gullett, the pragmatic newspaper man, would have frowned upon.

By the night of 30 September 1918 Turkish rule had virtually ceased in Damascus.[46] There has always been controversy as to who was the first into the

46 HS Gullett, *The Official History*, Volume VII, p. 758.

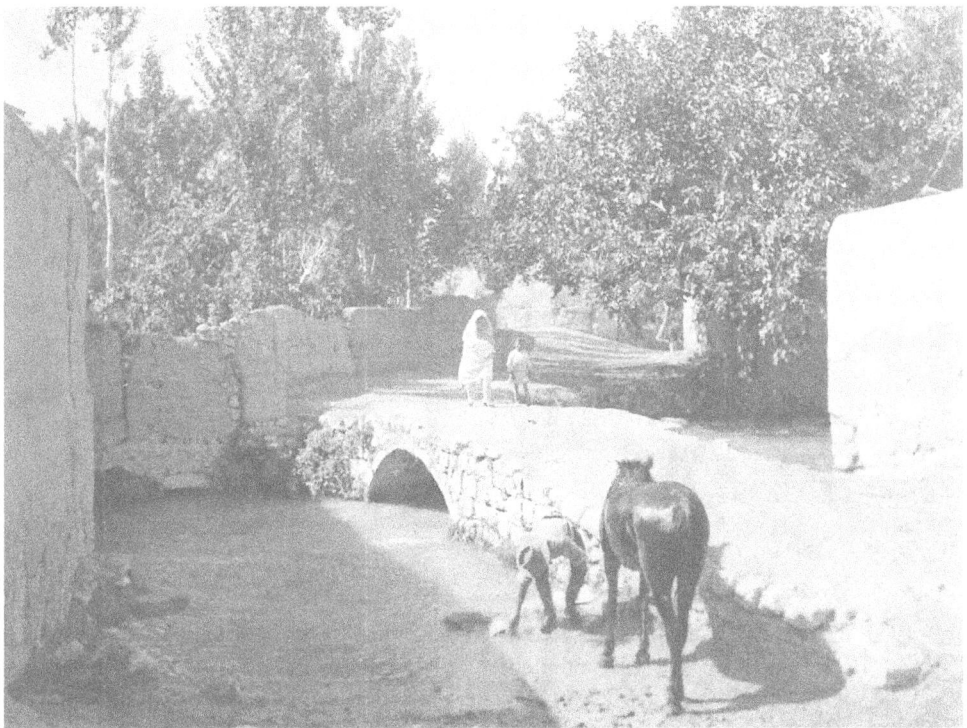

Fig. 127. 'No. 136. A Damascus Lane. (Dumar). Barada Gorge'.
(Courtesy of Falconer collection)

ancient city, the Allied troops or the Arabs. Historian Roland Perry argues strongly that it was members of the 10th Light Horse under Lieutenant Colonel Olden on 1 October, who, by taking a short cut from the Barada Gorge to the Homs Road north of Damascus, were the first into the heart of the city. They entered the town hall and in effect took formal control of the city from the officials present.[47] They

47 Ibid., pp. 759-61, Roland Perry, *The Australian Light Horse*, Hachette Australia, 2009, pp. 461-7, and Brigadier General LC Wilson, 3rd Light Horse Brigade, AIF, *Narrative of Operations of Third Light Horse Brigade (Including the Egyptian Rebellion 1919) from 27 October 1917 to 11 July 1919*, facsimile from the original, Naval and Military Press Ltd., East Sussex, & Imperial War Museum, London, date unknown, pp. 46-7. Perry explains the power play between Chauvel and TE Lawrence. The latter, argues Perry, was in essence an advocate for Arab interests in a tense situation, where the British and French were dividing up the Middle East. Lawrence claimed the Arabs were the first of the conquering force to arrive in Damascus, and it was advantageous for the British government for this to be perceived as such (Perry, p. 477). As the official correspondent, Gullett was asked to give the Arabs as much credit as possible, to soften them up for what was to come, the carve up of the Middle East by Britain and France. Gullett wrote an article saying the Australians (the 10th Light Horse) were the first into Damascus, but the censor altered it to read "first British troops", presumably after the Arabs (Perry, pp. 478-9).

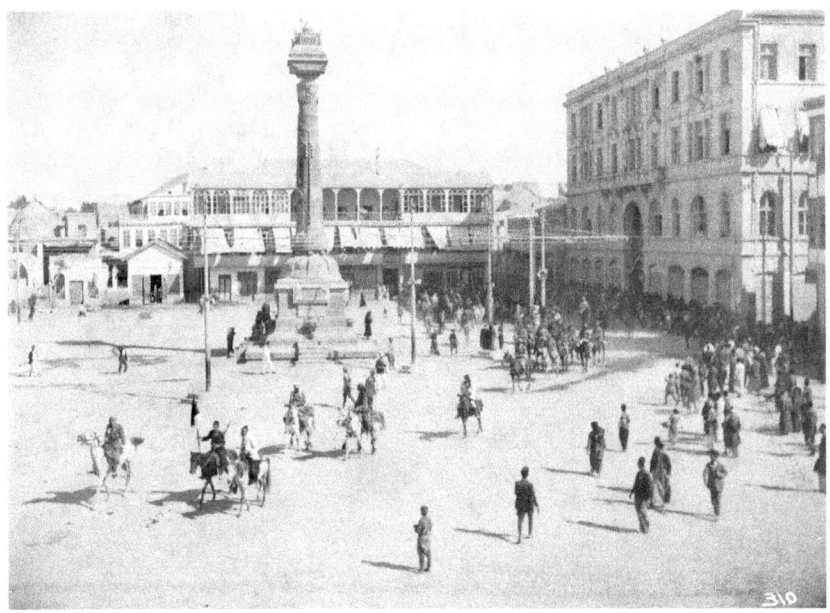

Fig. 128. Unnumbered. 'The Hedjaz party heading the triumphant entry into Damascus'. One of a series of images Campbell took of Chauvel's parade on 2 October 1918. (Courtesy of Falconer collection, AWM image B00310)

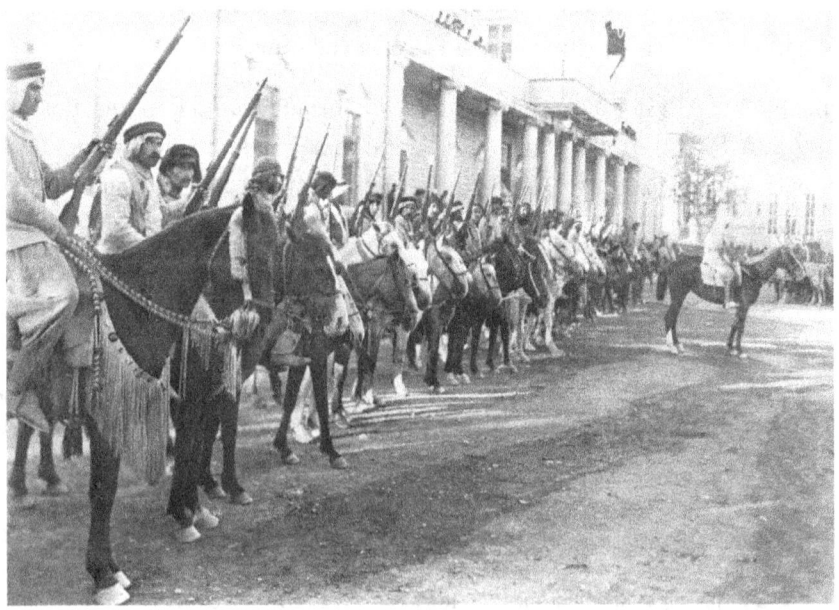

Fig. 129. 'No. 116. Hedjas Cavalry, Damascus, on occasion of visit of Gen. Allenby'. (Courtesy of Falconer collection, AWM image B00320)

then, along with the rest of the 3rd Light Horse Brigade, pursued the Turks north-east of Damascus, past Duma.

On 2 October the last Light Horse engagement in the campaign took place near Khan Ayash north-east of Damascus when the 9th Light Horse captured a large column of Turkish and German troops. The British handed over administration of Damascus to the Arabs on 2 October 1918. On the same day Chauvel marched through the streets as a show of strength, escorted by a squadron of Light Horsemen and representatives of three cavalry divisions, with Arabs at the head of the parade at the behest of TE Lawrence. The city, according to Gullett, was 'awed into silence' (Fig.128).[48] Campbell captured some of the grandeur of Damascus, a strung out parade, and a somewhat sparse crowd. His photographs became part of the illusion that the Arabs were being given the power they had fought for when they became allies of the British against their Turkish oppressors.

Allenby reached Damascus by motor car on 3 October 1918 and summoned the Arab leader Emir Feisal to the Hotel Victoria, informing him that the French were taking Syria as their protectorate, much to Feisal's amazement and Lawrence's disgust (Fig. 129). Feisal was to be Syria's administrator.[49] The Allies, and in particular the Australian Light Horse, argues Roland Perry, had evicted the Turks from the Middle East, and now it was being carved up under predetermined political agreements.[50] The final push to achieve this victory had not been costly as far as battle casualties were concerned. During the 'Great Ride', from 19 September to 2 October 1918, the Australian Mounted Division lost twenty-one killed and seventy-one wounded, and they took 31,335 prisoners. The other Allied Divisions had even less casualties.[51] The troops enjoyed the

---

48 HS Gullett, *The Official History*, Volume VII, pp. 764-70, and Roland Perry, *The Australian Light Horse*, p. 479.

49 Roland Perry, *The Australian Light Horse*, p. 481. Lawrence had led Feisal to believe that the Arabs would take over power in the Middle East. Campbell had photographed the leader of the Arab revolt against the Turks and collaborator with TE Lawrence, Emir Feisal (or Faisal, 1885-1933), at the Dead Sea Post of the Allies when he was in the Jordan Valley (AWM B00056). Feisal became the first King of the British mandated territory of Iraq in 1921. David Stevenson, *1914-1918*, p.436, pp. 526-7.

50 In the last chapter of *The Australian Light Horse*, titled 'Light Horse Legacy', Roland Perry writes: 'General Sir Harry Chauvel and his 34,000 horsemen . . . had the biggest impact on the defeat of the Ottoman Empire in the Middle East War 1914-18', p. 500. However, despite the important role of the Light Horse in the achievements of the Allies, there is doubt their victory in the Palestine campaign forced the Turks to seek an armistice. Rather, Germany's defeats on the Western Front and the fall of Bulgaria in September 1918 were more telling factors in bringing the Turks to the table. David Stevenson, *1914-1918*, pp. 437-8.

51 HS Gullett, *The Official History*, Volume VII, p. 772.

fecundity of Damascus after the bare plains. However, disease (mainly malaria and influenza) swept through the Allied troops and Turkish and German prisoners alike (Fig. 130 & Fig. 131). Many of the Australian soldiers survived

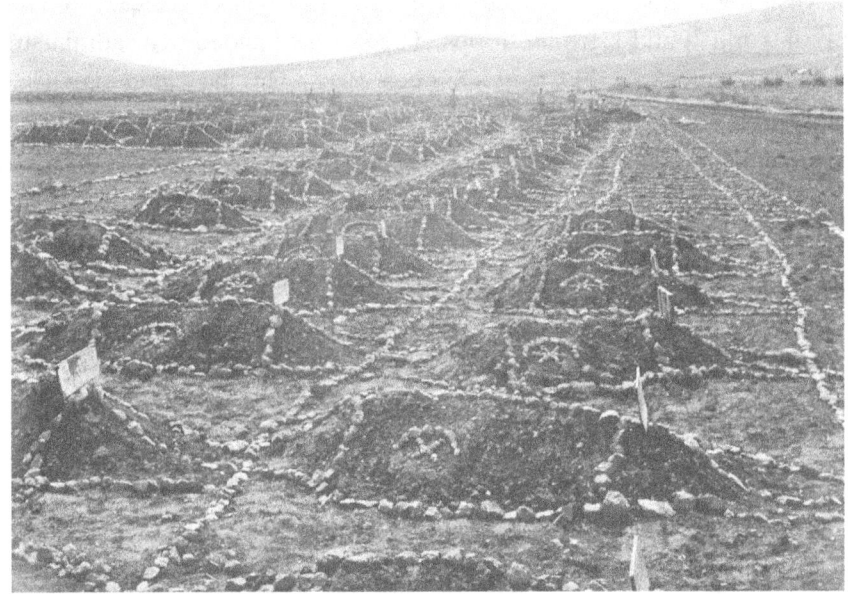

Fig. 130. 'No. 106. Enemy graves – 125 a day died at first – previously been Starved and with exhaustion and no medicine peggout quickly'.
(Courtesy of Falconer collection)

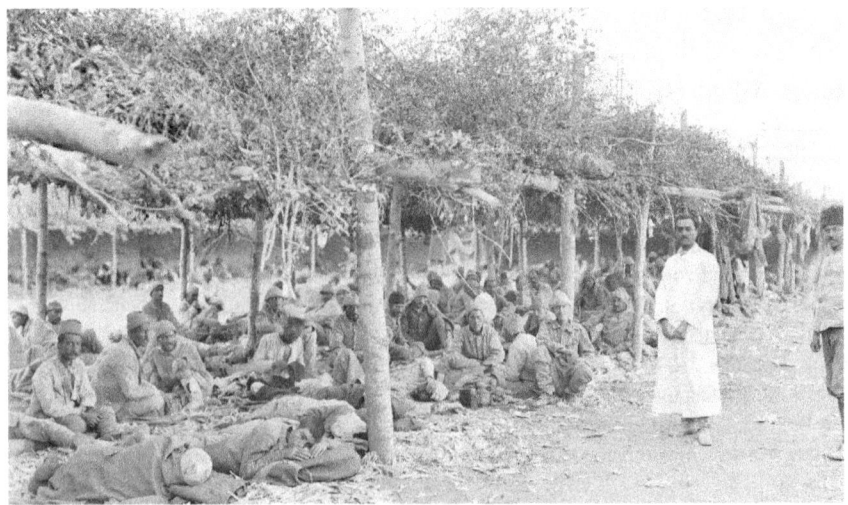

Fig. 131. 'No. 108. Part of the hospital arranged by the victors and in a short time deaths were nil'. (Courtesy of Falconer collection, AWM image B00364)

Gallipoli to finally reach Damascus and victory, only to die of disease in miserable squalor.[52]

Campbell was taking photographs, but the logistics of processing them was causing concern. As the days wore on, Dinning, writing on 11 October, lamented that he was yet to see photographs taken by Campbell since the push to Damascus began up the west coast.[53] He was, however, buoyed by a report from Gullett that Campbell had 'been able to get a very good lot of pictures'.[54] On reaching Damascus Campbell had organised for the plates to be developed at a local shop, having realised the urgent need to dispatch prints for publicity purposes. He then drove to the dark room in Jerusalem to do further work. Some of the glass plates were cracked and others spoiled from light penetrating into the damaged camera during the hectic push north. He eventually submitted a number of photographs to the censor at General Headquarters in Cairo. Campbell was happy with these, and equally pleased that they were despatched before any material produced by British official photographers. McPherson, Campbell's assistant, continued the darkroom work in Jerusalem and Campbell returned to Damascus.[55] The prints produced for record and publicity purposes, were sent to London, Cairo and Melbourne. Wherever possible the official correspondent, Gullett, wrote the captions, presumably from notes written about each image by Campbell and from his own perceptions of the subject. They were required to contain the words 'Australian' and, where possible 'Australian Light Horse'.[56] All this took time and contributed to delays in getting images to newspapers hungry for news.

As the campaign in Palestine and Syria drew to a climax Campbell was under great pressure from his superiors in the AWRS to produce quality images. In October he sent Lilian Pitts a postcard from Damascus wishing her:

> a Peace Xmas and consequent happier New Year. Hope to get to Cairo in a couple of weeks and send along a story of my tour – not possible to do these days. The scenery in Syria is "speechless" so are all the things I've

52 Ibid., pp. 771-4.

53 HW Dinning to J Treloar, 'Weekly Report 3', 11 October 1918, AWM 16 4379/5/4 Pt 1.

54 HW Dinning to J Treloar, 'Weekly Report 2', 4 October 1918, AWM 16 4379/5/4 Pt 1.

55 In early October 1918 Campbell 'rushed through [the censor] in post haste . . . 2 prints each of 16 subjects of the late push to Damascus' (along with a hand written description of each image dated 9 October 1918) to the Australian War Records Section office in London. JP Campbell to Australian War Records Section, London, AWM 16 4375/12/2. Also, JP Campbell to Commandant, Australian Headquarters, Cairo, 14 November 1918, AWM 16 4375/2/2.

56 HW Dinning, 'Instructions for Official Photographer, A.I.F. in Egypt', AWM 16 4379/5/4 Pt 1.

seen, and hope to see, and wont know where to commence a story or how to aptly describe. All that is best I wish you.[57]

There was little time to play the soldier-tourist, and there was bad news on the way. Gullett received notice from Lieutenant Colonel D Fulton of Australian Head Quarters in Cairo on the poor quality of many of the prints Campbell had produced, images that were intended to show the triumphant Light Horse finally achieving victory. In reply, Gullett agreed that the prints were inferior, conceding that the fault may have been either due to the camera or the developing process. But he criticised Campbell's photography, stating 'that the pictures even if clear are not of a kind which make much appeal to newspapers or be useful for exhibition or record purposes'.[58] Finally, unfortunately for Campbell, Gullett made a recommendation:

> To the extent that I am responsible for photographs of the A.I.F. here, I regret that I do not think Lieut. Campbell's work does the force justice and recommend that unless he can show that the indifferent work has been due to some circumstance for which he was not responsible, his services as Official Photographer should be discontinued with.[59]

Meanwhile, Campbell continued to record the war as the Allies pushed on north to Aleppo in pursuit of the rest of the Turkish army. Campbell photographed his former regiment strung out across the plains north of Damascus (Fig. 132). Chauvel waited at Aleppo with the 5th Cavalry Division for the Australian Mounted Division to come up from Damascus, but in the meantime the Turks signed an armistice on 30 October, and the exhausted troops, depleted by illness, were out of the war, their elation dampened by rampant disease.[60]

Gullett's perception of Campbell as an incompetent war photographer prevailed – his recommendation that he be removed from his position was accepted. Lt Col Newton, Commandant, Australian Head-Quarters, Egypt, delivered the blow in writing, to what now must have been a very depressed Campbell: 'It has been decided that you should for a time confine yourself to dark room work in Cairo',

---

57 Postcard, JP Campbell to LL Pitts, 22 October 1918. Whether he ever told Lilian Pitts the full story of his involvement in the 'Great Ride' to Damascus is not known.

58 HS Gullett to Lt Col D Fulton, Commanding, Australian Headquarters, Cairo, 29 October 1918, AWM 25 1013/38A.

59 Ibid.

60 HS Gullett, *The Official History of Australia in the War of 1914-1918*, Volume VII, p. 511.

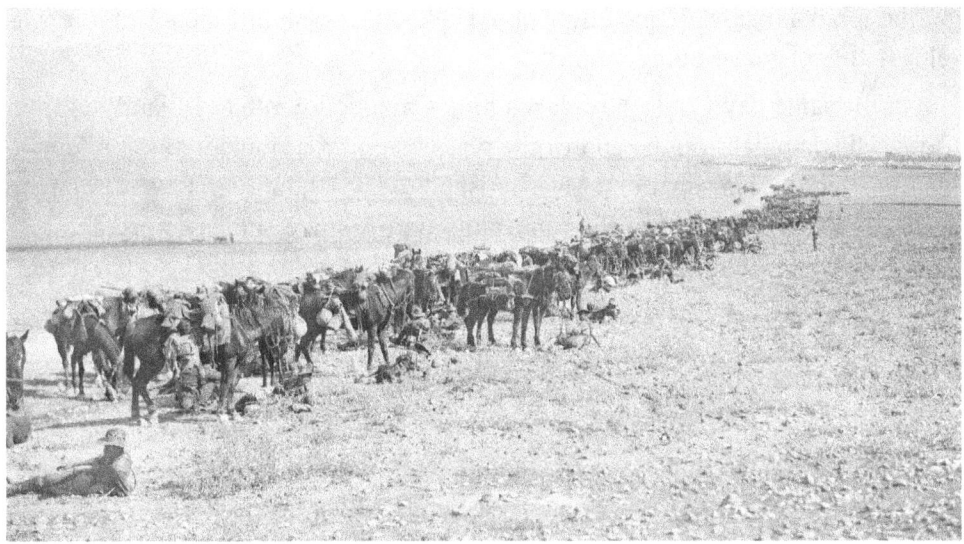

Fig. 132. 'No 147. 8th LH Smokeho – approaching Kuteife, Homs Road [north of Damascus]'.
(Courtesy of Falconer collection, AWM image B00342)

despite the fact the AWRS did not have a dark room in Cairo. He was to establish one immediately.[61] Newton also demanded Campbell hand over prints of the photographs he had taken with his own 'small post-card camera' when he was official photographer, claiming the negatives were the property of the Australian War Records Section.[62]

On 11 November 1918, Armistice Day, Oswald H Coulson, a lithograph artist and photographer in civilian life, was promoted to Honorary Lieutenant and appointed official war photographer in Campbell's place.[63] Authorities were keen to establish a 'good' photographic record before Australian troops disembarked for London and back home. Campbell was considered too much of a ditherer to

---

61 Lt. Col. Newton to JP Campbell, 9 November 1918, AWM 25 1013/38A. Campbell established the darkroom before he departed for Australia in mid January 1919. Australian War Records Section, Cairo, Circular Memorandum No. 37 'Sale of Official Photographs', 11 January 1919, AWM 25 1013/37.
62 Lt. Col. Newton to JP Campbell, 9 November 1918, AWM 25 1013/38A.
63 NAA: B2455, Coulson OH. Coulson enlisted on the 1 April 1916 and on 25 August 1916 was reporting for duty at Heliopolis as a photographer with the Australian Flying Corps. On 1 September 1917 he became a corporal and a 1st Class Air Mechanic. He was promoted to Flight Sergeant on 13 March 1918. Gullett had tried to induce Sergeant Coulson to take up the official photography work as temporary assistant with his existing rank, on loan to the Australian War Records Section, but Coulson was happy where he was. Gullett had then recruited McPherson, although, as pointed out above, Campbell claims credit for finding the Warrant Officer.

get the job done quickly and efficiently. He kept his rank of Lieutenant, but was relegated to the developing room.[64]

On the same day Coulson replaced him, Campbell wrote to Lilian Pitts from Cairo. His comment on the end of the war is somewhat muted, possibly due to his treatment by his superiors: 'War finished today – hooray'. He was happy to be back in Cairo and out of the 'unhealthy parts' where soldiers were dying of disease. He had left Damascus on 31 October 1918, the day Turkey surrendered.[65] Whether he told Lilian of his fall from grace is not known.

Gullett set out his case against Campbell in a letter to Treloar. He believed Campbell was slow, showed little initiative and produced poor images. Ill health, age and temperament contributed to this, making him unsuitable for the position. He judged the hapless photographer's work overall as disappointing, but particularly so during the advance to Damascus, where it exceeded his 'worst anticipations', although he agreed that Campbell was 'handicapped' by malaria and the lack of glass plates.[66] He thought Campbell had every opportunity to perform 'wonderful work', but let everybody down. Gullett claimed he obtained the services of Warrant Officer McPherson from another unit, who obtained excellent pictures working with a half-plate camera while attached to the Anzac Mounted Division.[67] He supported the decision to replace Campbell with Coulson, stating that if a choice had to be made between Coulson's and Campbell's commission, 'the latter must be the one to go'.[68]

Campbell did not go without a fight. He set out his defence in a long letter to the Commandant, reminiscent of his attempts to keep his job with the External Affairs Department. He had been reluctant to ride in the car with Gullett at Megiddo but,

> I did through to Damascus and [words crossed out] unfortunately I found
> him at times a most unpleasant, selfish companion and interfered as

---

64 Interestingly, Campbell may already have known Coulson. This is who he may have been referring to in a postcard to Lilian Pitts dated 24 December 1917: 'Spent yesterday afternoon and evening with a couple of mechanics from the Flying Corps from the front in on leave. One handles a camera decently and had some interesting snaps and incidents to pass around'. Some of Coulson's photographs appeared in *Kia Ora Coo-ee* under the title 'Photos by the Photo Section A.F.C.'. *Kia Ora Coo-ee*, June 1918, p. 12.

65 Postcard, JP Campbell to LL Pitts, 11 November 1918.

66 HS Gullett to J Treloar, 12 November 1918, AWM 16 4375/2/12.

67 Ibid.

68 Ibid.

regards position for the camera for a subject; camera possibilities being unknown to him; consequently I said things and got disliked.[69]

Campbell was adamant the poor prints of his images seen by the Commandant had not been caused by his photographic skills, and he believed Gullett was aware of this. He attributed the poor quality of the prints to deficient plates and a damaged camera. When developing he found cracked plates, and some damaged by leakage of light into the camera, through no fault of his. Later he found that

> several of the whole plate prints sent were faulty by reason of not being in proper contact with the negative and as a consequence I am given credit for making a bad <u>negative</u>'.[70]

He considered Frank Hurley had also let him down by failing to forward a camera suitable 'for rapid instantaneous work', forcing him to 'pass hosts of snappy rapidly moving scenes', as it took time to erect his cumbersome large-stand camera.[71] Campbell claimed it was he who found McPherson, providing him with his (Campbell's) own personal photographic equipment, which he had used himself prior to whole plates arriving from London. This equipment, he claimed, was returned to him in a poor state.

Campbell thought he had 'expended a good deal personally to help things along'. After all he did not get the extra £1 a week that Gullett received, and it seemed to him that Gullett had 'turned me down for daring to roar when treading on my corns'.[72] Finally, Campbell had 'no kick against anyone thinking my selection of scenes should have been different; that is a matter of opinion, apparatus and circumstances', but he was upset that people were judging him before all his work was seen.[73] He scrawled a memo to Treloar in freehand at the bottom of this typed letter. He had sought approval for his work in a 'higher place' by sending a set of 130 prints to General Chauvel, 'and in the words of

---

69 JP Campbell to Commandant, Australian Headquarters, Cairo, 14 November 1918, AWM 16 4375/2/2.

70 Ibid.

71 JP Campbell to J Treloar, 14 November 1918, AWM 16 4375/2/2.

72 JP Campbell to J Treloar, 14 November 1918. Campbell had a point given the hardships he experienced in the field. HS Gullett, before accepting the position of war correspondent, Palestine, requested a permanent travelling allowance additional to his field allowance 'owing to the wide front he must cover' and the high cost of living. He requested a 'compounded field and travelling allowance of £1 a day'. This was approved. From: Adminaust, London, to Defence, Melbourne, 5 September 1918, AWM 16 4353/1/3.

73 JP Campbell to J Treloar, 14 November 1918.

A.D.C. [*Aide-de-Camp*] Lyons, 'he was delighted'.[74] Campbell commented on Gullett:

> Mr Gulletts greatly exaggerated language [and] opinion of me does not matter as the evidence I have to show will keep me in continued good books in other quarters, however, I am sorry he is an impossible character for me to work with.[75]

Gullett was not impressed with Campbell's letter, as he told Treloar:

> It is unnecessary I think to comment on Campbell's ravings. Had he carried out his philosophy [with] some of the enthusiasm with which he now abuses me the trouble would not have arisen.[76]

When Coulson's appointment became official Treloar sent Gullett the extract from the AIF List, stating: 'You will be pleased to see the following'.[77]

Treloar reflected on the lack of suitable official photographs taken during the drive to Damascus in the latter days of the war. Initially photographs were processed quickly and passed to Australia House for distribution to the press, but the supply dried up, caused, he thought, by 'the difficulty experienced with Lieut. Campbell during these operations'. The 'difficulty', presumably, referred to Campbell's perceived slowness and general inefficiency, and his relationship with Gullett. Treloar did not mention the crucial lack of materials. By now he had fully accepted Gullett's assessment of Campbell.[78]

Had Campbell been too preoccupied with the antiquities around him, too intent on capturing images of the Holy Land and contributing to *Kia Ora Coo-ee*? He had suffered from a lack of photographic supplies, particularly glass plates, and

---

74 Chauvel ordered the prints at Campbell's instigation. Campbell produced a set for Chauvel and a private set for himself. Some of the photographs Campbell gave to Chauvel ended up in volume two of a large 'scrap' album put together lovingly by his wife, Sibyl Chauvel (nee Jopp), after the war from his letters, photographs and press cuttings. There are approximately 35 of Campbell's official photographs in the album; all in volume two covering Chauvel's service from late 1917 to 1919. Again the captions vary, and are often more detailed. The first volume covers the period 1914 to 1917. Papers of General H Chauvel, AWM PR00535.

75 Campbell to Treloar, 14 November 1918. This was a freehand addendum scrawled at the bottom of his typed letter to Treloar.

76 HS Gullett to J Treloar, 26 January 1919, AWM 16 4375/2/2.

77 J Treloar to HS Gullett, 30 January 1919, AWM 16 4375/2/12.

78 J Treloar to HW Dinning, 10 February 1919, AWM 16 4379/5/4. As a result of what Gullett saw as a lack of suitable material on the advance to Damascus, cinema film had to be obtained from the British official photographer in Palestine.

both Gullett and Treloar had conceded this. It was a case of history repeating itself. To his ultimate detriment Campbell had used his own photographic equipment when the External Affairs Department had failed to provide him with adequate materials back in 1912 in the Northern Territory. He had resented bureaucratic interference in his work then, and he had become even more resentful under the watchful eyes of Gullet on the turbulent road to Damascus, which had led to his sacking. Ironically, despite the fact he was no longer the official photographer, Campbell was sent to Kantara in late November 1918 to photograph the 7th Light Horse prior to its return to Gallipoli on an exploratory mission. He also took a series of photographs of the Australian Base Post Office at Kantara.[79] The official photographs taken on these assignments were possibly his last as a member of the AIF.

On 15 January 1919 Campbell embarked for Australia on the transport *Berrima* at Suez, arriving on 17 February 1919. He kept his rank as Honorary Lieutenant but returned to Australia attached to AA Pay Corps.[80] However, he could safely say that, to the end of the war, he was the official war photographer in Egypt. Fifteen days after he set foot back in Melbourne Campbell was being conveyed through the main street of Mansfield in a bunting-decorated car driven by his old friend, HJ Vallance. Sister A King and Private AJ Pollard also paraded in separate cars, in what the *Mansfield Courier* said was one of the largest gatherings to welcome home returned soldiers. Praise was lavished on the returnees by a representative of the Mansfield Patriotic League who congratulated Campbell on his war photography: 'they all knew, from what they had seen him do in Mansfield [with Vallan Studio], that his photos would be unapproachable'. At least the Mansfield community appreciated his work.[81]

After the Mansfield reception he visited his family in the Heyfield district of Gippsland, and addressed a 'Welcome to Returned Soldiers' function in Seaspray. According to the *Gippsland Mercury* reporter, Campbell explained his connection to Gippsland, saying how 'his 4½ years' [military] service had been of thrilling interest in foreign lands, the interest being added to by his having for the last 25 years been an enthusiastic photographer'. Further, it was a privilege 'to see and photograph many scenes of sacred history in the Holy Land of Palestine and

---

79 JD Richardson, *The History of the 7th Light Horse Regiment AIF*, Sydney, 1919, p. 107, and Australian War Memorial images B00144-190.

80 NAA: B2455, Campbell JP.

81 *Mansfield Courier*, 8 March 1919.

Syria [and he was] duly thankful to the powers that be for [this as] he [valued] his trophies from Gallipoli, the Holy Land and Egypt'. These made up 'a personal collection of about 2000 negatives', one he felt was an 'asset worth risking one's life for from shot and shell, and the terrors to health of the deadly Jordan Valley in summer'.[82]

In April the people of Mansfield followed up with a lavish welcome home function in the public hall for the returned nurses and soldiers of the district, including Campbell. In a speech thanking the Mansfield people on behalf of himself and the other returnees, Campbell offered to deliver an illustrated 'lecturette (*sic*)' dealing with his travels and experiences on Gallipoli and in the Holy Land.[83] He was discharged from the Army on 18 April 1919, but re-enlisted four days later in the Citizen Forces (or Home Service) as a Sergeant in the Pay Corps, again giving his age as forty-nine. He gave his address as 'St Ivans', Westgarth Street, East Malvern, the home of his wife, Elizabeth. In May he suffered a relapse of malaria and had two weeks off work, another indication that his poor health was ongoing and had hindered him towards the end of the war.[84]

While he was ill an edition of the *Bulletin* praised his war photography. The *Mansfield Courier* reproduced the piece which acknowledged the good quality of Campbell's work after he succeeded Hurley as official photographer in the Middle East. It highlighted his photographs of Mena camp in Egypt and, in an advertising coup for Campbell, stated 'it is to be hoped that the proposed War Museum or the Mitchell Library will secure these later on'.[85]

In June Campbell attended a welcome home function of another, perhaps more sophisticated kind. The Working Men's College Photographic Club held a social evening for returned club members at Hooker's Café in Flinders Lane, Melbourne.[86] He was back in the fold enjoying his old haunts in Melbourne. He

---

82 *Gippsland Mercury*, 18 March 1919.

83 *Mansfield Courier*, 19 April 1918. I have not found recorded evidence of Campbell giving a lecture on his war experiences in Mansfield. Nurse Lester (nee Ritchie), who had nursed the wounded Campbell in 1915, was one of the apologies for non-attendance at this function. It was the Lester and Ritchie family who were to each receive one of Campbell's Gallipoli albums, one now held by the Mansfield RSL, the other by the National Library of Australia.

84 NAA: MT1486/1, Campbell/James Pinkerton, and Cameron Simpson, *Maygar's Boys*, p. 50. Elizabeth had left their old home at 12 Hunter Street, Malvern, in 1916 and moved to Halstead Street, Caulfield. In February 1919 she advised the Defence Department that she now lived at 'St Ivans', Westgarth Street, East Malvern. NAA: B2455, Campbell JP.

85 *Mansfield Courier*, 17 May 1919.

86 Alan Elliot, *A Century Exposed: One Hundred Years of the Melbourne Camera Club*, The Melbourne Camera Club, 1991, p. 4.

was finally discharged from the Citizen Forces at his own request, on 1 September 1919, after a total of five years military service.[87]

Campbell was not yet finished with his war photographs. The Australian War Museum (later Memorial) was created in Melbourne after hostilities ceased, using the material amassed by the Australian War Records Section as the basis of its collection.[88] In August 1923, when Campbell was employed as a clerk with the State Electricity Commission at Yallourn in the Latrobe Valley, the Director of the Museum, his old AWRS boss John Treloar, instructed the Assistant Director to obtain more war photographs from Campbell. Perversely, after humiliating him in the Middle East, the Australian War Museum wanted more of his photographs, as they now regarded Campbell as a 'good photographer'. The museum thought they had all his Gallipoli photographs, but wished to know if he had others 'which you could lend for copying for record purposes'.[89] Campbell responded:

> [When] I see what you have I will know whether there are any other Anzac negs I can lend. I have a large number of private scenes of Palestine, Syria and Egypt which though of interest to ex-soldiers are not War Records.[90]

Here was another clear admission of the reason he carried a private camera as well as his official one whilst on duty in Palestine and Syria:

> It was my intention to market [my private photographs of Egypt, Palestine and Syria] when demobilised but I have not had the time to even properly assemble the negatives. Could the marketing be done through the Museum with a share of the profits to myself?[91]

The Acting Director replied in the negative to this request, as 'much as we

---

87 NAA: MT1486/1, Campbell/James Pinkerton. Elizabeth had left their old home at 12 Hunter Street, Malvern, in 1916 and moved to Halstead Street, Caulfield. In February 1919 she advised the Defence Department that she now lived at 'St Ivans', Westgarth Street, East Malvern. NAA: B2455, Campbell JP.
88 Anne-Marie Condé, Australian War Memorial, 'John Treloar, Official War Art and the Australian War Memorial', *Australian Journal of Politics and History*, Volume 53, Number 3, 2007, p. 454.
89 Acting Director, Australian War Museum, to JP Campbell, 20 August 1923, Commonwealth of Australia Home and Territories Department file, 'Mr Campbell re photo's of Gallipoli', AWM93 17/3/294. Campbell had 'lent' the Museum photographs for copying, and they had the JP Campbell 8th Light Horse/Gallipoli album presented to them by Justice Higgins, as previously discussed.
90 JP Campbell to Acting to Director, Australian War Museum, 22 August 1923, Commonwealth of Australia Home and Territories Department file, 'Mr Campbell re photo's of Gallipoli', AWM 93 17/3/294.
91 Ibid.

would like to be of service to one who has so helped the Museum'.[92] He had been ordered to hand his private photographs to the AWRS, but kept copies for himself. Now he was hoping to profit from them, as he had in 1912 when he produced postcards from photographs he had taken while with the External Affairs Department.

Campbell was caught up in the great grab for war memorabilia commenced by the Mitchell Library, rival to the fledgling Australian War Museum, in early 1919. The Mitchell Library advertised for material, offering money, mainly for diaries and suitable on-the-spot accounts of the war.[93] Loyalty to the Australian War Records Section, his old employer and precursor to the Australian War Museum/Memorial, may have prompted Campbell to donate his private Gallipoli negatives to the Australian War Museum, a non-payer for material, rather than profiting from them via the Mitchell Library.

The other source for some of his private images, held today by the Australian War Memorial, is listed as A Campbell, presumably his son Aubrey, who may have donated further photographs after his father's death. Hundreds of JP Campbell's official and private war photographs are held by the Australian War Memorial. Many have been attributed to him, and others are gradually being identified and acknowledged as Campbell's. While many do not have the action qualities of Hurley compositions, the official images mostly conform to Bean's original aim of true, un-adulterated records, despite Campbell's adherence to pictorialism. In *Contact*, a book on the Australian War Memorial's photography collection, Shaune Lakin, a former curator of photography at the Memorial, states Campbell spent 1918 'producing some of the most beautiful photographs of the war', pictures that were 'atmospheric and technically superior' (Fig. 133).[94] Lakin maintains that Campbell's pictures 'differed little' from Frank

---

92 Acting Director, Australian War Museum, to JP Campbell, 27 August 1923, Commonwealth of Australia Home and Territories Department file, 'Mr Campbell re-photos of Gallipoli', AWM 93 17/3/294.

93 Anne-Marie Condé, 'The Records of War: Collecting at the Mitchell Library and the Australian War Memorial', *Australian Historical Studies*, Volume 37, Number 125, April 2005, pp. 139-41.

94 This is a private war photograph of Campbell's, also in the Australian War Memorial collection (H03022). There is an official photograph (B00026) of the same subject, but taken a bit closer (the bushes, backdrop etc, are the same, the Light Horse column in a slightly different position). This is another case of Campbell taking private photographs during his official duties, possibly using army materials.

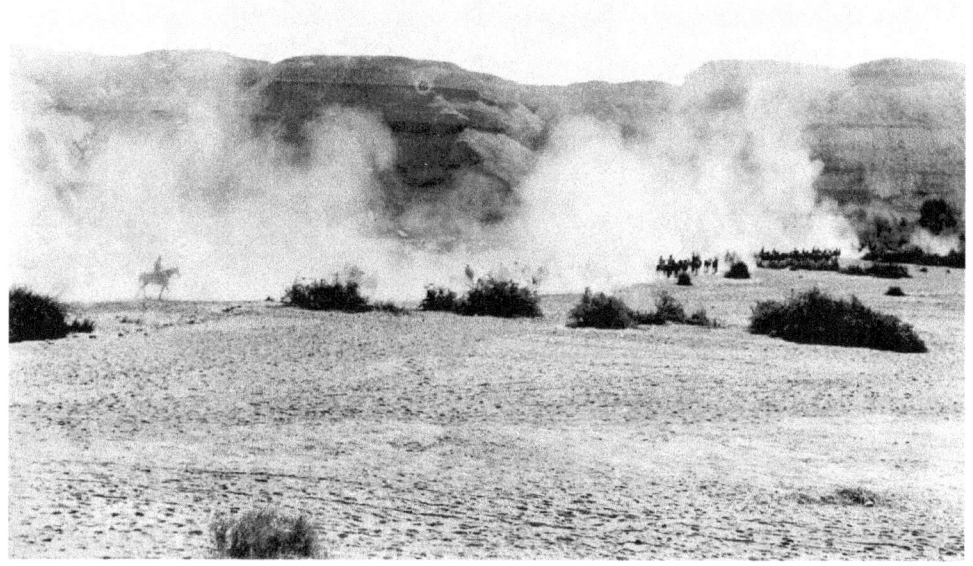

Fig. 133. 'No 49. 8th LH going to water. Jordan River. Auja Ford', another example of
Campbell's 'atmospheric' photography.
(Courtesy of Falconer collection, AWM image H03022)

Hurley's, although he points out that Gullett saw them as neither good as records
nor as 'stirring' as Hurley's work, leaving them in some sort of twilight zone.[95]

* * *

As Campbell took the long, slow voyage back to Australia in early 1919, he
must have felt downcast at his treatment at the hands of his superior officers,
but also a sense of pride at his achievements as a photographer during wartime.
Like all soldiers serving overseas he faced the process of repatriation back into
his own country, a process that could be long and painful. An unknown future
loomed before him, but he had his photography to fall back to, a crux to hold
on to in turbulent times. It was a matter of finding a job back in civilian life to
support his ongoing passion.

---

95 Shaune Lakin, *Contact*, p. 74.

10

YALLOURN

*Back to Gippsland – The Beginnings of the SEC – Chief Clerk and SEC
Photographer – Model Town – Propaganda – Machine Age Photography
– The Panorama*

On 5 February 1921, amidst a period of industrial turmoil in Victoria, a symbolic sod was turned for a major state infrastructure project, the construction of a power station near Yallourn in the Latrobe Valley. It was the first step in providing Victoria with a state-wide electricity supply. JP Campbell was there to record the moment (Fig. 134).[1] Sir John Monash, a revered military commander during the First World War, and now Chairman of the State Electricity Commission of Victoria (SECV, or SEC as it was commonly known), fronted the camera, along with other commissioners and SEC officials, including Campbell's long-time friend, Roy Liddelow, SEC Secretary. The workers hung around in the background.

After discharge from the Home Service in September 1919, Campbell obtained employment with the Mines Department as chief clerk at the government-run brown coal mine north west of Morwell in Gippsland, and close to the site of the proposed new power station. This clerical position with the Mines Department eventually led to his employment with the SEC as a clerk, store manager and photographer.[2] He was back in a part of Victoria he knew well, and he was to stay there for the rest of his life.

Brown coal deposits, later proven to be some of the largest in the world, were discovered in the Latrobe Valley in the early 1870s, and their sporadic exploitation was driven by Victoria's dependence on black coal, mainly from NSW, and the constant disruption to supplies by strikes and transport problems.

---

1 Cecil Edwards, *Brown Power: A Jubilee History of the State Electricity Commission of Victoria*, State Electricity Commission of Victoria, Melbourne, 1969, p. 59.

2 *Live Wire* , 11 September 1935; Prue McGoldrick, *"Yallourn was . . ."*: *A Historical and Pictorial record of the functions, life and people of this "deceased" town*, Gippsland Printers Pty Ltd, Morwell, 1984, p. 8; Kath Ringin, *The Old Brown Coal Mine*, Moe and District Historical Society, Moe, 1986, p. 12, and State Electricity Commission of Victoria (SECV), Office of the Administrator, Melbourne, employment records of JP Campbell obtained under freedom of information.

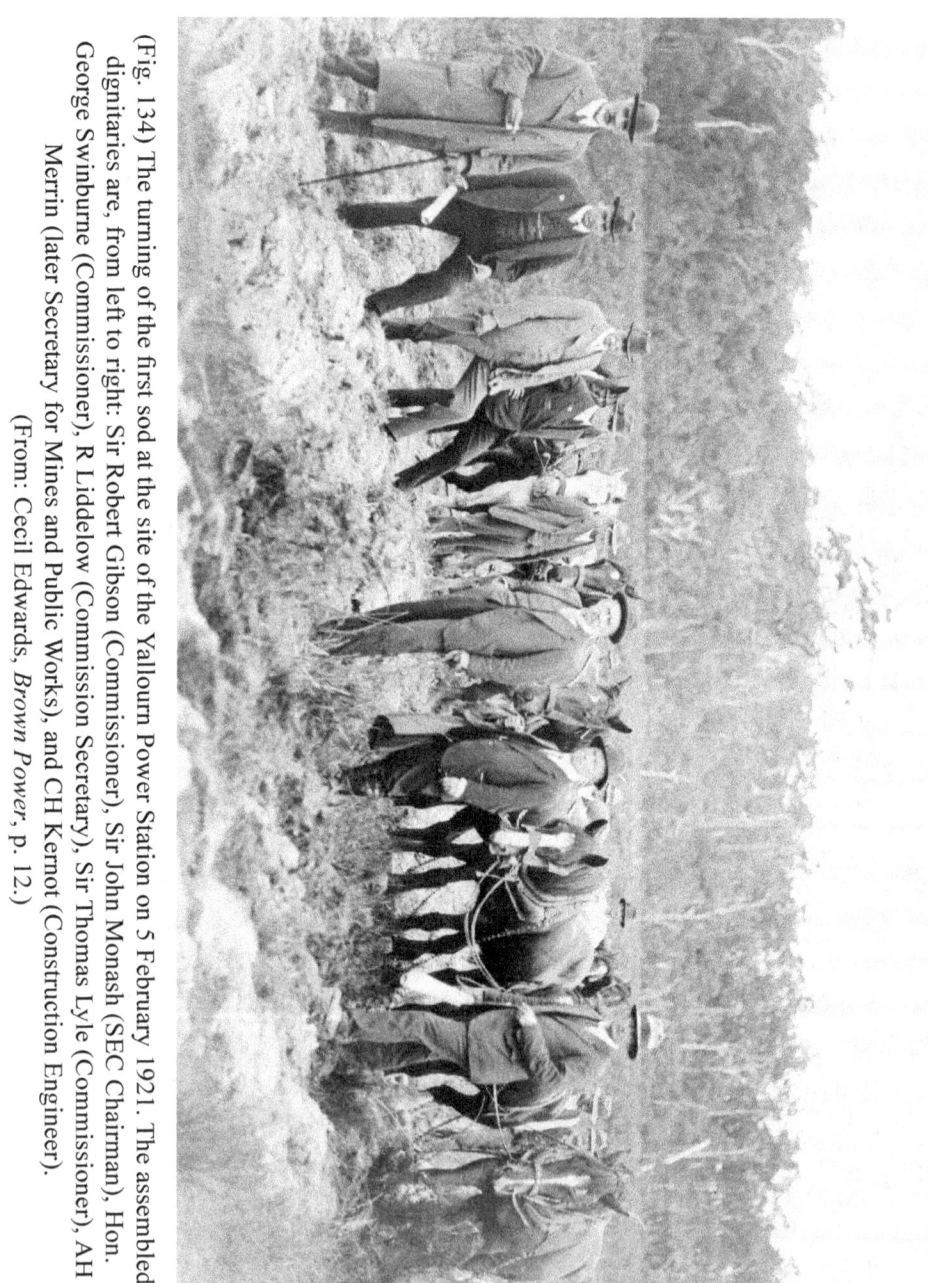

(Fig. 134) The turning of the first sod at the site of the Yallourn Power Station on 5 February 1921. The assembled dignitaries are, from left to right: Sir Robert Gibson (Commissioner), Sir John Monash (SEC Chairman), Hon. George Swinburne (Commissioner), R Liddelow (Commission Secretary), Sir Thomas Lyle (Commissioner), AH Merrin (later Secretary for Mines and Public Works), and CH Kernot (Construction Engineer).

(From: Cecil Edwards, *Brown Power*, p. 12.)

The Great Morwell Coal Mining Company established an open-cut mine on the north side of the Latrobe River in the late 1880s. It closed in 1899, but was re-opened by the Victorian Government in 1917, during the First World War, to boost Victorian coal supplies because of an interstate coal mining strike.[3] The re-opening of the Brown Coal Mine, as this open-cut mine came to be called, was also a war-time stop-gap measure until larger, easily accessible coal deposits, close by on the south side of the river, could be mined.

Elaborate plans to use these vast coal deposits to generate electricity were disrupted by the First World War.[4] As early as 1908, the Victorian Government had received expert advice that a power station could be built on the Morwell brown coal fields, utilising the abundant brown coal to produce electricity for Melbourne. In 1917, while Campbell marked time as an army pay clerk in Cairo, a Brown Coal Advisory Committee appointed by the state government recommended that a power station be established on the southern side of the Latrobe River north of Morwell. By the end of 1919 a Bill was passed in Parliament creating the Electricity Commissioners, with the mandate to electrify Victoria, and bring it into the modern age. The Morwell project, later known as Yallourn, was to be a massive government-funded undertaking, unique in the British Empire in its application of science and engineering.[5]

By the end of 1920 Sir John Monash, engineer and soldier extraordinaire, was Chairman of the Commissioners. Monash had excelled as a commander on the Western Front during the First World War, and in overseeing the demobilisation of Australian troops after the war. Now he was to use his leadership skills to oversee the operation of a power station, briquette factory and model town. German engineering and Monash's standing in the Australian community played major roles in the success of the SEC in its early years. Monash was the face of the SEC, he oversaw how it was promoted. Photography played an important role in its portrayal, with JP Campbell there from the beginning to document the project's progress.[6]

---

3 Cecil Edwards, *Brown Power* p. 9, 18, and Kath Ringin, *The Old Brown Coal Mine*, pp. 1-6, 10-11.

4 Cecil Edwards, *Brown Power*, pp.8-10, 15-18; Kath Ringin, *The Old Brown Coal Mine*, pp. 1-11.

5 Meredith Fletcher, *Digging People Up for Coal: A History of Yallourn*, Melbourne University Press, Melbourne, 2002, pp. 15-17.

6 Ibid., pp. 33-48. An obituary for JP Campbell in the *Australian Traveller* states 'On returning to Melbourne, Sir John Monash, who had not lost sight [of Campbell,] secured his services for Yallourn in connection with the Electricity Commission's business activities'. *Australian Traveller*, 7 October 1935, p.28. I have not found any evidence to suggest Monash knew Campbell personally prior to joining the SEC, although he did photograph one of his engineering structures prior to the war, and he was on Gallipoli with him, albeit separated vastly by rank and in different units. It is more likely that Roy Liddelow recommended Campbell to Monash if indeed that was required to get him the job of chief clerk. Monash may have personally overseen recruitment of staff when the SEC was in its embryonic stage.

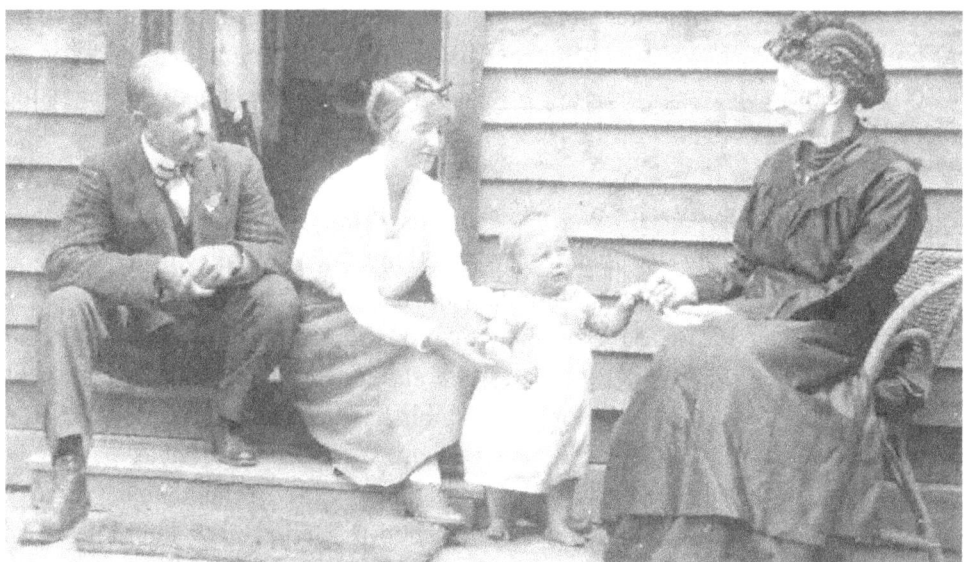

(Fig. 135) 'The 4 Generations. 8.2.20'. JP Campbell with his daughter Ada Falconer, his grandson Derek Falconer, and his mother Margaret. Margaret died two months later, aged 90. (Courtesy of Falconer collection)

How Campbell came to obtain a job with the Mines Department is not known. It is possible that he renewed contact with Roy Liddelow, one of the sons of his old mentor, the teacher Arthur Liddelow.[7] In early 1919 Liddelow became secretary to the newly appointed Electricity Commissioners overseeing electricity generation and distribution in Victoria.[8] Liddelow may have advised Campbell of the impending development in the Latrobe Valley, suggesting he apply for the clerical position with the Mines Department at the Brown Coal Mine. During the maritime strike of 1919 Victoria could not obtain black coal from NSW so the demand for brown coal increased dramatically. The mine's workforce grew rapidly as a consequence. More clerical staff were required on location by the Mines Department. Campbell was recruited 'to organise the office'.[9] The location was attractive to him: it was not far from Heyfield and district, home of his ailing elderly mother and other family members, and it was in the bush which appealed to his instincts as a landscape photographer (Fig. 135).

7 Roy Liddelow had worked in administrative positions in the mining industry in New Zealand and Broken Hill, NSW. Cecil Edwards, *Brown Power*, p. 30.

8 NAA: B2455, Liddelow Ray (first name listed as Ray instead of Roy), and Cecil Edwards, *Brown Power*, p. 30.

9 *Morwell Advertiser*, 3 November 1932.

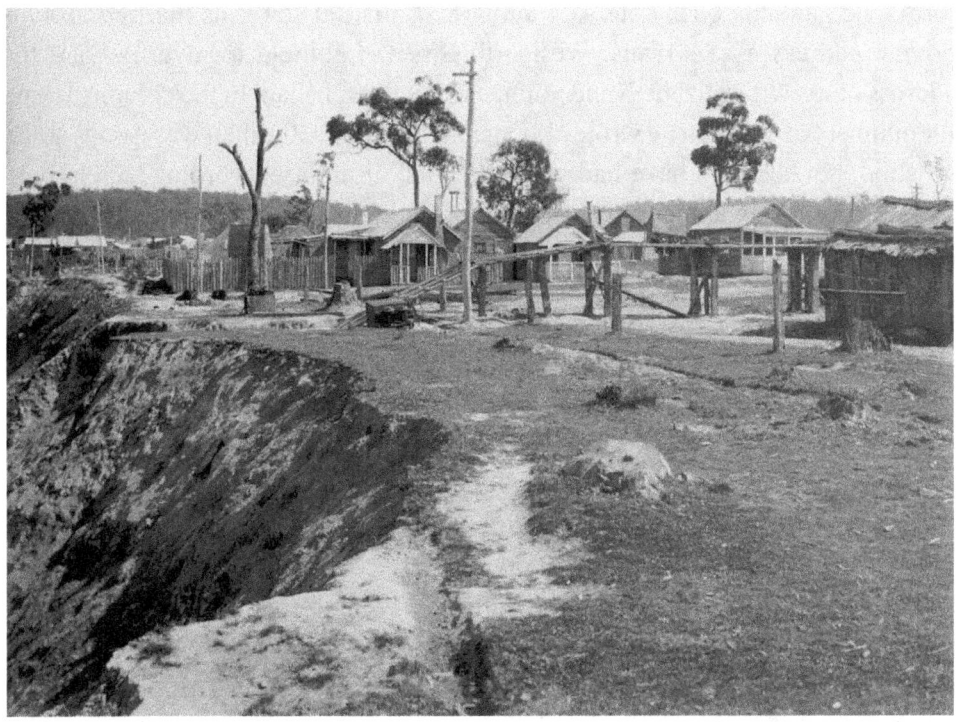

(Fig. 136) 'Brown Coal Township 1919'. The township teetered on the edge of the open cut.
(Courtesy of State Library of Victoria, H2009 18/342)

So demanding was the job that he never visited 'home' in Melbourne for six months. Conditions were trying. Twice Campbell's new office was destroyed by landslips, but he was determined to make himself comfortable.[10] Eventually a reasonable building was erected; compared to the ramshackle structures built to house the workers, ironically known as 'Toorak', the main stores-cum-office building at Brown Coal Mine was rather flash – the chief clerk installed a frilled blind on a window to augment its status. As a result Campbell gained a reputation as being rather fastidious.[11] Two Campbell photographs show the housing and the open cut at the Brown Coal Mine, (Figs. 136 & 137).

True to form, when he applied for the job Campbell gave his age as forty-six, when he was actually fifty-four. Later, on Electricity Commissioners employment

---

10 *Morwell Advertiser*, 3 November 1932.

11 This is documented in detail in *The Age*, 16 April 1920, and mentioned briefly in Cecil Edwards, *Brown Power*, p. 60. A year later the seven huts erected for Commission staff near the site of the new temporary power station were known as 'Little Toorak'. Colin Harvey, *Yallourn Power Station: A History 1919 to 1989*, State Electricity Commission, Morwell, 1993, p. 37.

forms, he gave his birth date as 4 July 1870, marital status as married and his private address as St. Ivans, Westgarth Street, Caulfield (Malvern) East, the address of his wife Elizabeth and youngest daughter, Lilian. In the column asking for numbers of children he wrote '1 dependant'.[12] In 1920 Lilian was twenty-four, no child, but she may have had an intellectual disability according to relatives, and it is possible Campbell was helping provide for her. Again Campbell chose to live apart from his wife. He was relatively close to Caulfield East with easy access by train, and his grand-daughter, Noel Fethers, maintains he regularly visited his wife Elizabeth. He seemed, however, to have a preference for going his own way – the clerical position in the Latrobe Valley suited him.

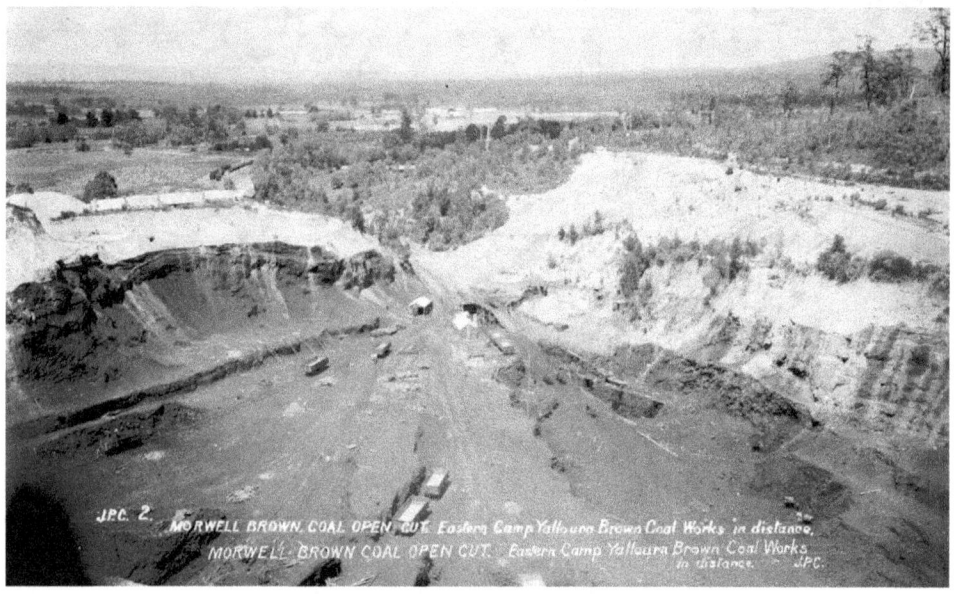

(Fig. 137) 'JPC 2 MORWELL BROWN COAL OPEN CUT. Eastern Camp Yallourn Brown Coal Works in distance. JPC.' Campbell seems to have been practising his printing on this damaged print. (Courtesy of State Library of Victoria, H2009 18/346)

Preliminary work began on the first experimental power station at Yallourn in April 1920. In May, Campbell was recruited from the Mines Department to perform the dual job of clerk-in-charge at both the old Brown Coal Mine and the Commissioners' office on the new site south of the river.[13] In November 1920 Campbell commented to a journalist on the more than 300 employees who had downed tools at the mine over a wage dispute. The men had returned to work in

---

12 JP Campbell, personnel record, SECV Office of the Administrator.
13 *Live Wire*, 18 June 1931 and JP Campbell, personnel record, SECV Office of the Administrator.

July after a protracted strike, and he expressed surprise that they had again gone out again only three months later.[14] The frequent industrial disputes may have hastened Campbell's decision to take up a full time job with the SEC, as the strike did not affect the 100 or so people employed on preparatory work at the new power station site. Another reason was the rapid increase in the workforce on the construction site, and associated explosion in clerical work with more people to pay.[15]

From 16 December 1920 Campbell was employed full time on staff with the SEC as clerk-in-charge, 'the only senior residential officer on the field for some time'.[16] Accommodation was in tents until old army buildings were re-located from Langwarrin. As a staff member Campbell occupied a section of the temporary head office building which acted as office, bedroom and – importantly for his photography – darkroom.[17]

His status as a returned soldier with the rank of lieutenant and experience as a senior army payroll clerk quickly elevated him to positions of responsibility.[18] In the same month he officiated at the opening of the new Eastern Camp, on behalf of the Electricity Commissioners. His speech expressed his adherence to Commission ideals and revealed aspects of his own personality:

> Mr Campbell gave a brief outline of the Commissioners desire in as much as they were out to study the interests of their employees in every way. The accommodation as could be seen was remarkably good and this could be considered as only one direction in which their desire ran, but it was the first and important. These buildings although temporary were elaborate and the whole work as presented to the visitor, could be looked upon as a mere ABC to a school child as a prelude to his merit certificate. Nobody could foreshadow the vastness of the electrification scheme therefore the importance to the State could not be over estimated.

---

14 *Morwell Advocate*, 12 November 1920. Campbell may have been temporary manager for some reason as this certainly was not his permanent job.

15 Ibid., and *Live Wire*, 18 June 1931. Campbell may have still continued overseeing clerical operations at the Brown Coal Mine, which was eventually taken over by the SEC in 1924.

16 JP Campbell, personnel record, SECV Office of the Administrator; *Live Wire*, 18 June 1931, and *Morwell Advertiser*, 3 November 1932.

17 *Live Wire*, 18 June 1931.

18 In November 1920 he was appointed a commissioner for taking declarations and affidavits under the Evidence Act 1915. Letter, Secretary to the Law Department to Secretary, Electricity Commissioners, 16 November 1920, 'General Correspondence Files and File Registration Cards', VPRS 8892/P1 Box 259, PROV.

Consequently the Commissioners were out to secure the hearty co-operation of their employees in every way. To his mind three things were most important as regards the successful running of the accommodation buildings, they were sobriety, careful use of language and the desire to improve the surroundings. With these three working together he felt sure we would be a happy and contented people.[19]

Campbell had always found swearing and un-gentlemanly behaviour abhorrent. On one occasion, whilst he was paying workers, a drunken man used insulting language in demanding money he was not entitled to. The police were called, the man was charged and the case went to court. In giving evidence Campbell would not repeat the swear words used by the accused, writing them down instead.[20] His personality was suited to the military life, and this new scheme reflected a military structure under its leader, Sir John Monash. Returned soldiers were welcomed in its ranks, as they were in all primary and secondary industries throughout Australia.

Monash made it clear that the Commission was proud of its preferential treatment of returned soldiers.[21] Commission paper work reflected this, as personnel forms were pre-printed with, among other things, 'R.S.' ['Returned Serviceman'] (Yes or No) at the top.[22] Satisfactory overseas service enhanced promotional prospects. The Commission, particularly Monash, deemed hierarchical discipline necessary, with a workforce recently set free from the army, and restless in the civilian world.

Photography was used to record the progress of the project from its beginning. In mid 1921 the construction engineer, CH Kernot, requested photographic materials from the Commissioners for JP Campbell, at the same time recommending an increase in his salary for the photographic services he was providing in addition to his normal job.[23] Campbell set up a dark room in the newly constructed stores and administrative building located at the Eastern Camp.[24] In early 1921 a boat

19 *Morwell Advertiser*, 26 November 1920.
20 *Morwell Advertiser*, 29 June 1923.
21 Meredith Fletcher, *Digging People Up for Coal*, pp. 55-6.
22 JP Campbell's Staff card, personnel record, SECV Office of the Administrator.
23 Letter from Construction Engineer, 1 July 1921, 'File Registration Card', VPRS 8892/P1 Box 309, PROV. Campbell may have approached the project's hierarchy, suggesting he document the schemes progress via the photographic medium, for a fee of course. After all, he had been an official photographer before and during the war. And he was taking photographs anyway, always, and may as well be paid for it as it was a costly passion.
24 *Live Wire*, 2 July 1931.

arrived and Campbell, Roy Liddelow and two 'deckhands' carried it through rough terrain on the southern banks of the Latrobe River, taking it above the rapids and launching it with the appropriate bottle of champagne 'duly recorded by camera'. Thereafter many 'happy summer time weekend-river picnics' were spent on the bush-lined Latrobe River until the weir drowned the picnic site.[25]

Monash announced the name of the electricity project and its town in December 1920, as Yallourn, a combination of two Aboriginal words meaning brown fire.[26] The garden town project for housing the workers was underway. Monash went so far as to instruct the construction engineer 'not to slaughter the forests', as every tree was potentially precious.[27] On 10 January 1921 the Electricity Commissioners became the State Electricity Commission of Victoria.[28] The head of the spur railway line at the Eastern Camp, resembled, in Campbell's words, 'a head of the line war dump during the building of the military railway from the Suez Canal to Palestine for train loads of material were arriving apace'.[29] Much photographic attention was paid to the Ruston shovel awaiting assembly before its assault on the overburden covering the brown coal (Fig. 138).[30]

Yallourn was to be a model town for housing the workers, built on garden city lines, a concept originating in Britain in the 1890s. In Australia the garden city movement was linked to the reform of industrial areas and provided a new start for many damaged returned soldiers. Beautiful surroundings were thought to induce industrial harmony. To ensure the contentment of the workforce, modern conveniences were to be provided. Well designed gardens blended with houses and surrounding bush. Built on high ground with good drainage and away from easily winnable brown coal deposits, the town of Yallourn had a handsome town square with streets radiating out from it, conforming to the contours.[31]

---

25 *Live Wire*, 6 August 1931.

26 Meredith Fletcher, *Digging People Up for Coal*, p. 7.

27 Cecil Edwards, *Brown Power*, p. 58.

28 Cecil Edwards, *Brown Power*, p. 51.

29 *Live Wire*, 2 July 1931. In 1931, as editor of the *Live Wire*, Campbell wrote a series of articles under the title 'Old Yallourn Days', documenting the first two or three years of the scheme.

30 There is a similar image, titled 'New Bucyrus', with a woman and two men standing in the bucket, in an album held by the State Library of New South Wales. Album title: 'Yallourn, 9th March 1924'; Call No: PXA 602 (v.2), State Library of New South Wales. This album is attributed to JP Campbell, but the captions are not in his handwriting. The album includes an image of Campbell himself, suggesting the photographs were taken by a friend or relative.

31 Meredith Fletcher, *Digging People Up for Coal*, p. 9, pp. 22-5.

As all houses were owned by the SEC, the Commission decided who would live there, excluding those seen not to be compatible with its aims. Only SEC employees, their dependants, and those providing essential services were to reside in the place: only much later would such rules be relaxed.[32] The general store was owned and run by the Commission; there was to be no private enterprise in the town. Essentially, Yallourn was a town of public servants controlled by the SEC. Campbell was to settle into this bureaucratic environment and thrive on it, despite his turbulent experiences with earlier employers.

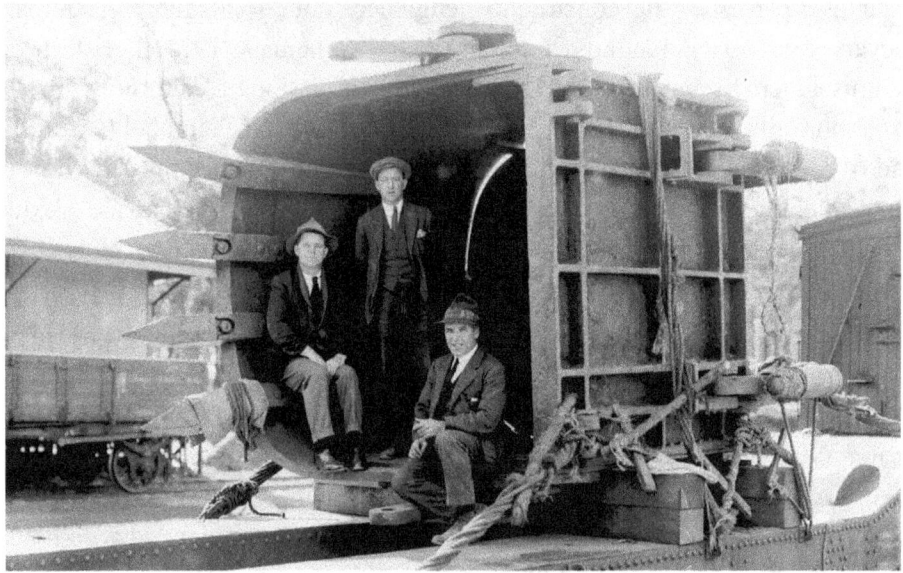

(Fig. 138) A Ruston Bucket on the back of a railway truck. Campbell noted how people were fascinated by the huge machine when it arrived in bits, watching in awe as it was assembled, and many 'snaps' were taken of people posing in the bucket. (Courtesy of State Library of Victoria H2009 18/822)

The designers and architects aimed for 'a community of homes'. Housing was classified to reflect the SEC's hierarchy, with staff getting the better housing, the rank-and-file employees the worst, and all, of course, were connected to the electricity supply.[33] SEC employees were divided into the two categories of staff and wages. Staff, with the engineers at the pinnacle, wore grey coats, wages wore blue overalls. Campbell became firmly entrenched on the staff side, who led the SEC and the community.[34]

---

32 Ibid., pp. 20-1.
33 Ibid., pp. 26-7.
34 Ibid., pp. 53-5.

In early 1921 the temporary power house was under construction, with Campbell documenting every move with his camera. It began operating in June 1921, providing power and light for the construction of the main power station and the emerging township of Yallourn.[35] Between 1921 and 1922 thirty-four four-roomed houses were erected in Yallourn on a rise to the south of the temporary power house. For the first time the SEC's annual report included photographs taken by Campbell, one of which was an image of Maiden Street showing houses in the bush divided by a dirt road cut through woodland. Conveniences were being provided to the workers. Campbell photographed the construction in this street, men labouring amidst the trees and dense scrub, a pictorialist's dream (Fig. 139). The scrub in the background seems to be immersed in fog, a trademark in Campbell's early work.[36]

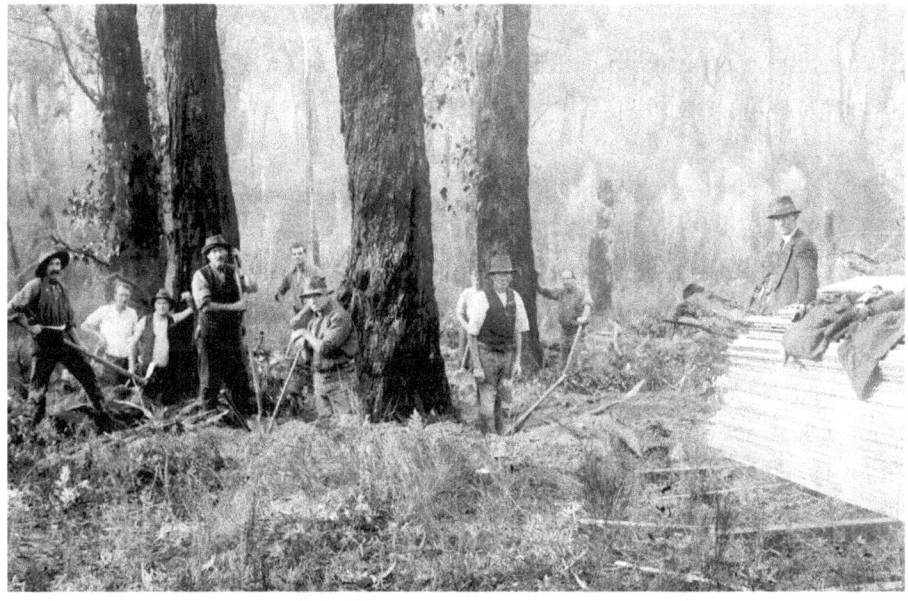

(Fig. 139) 'First clearing – for houses in Maiden St'.
(Courtesy of State Library of Victoria H2009 18/304)

It was not until December 1921 that a pictorial weekly, the *Weekly Times*, published a two-page illustrated feature article on all aspects of the scheme, with an additional two pages of photographs.[37] Portraits of four stern-faced

35 Cecil Edwards, *Brown Power*, p. 61.
36 He also took a series of images of the construction of a railway branch line to Yallourn in 1921, a project his brother William was involved in as a supervisor. Prue McGoldrick, *"Yallourn Was . . ."*, p. 11.
37 *Weekly Times*, 3 December 1921, p. 5.

commissioners graced the first page, including a larger one of a portly Chairman Monash sitting at his desk in his Melbourne office, glaring at the camera while poised to write, a picture of the head of a modern organisation. The *Weekly Times* journalist viewed the works site from a high vantage point, describing it as primeval bush mixed with farmland, and below it lay 'the marvellous civilising power [of brown coal] locked away in the earth'. This landscape was being disturbed:

> the troops of industry are on the march in a great invasion of nature. Soon nature will capitulate and yield an illimitable ransom. A typical Gippsland landscape, mangled by the wheels of industry, hills and dales as verdant as a Flanders hop-field eaten into by invading Science. Relentless progress is there, in strange contrast to peaceful, slumbering settlement.[38]

The article contrasted the old Brown Coal Mine on the north side of the river to the new mine where 'the miner will not have to scratch like the primeval stone-man'.[39] Instead, the machine would dominate: the power of the Bucyrus steam shovels used for excavating the overburden was described in rapturous detail, along with the other major features of the project: the harnessing of the river to supply water for the power station; the future transmission of electricity to Melbourne and beyond; the brick works; and the building of the town.[40]

When the first passenger train steamed into Yallourn's railway station on 7 December 1921, Campbell was there with his camera to greet it, along with CH Kernot, construction engineer for the SEC, and railway and local government dignitaries. The passengers included the Governor General, Henry Forster, the State Governor, Colonel George EJ Mowbray, the third Earl of Stradbroke, Countess Stradbroke, SEC and Railway Commissioners (including Sir John Monash), politicians and SEC officers (including Campbell's friend, Roy Liddelow). Campbell photographed the party near the locomotive and at various stages of their tour of the SEC works and town.[41]

As the Yallourn project got under way photographs began appearing on a more regular basis in the pictorial weeklies. They were carefully selected to impart the

---

38 Ibid.
39 Ibid.
40 *Weekly Times*, 3 December 1921, p. 8.
41 *Morwell Advertiser*, 9 December 1921.

best impression of a venture funded by the public purse. It was in this controlled environment that Campbell had to operate as a photographer. In May 1922 Sir John Monash led, 'in military fashion', a tour of the Yallourn project by a group of Victorian journalists, taking them on 'a series of forced marches [cramming] into one long afternoon a tour of inspection that might have taken a week if it had been conducted by a leisurely civilian'.[42] They scrambled up and down steep embankments, with occasional halts called by Monash, who would order them to take out their notebooks, explain briefly the importance of the scene before them, and then rush on to the next site. Five hours later they staggered back on to the Melbourne-bound train. The *Australasian* accompanied its article on the visit with eight photographs.[43] As the use of cameras was strictly controlled in the works area, one suspects outside cameras were not allowed on the visit, and SEC photographs taken by Campbell were released to accompany the reports of the touring journalists.

When a party of Rotarians visited Yallourn in October of the same year, Monash instructed the tour guide to blow a whistle as a signal for the party to gather around him, and to make sure the visitors did not straggle during the walk of 'under 3 miles'.[44] Control was essential: the straying eyes of stragglers or lost visitors may have seen something they should not, and Monash could not afford to give enemies of the project ammunition.[45] A Rotarian himself, he ensured the *Australasian* carried a series of four SEC official photographs taken by Campbell to commemorate the visit, associating the prestige of the organisation with the importance of the project.[46] Similarly, when a group of delegates from the Empire Press Union, in Melbourne for a conference, visited Yallourn led by Monash, the *Australasian* published a lavish ten photograph spread of the eminent visitors under the SEC chairman's instruction as they viewed the power

---

42 *Australasian*, 3 June 1922.

43 Ibid.

44 'Visit to Yallourn by Rotary Club – October 4th 1922', Correspondence, Papers and Memorabilia of Sir John Monash, VPRS 9673/P1 Unit 7, PROV.

45 The SEC received a steady stream of criticism in its early years, particularly from *The Age*, *Smith's Weekly* and some State MP's. Monash and the SEC were almost constantly under siege. The criticism was about everything from perceived poor coal deposits and excessive construction costs, to the high cost of electricity tariffs. All resulted, claimed the critics, in a heavy burden on the taxpayer. Cecil Edwards, *Brown Power*, pp. 92-3.

46 *Australasian*, 14 October 1922. These were: Yallourn Railway Station; Discharge conduit at weir; Turbine house; and Weir Across Latrobe River (the latter appeared in the 1922 annual report).

station and surrounding infrastructure.[47] In this way, photography, whether by Campbell or newspaper photographers, was used to reinforce the status of the electricity generating venture. This coverage extended to recreational occasions, like the Yallourn gymkhana of November 1922 (Fig. 140).

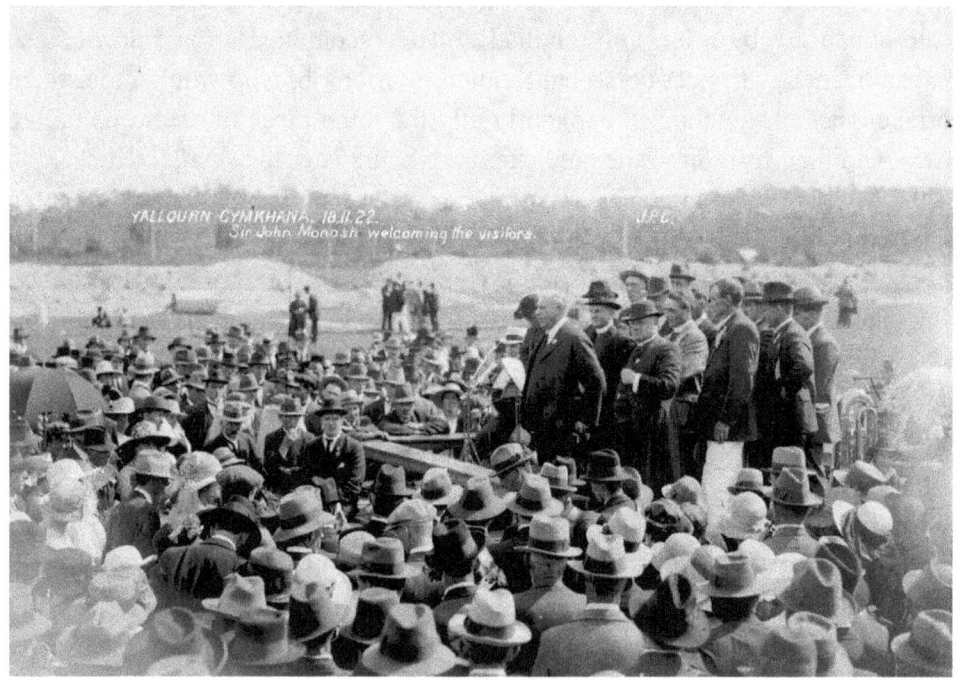

(Fig. 140) Sir John Monash addressing the crowd at the Yallourn gymkhana in 1922.
(Courtesy of State Library of Victoria H2009 18/3)

In May 1923 two 'J.P. Campbell Yallourn photos' appeared in the *Argus* under the heading MACHINE-MADE MOUNTAIN AT YALLOURN. One showed the mountain of over-burden, referred to as 'Mount Monash', material taken from the top of the brown coal open cut. The other was a panorama with the main features labelled from one to seven, showing the giant Bucyrus shovels digging in the foreground, the site of the powerhouse, the 'Yallourn Alps' (over-burden) in the background, and a cleared gap showing the route the electricity transmission line would take transmitting energy to Melbourne.[48] The images were a compact overview of the project produced to impress the public – Campbell's skills were being put to good use.

47 Australasian, 10 October 1925. These may or may not be Campbell's photographs.
48 *Argus*, 15 May 1923.

'Propaganda' was a word freely used in the SEC when Stretton Morgan was appointed the first publicity officer in June 1923, largely one suspects to take some of the pressure off Monash who was a one-man publicity machine.[49] Morgan's role was to:

> conduct continuously a general propaganda by utilising all legitimate agencies, in order to popularise: (a) the use of electricity; (b) the use of brown coal and briquettes; and (c) the policies and proposals of the Commission in regard to all its activities.[50]

If propaganda was used against the SEC, Morgan was to 'undertake a counter-propaganda'. Beside keeping up with parliamentary debates, he was to observe press opinion of the Commission and the 'public utterances by public men' and to 'contradict, controvert, or correct statements and reports adverse to the interests of the Commission'.[51] His duties also involved supplying the press with information on SEC activities, and, importantly for Campbell's official photography duties, arranging 'for cinema pictures of the Commission's operations and works to be taken and publicly exhibited', and also arranging for photographs to be used by the press.[52]

Monash left it to Morgan to communicate with the press except in special cases. He reminded heads of branches that existing rules debarred officers of the SEC from giving information to the press. It was up to the heads of branches to supply suitable material for publicity.[53] In his role as official photographer Campbell was therefore under the direction of the publicity officer. Official photographs were released for specific purposes, for example lantern slides produced from Campbell's photographs were used in public lectures delivered by Monash to promote the SEC, at a time when Monash was fighting to ensure the organisation had a monopoly of electricity production and sales.[54]

How these restrictions affected Campbell's private photography is not clear.

---

49 WR Armstrong, 'History of the State Electricity Commission of Victoria', Unpublished Manuscript, 1938, MS 13064, MS Box 3747/7-8, State Library of Victoria, p. 421.

50 File: Staff General Press Statements, January 1924–December 1925, Correspondence, Papers and Memorabilia of Sir John Monash, VPRS 9673/P1, Unit 7, PROV.

51 Ibid.

52 Ibid.

53 File: Staff General 1922-23, 'Monash letter to Heads of Branches, 9 July 1923', Correspondence, Papers and Memorabilia of Sir John Monash, VPRS 9673/P1, Unit 7, PROV.

54 Roland Perry, *Monash: The Outsider Who Won a War*, Random House Australia, paperback edition, 2005, p. 479.

Was he free to wander through Yallourn and the SEC works taking photographs on weekends, or did his private and official photography of Yallourn and environs blur into one? He produced composite postcards of Yallourn scenes under his own copyright, but this may have been within SEC guidelines, as some of these were sold to raise money for Yallourn institutions, and they promoted the town and the SEC.[55] Campbell was a trusted, loyal SEC staffer, committed to its goals. But as we have seen, he combined his art with his official photography wherever he could. Did he 'self' censor images that may have been detrimental to the SEC, or did the publicity officer act as censor, or both?

The briquetting plant came from Germany, the only country to have the specialised manufacturing capabilities to supply the project with the technology necessary to make it viable. In August 1922, despite the reluctance of the Commonwealth government to let former enemy aliens into the country, six German experts arrived to supervise the installation of the briquette plant.[56] They were isolated in the southern camp away from the other workers in case of trouble.[57] As well as pioneering the use of high moisture brown coal in briquette manufacturing and electricity generation, the Germans were experts at using of factory photography for promotional purposes. Photography created an industrial identity in countries like Germany, England and America. Progressive German industrialists, for example the Krupp family, used photographic propaganda to promote their steel empire sixty years before the Yallourn project began.[58] Such trends in the use of photography ultimately spread to Australia. Growth showing return for capital invested is important in private and government ventures, being recorded in statistics, words and pictures.[59] Bland figures were too dry as a measurement of growth, so photography was chosen as a medium to demonstrate it.[60]

---

55 This will be discussed in more detail later in this chapter.

56 Cecil Edwards, *Brown Power*, p. 67.

57 Colin Harvey, *Yallourn Power Station*, p. 25.

58 Klaus Tenfelde's edited book *Pictures of Krupp*, using material from the Krupp Historical Archive at Villa Hugel in Essen-Bredney, takes photography seriously as a source for historical purposes and aims 'to debate the connection between photography and history in the Industrial Age from as many different aspects as possible'. *History of Krupp* confines itself mainly to the pre-1914 period, only touching on the First World War when the Krupp influence was at its height. Klaus Tenfelde, Introduction, in Klaus Tenfelde (ed.), *Pictures of Krupp: Photography and History in the Industrial Age*, Philip Wilson, London, 2005, pp. 9-10.

59 Ulrich Borsdorf and Sigrid Schneider, 'A mighty business: factory and town in Krupp photographs', in *Pictures of Krupp*, p. 123.

60 Ibid., p. 127.

Post war Campbell was coming to terms with the Machine Age, like many other photographers. While he was immersed in Yallourn documenting the wonders of modern industrial technology, photography as art and practice was changing. Was Campbell influenced by these trends during the 1920s? The Machine Age, which had started in the nineteenth century, peaked in the 1920s.[61] Dominated by the assembly line, the steel bridge, the railroad, the automobile and the power station, it was a revolution in technology. Factories and tools became symbols of the industrial world, and photographers rose to the challenge, particularly in Germany and America, two of the most industrialised nations.[62] By the 1920s, the photograph 'had become the most popular and powerful medium for creating icons of machine-made products'.[63] The period after the First World War 'proved a boom time for machine art'.[64] Artists believed that technology would improve the world – the machine was a new God. Germany, the UK and the USA 'incorporated photography into their industrial projects'.[65] The Depression dampened the enthusiasm of lovers of the machine, and, after World War Two, industry was equated with mass carnage and the power of industrial imagery waned.[66]

Between the wars, the American photographer Margaret Bourke-White, with her 'lingering pictorialism', allowed 'steam and smoke to obscure the sharp edges of the machine-made environment, giving her images a sense of drama', in the promotional photographs she took for industrialists.[67] Charles Sheeler, a painter as well as photographer, portrayed the factory as a spiritual entity, a cathedral in which to worship the machine. Paul Strand also wrote of the machine as the 'New God'.[68]

Campbell's approach to photographing the industrial landscape of the 1920s was however more akin to pictorial photography in the early 1900s, when artists

61 Kim Sichel, 'From Icon to Irony: German and American Industrial Photography', in Kim Sichel, with additional essays by John Stomberg and Judith Bookbinder, *Icon to Irony: German and American Industrial Photography*, Boston University Art Gallery, 1995, p. 1.

62 Ibid.

63 Ibid., p. 3.

64 Ibid., p. 4.

65 Ibid., p. 5.

66 Ibid., pp. 8-9.

67 John Stomberg, 'A "United States of the World": Industry and Photography between the wars', in Kim Sichel, *Icon to Irony: German and American Industrial Photography*, Boston University Art Gallery, 1995, p. 19-20.

68 Ibid., p. 21.

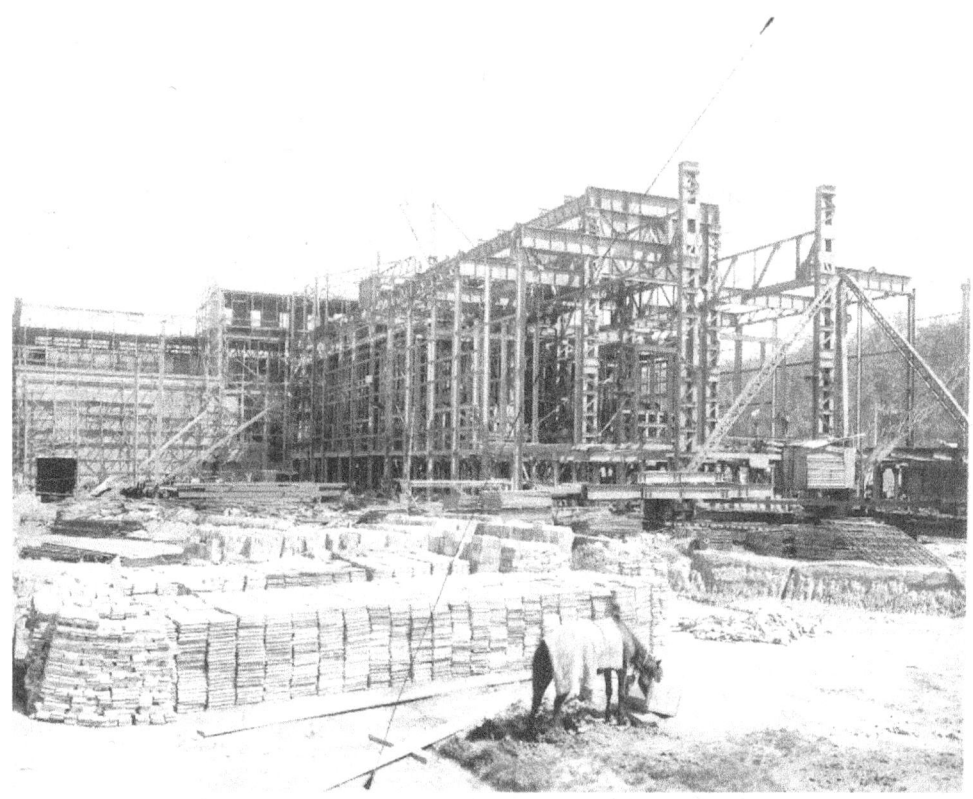

(Fig. 141) Yallourn A Power Station under construction, 20/3/1923.
(Courtesy of Centre for Gippsland Studies, P1/2-3-6/2772)

interested in the industrial world saw a 'strange picturesqueness' in the new structural forms rising in cities. American photographer Alfred Stieglitz observed a New York city building he initially disliked in a different vein when it snowed, 'a picture of new America in the making', and tried to create this impression in his photograph, using a tree in the foreground to give the building an organic feel, and park benches in front of it, along with a rugged-up pedestrian, to provide a human touch.[69]

An example of Campbell observing the Machine Age through the eyes of a pictorialist can be seen in his use of a similar approach to Stieglitz's, the use of trees and even horses to soften the industrial images. This may have been an attempt to make the building more amenable, or to hanker back to the world of the landscape image, the picturesque, the quieter days of the horse, and suggests an underlying 'resentment of modernity, a reluctance to accept its inevitability'

69 Karen Lucic, *Charles Sheeler and the Cult of the Machine*, Reaktion, London, 1991, pp. 23-4.

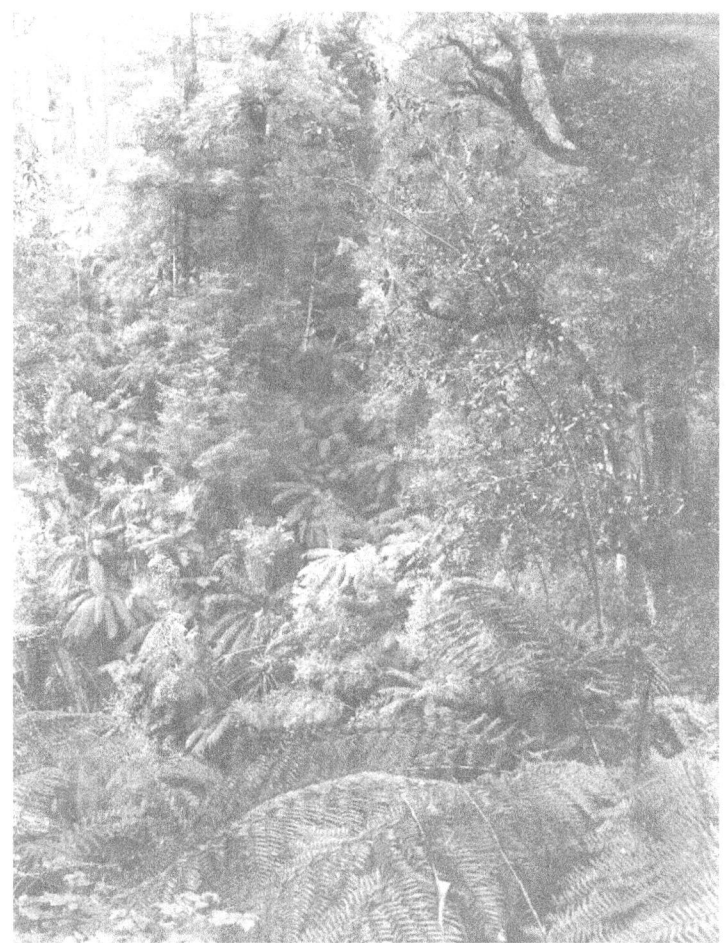

(Fig. 142) 'Fern Dell Yarram Road.' 1926. This scene could be a tribute
to Nicholas Caire, and is from one of Campbell's private albums.
(Courtesy of Falconer collection)

(Fig. 141).[70] Thus an apparent expression of solidarity with modernity could in fact indicate rejection of it in this post World War One industrial world. Stieglitz and some of his circle believed the 'fragmenting, dehumanising effects of the machine' needed to be counteracted.[71] Campbell's photographic philosophy still embraced the tree-fern fairy dell, so the industrial world he found himself in, despite his adherence to SEC protocol, must have tested all his artistic sensibilities (Fig. 142).

70 Ibid., p. 26.
71 Ibid.

Perhaps the bush setting of Yallourn, its worship of the garden and its location in Gippsland, softened the Machine Age for Campbell. His location was fortuitous. If he was to be caught up in industrialisation, Yallourn was the place to be, not some stark industrial estate on the edge of a large city. Australia, like America, was part of the New World, pioneering 'a new, completely modern style of personal and social life free of historical baggage', as Karen Lucic said of industrialism in the USA. There was something wholesome 'about a country dominated by the values of industry, commerce and engineering', and with it new art forms would develop.[72] But Campbell had one foot firmly placed in the nineteenth century.

In the late 1920s, the American Charles Sheeler was contracted to photograph the large Ford factory on the Rouge River near Detroit. Ford used the images for publicity and Sheeler was free to publish them himself as works of art. His interior shot 'Ladle Hooks, Open Hearth Building', showing the inside of a massive factory building with a large steel hook suspended from the ceiling and the whole scene mysteriously lit by rectangular windows, was likened to a cathedral.[73] Whether Campbell was exposed to such influences as these through photography magazines and journals is unknown, but his photograph 'Boiler House, Yallourn Power Station' radiates this same sense of industrial worship (Fig. 143).

Pulpit-like structures either side in the foreground draw the eye along a grate-like floor past large sloping columns to an interior of webbed steel, ending in swirling steam while light streams down from a skylight above. A narrow beam of light from a window or gap slices through the middle of the image from the right, and a face-like instrument panel stares with its many eyes at the camera. It is a surreal image elevating the boiler house to holy status, a celebration of Campbell's impressionistic pictorialism. In Germany in the 1920s machine imagery became controversial 'as enthusiasts described the spiritual qualities they found in technology'.[74] What viewer of this image of Campbell's could not admire the achievements of engineers and the SEC, or wonder at the magic of the Machine Age?

---

72 Ibid., pp. 28-9.

73 Ibid., p. 92.

74 John Stomberg, 'A "United States of the World": Industry and Photography between the wars' in Kim Sichel, *Icon to Irony: German and American Industrial Photography*, Boston University Art Gallery, 1995, p. 18. 'Machine imagery' means any artistic interpretation of machines, including photography.

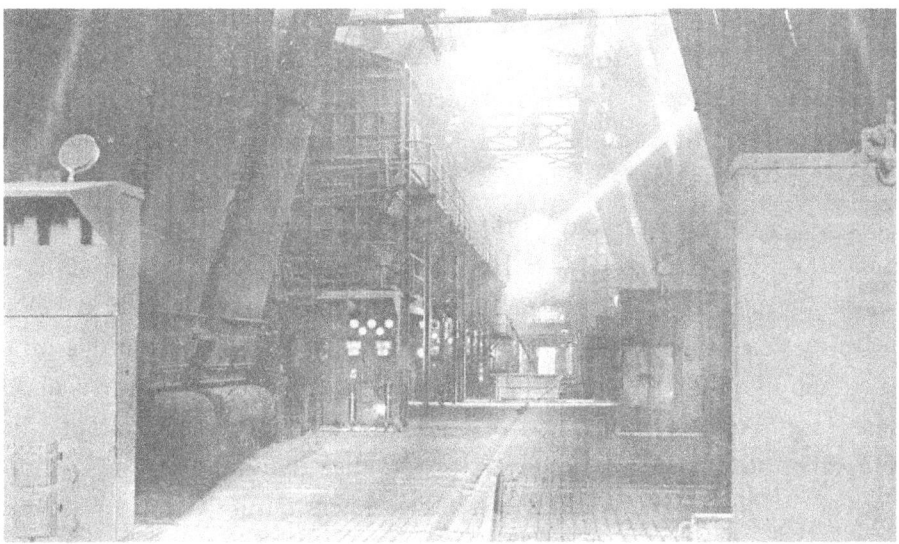

(Fig. 143) 'Boiler House, Yallourn Power Station'. From *Power and Heat: Victoria's National Scheme Electricity & Briquette Production*, SEC, Melbourne, March 1928, p. 30. (Courtesy of Falconer collection)

In Australia, as photography historian Gael Newton wrote, 'by 1928 the Machine Age was felt to herald a new aesthetic'.[75] Photographers like Max Dupain were photographing wheat silos, showing the 'abstract formal structure'.[76] Pictorialists, too, devoured industrial subjects in the 1920s and 1930s 'as they sought to find in the new age pictorial beauty with which they were familiar', however, 'the picturesque atmosphere of the subject was accentuated – not the machine age forms'.[77] This is a fitting description of Campbell's work at the time, the pictorialist in his mid-fifties struggling to embrace the new age. Dressing up industrial subjects with pictorial elements was not in line with the New Photography coming out of Germany and America, with its objectivity, clean, sharp lines and geometric patterns, with the subject focused on for what it was, not dressed up with 'impressionistic effects'.[78]

By 1932 the *Australasian Photo-Review* called for support for the New Photography after concluding that pictorialism had limitations.[79] The pictorialists

75 Gael Newton, *Silver and Grey*, p. 5.

76 Ibid.

77 Ibid.

78 Ibid.

79 Ibid., p. 6.

were bewildered by the embrace of the New Photography. The renowned photographer Harold Cazneaux and his pictorialist friends found it hard 'to accept either abstract or distorted imagery. They remained faithful to the idea of beauty formed in a pre-industrial society and notions of the romantic and picturesque formed a century earlier'.[80]

The clash between the old world and the new seems to be at the heart of Campbell's SEC photography [81] He could not deny photographic skills and a way of observing the world through a camera lens assiduously developed over thirty years. Separating Campbell's private photography from his official photography is difficult without an inventory documenting the provenance of images in various collections. The SEC did not keep a definitive record of official photographs used for promotional purposes; rather, they were scattered amongst a variety of files. There were other photographers during Campbell's time of employment with the SEC, but they were concerned with the more technical and mechanical aspects of operations, rather than the general scenes produced by Campbell.[82]

During the early days of his employment in the Latrobe Valley, Campbell took numerous photographs of the Brown Coal Mine and its environs, before turning his attention to the approximately 3000 acre site acquired by the Commissioners across the river.[83] He photographed the establishment of the various camps and buildings, the excavation of the open cut, the completion of the temporary power house and laboratory, the beginnings of the Yallourn model town, and the construction of the main power station and briquette factory. He also documented

---

80 Ibid., p. 7.

81 Mark Crinson, 'Pictorialism and Industry: Alvin Langdon Coburn in Manchester', *History of Photography*, Volume 30, Number 2, Summer 2006, p. 155. This article discusses a photographer adapting to the industrial world in England during the early 1920s. Alvin Langdon Coburn accepts a commission from industrialists, the city council and a club to photograph industrial and other activities in Manchester for inclusion in promotional booklets. A renowned pictorialist, he has to balance photography as record whilst retaining his own integrity as a pictorialist. Like Campbell, Coburn was a Freemason. He also dabbled in mysticism. Campbell belonged more to the first wave of pictorialists obsessed with the beauty in nature, whereas Coburn, about fifteen years younger, belonged to the second wave, fixated on modern subjects like industrial buildings, with an emphasis on sharper vision and modern styles like Cubism.

82 For the purposes of identifying Campbell's Yallourn photographs, I have tended to rely on his caption writing on the front or back of an image. His initials may be present, and there may be a date (i.e. between 1920 and 1928 when he was the official photographer) or, in rare cases, the style of the photograph may be used to connect him to the picture.

83 Meredith Fletcher, *Digging People Up for Coal*, p. 17.

floods and fires in the open cut, recording the hazards involved in the project as well as the grandeur as it progressed.

One of the principal photographic tools to achieve this was the panorama, sweeping views of factory-like buildings and landscapes. These broad views were widely disseminated by appearing in SEC annual reports, weekly pictorial newspapers, SEC publications such as *Power and Heat*, or used by Monash in the form of lantern slides on the promotional lecture circuit. They conveyed the enormity of the scheme in enhancing future prosperity for Victoria. They also went some way to legitimising the semi-entrepreneurial activity of the scheme.[84]

Campbell did not have the best equipment and facilities for photography. He had to be content with a darkroom attached to the main office in Yallourn, and had to balance photography duties with clerical work. Nevertheless he applied his skills to the best of his ability by utilising available facilities. To obtain wide-angled views of the SEC works it was necessary to obtain an elevated vantage point, something Campbell was familiar with from his early days as a landscape photographer. As the SEC plant was erected, various buildings provided convenient viewing platforms, particularly the briquette factory chimney. It is a testament to Campbell's fitness that, at about sixty years of age, he held the record for the fastest climb to the top of the 330 foot-high chimney, an ascent he made regularly 'in the course of his photographic duties' (Fig.144).[85]

Campbell's name was generally not appended to his official photographs, again a condition he was accustomed to after employment with the External Affairs Department and the army. However, there were rare cases when photographs appearing in the press promoting the SEC had Campbell's name attached, as in the *Argus* in May 1923 showing the open-cut. In August 1923 the *Argus* published single SEC photographs with his name underneath in two separate editions. The first was a picture of the new weir on the Latrobe River, built to provide water to the power station.[86] The second image was of the briquette factory under construction, with text quoting Sir John Monash, declaring proudly that the

---

84 Klaus Tenfelde, *Pictures of Krupp*, p. 313. The Yallourn SEC project was, of course, ultimately of immense economic benefit to Victoria.

85 WR Armstrong, 'History of the State Electricity Commission of Victoria, 1927-1947', MS 13064, MS Box 3747/7-8, State Library of Victoria, p. 87. Whether he was carrying his photographic equipment is not mentioned.

86 *Argus* , 1 August 1923.

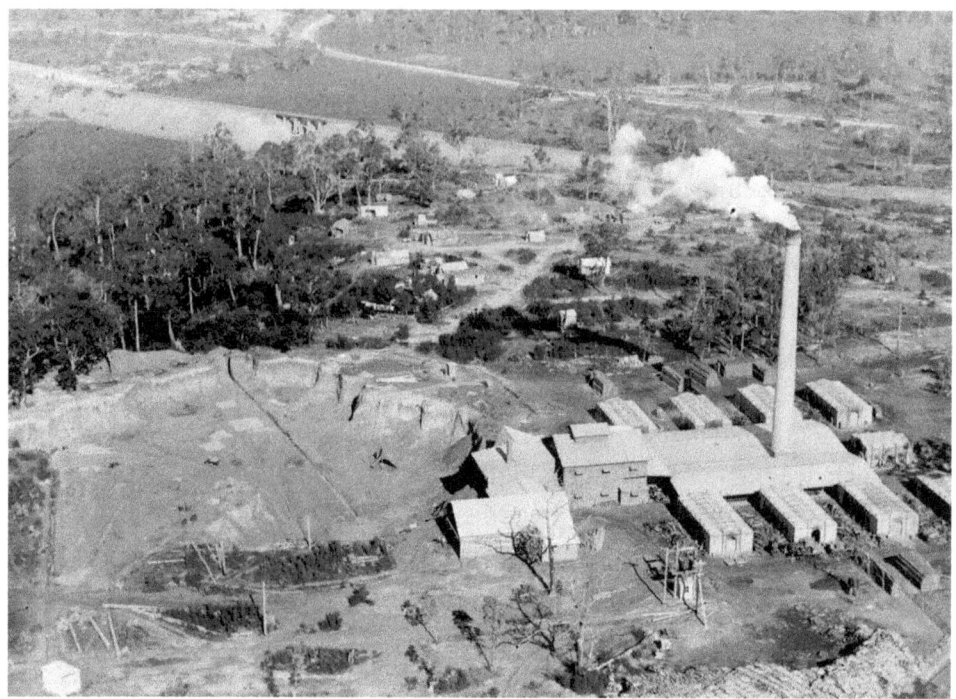

(Fig. 144) The Yallourn Brickworks from the briquette factory chimney. This image is also in the Latrobe City JP Campbell album as 'Birds-eye view of Brick, Tile and Pipe works'. (Courtesy of State Library of Victoria H2009 18/276)

factory would be producing briquettes in the New Year.[87] Monash was anxious to demonstrate the satisfactory progress of the whole project in order to allay fears of delays and wastage of public money, views promulgated in the Melbourne *Age* newspaper, 'a bitter and often intemperate critic' of the SEC.[88] Images of Yallourn buildings approaching completion were evidence of a project coming to fruition. In this case Campbell received recognition for his photographic work, something rarely seen during his previous periods of employment as a public servant and soldier.

Campbell had a positive approach to his role, trying to make his record images as interesting and artistic as possible. Comfortable in his position within a large organisation, he could have succumbed to a photographic methodology of objectivity and blandness. Some of the official images appeared in his private albums with different captions, presented as gifts to people departing Yallourn,

---

87 *Argus*, 4 August 1923.
88 Cecil Edwards, *Brown Power*, p. 82.

or in photographic booklets sold for charitable purposes at the general store. These were under his name, an indirect way of gaining credit for photographic output. He was largely able to overcome the tension between pictorialist and record photography, as an analysis of his SEC photographs shows. Postcards compiled by Campbell provided cheap mementoes for Yallourn workers and visitors to take away. They reinforced pride in the Yallourn venture community and Campbell's fondness for it. (Fig. 145).

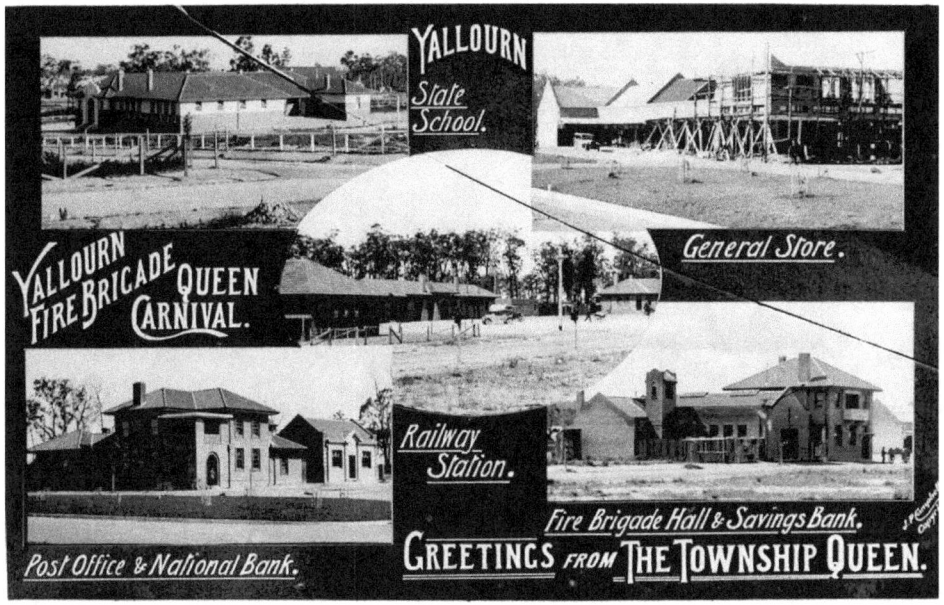

(Fig. 145) One of JP Campbell's composite postcards of Yallourn produced for commercial purposes. (Courtesy of State Library of Victoria H2009 18/503)

11

MAKING AN IMPRESSION

SEC Annual Reports – Power & Heat – *A Life in Yallourn* – *Store Manager and* Live Wire *Editor – Photography and Impressionism – Illness, Retirement and Death*

Campbell dutifully performed his various roles for the SEC. He was a dedicated Mason, and had joined the Morwell Lodge early during his time in the Latrobe Valley, rising to Worshipful Master within its ranks in 1925. By the end of the 1920s he was a member of the Royal Arch Chapter and associated with a number of lodges throughout Gippsland. He reached the Rose Croix level of Masonry in 1927 and was chaplain of the Morwell Lodge in 1929. In 1930-31 he became a Grand Standard Bearer within the Grand Lodge at State level.[1] As a single man with grown up children, involvement with the Masons and in the general community may have filled a void in his life. He regularly attended church, was a proud returned soldier and believed in the SEC's goals.

In February 1930 Sir John Monash eagerly awaited an article on the communal life of Yallourn in the Saturday *Argus'* Camera Supplement.[2] Titled 'The Spirit of Yallourn: Contentment, Civic Pride and Progress', and written by Norman McCance, the piece extolled the virtues of the SEC town, with the text accompanied by five photographs supplied by the SEC's publicity officer. An image showing houses in the background and extensive gardens in the foreground was captioned: 'A corner of the Yallourn township to-day. There are no cliques or opposing sections of the community here. The pretty little villas illustrated are let at a moderate weekly rental to employees of the Commission, and the artisan and the superintendant live in adjoining houses'.[3]

Providing a contrast, and illustrating the starting point of the town, was Campbell's much-used photograph of Maiden Street in 1922, part of the caption

---

1 JP Campbell's 'United Grand Lodge' book courtesy of Noel Fethers. *Argus*, 6 September 1935, *Gippsland Times*, 21 January 1929, and *Morwell Advertiser*, 17 May 1929.
2 'Correspondence, Papers and Memorabilia of Sir John Monash', VPRS 9673, Unit 8, Staff General Statements for Press, 1929-30, Memo Chairman to Chief Clerk, 24 February 1930, PROV.
3 *Argus*, 8 March 1930.

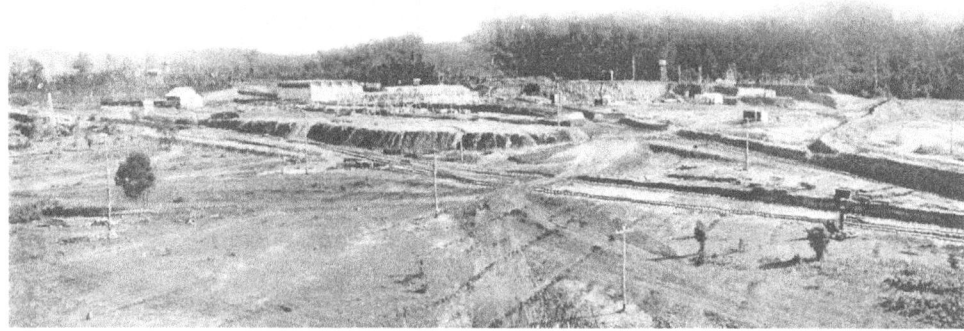

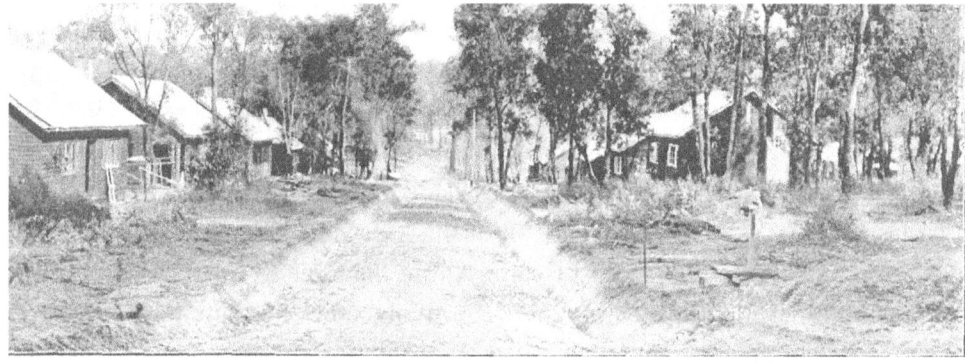

(Fig. 146) Two of Campbell's photographs in the 1922 SEC Annual Report. On the bottom is Maiden Street. (Courtesy of the PROV, VPRS 1382/P1 Unit 1, File SEC of Vic. 3rd Annual Report, 1922)

stating: 'Homes were carved for the workmen out of virgin bush'. The other three photographs showed hospital facilities, the fire brigade, and healthy children in a playground.[4] Campbell's early SEC photographs were frequently used in tandem with 'modern' images to demonstrate perceived progress. In this way change was recorded and tradition cultivated within the organisation. As the temporary power house, offices and accommodation buildings at Yallourn were torn down and replaced with more permanent structures, they were photographed as historical record, contributing to the progressive image of the SEC.

The annual reports were used as one of the SEC's main publicity strategies, being tabled in Parliament and distributed to the press and beyond. The annual report's presentation influenced future funding by the government, particularly in the early years when Monash was fending off critics. Visual evidence of a successful scheme was important in an era when the photograph was generally

---

4 Ibid.

perceived as reality. The first annual report containing photographs was that of 1921-2.[5] There were eight photographs, including five of the Yallourn works and environs in an appendix. 'Yallourn Township – Typical Street View' (Lower image, Fig. 146) proudly displayed new houses sprouting amongst the bush. A deeply cut road leads into and dissects the picture, a favourite Campbell format. This was Maiden Street, the first street constructed.[6] The picture above displayed the site of the main power station.

Of the other six photographs two show the removal of overburden at the open cut, and one is a distant shot of weir construction on the Latrobe River. The 1923 annual report again showed wide views of the open cut and power station construction sites, and this time showed the briquette factory under construction. Housing construction had increased and there were three views of the Yallourn township, showing neat rows of houses. There was also an image of the weir on the Latrobe River with the partly completed power station and horses in the background, contrasting the new and old worlds, probably an intentionally inclusion by Campbell.[7]

After the main power station and briquette factory were completed, the focus shifted to industrial photography. These photographs included indoor scenes of machinery, such as the first turbo-generator in the power station and presses in the 'Briquetting Factory'. These looked like artillery lined up in a large hall, symbols of power and engineering might (Fig. 147).[8]

Despite this enthusiasm for machinery, sweeping panoramas remained apparent, such as an elevated view of Yallourn township surrounded by bush (Fig. 148).[9] Houses spread out across the landscape imposing order on it, the remnant bush dark and ominous on either side.

The 1925 annual report contained an image of the first train load of briquettes leaving Yallourn, taken from the top of one of the trucks or the guard's van, with station staff and workers looking at the camera. This was an old technique of Campbell's, used prior to the war when he photographed rail trucks full of wheat

---

5 3rd Annual Report, 1922, VPRS 13872/P1, File: SEC of Vic., PROV, pp. 23-6.

6 This photograph was also located in VPRS 15785/P3 Box 1, PROV, mounted on cardboard with two other photographs, with Campbell's writing visible and the date 31 March 1922.

7 4th Annual Report, 1923, VPRS 13872/P1 Unit 1, File: SEC of Vic., PROV, pp. 27-33. The last three pages show scenes from other areas.

8 5th Annual Report, 1924, VPRS 13872/P1 Unit 1, File: SEC of Vic., PROV, pp. 29-32.

9 5th Annual Report, 1924, PROV, p. 29.

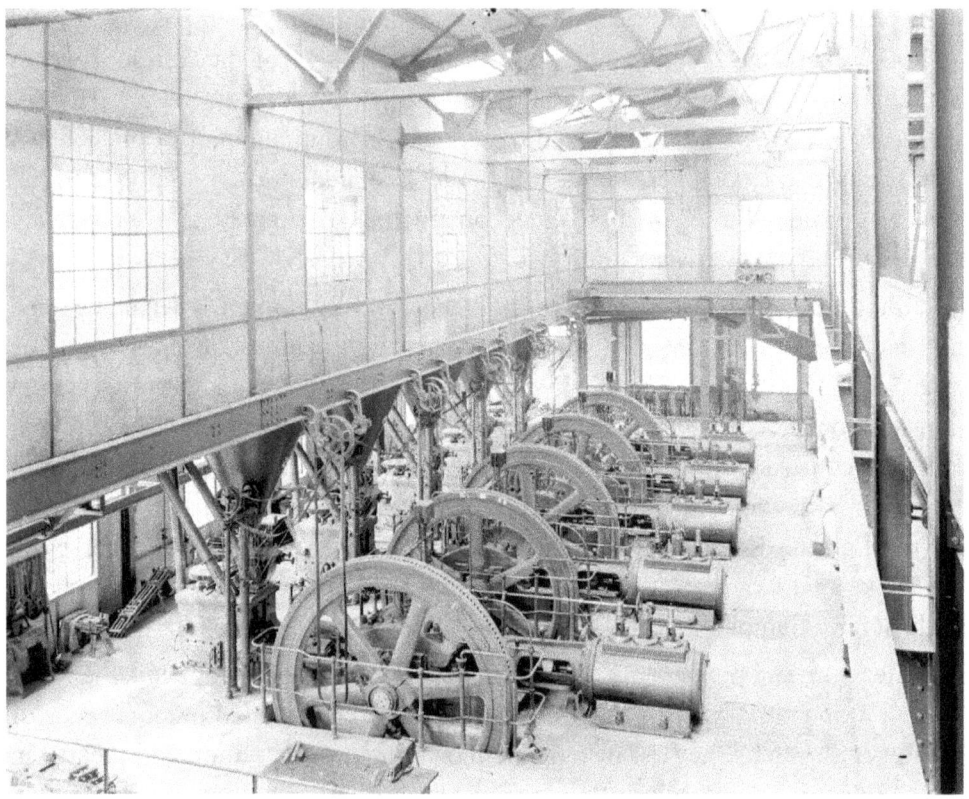

(Fig. 147) Interior of the Briquette Factory showing the presses. This image was included in the SEC's 1924 Annual Report. (Courtesy of State Library of Victoria, H2009 18/1059)

bags at Merrigum Railway Station. One other image in this report stands out, a landscape view of a transmission line easement littered with the remnants of fallen trees, with a bullock driver urging his charges up a rise in the foreground.[10]

A two part panorama published in the 1927 Annual Report showing Yallourn through coppicing eucalypts recovering from a bushfire displays Campbell's skills in obtaining good composition and balance (Fig. 149). Using a pictorialist technique, the regenerating bush is used to soften the view, with the trees towering over the town in the foreground, almost diminishing it.

Retrospective material dominated the tenth annual report, with photographs dispersed amongst the text for the first time, rather than placed in an appendix. These included 'Turning the First Sod' and views of the town and open cut.[11]

---

10 6th Annual Report, 1925, VPRS 13872/P1 Unit: 1, File: SEC of Vic., PROV, pp. 51-6.
11 10th Annual Report, 1929, VPRS 1382/P1 Unit 1, File: SEC of Vic., PROV, pp. 3-11.

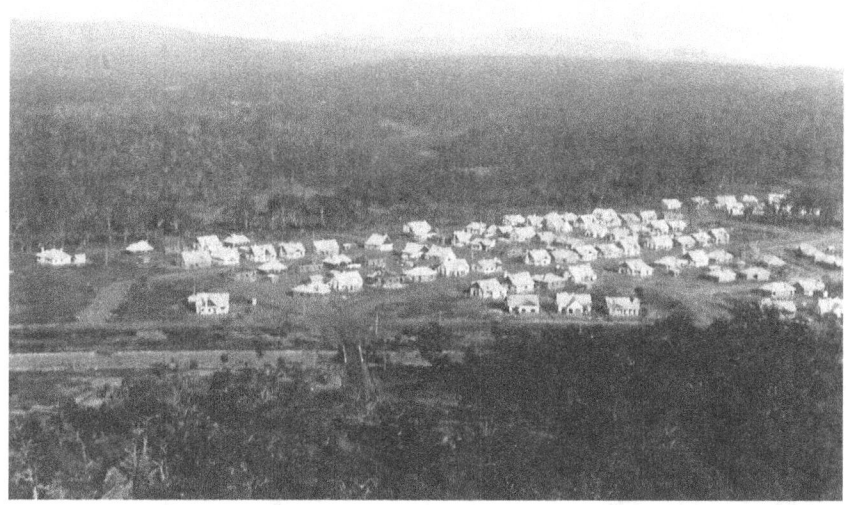

(Fig. 148) An elevated view of Yallourn, part of a panorama view
which appeared in the SEC's Annual Report of 1924.
(Courtesy of PROV, VPRS 15785/P3 Unit 5)

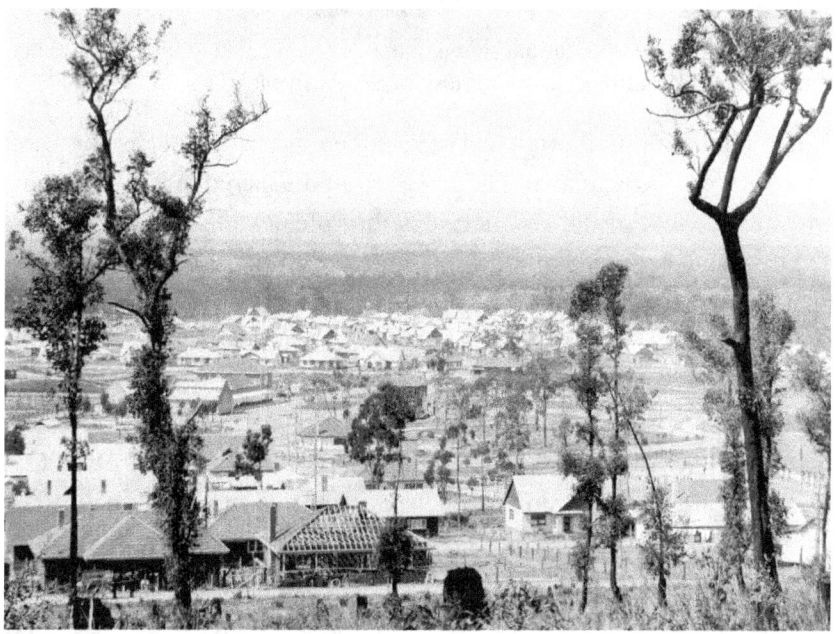

(Fig. 149) Yallourn Township shown through coppicing trees. With these shots
Campbell showed Yallourn within the wider landscape. This is similar to part of
a panorama in the 1927 Annual Report.
(Courtesy of State Library of Victoria, H2009 18/856)

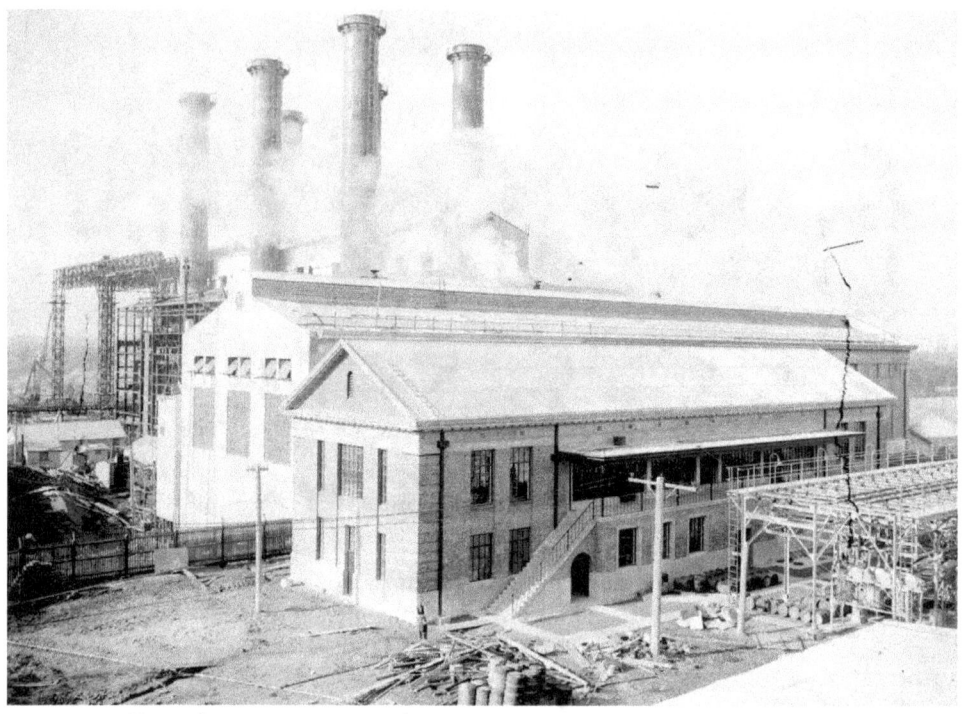

(Fig. 150) Yallourn A Power Station, showing the Telpher coal handling plant, boiler house, turbine house and control room. (Courtesy of State Library of Victoria, H2009 18/651)

Thereafter photographs diminished in number in the annual reports, replaced with more graphs and statistics. The 1930 report displayed only two photographs, one an exterior view of the Briquette Factory plus extensions, showing a stark, spindly tree smack in the middle, a hint the photographer was Campbell.[12] Visual reassurance of progress was by this stage probably no longer necessary: the venture was established and returning an income, loosening dependency on government grants. Unassumingly and without public recognition Campbell had made an important contribution to the promotion of the SEC. A Campbell photograph of the Yallourn A power station appeared in the 1924 SEC Annual Report (Fig. 150). Transmission of electricity to Melbourne commenced in 1924.

The SEC also produced promotional booklets, such as the eighty page *Power and Heat: Victoria's National Scheme of Electricity & Briquette Production* published in 1928.[13] Besides the extensive text, it contained a

12 11th Annual report, 1930, VPRS 13872/P1 Unit 1, File: SEC of Vic., PROV, pp. 27-8.
13 *Power and Heat: Victoria's National Scheme of Electricity & Briquette Production* , SECV, March 1928, Melbourne.

number of photographs, many of them Campbell's. Its publication coincided with the commencement of the Lower Rubicon Hydro-electric Power Station in Victoria. Many images of this scheme had already appeared in annual reports. Campbell also incorporated some of the photographs in his own private albums. This provides a rare opportunity to compare the use of a particular image as promotional record and pictorial art, demonstrating the two were compatible. Photographs that performed both functions were landscapes, in this case two ways of looking at the same river (Figs. 151 & 152).

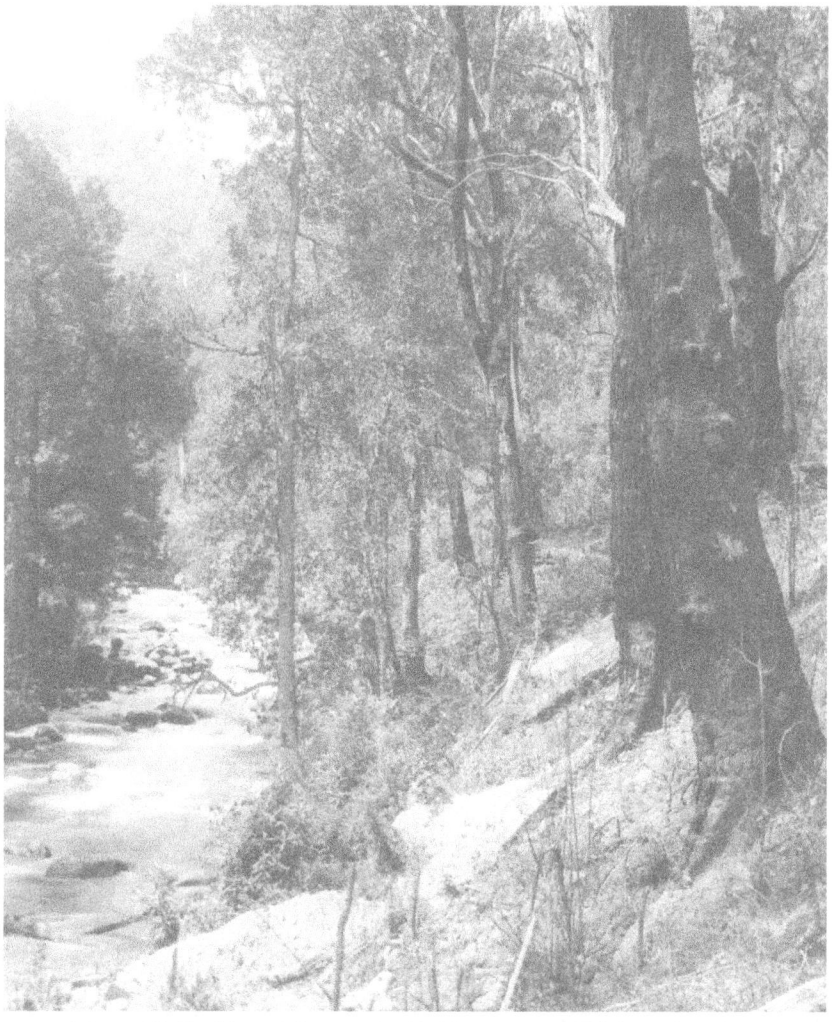

(Fig. 151) 'Rubicon River. 1926'. This is a beautiful forest scene in Campbell's private album, but in Fig. 172 it is invested with a different meaning. (Courtesy of Falconer collection)

271

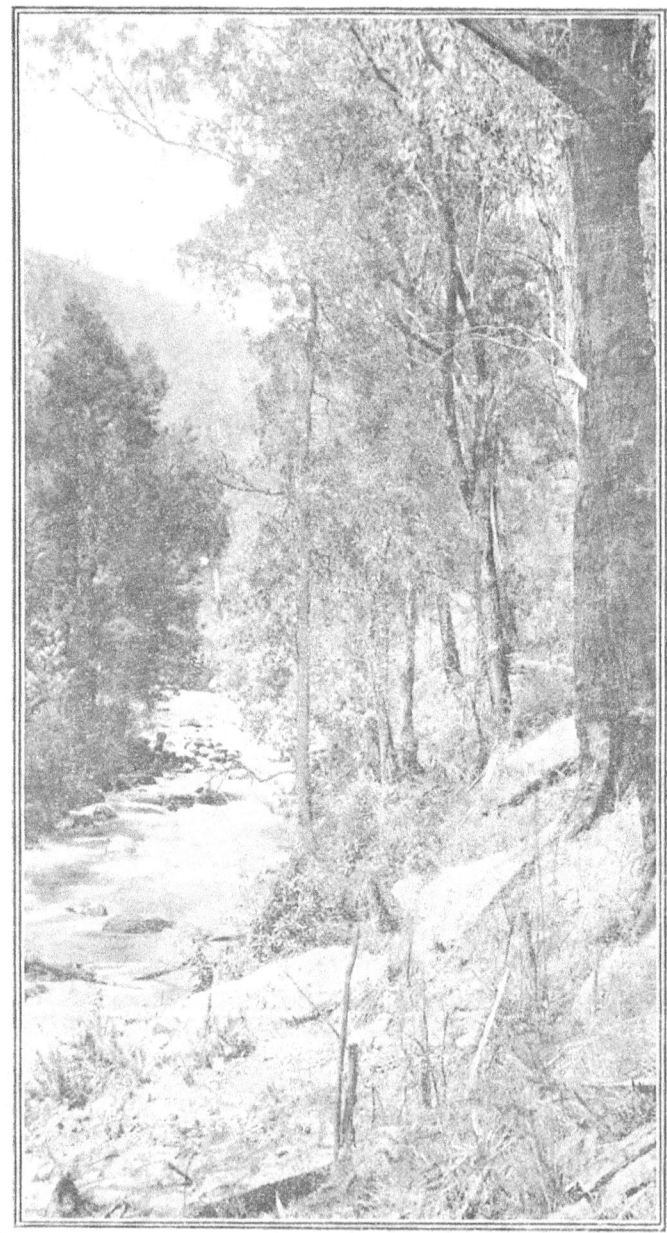

The Royston River—Site of Diversion Dam.—Sugarloaf-Rubicon Hydro-Electric Scheme.

(Fig. 152) The Rubicon River, 1926, photograph as it appears in the 1928 SEC promotional Booklet, *Power and Heat*, renamed the Royston River. The caption invests it with a whole new meaning. (Courtesy of Falconer collection)

In *Power and Heat* the caption invited the viewer to imagine a dam on a river: the site was for practical, industrial purposes. In Campbell's album the image was simply a scenic portrayal of a river flowing through a forest. As in the past in the Northern Territory and the Middle East he was cleverly using his employer's resources to achieve a result which satisfied his own and their demands.

Campbell's ability to create a balanced, absorbing image is proven time and again. In the photograph 'Elevated Electric Railway', published in *Power & Heat*, Campbell captured the elegant sweep of the railway in contrast to the bulk of the bunker (Fig. 153). The linear aspect of the picture draws the viewer into the image, a frequent Campbell technique. In the image 'Conveying Coal from the open cut to Briquetting Factory', a lone employee can be seen walking behind one of the trucks, dwarfed by it, showing the dominance of the machine. There is also the poignant contrast between the bush on the left and the briquette factory

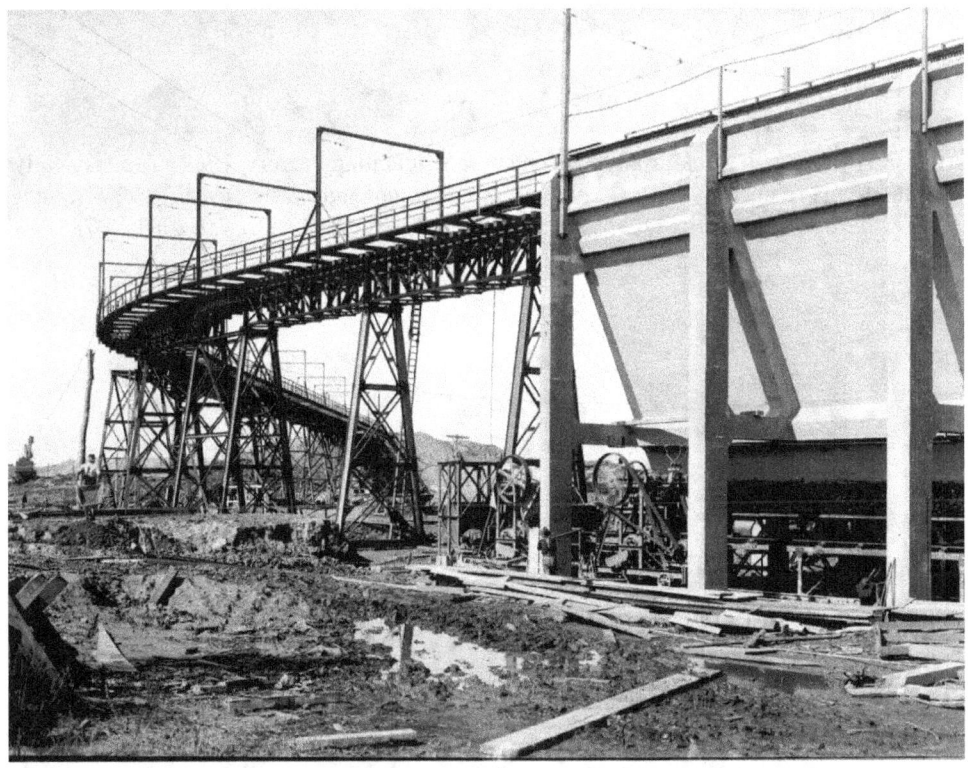

(Fig 153.) 'Elevated Electric Railway'. From Power and Heat: Victoria's National Scheme of Electricity & Briquette Production, SEC, Melbourne, March 1928, p. 26.
(Courtesy of State Library of Victoria, H2009 18/760)

on the far right (Fig. 154). The grandeur of the project is shown in Campbell's image of the weir gates with the power station in the background (Fig. 155). The waters of the Latrobe River had been harnessed, but Campbell had his own view of its tranquillity amidst industrialisation (Fig. 156).

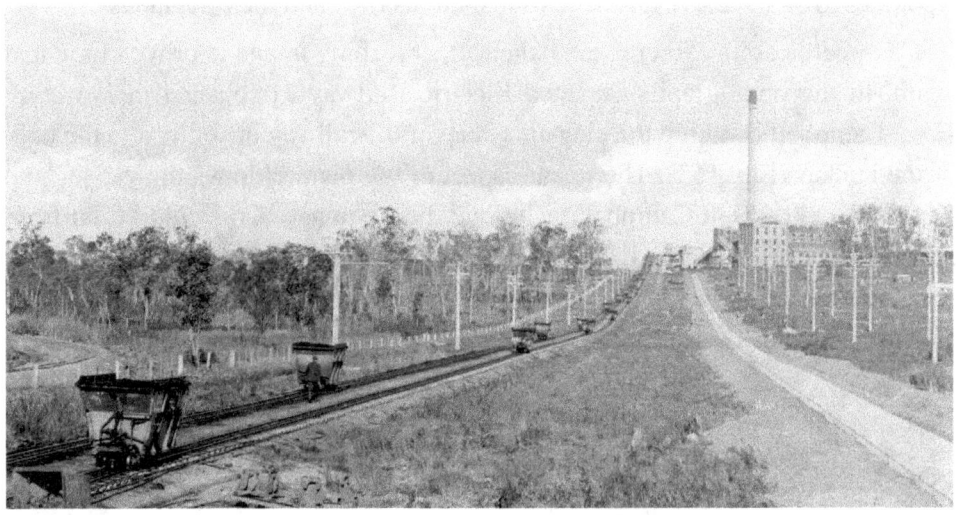

(Fig 154) 'Conveying Coal from the open cut to Briquetting Factory. The haulage is nearly a mile long'. From: *Power and Heat: Victoria's National Scheme of Electricity & Briquette Production*, SEC, Melbourne, March 1928, p. 65. (Courtesy of SLV, H2009 18/786)

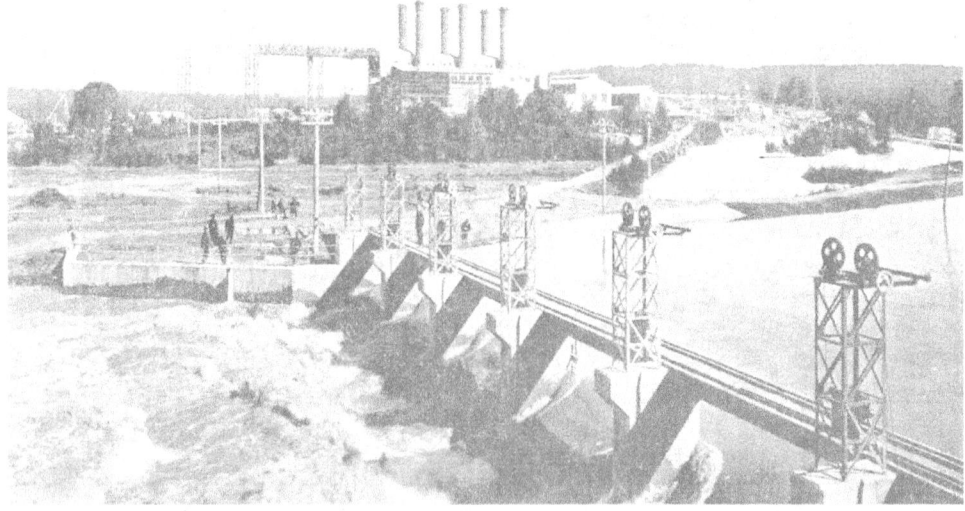

(Fig. 155) 'Weir and Cold-Water Storage, Latrobe River, Yallourn, showing Power Station in background'. From *Power and Heat: Victoria's National Scheme of Electricity & Briquette Production*, SEC, Melbourne, March 1928, p. 29. (Courtesy of Falconer collection)

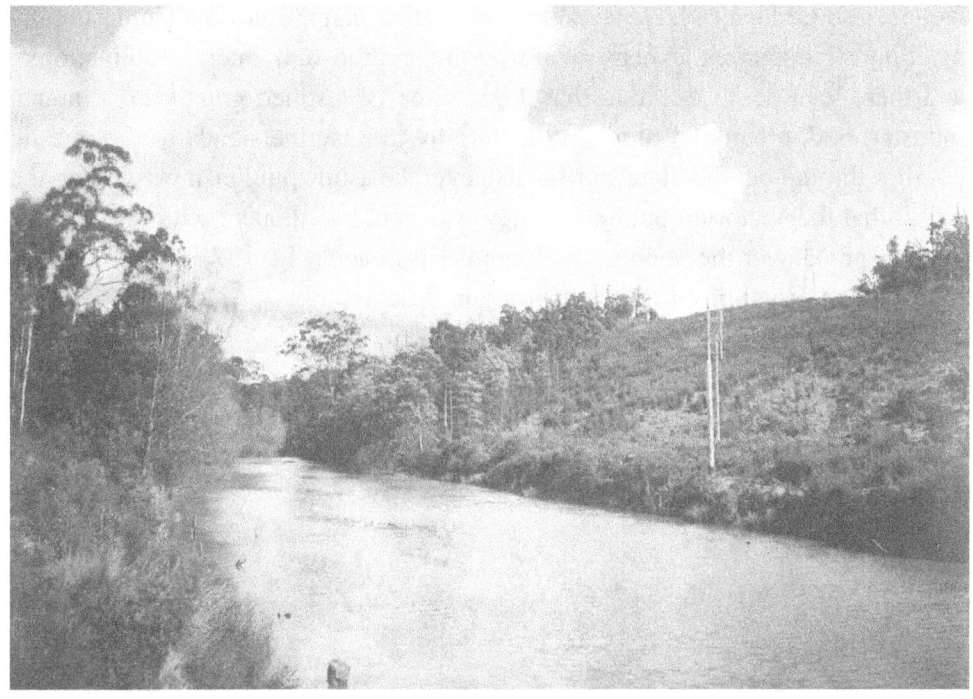

(Fig 156) 'Latrobe River. Yallourn'. (Courtesy of Falconer collection)

In November 1926 Monash requested three photographs of the SEC operations at Yallourn from the publicity officer. He needed a photograph to accompany a 1200 word article he was writing for a supplement on Australia to be published by the London *Times* in May 1927, commemorating the first sitting of Federal Parliament in Canberra.[14] The photograph selected was a panoramic view of the Yallourn Power Station, possibly at 'knock off' time, a classic Campbell shot (Fig. 157).[15]

The wide road is scattered with workers, drawing the line of sight into the scene. The right side is dominated by factory buildings, the left with foliage in the foreground and the impressive chimneys and structural outline of the station building in the background. Monash's article trumpeted Victoria's vast brown coal deposits and their utilisation for electricity generation. He also lauded the SEC's construction of the Yallourn and Newport Power Stations on which £10,000,000

---

14 Correspondence, Papers and Memorabilia of Sir John Monash, VPRS 9673/P1, Unit 7, File: Press Statements, January 1926 – December 1926, Letter to Publicity Officer, 8 November 1926, PROV.
15 London *Times*, 9 May 1927. Although the photograph is not attributed to Campbell, he was the official photographer for the SEC in Yallourn at the time, and it has all the hallmarks of his work.

had been so far invested. He concluded by stating that the 'investment is already meeting all operating expenses and administration and interest obligations', and there 'can be no question that the scheme is destined greatly to stimulate industry, both urban and rural, and materially to raise the standard of domestic comfort throughout the State'.[16] Monash, ever the astute publicist, was telling the world that the Victorian public's money was being well spent with the benefits evenly spread over the population. Campbell's image (Fig. 157) went some way in providing visual proof for these pronouncements.

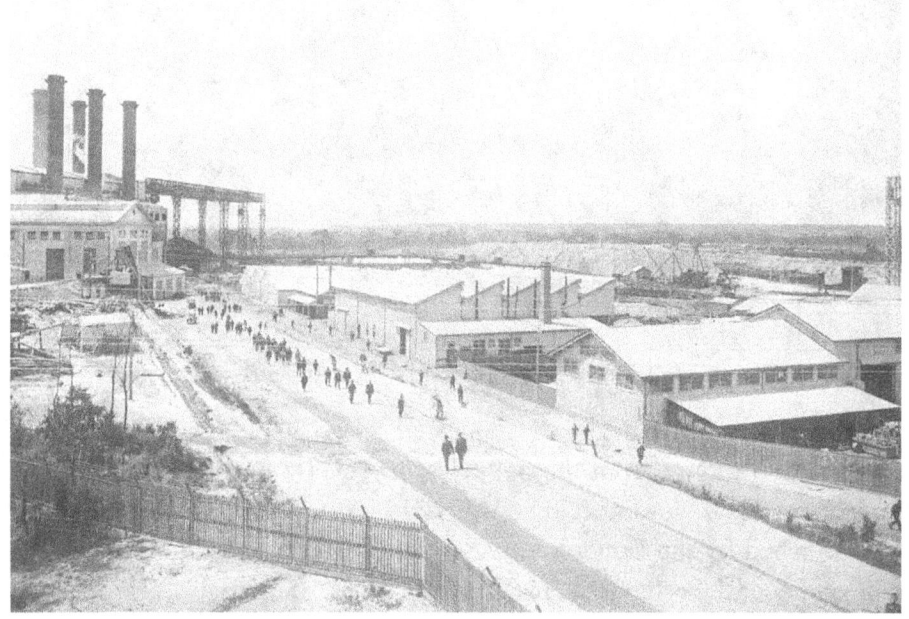

(Fig. 157) 'ELECTRICITY IN VICTORIA' The photograph accompanying Sir John Monash's article on the SEC in the London *Times* of 9 May 1927. (Courtesy of State Library of Victoria, H2009. 18/1018)

As Yallourn grew during the 1920s Campbell found himself increasingly busy, juggling the roles of clerk-in-charge, official photographer, and between 1921 and July 1923 manager of the Yallourn General Store. Energetic as he was, Campbell could not do everything. Ex SEC engineer turned historian, JW McMahon, relates how another SEC photographer began operating at the construction site of the main Yallourn Power Station, mainly in the field of internal plant and machinery photography, but was dismissed when Head Office

---

16 Ibid.

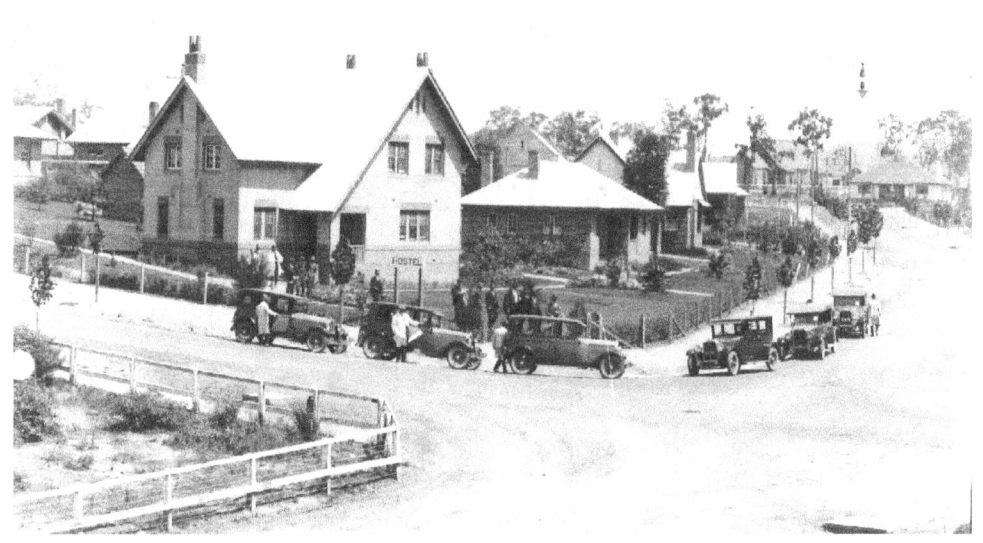

(Fig. 158) The Yallourn Hostel. This image is also in Noel Fethers' collection, dated August 1928, about the time Campbell was moving out into his own private accommodation.
(Courtesy of Centre for Gippsland Studies, P1/2-3-6/2080)

ruled Campbell to be the official photographer, with time to spare from his two main occupations, chief clerk and store manager, to do the job. Campbell tried valiantly to catch up with a backlog of photography, work which sometimes involved getting into dangerous positions. When asked to take a photograph inside a boiler drum at the top of steel columns, he refused to squeeze through the man-hole, and as a result the other photographer was reinstated.[17] By this time Campbell was in his late fifties and although still very fit for his age, would not have been as flexible as he used to be in confined spaces.

Accommodation in the town improved and finally Campbell was able to move into the newly built staff hostel (Fig. 158). Campbell may well have organised this image, with the cars parked in unusual positions. It shows a neat garden town with newly planted trees, modern houses, wide streets and remnant eucalypts rising up in the background between the houses. Campbell led an active social life. From his early days in Yallourn, he took part in improving the living standards of its inhabitants, having firstly represented the Commissioners on a Progress and

17 JW McMahon, 'The Early Years at Yallourn', 1919-1926, typescript, SEC, 1968, p. 88.

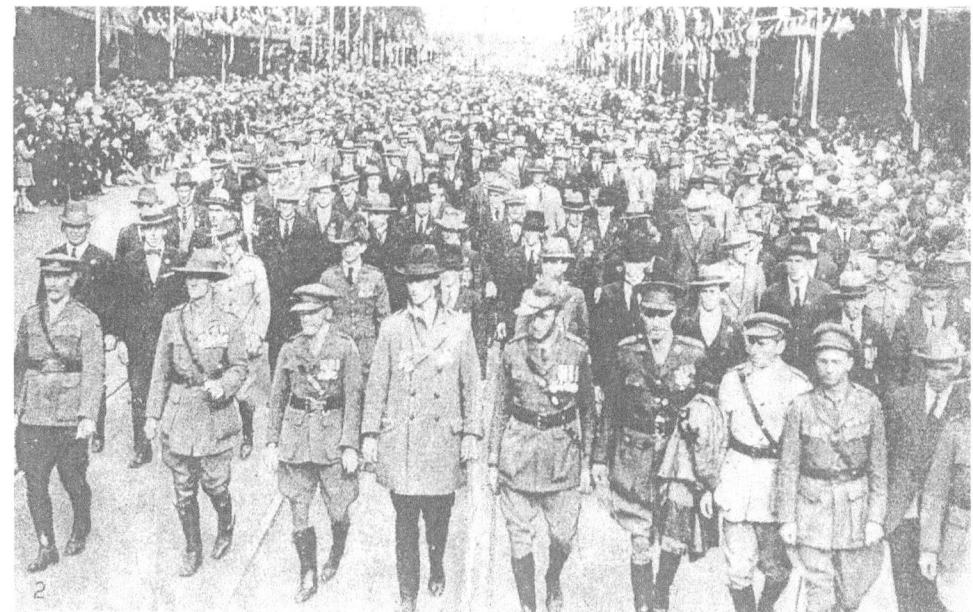

(Fig. 159) JP Campbell (front, far left) striding out in the 1927 Anzac Day march down Swanston Street, Melbourne. Erect, eyes forward, he looks solemn and proud. He wore his lieutenant's uniform and appears to have found himself a position at the head of the mass of veterans, estimated at 28,000 in number. *Leader*, 7 May 1927.

Welfare Association committee at the Eastern Camp.[18] By the mid 1920s he was involved with the Yallourn Fire Brigade Cricket Club as vice president, and also the Yallourn Brass Band.[19] He photographed the local football team and many other town organisations.[20] As well as involvement with the Masons, he was a trustee of the Yallourn Branch of the Australian Natives Association (ANA).[21] Although he was a member of the local Returned Sailors', Soldiers' and Imperial League of Australia (RSSILA) he preferred to go to Melbourne for the Anzac Day march (Fig. 159). He was also a member of the Yallourn sub-branch of the League of Nations Union, an organisation which hosted speakers on world affairs in line with its dedication to promoting peace throughout the world. Campbell was auditor for the sub-branch in the early 1930s.[22]

Campbell's chosen sport, approaching old age, was bowls; he donated trophies

18 *Live Wire*, 20 August 1931.
19 *Live Wire*, 17 September 1925 and 19 November 1925.
20 *Live Wire*, 12 August 1926.
21 *Live Wire*, 11 September 1935.
22 *Morwell Advertiser*, 16 January 1931 and 22 December 1932, and the *Live Wire*, 14 December 1933.

to his club for tournaments.[23] He could afford to do so, as his salary rose from £364 per annum in 1920, when he commenced with the SEC as clerk-in-charge, to a peak of £650 in 1927. Thereafter it fell away to £480 in 1931, due to the Arbitration Court reducing award wages by 10 per cent during the Depression and an SEC policy of reducing salaries for the good of the organisation.[24]

In July 1933 Campbell's name appeared in a list, along with 149 others, in an indignant article published by the *Age*, exposing SEC employees who earned over £400 a year (Campbell was on £480). The article suggested that during a time of general austerity in the community those funded by the public purse should have their incomes reduced.[25] In 1931, for example, the award wage for a male in the textile industry was approximately £200 per annum after the 10 per cent Arbitration Court reduction.[26] This relative affluence allowed Campbell to contribute to the Yallourn community with his photography and his work in numerous organisations. It was a commitment expected of SEC staff, and he did not disappoint.

Campbell's life changed considerably in 1927. His wife, Elizabeth Campbell, died aged seventy-five at her residence 'St. Ivans' in Young [Westgarth] Street, East Malvern on 14 September 1927, after three months' illness. She had never lived at Yallourn. Her death notice read 'loved wife of J.P. Campbell, Yallourn', making it clear that this was the case.[27] Noel Fethers maintains that Elizabeth was an invalid who required a home nurse, although no mention of any serious illness is made on the death certificate.[28] She left nothing to her husband in her will.[29]

Towards the end of 1927 Campbell became embroiled in an attempt by the SEC to establish a hotel in Yallourn. The aim of the Commission was to control

---

23 *Live Wire*, 12 January 1933

24 JP Campbell, personnel record, SECV Office of the Administrator, and Stuart Macintyre, *The Oxford History of Australia, Volume 4, 1901-1942*, Oxford University Press, Melbourne, 1986, p. 261.

25 *The Age*, 20 July 1933. Article reproduced in Colin Harvey *Yallourn Power Station*, p. 434. The list of employees was given to a Country Party MP in the Victorian Legislative Assembly by the Minister in charge of Electrical Undertakings.

26 Michael Cannon, *The Human Face of the Depression*, Published by the Author, Mornington, 1996, p. 31.

27 *Argus*, 15 September 1927. There is no Young Street in East Malvern.

28 Interview with Noel Fethers, 20 April 2005, and death certificate of Elizabeth Blanche Campbell. There may have been some long term illness of a non-death threatening kind that required constant nursing assistance.

29 Will and Probate and Administration Files of Elizabeth Blanche Campbell, VPRS 7591/P0002/760, and VPRS 28/P0003/1783, PROV. This may have been because of his relative affluence and perhaps at his request, other members of the family being more in need.

the illicit sale of liquor in the Yallourn community by confining the sale of alcohol to a single, legal outlet.[30] The Licensing Court ruled that the SEC was entitled to hold a licence to run the hotel. Campbell and other concerned residents objected to the granting of a licence for the hotel on the grounds it was near a 'place of public worship', school and hospital, that it would disturb the peace of the neighbourhood, and, finally, that the SEC had no power to hold a licence. Campbell took the matter on appeal to the Full Court of Victoria and it was upheld, only to have it referred back to the Licensing Court the next day by a judge of the Practice Court in order to consider the case of a second applicant for the licence, George Dickson Brown. The Licensing Court overruled the objections and granted the licence to Brown.[31] The hotel opened in October 1928. JP Campbell had again shown his puritan side.[32] Six years later, on retiring as manager of the Yallourn general store and from the SEC, he entertained departmental managers at the hotel, presumably having come to terms with its existence.[33]

He got on with his life, purchasing a car and moving out of the hostel into a new Yallourn brick home on Railway Avenue (Fig. 160). Campbell did not abandon the bicycle entirely for the car; he continued to keep up with cycling technology, obtaining the latest rally bicycle in the last years of his life.[34] He set himself up in his new home, entertaining people with musical evenings, an activity he also pursued in the hostel. He had a substantial record collection of His Masters Voice albums, all meticulously indexed, and 'he would make up a program . . . and write down the words for various musicals, such as Gilbert and Sullivan, so guests could follow them. It was a good way of entertaining and invitations were sought after'.[35] He also established a showy garden in the Yallourn tradition. His grand-daughter remembers visiting him in the early 1930s, walking with him in his garden admiring the tulips, and then strolling down to the store together to buy meat to feed the kookaburras.[36]

Campbell regularly travelled to south Gippsland through the Strzelecki Ranges to see his friends, the Wheelers, who had a guesthouse in Welshpool. They also

---

30 Meredith Fletcher, *Digging Up People for Coal*, p. 93.

31 *Argus*, 14 December 1927, 16 December 1927, 17 December 1927 & 24 December 1927.

32 *Argus*, 1 October 1928.

33 *Morwell Advertiser*, 13 December 1934.

34 Conversation with Noel Fethers, 5 August 2004. Indeed Noel said she was jealous that her grandfather had a better bike than her.

35 Interview with Noel Fethers, 20 April 2005.

36 Ibid.

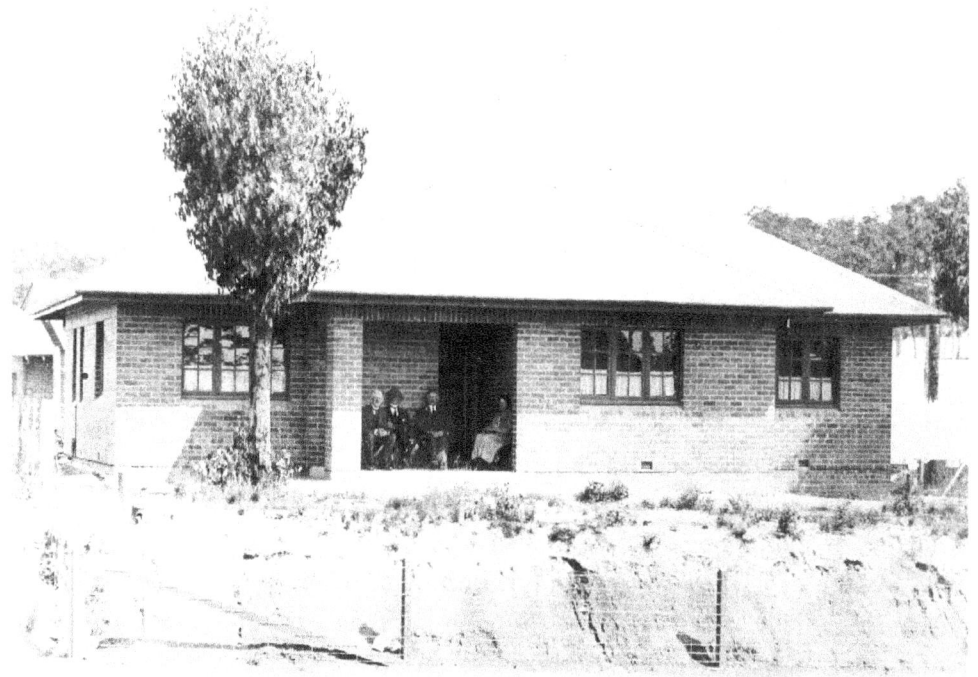

(Fig. 160) JP Campbell's new brick house in Yallourn, c1928.
(Courtesy of State Library of New South Wales)

had a boat by which guests would be taken to Wilson's Promontory across Corner Inlet. Campbell took his car as far as the Promontory, laying mats across sandy patches to avoid getting bogged. He took some beautiful photographs of the light house and its surrounds.[37] The extended Campbell family would often come on these trips. Other friends included a young couple, Clive and Winifred Miller. As a schoolgirl, Winifred Murphy had knitted socks for soldiers and Campbell had been one of the lucky recipients on Gallipoli. He wrote to thank her and it started a life-time correspondence. She later visited him in Yallourn, met a young engineer working there, Clive Miller, and they married. Photographs taken by Campbell of this wide circle of friends are scattered among family memorabilia. Some show people bathing in the crystal clear water of a bush stream in the south Gippsland hills.[38] His friendship with Lilian Louisa Pitts continued. He was still sending her gifts as late as 1933, two years before his death.[39]

---

37 These can be seen among Campbell's SEC images held by the State Library of Victoria: Images H2009 18/32, H2009 18/33, H2009 18/34, and H2009 18/35.
38 Ibid., and the marriage certificate of the Millers.
39 In this case a book, *In Search of Wales*.

The position of clerk-in-charge was abolished in August 1928 and with it went Campbell's job as official photographer. He had held both positions since joining the Yallourn project in 1920. Instead, he was appointed to a new position taking control of all trading activities in Yallourn, which included the SEC-controlled general store and Western Branch Stores.[40] When WC Mead, manager of the general store and founding editor of the SEC's newspaper *Live Wire*, was sacked in January 1929 due to apparent poor management, Campbell took over both roles, relinquishing the trading manager position. The store, with its multi-faceted departments, had made a loss in the financial year 1926-7 and Mead was considered responsible, particularly by the secretary Roy Liddelow.[41] Campbell was involved in Mead's dismissal, having been asked by the assistant general superintendent, RD Dixon, in November 1928 for comments on Mead's performance, as it was 'not considered that the Store can carry yourself as Trading Manager in addition to a Stores Manager'.[42] Campbell replied that upon taking up an office in the store as trading manager he 'would recommend either the dispensing of Mr. Mead's services or retaining them in a minor capacity' (Fig. 161).[43]

Campbell revelled in being editor of the *Live Wire*, the circulation of which reached 600 copies in early 1928.[44] Up to six pages in size at the end of 1928, it was full of community news, sport, film notices, lists of SEC holidays, garden advice from the SEC's head gardener, advertisements for the store, and notices of lectures put on by the Workers Educational Association. The *Live Wire*, published by the general store, became a forum for the SEC to promote good behaviour, hard work and the continued upkeep of the town. Not surprisingly, as an SEC paper nothing controversial was reported such as strikes or work place accidents, unlike its short-lived rival from the Brown Coal Mine, the *Electric Spark*, which

---

40 WR Armstrong, *History of the State Electricity Commission of Victoria, 1927-1947*, p. 87; *Live Wire*, 14 February 1929.

41 Ibid., and memos between RD Dixon, Assistant General Superintendent, SEC Yallourn, and Roy Liddelow, Secretary, SEC, and later Commercial Manager, 17 March 1928 to 6 February 1929. VPRS 9936/P/1 File Mr. Mead Provision Store, PROV. The *Live Wire* report said Mead 'had tendered his resignation'. In fact he was told his services 'will not be required after 31st March [1929]', but was allowed to resign due to his good community service. He wanted another position in the SEC but was refused, and duly served out his notice.

42 Memo RD Dixon to JP Campbell, 23 November 1928, VPRS 9936/P1 Unit 11 File Provision Store, PROV.

43 Ibid., memo JP Campbell to RD Dixon, 26 November 1928.

44 *Live Wire*, 16 February 1928.

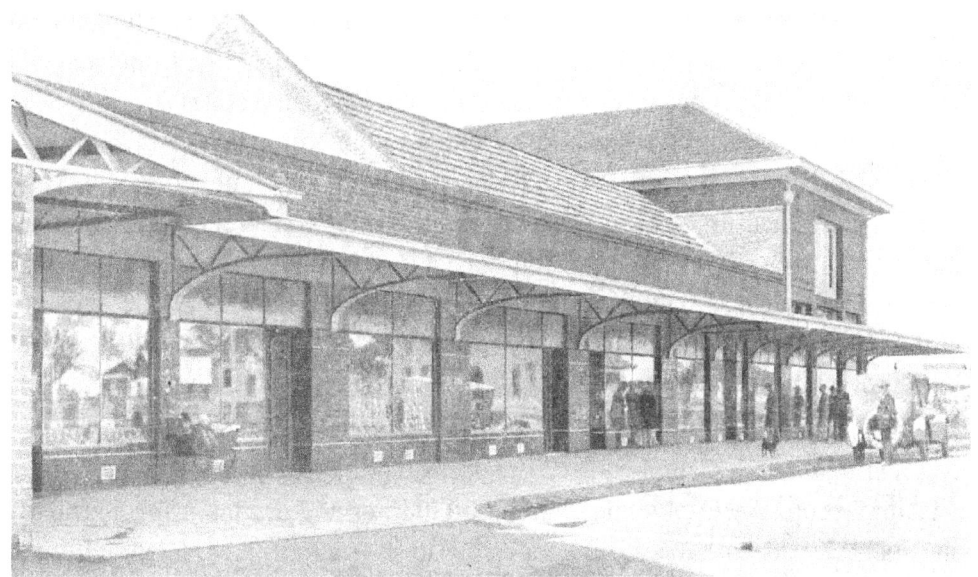

(Fig. 161) The Yallourn General Store as it appears in the 1928 booklet *Power and Heat*.
(Courtesy of the Falconer collection)

reported everything, as did the *Trafalgar and Yarragon News*.[45] Campbell, a good SEC man, supported paper functioning as an organ of propaganda. He had often been associated with journalism, writing about photography or travel, and illustrating his prose with his own photographs. Now he had a whole paper in which to do this.

Descriptive advertisements for Campbell's photographic views of the Yallourn site, on sale at the general store, appeared regularly in the *Live Wire*, even when he was no longer official SEC photographer.[46] Campbell was financially astute, whatever circumstances he was in. People visiting the town to marvel at the works could take away postcards, which came 'in folders of 6, making a nice souvenir to send to friends'.[47]

The first edition of the *Live Wire* under Campbell's editorship appeared on 1 May 1929. Unsigned 'scraps of paper' were being handed to 'juniors' in the store for passing to the editor, but now 'to ensure publication', *Live Wire* clients were to 'comply with our request' to send material directly to the editor.[48] The

45 Meredith Fletcher, *Digging People Up for Coal*, pp. 102-3.
46 For example the *Live Wire*, 25 October 1928.
47 Ibid.
48 *Live Wire*, 1 May 1929.

Returned Sailors, Soldiers' and Airman's Imperial League of Australia featured prominently, given the editor was a member of that organisation. Little changed in the style of the paper during the first year of Campbell's editorship.[49] In May 1930 there was a noticeable increase in letters-to-the-editor, contrasting with the occasional letter by one of the local vicars previous to Campbell's editorship. The paper livened up considerably – a spirited letter war broke out over about the management of the Yallourn Mothers' Club.[50] In June that year the Rev. PH Dicker, an Anglican friend of Campbell's from the early 1920s, wrote a history of the Yallourn Boy Scouts for the paper. It began an emphasis on the history of Yallourn, and was the precursor to a series of articles on the town and the SEC written by Campbell himself.

Later that month Campbell used the occasion of a lecture on photography by a visiting professor to give his own dissertation on the origins of photography, and its chemistry and mechanics, referring to it as an art, and encouraging the 'average humble worker [to get] a lot of pleasure out of a No. 2 Brownie [camera, as the] No. 2 can be made to do wonderful things in the hands of an expert'.[51] The store sold the No. 2 Box Brownie.

In April 1931, aged sixty-five, Campbell again publicly set out his ideas regarding pictorial photography under his nickname 'Kam':

> Likeness is not everything in picture making, although valuable enough at times [and there are] two kinds of likeness – in one every detail is shown; another kind gives us only a selected few of the features or details. [Further, in] a picture that impresses us and which we remember easily we can, with little effort, recall to the mind's eye the principal features; first, because they are few, secondly because they impressed themselves on our attention by reason of their form, arrangement, position or light and shade.
>
> Many subjects are photographed for record purposes only and by reason of their position [it is] difficult to make a photograph pleasing to the eye and the only thing to be done is to observe perspectives, balance, and the most effectual lighting to give harmony to the scene. Thus many photographs have been taken with an aim in view, but not necessarily a strictly pictorial one. A record of facts is one thing, and a record of an

---

49 In the 1 May 1930 edition of the *Live Wire*, Monash's Anzac day address appeared verbatim on the front page, taken from the *Age* of 26 April 1930.
50 *Live Wire*, 22 May 1930 to 29 May 1930.
51 *Live Wire*, 26 June 1930.

impression which certain facts have made on us is another. If we can get that impression into our print so that another person looking at the picture feels the same sensation as we had when we looked at the scene, then we have secured our effect.[52]

The last two sentences summarize the photographic philosophy Campbell had pursued throughout his life. Here, as in his Working Men's College days, he stressed the importance of mastering photographic technique.

It was not until June 1931 that the first photograph by Campbell appeared in the paper, an image of pupils at Yallourn's first State School.[53] In this month Campbell's history series on the 'Old Yallourn Days' also commenced, inspired, he wrote, by criticism of the SEC and Yallourn, mainly from outsiders. The history was designed to dispel such views as Yallourn 'being a veritable cesspool tenanted by the dregs of humanity' and 'if the whole position and the activities of the Commission in connection with Yallourn are examined in a proper manner, it will be found that in nearly every case gross exaggeration has been indulged in'.[54] The series appeared in seven instalments, including two articles on the history of the Church of England in Yallourn, inspired no doubt by Campbell's friendship with the Rev. Dicker and his association with the church. When a visiting lecturer at Yallourn gave a talk on the future of Palestine it inspired Campbell to write a lengthy report on the subject, advising readers of an upcoming display of photographs of Jerusalem and Palestine taken during the war, to be put in the store window, probably his own.[55]

Some of Campbell's articles were becoming eccentric, none more so than a front page spread on 'Hippopotami in the Morwell River'. Cattle in a paddock adjoining the Morwell abattoir were wallowing in the river bed and became stuck in the mud. Campbell, with his strange sense of humour, filled two front page articles with this, including photographs.[56] He was also slowing down, a sign his health was not good. Despite this, he published a booklet of seventeen Yallourn and SEC works photographs.[57] On 7 June 1932 Campbell 'underwent a serious

---

52 *Live Wire*, 9 April 1931.

53 *Live Wire*, 11 June 1931. This may have been the first picture to appear in the paper.

54 *Live Wire*, 18 June 1931.

55 *Live Wire*, 24 September 1931.

56 *Live Wire*, 14 & 21 January 1932.

57 *Live Wire*, 9 June 1932 and Prue McGoldrick *"Yallourn was . . . ."* pp. 54, 89. Proceeds from the sale of this booklet went to the Yallourn hospital.

but successful operation in Melbourne' for cancer, and it was not until October 1932 that he returned to work.[58]

In January 1933 he increased the size of the *Live Wire* to eight pages. Suddenly there were more photographs, portraits of celebrities, pieces on international sport and news mixed with local material, even a picture of the Geological Museum in London. This was a radical change for the *Live Wire*, which had not until now developed much beyond being an SEC newsletter. It was, however, too much for some. After suffering several issues of the new *Live Wire*, the SEC's publicity officer, WR Armstrong, an experienced journalist based at head office in Melbourne, wrote to the SEC manager Roy Liddelow stating that he 'heartily' disliked 'the form which the "Live Wire" is taking':

> It is unnecessarily large and expensive, and its pretensions to cater for the general reader are not only making it look ridiculous and eccentric as a local newspaper, but are also destroying its local colour.[59]

Armstrong made a number of suggestions regarding alterations to the paper, including confining Campbell to store management only, and appointing an experienced person to work as editor. Further, in a criticism of Campbell, he suggested the new editor should be 'relied upon to divorce his own personality from the paper – to display a judicial detachment of mind on all occasions'.[60] Armstrong suggested a replacement for Campbell, concluding that the new editor should aim for 'a well-written, newsy and happy little journal that local people will be pleased to have and to send to their friends in other places'.[61]

The SEC felt Campbell had overstepped the mark. Liddelow, in writing to the general superintendent at Yallourn, agreed that 'alteration seems necessary' to the paper. On top of all this, Campbell was struggling with his illness, a double blow. Liddelow probably felt a touch of sadness at the demise of an old family friend, but presumably the SEC came first. Campbell was stripped of the *Live Wire* editorship, retaining his job as store manager.[62] Yet another report

---

58 *Morwell Advertiser*, 10 June 1932 & 3 November 1932.

59 Publicity Officer to SEC Manager, 26 January 1933, VPRS 9936/P/1 Unit 11 File Administration, PROV.

60 Ibid.

61 Ibid.

62 In the *Live Wire* of 21 December 1933 the new editor wrote: 'We join the manager of the General Store in [wishing everyone a Merry Christmas]', that is, the editorship and store manager positions were now separated.

was completed on the financial viability of the Yallourn General Store in July 1934, and, like Mead before him, Campbell was under criticism for the store's poor performance.[63] Locals were flocking to nearby towns to shop because of outmoded stock at Yallourn. One outraged woman, a leading light in the Housewives Association, reportedly attacked Campbell with an umbrella for not listening to her complaints about the store.[64] Resignation from the SEC must have looked an attractive option for Campbell, who was a very ill man.

Despite his illness, Campbell doggedly pursued his photography. On a wet Saturday in October 1934 the Duke of Gloucester, in Australia to participate in Victoria's centenary celebrations, visited Yallourn. Campbell was on the spot to record the occasion. He scrambled 'up and down a ladder [with his glass plate camera] disappearing under his black cloth, taking photographs of the Duke' and his party as they appeared briefly in the Yallourn town square. His daughter Ada and granddaughter Noel watched from a vantage point in the store window, marvelling at his courage and perseverance in the face of serious illness.[65]

In November 1934 JP Campbell resigned from the SEC.[66] His declining health was clearly a major reason for this, compounded by the poor performance of the store under his management. He spent some time in the Yallourn Hospital, and was transferred to the Austin Hospital, Heidelberg, in February 1935.[67] In 1948, when the retired publicity officer WR Armstrong wrote a lengthy manuscript of the history of the SEC, he respectfully devoted almost a page to Campbell's career and life at Yallourn.[68] Campbell had survived in the SEC up to this point by his usual method of combining his love of photography with his work. This was as an official photographer up until 1928, and then unofficially in the latter part of his SEC career. It was his passion for photography as art that contributed yet again to his downfall. Given this illness, and his war experiences, it is remarkable that he was able to keep up such a hectic pace for so long.

After devoting fifteen years to the SEC, Campbell's working life and his career as a photographer were finished. His photographic legacy is invaluable as the SEC contributed so much to the economic prosperity of Victoria. His pictures

63 Meredith Fletcher, *Digging People Up for Coal*, p. 105.
64 Prue McGoldrick, *"Yallourn Was . . ."*, p. 175.
65 Interview with Noel Fethers, 20 April 2005; *Live Wire* 25 October 1934 & 1 November 1934.
66 *Live Wire*, 29 November 1934.
67 *Morwell Advertiser*, 21 February 1935.
68 WR Armstrong, 'History of the State Electricity of Victoria', 1948, p. 87.

of Yallourn, a model garden city, are important as the town was demolished in the 1970s to obtain the coal underneath it. Two images, one of himself with his camera in the bush, and another typical pictorialist 'snap' (as he liked to call them), go a long way to defining Campbell's time at Yallourn (Figs. 162 & 163).[69]

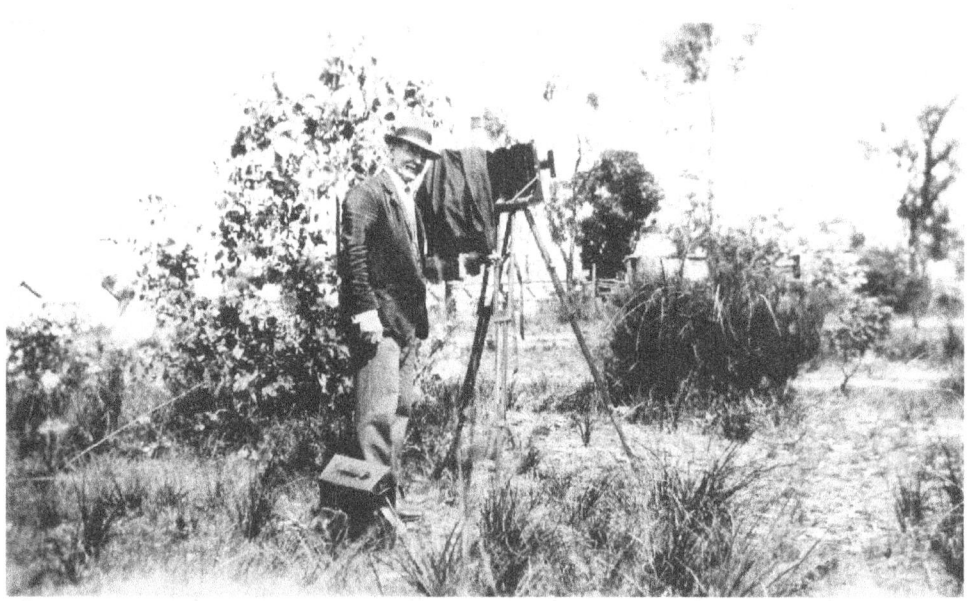

(Fig. 162) 'J.P.C.'. JP Campbell and his glass plate camera in the scrub, probably near Yallourn. Photographer unknown. (Courtesy of State Library of New South Wales)

Campbell's condition deteriorated quickly after his resignation from the SEC. His friends were amazed at 'the unfailing optimism and fortitude with which he met his affliction and suffering'.[70] He was bedridden towards the end of his life, and his granddaughter, Noel Fethers, remembers taking him drinks as he lay ill. JP Campbell died at his son Aubrey's home in Murrumbeena on 5 September 1935 aged seventy, from carcinoma of the rectum and heart failure. There was no will, suggesting he had already dispersed his estate prior to his death. He was

---

69 Fig. 162 is in an album titled 'Yallourn, 9th March 1924', PXA 602 (v.2), State Library of New South Wales, and an album attributed to Campbell, but consisting of images taken by a relative or friend, as previously discussed. Fig. 163 is included in the album 'La Souvenir, J.P.C.', PXA 602 (v.4), State Library of New South Wales.

70 *Live Wire*, 11 September 1935.

buried in the Yallourn cemetery on 6 September 1935, in the bush as he wished. As he was a prominent Mason, the Masonic brethren from the Morwell Lodge acted as pall-bearers.[71] Herbert Vallance was there to say goodbye, but there is no record of whether Lilian Pitts attended.

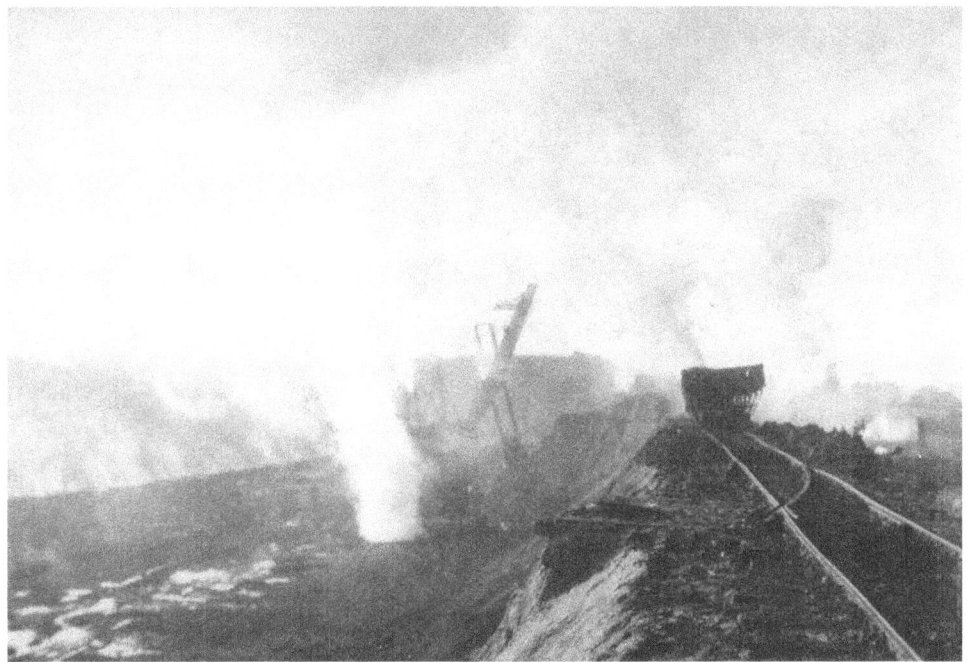

(Fig. 163) 'Winter's Morning, Yallourn'. The open cut.
(Courtesy of State Library of New South Wales)

---

71 Ibid., and JP Campbell's death certificate.

BIBLIOGRAPHY

UNPUBLISHED SOURCES

JP Campbell's Photographs

Privately Held War Photographs

The majority of the photographs reproduced in chapters eight and nine are from a collection JP Campbell bequeathed to his grandson, Derek Falconer. On Derek's death a substantial proportion of this collection went to his son, Rod. The Falconer collection has upwards of 200 photographs in it from Campbell's time in Egypt, Palestine and Syria during World War One. It includes both official war photographs – contact prints kept by Campbell for his own private collection – and private images he took as a soldier-tourist. Most of the official war photographs in the Falconer collection have a number and brief description written in pencil on the back by Campbell, and these are typed in quotation marks under each reproduced photograph in this chapter, and anything else outside these inverted commas is my own contribution. The contact prints are the same size as the original negative, and an enlarger was needed to change the size, which Campbell had access to in the various makeshift dark rooms he used.

When organised in numerical sequence the collection is approximately in chronological order, covering Campbell's movements right up to the end of the war and Light Horse operations north of Damascus in October 1918. They are in good condition, as can be seen from those reproduced in this book, having been in the dark for over eighty years. The Australian War Memorial has the negatives of these same official photographs, plus many more of Campbell's official photographs. In addition they have his private photographs of this period, some similar to the official photographs. Where a number is given it is Campbell's original numbering system, e.g. No. 4; within inverted commas, it means the image is an official photograph unless otherwise stated. Where necessary I provide the Australian War Memorial image reference number (beginning with the prefix 'B' for an official war photograph taken in the Middle East, and 'H' for a private image for the equivalent photograph). Campbell often created parallel sets of his own, private images shadowing the official photographs he took, the same subject often with only slight variation. If the photograph is a private Campbell image, I indicate it as such.

Australian War Memorial

The Australian War Memorial holds the negatives of the official war photographs taken in the various theatres of war during and immediately after the First World War, including those taken by JP Campbell in the Middle East. In addition they have Campbell's private photographs of this period, and his Gallipoli images, but not in album form. A large number of the images in the Australian War Memorial's photographic collection are digitised and available for viewing on their website. As already mentioned they use a 'B' prefix to indicate the official war photographs taken in the Middle East, and 'H' to indicate those privately taken and donated to the Memorial. Many of Campbell's official photographs are attributed to him, some are not. By performing a search of the War Memorial's online, digitised photographic collection, using Campbell's name in a variety of ways (for example, James P Campbell, or JP Campbell) one can view many of the hundreds of photographs he took during his war service.

Centre for Gippsland Studies, Gippsland Campus, Monash University, Churchill (now Federation University)

The Centre for Gippsland Studies holds a collection of State Electricity Commission of Victoria photographs consisting of contact prints of the early years of Yallourn power station and township. These were in seven folders, all of which contain images by JP Campbell. The SLV now holds this collection.

Euroa Historical Society

Photographs, particularly postcards, produced for the Euroa Hotel for promotional purposes by JP Campbell representing Vallan Studio in 1911.

Falconer Collection

Held by Rod Falconer, JP Campbell's great grandson, this collection consists primarily of both Campbell's official and private photographs in a variety of forms. It includes images from all phases of his career as a photographer, apart from his sojourn on Gallipoli. The rest of the collection is made up of general private pictorial compositions of various subjects, and family images taken both before and after the First World War, in single print and album form, including postcards.

Fethers, Noel

Extensive collection of Campbell private and official photographs mixed with Campbell family images.

Gillespie, Greg

Photograph album, 'On Active Service with a Camera: A remarkable set of photographs taken with a hand camera by Private J.P. Campbell of Malvern, Victoria, under all kinds of circumstances whilst on service as a signaller with A Troop, B Squadron, 8th L. Horse Reg. 3rd L.H. Brigade. This Album will serve as a History of The Glorious 8th L. Horse whose memory will ever bring feelings of pride to the hearts of all British Australians. Compiled by Aubrey J. Campbell'.

Harding, Alan

Extensive collection of postcards, particularly of Campbell's images of north-east Victoria.

Latrobe City Council, Morwell

'Yallourn Views', an album of 49 panoramic photographs of Yallourn taken between 1919 and 1925.

Mansfield Historical Society

This organisation has many JP Campbell and Vallan Studio images. Of particular value was the 'Little Laddie Adam' series of Vallan Studio postcards documenting the search for a little boy lost in the Mansfield district in 1909.

Mansfield RSL

Photograph album, 'The Eighth Light Horse Book: A Collection of Photographs taken by Signaller J.P. Campbell whilst on Active Service with the Regiment in Egypt and Turkey'.

Mossop, Marjorie

A small collection of Bramley family photographs taken by JP Campbell.

National Gallery of Australia

"Untitled album", Campbell, J.P., Accession No. NGA 83.1372.1-24, NGA IRN 91540.

National Library of Australia

Souvenir of the visit of the Federal Parliamentary Party to the Northern Territory, April – May, 1912, PIC PIC/7459/1-133 LOC Album 1017.

Campbell, J.P. (James P.) 'The Great War, 1914-1915: A Collection of Photographs taken by Signaller J.P. Campbell whilst on Active Service with the Glorious 3rd Brigade of Light Horse'. Call Number PIC/6109/1-184 LOC Album 1009.

Nicholas, Jim

Collection of JP Campbell glass plate negatives of the Upper Murray and north-east districts of Victoria.

Northern Territory Library

Album titled: 'Souvenir of the Visit of the Federal Parliamentary Party to the Northern Territory, April-May, 1912' consisting of 135 images.

Pickerd, Jeff

A small collection of Vallan Studio postcards, produced by JP Campbell, of the Australian Light Horse in camp and on manoeuvres near Broadford in March 1914.

Pinkerton, Peter

JP Campbell album of general pictorial views taken in Victoria, and Campbell family photographs.

Pitts, Frank

Postcards bequeathed to Frank Pitts by Lilian Pitts, his aunt. There are images by both Lilian and JP Campbell of the Merrigum and Mansfield districts, before the First World War.

Public Record Office of Victoria

SECV Photographic Images, Prints, Subject Headings, VPRS 15785.

State Elecricity Commission of Victoria (SECV), Office of the Administrator, Melbourne

Large 92 leaf photograph album containing images of the construction of the Yallourn power station and associated infrastructure in the early 1920s. Many of the images are by JP Campbell. Reference SEC01774.

There are four other albums containing JP Campbell images in Series YAPS0009, Box No's A0004, A0006, A0007 and A0009.

State Library of New South Wales

Souvenir of Yallourn [album of photographs by J.P. Campbell, 1926], Call No. PXA 602 (v.1).

Yallourn, 9 March 1924, Call No: PXA 602 (v.2).

Yallourn photographs, Call No. PXA 602 (v.3).

La Souvenir, J.P.C. [album of photographs of Victoria], Call No. PXA 602 (v.4).

State Library of Victoria

The SLV has a substantial holding of Campbell's Yallourn images known as the 'J.P. Campbell collection of glass negatives documenting [the] industrial enterprise at Yallourn'. They also hold an album of his Northern Territory photographs known as the 'Kirbride collection', Accession No. H2744.

Tyson, Nance

Collection of sixty postcards, sent to Lilian Pitts by JP Campbell during his period of service overseas with the AIF during the First World War. The collection also includes an album of Omeo and district images, some of which were taken by Campbell, and also sundry postcards of subjects taken in Victoria and beyond before the First World War.

Archival and Manuscript Sources

Australian War Memorial

The appointment of Lieut HS Gullett as War Correspondent, AWM 16 4353/1/3.

Re appointment of Lieut Campbell as official photographer – Egypt vice Capt Hurley, AWM 16 4375/2/2.

Appointment Lieut OH Coulson as official photographer vice Lieut Campbell, AWM 16 4375/2/12.

Photographs: photographs from official photographers – Official Photographs – Palestine & Egypt, AWM 16 4375/12/2, Folders 1 & 2.

Official Records Weekly Reports from Egypt Expeditionary Force, AWM 16 4379/5/4 Pt 1 & 2.

Corrrespondence between Officer in Charge Egypt Expeditionary Force Sub-section, Australian War Records Section, AWM 16 4379/5/21.

[War Records Section] Notes in connection with War Record work in Egypt and Palestine, 1917-1918, AWM 25 1013/36.

Correspondence and weekly reports to Australian War Records Section (London), August-September 1918, AWM 25 1013/37.

Correspondence – Re Photography, AWM 25 1013/38A.

[Australian War Memorial registry file]: Mr Campbell re photos of Gallipoli [correspondence only], AWM 93 17/3/294.

JP Campbell camera, AWM REL32968.001, and case, AWM REL32968.002.

Papers of General H Chauvel, AWM PR00535.

Papers of GF Langley, AWM PR00096.

Campbell, Archibald Bryan

'The Diary of Archibald Campbell, 1817-1872: An early Port Phillip Resident, 1840-1872', foreword by Archibald Bryan Campbell, December 2005.

Falconer Collection

Campbell – Pinkerton family tree.

Kissock, Margaret, 'A Pioneering Family', a short Pinkerton and Campbell family history manuscript, 1931.

Pinkerton and Campbell family history manuscript, author and date unknown.

Gillespie, Greg

First World War letters of troopers John, Stanley and Ernest Mack of A Troop, A Squadron, 8th Light Horse Regiment, 3rd Light Horse Brigade.

Greany, Laurie and Francis, Heather

Campbell, Willam Burne, 'Doings and Experiences', East Malvern, 1955.

Mansfield Masonic Lodge

Appearance Book, Mansfield Masonic Lodge No. 158.

National Archives of Australia

Campbell, James Pinkerton, Defence Service Record, hardcopy, Series B2455, Item 1854272, National Archives of Australia, Canberra.

'J.P. Campbell – Cmth. Photographer', digitised file, Series number A1, Series accession number A1/15, Item 16281, National Archives of Australia, Canberra.

Coulson, Oswald Hillam, Defence Service Record, digitised file, Series B2455 Item No. 455, Barcode No. 3430799, Digital copy, National Archives of Australia.

McPherson, Duncan, Defence Service Record, digitised file, Series B2455, Item No. 1958660, National Archives of Australia.

National Library of Australia

Hurley, Frank, 'My diary official War Photographer Commonwealth Military Forces, from 21 August 1917 to 31 August 1918, (220 parts), entries for 29-31 December 1917, Parts 128-130, Digital Collections Manuscripts On Line, MS 883 Papers of Frank Hurley, Series 1: Diaries, 1912-1961, Item 5, National Library of Australia, Canberra.

Pickerd, Jeff

'More Majorum: Chronological History of the 8th Light Horse Regiment, 3rd Light Horse Brigade, A.I.F., 1914-1919', work in progress.

Public Record Office of Victoria

Agency VA 714 – Education Department

Teacher Record Number 7505, Seaton Roll No. 1649, Teacher Record Books, VPRS13718, PROV.

Agency VA 2620 – Registrar of Probates, Supreme Court

Will of John Parsons, VPRS 7591/P0002/122, PROV.

Probate and Administration Files for John Parsons, VPRS 28/P0002/216, PROV.

Will of Elizabeth Blanche Campbell VPRS 7591/P0002/760, PROV.

Probate and Administration Files for Elizabeth Blanche Campbell, VPRS 28/P0003/1783 PROV.

Agency VA 1002 – State Electricity Commission of Victoria (previously known as the Electricity Commissioners)

General Correspondence Files and File Registration Cards, VPRS 8892.

Correspondence, Papers and Memorabilia of Sir John Monash, VPRS 9673.

Correspondence, Papers and Memorabilia of Sir John Monash, VPRS 9673.

SEC Annual Reports,1922-1930, VPRS 13872.

Subject Correspondence Files: Manager (Roy Liddelow), VPRS 9936.

Royal Melbourne Institute of Technology (RMIT) Archives

Student Attendance Registers 1887-1935.

The College Quarterly: The Official Organ of the Working Men's College Melbourne, 1900; 1909-1912, Series 326.

Details of 'The College Photo. Club' exhibition of the photographs exhibited in Dresden, Germany, by AJ Campbell and JP Campbell, 1909, Series 326/1.

Prospectus of the Working Men's College, Melbourne Technical College and Royal Melbourne Technical College 1887-1960, Series 390.

State Electricity Commission of Victoria (SECV), Office of the Administrator, Melbourne.
Employment records of JP Campbell, obtained under freedom of information.

State Library of Victoria
Armstrong, WR, SEC Publicity Officer 1927-1947, 'History of the State Electricity Commission of Victoria 1937-1948', 1948, MS 13064, MS Box 3747/7-8, State Library of Victoria.
McMahon, JW, 'The Early Years of Yallourn', 1919-1926, typescript, SEC, 1968, State Library of Victoria.

Victorian Registry of Births, Deaths and Marriages
The Victorian Pioneers Index 1837-1888, Federation Index Victoria 1889-1901, Edwardian Index Victoria 1902-1913, Great War Index Victoria 1914-1920, and the Death Index Victoria 1921-1985, all on CD-ROM, were valuable in researching Campbell family members, friends and associates. The relevant information could be taken from these to request full birth, death or marriage certificates from the Victorian Registry of Births, Deaths and Marriages in the Department of Justice.

Sundry Manuscripts
Walter, James, "The Solace of Doubt'?: Biographical Methodology after the Short Twentieth Century', Seminar paper, date unknown.

Theses
Cook, Valda Dorothy, 'Women? The Life and Times of Lilian Louisa , Photographer', Master of Arts in Public History, Monash University, 1992.
Dowling, Peter, 'Chronicles of Progress: the Illustrated Newspapers of Colonial Australia, -1896', PhD Thesis, Monash University, 1997.
Ebury, Francis, 'Pictures: Australian Pictorial Photography as Art 1897-1957', PhD Thesis, University of Melbourne, 2001.
Fewster, Kevin J., 'Expression and Suppression: Aspects of Military Censorship in Australia During the Great War', PhD Thesis, University of NSW, 1980.
Jolly, Martyn, 'Fake Photographs: Making Truths in Photography', PhD Thesis, University of Sydney, 2003.

Lydon, Jane, 'Regarding Coranderrk: Photography at Coranderrk Aboriginal Station, Victoria', PhD Thesis, Australian National University, 2000.

Sassoon, Joanna, 'An Archaeology of Memory: A Cultural Biography of the Photographs of EL Mitchell 1900-1930', PhD Thesis, University of Western Australia, 2001.

Interviews

Stella Andrews, 10 January 2005.

Noel Fethers, 20 April 2005.

Greg Gillespie, 11 February 2005.

Marjorie Mossop, 28 December 2003.

PUBLISHED SOURCES

Newspapers

Daily Herald, (Adelaide), 1912.

Adelaide Register, 1912-1913.

Age (Melbourne), 1927, 1935.

Argus (Melbourne), 1913, 1923.

Australasian (Melbourne), 1894-1928.

Barrier Miner, (Broken Hill), 1913.

Canberra Times, 1991.

Corryong Courier, 1907-1909, 1914.

Daily Telegraph (Sydney), 1913.

Examiner, (Launceston), 1913.

Gippsland Independent, 1904, 1908.

Herald (Melbourne), 1915.

Heyfield Herald, 1912, 1915-1920.

Live Wire (Yallourn), 1925-1934.

Maffra Spectator, 1907.

Mansfield Courier, 1908-1930.

Melbourne Leader, 1899-1928.

Northern Territory Times, 1912.

Omeo Standard, 1906-1907

Walhalla Chronicle, 1912.

Weekly Times (Melbourne), 1899-1901, 1909-1910, 1913, 1921-1924.

Journals

Australasian Photo-Review, 1912.

Australian Cyclist, 1897, 1898.

Australian Photographic Journal, 1896, 1898, 1909.

Australian Traveller, 1935.

Camera House Beacon, 1907, 1909.

Photographic Review of Reviews (Australian edition), 1894.

Books, Articles, Government Reports

Across the Alps to Omeo, The Omeo Tourist Association, Omeo, 1906.

Adams, Ansel and Alinder, Mary Street, *Ansel Adams: An Autobiography*, New York Graphic Society, Little, Brown and Company, Canada, 1985.

Anderson, Warwick, *The Cultivation of Whiteness: Science, Health and Racial Destiny in Australia*, Melbourne University Press, Melbourne, 2005.

Ashton, Paul, 'Evidence: Photography & the Bush', *Locality*, Volume 6, Number 5, 1994, pp. 206-9.

Ashton, Paul and Blackmore, Kate, *On the Land: a Photographic History of Farming in Australia*, Kangaroo Press, Kenthurst, 1987.

Atwood, Margaret, *The Blind Assassin*, Virago Press, London, 2001.

Attwood, Bain, *A Life Together, a Life Apart: a History of Relations between Europeans and Aborigines*, Melbourne University Press, Carlton, 1994.

Auchmuty, J.J., *Problems of Nineteenth Century Biography: Wyse–Acton–Lecky*, Canberra, 1963.

Auchterlonie, Gloria, *'Dad's War Stuff' – The Diaries: The Complete Personal Diary Entries and Selected Photographs of George Auchterlonie, an Australian Lighthorseman, who served in the 8th Lighthorse Regiment in Egypt, Sinai and Palestine during World War 1*, Advance Morwell Inc. and Gloria Auchterlonie, Morwell, 2001.

Bair, Deidre, 'The "How-To" of Biography', in James Walter and Raija Nugent (eds.), *Biographers at Work*, Griffith University, Institute of Modern Biography, 1984, pp. 36-42.

Baly, Lindsay, *Horseman, Pass By: The Australian Light Horse in World War 1*, Kangaroo Press, Sydney, 2003.

Barrie, Sandy, *Australians Behind the Camera: Directory of Early Australian Photographers 1841 to 1945*, S Barrie, 2002.

Batchen, Geoffrey, *Each Wild Idea: Writing Photography History*, Massachusetts Institute of Technology, 2001.

Batty, Phillip, Allen, Lindy and Morton, John (eds.), *The Photographs of Baldwin Spencer*, The Miegunyah Press and Museum Victoria, Carlton, Victoria, 2007.

Bazley, AW, 'Obituary, CEW Bean', *Historical Studies*, Volume 14, Number 53, October 1969, pp. 147-54.

Bean, Charles Edwin Woodrow, *Anzac to Amiens*, Australian War Memorial, Canberra, Second Edition, 1947.

Bean, CEW and Gullett, HS, *Photographic Record of the War: Reproductions of Pictures taken by the Australian Official Photographers*, Volume X11, Angus and Robertson, Sydney, Seventh Edition, 1937.

Bean, CEW, *Frontline Gallipoli: CEW Bean's Diary from the Trenches*, Selected and annotated by Kevin Fewster, Allen and Unwin, Sydney, 1990.

Bean, CEW, *The Official History of Australia in the War of 1914-1918*, Volume 1, *The Story of Anzac from the Outbreak of War to the End of the First Phase of the Gallipoli Campaign, May 4, 1915,* , Angus and Robertson, Sydney, Sixth Edition, 1937.

Bean, CEW, *The Official History of Australia in the War of 1914-1918*, Volume 11, *The Story of Anzac from 4 May, 1915, to the Evacuation of the Gallipoli Peninsula*, Angus and Robertson, Sydney, Fourth Edition, 1936.

Beaumont, Joan (ed.), *Australia's War, 1914-18*, Allen & Unwin, St Leonards, NSW, 1995.

Berger, John, *About Looking*, Writers and Readers Publishing Cooperative, London, 1980.

Berman, Marshall, *All That is Solid Melts into Air: The Experience of Modernity*, Penguin, New York, 1988.

Bickel, Lennard, *In Search of Frank Hurley*, Macmillan, South Melbourne, Vic., 1980.

Blainey, Geoffrey, *A History of Victoria*, Cambridge University Press, Melbourne, 2006.

Blainey, Geoffrey, *Black Kettle and Full Moon: Daily Life in a Vanished Australia*, Penguin/ Viking, Camberwell, 2003.

Blake, Robert, 'The Art of Biography', in Eric Homberger and John Charmley (eds.), *The Troubled Face of Biography*, Macmillan Press, London, 1988, pp. 75-93.

Bloxham, Donald, *The Great Game of Genocide: Imperialism, Nationalism, and the Destruction of the Ottoman Armenians*, Oxford University Press, New York, 2005.

Bostock, Henry Phillips, *The Great Ride: The Diary of a Light Horse Brigade Scout, World War I*, Artlook Books, Perth, WA, 1982.

Bradley, Anthony and Smith, Terry, *Australian Art and Architecture: Essays Presented to Bernard Smith*, Oxford University Press, 1980.

Brady, Edwin James, *Australia Unlimited*, George Robertson and Co., Melbourne, 1918.

Britain, Ian 'Undertaking a Life', in *Australian Book Review*, Number 298, February 2008, pp. 7-9.

Broome, Richard, *Tracing Past Lives: The Writing of Historical Biography*, History Institute of Victoria Inc., Carlton, 1995.

Brothers, Caroline, *War and Photography: A Cultural History*, Routledge, London, 1997.

Brugger, Suzanne, *Australians and Egypt 1914-1919*, Melbourne University Press, Melbourne, 1980.

Burgin, Victor (ed.), *Thinking Photography*, Macmillan, London, 1982.

Burness, Peter, *The Nek*, Kangaroo Press, Kenthurst, NSW, 1996.

Callister, Sandy, 'War, Seen Through Photographs Darkly: Visual Traces and Interpretative Possibilities in the Photographic Representations of Gallipoli', Conference paper presented at *Frontlines: Gender, Identity, and War*, Monash University, July 12-13, 2002, p. 1-5. <http://www.arts.monash.edu.au/history/events/genidwar/papers/callister.html>

Campbell, James Pinkerton, 'How to Spend your Holiday in the "Queen City" of the South and its surrounding', in *The Australian Photographic Journal Annual*, Harrington and Co., Sydney, 1998, pp. 163-72.

Carlyon, Les, *Gallipoli*, Pan Macmillan Australia Pty. Ltd., Sydney, 2001.

Carmichael, Jane, *First World War Photographers*, Routledge, London, New York, 1989.

Carmody, Jean, *Early Days of the Upper Murray*, Shoestring Press, Wangaratta, 1981.

Carroll, John (ed.), *Intruders in the Bush: The Australian Quest for Identity*, Oxford University Press, Melbourne, 1982.

Cato, Jack, *I Can Take It: The Autobiography of a Photographer*, Georgian House, Melbourne, 1947.

Cato, Jack, *The Story of the Camera in Australia*, Institute of Australian Photography, Second Edition, 1977.

Commonwealth of Australia Parliamentary Debates, House of Representatives, July 1912.

Condé, Anne-Marie, 'the Records of War: Collecting at the Mitchell Library and the Australian War Memorial', *Australian Historical Studies*, Volume 37, Number 125, April 2005, pp. 134-52.

Conrad, Peter, *At Home in Australia,* National Gallery of Australia, Canberra, 2003.

Cook, David, *Picture Postcards in Australia 1898-1920*, Pioneer Design Studio, Lilydale, Vic., 1986.

Cook, Tim, 'Documenting War and Forging Reputations: Sir Max Aitken and the Canadian War Records Office in the First World War', *War in History*, Volume 10, Number 3, 2003, pp. 265-95.

Crick, Bernard, *George Orwell: A Life*, Secker & Warburg, London, 1980.

Crinson, Mark, 'Pictoralism and Industry: Alvin Langdon Coburn in Manchester', *History of Photography*, Volume 30, Number 2, Summer 2006, pp. 155-72.

Daley, Paul, *Beersheba: A Journey Through Australia's Forgotten War*, Melbourne University Press, Melbourne, 2009.

Daunton, Martin, and Rieger, Bernhard (eds.), *Meanings of Modernity: Britain from the Late-Victorian Era to World War II*, Berg, Oxford, 2001.

302

Davidson, Bruce Robinson, *The Northern Myth: A Study of the Physical and Economic Limits to Agriculture and Pastoral Development in Tropical Australia*, Melbourne University Press, Melbourne, Third Edition, 1972.

Davies, Alan and Stanbury, Peter, *The Mechanical Eye in Australia: Photography 1841-1900*, Oxford University Press, 1985

Davison, G., Hirst, J., and Macintyre, S., *The Oxford Companion to Australian History*, Oxford University Press, Melbourne, 1998.

Dixon, Miriam, *The Imaginary Australian: Anglo Celts and Identity – 1788 to the present*, University of New South Wales Press, Sydney, 1999.

Douglas, Louise, Roberts, Alan, and Thompson, Ruth, *Oral History: A Handbook*, Allen & Unwin, Sydney, 1988.

Dowling, Peter, *The Culture of Newspapers: The Slow Birth of the Modern Newspaper in Australia, 1890-1940*, paper presented to the History of the Book in Australia conference, Sydney, August 1996, viewed online 1 September 2005, <http://idun.itsc.adfa.edu.au/ASEC/HOBA96_Papers/dowling.html>

Dunstan, Keith, *The Confessions of a Bicycle Nut*, Information Australia, Melbourne, 1999.

Ebury, Francis, 'Illuminatthe Subject: Towards a Distinctive Australian Pictorial Photography', *History of Photography*, Volume 26, Number 1, Spring 2002, pp. 34-41.

Ebury, Francis, 'James Campbell: Photographing the Australian Environment', *History of Photography*, Volume 28, Number 1, Spring 2004, pp. 1-14.

Edel, Leon, *Writing Lives: Principia Biographica*, Norton, New York, 1984.

Edmonds, Penelope, and Furphy, Samuel (eds.), *Rethinking Colonial Histories: New and Alternative Approaches*, History Department, Melbourne University, Melbourne, 2006.

Edwards, Cecil, *Brown Power: A Jubilee History of the State Electricity Commission of Victoria*, State Electricity Commission of Victoria, 1969.

Elliot, Alan, *A Century Exposed: One Hundred Years of the Melbourne Camera Club*, The Melbourne Camera Club, 1991.

Ennis, Helen, *Intersections: Photography, History and the National Library of Australia*, National Library of Australia, Canberra, 2004.

Epstein, William H (ed.), *Contesting the Subject: Essays in Postmodern Theory and Practice of Biography and Biographical Criticism*, Purdue University Press, 1991.

Fitzpatrick, Jim, *The Bicycle and the Bush: Man and Machine in Rural Australia*, Oxford University Press, Melbourne, 1980.

Fletcher, B.J. (ed.), *Broadford: A Regional History*, Lowden Publishing Co., Kilmore, 1975.

Fletcher, Meredith, *Digging People up for Coal: A History of Yallourn*, Melbourne University Press, Carlton, 2002.

Folco, John di, Terrain, 'Landscapes of the Great War', *History of Photography*, Volume 28, Number 3, Autumn 2004, pp. 261-5.

Forster, Colin, *Industrial Development in Australia 1920-1930*, Australian National University, Canberra, 1964.

Foss, Paul (ed.), *Island in the Stream: Myths of Place in Australian Culture*, Pluto Press, Leichhardt, NSW, 1988.

Freund, G., *Photography and Society*, London, 1980.

Friedson, A. M. (ed.), *New Directions in Biography*, Hawaii, 1981.

Fullerton, Mary E., *Bark House Days*, Melbourne University Press, Melbourne, 1964.

Gammage, Bill, *The Broken Years: Australian Soldiers in the Great War*, Penguin, Ringwood, 1975.

Garden, Donald S, *Victoria: A History*, Thomas Nelson Australia, Melbourne, 1984.

Gillison, Joan, *Colonial Doctor and his Town*, Cypress Books, Melbourne, 1974.

Glendinning, Victoria, 'Lies and Silences', in Eric Homberger, and John Charmley (eds.), *The Troubled Face of Biography*, Macmillan Press, London, 1988, pp. 49-62.

Gullett, Henry Somers, *The Official History of Australia in the War of 1914-1918: The Australian Imperial Force in Sinai and Palestine,* VII, Angus and Robertson, Sydney, Fourth Edition, 1937.

Gullett, Henry Somers, *The Opportunity in Australia*, The Field and Queen, London, 1914.

Guy, Albert, *A Brief History of Some of the Features of Public Electricity Supply in Australia: and the Formation and Development of the Electricity Supply Association of Australia*, Electricity Supply Association of Australia, Melbourne, 1958.

Hall, Barbara, and Mather, Jenni, *Australian Women Photographers 1840-1960*, Greenhouse Publications Pty Ltd, Richmond, Vic., 1986.

Hall, Rex, *The Desert Hath Pearls*, Hawthorn Press, Melbourne, 1975.

Hamilton, John, *Goodbye Cobber, God Bless You: The Fatal Charge of the Light Horse, Gallipoli*, August 7th 1915, Macmillan, 2004.

Hamilton (Duchess of), Jill, *First to Damascus: The Great Ride and Lawrence of Arabia*, Kangaroo Press, Sydney, 2002.

Hammond, Anne, *Ansel Adams: Divine Performance*, Yale University Press, New Haven and London, 2002.

Hansford, Brian, *Always Believe Your Grandfather*, Post Pressed, Teneriffe, Queensland, 2008.

Harding, Alan, and Ries, Roger, *Toongabbie Gippsland: A Gateway to the Walhalla Goldfields,* Roger Ries, Toongabbie, 2003.

Harvey, Colin, *Yallourn Power Station: a History, 1919 to 1989*, State Electricity Commission of Victoria, Melbourne, 1993.

Heathcote, RL, 'Early European Perception of the Australian Landscape: the First Hundred Years', in Seddon, and Mari Davis (eds.), *Man and Landscape in Australia: Towards an Ecological Vision,* from a symposium held at the Australian Academy of Science, Canberra, 30 May – June 1974, Australian National Commission for Unesco, Canberra, 1976, pp. 40-1.

Hibbins, G.M., Fahey, C., and Askew, M.R., *Local History: A Handbook for Enthusiasts,* Allen & Unwin, Sydney, 1985.

Hill, Alec, *Chauvel of the Light Horse: a Biography of General Sir Harry Chauvel,* Melbourne University Press, Carlton, 1978.

Hinckfuss, Harold, *Memories of a Signaller: The First World War, 1914-1919,* University of Queensland Press, Brisbane, 1982.

Hirsch, J., *Family Photographs: Content, Meaning and Effect,* New York, 1981.

Hirst, John, *The Sentimental Nation: The Making of the Australian Commonwealth,* Oxford University Press, South Melbourne, 2000.

Holmes, J Macdonald, *Australia's Open North: A Study of Northern Australia Bearing on the Urgency of the Times,* Angus and Robertson, Sydney, 1963.

Homberger, Eric and Charmley, John (eds.), *The Troubled Face of Biography,* Macmillan Press, London, 1988.

Howell, Brian, *The Seaton Story,* Penultimate Publication Services, Carlton, 1998.

Hunter, Jefferson, *Image and Word,* Harvard University, Massachusetts, 1987

Hutchinson, Garrie, *Pilgrimage: A Traveller's Guide to Australia's Battlefields,* Black Inc., Melbourne, 2006.

Idriess, Ion L, *The Desert Column: Leaves from the Diary of an Australian Trooper in Gallipoli, Sinai, and Palestine,* Angus and Robertson, Sydney, 1951 Edition.

James, Lawrence, *The Golden Warrior: The Life and Legend of Lawrence of Arabia,* Weidenfeld and Nicolson, London, 1991.

James, Robert Rhodes, 'Study of Churchill from 1900 to 1939', in Eric Homberger, and John Charmley (eds.), *The Troubled Face of Biography,* Macmillan Press, London, 1988, pp. 88-93.

Jenks, Chris (ed.), *Visual Culture,* Routledge, London, 1995.

Jolly, Martyn, 'Australian First-World-War Photography: Frank Hurley and Charles Bean', *History of Photography,* Volume 23, Number 2, Summer 1999, pp. 141-8.

Jolly, Martyn, 'Composite Propaganda Photographs during the First World War', *History of Photography,* Volume 27, Number 2, Summer 2003, pp. 154-65.

Jones, Shar, *J.W. Lindt: Master Photographer,* Currey O'Neil Ross Pty Ltd for Curry O'Neil on behalf of the Library Council of Victoria, 1985.

Joyce, Roger, 'Samuel Griffith, the Biographer and the Matter of Sources', in James Walter, and Raija Nugent (eds.), *Biographers at Work,* Griffith University, Institute of Modern Biography, 1984, pp. 17-25.

Kent, David, *The Kia Ora Coo-ee*, Cornstalk Publishing (A & R Publishers), 1981.

King, Jonathan, and Bowers, Michael, *Gallipoli: Untold Stories from War Correspondent Charles Bean and Front-line Anzacs*, Doubleday, Transworld, Milsons Point, NSW, 2005.

King, Michael, 'The Compassionate Truth', *Meanjin*, Volume 61, Number 1, 2002, pp. 24-34.

Kovacic, Leonarda, 'What Photographers Saw: Aboriginal People and Australian Colonial Experience', in Penelope Edmonds, and Samuel Furphy (eds.), *Rethinking Colonial Histories: New and Alternative Approaches*, History Department, Melbourne University, Melbourne, 2006, pp. 89-104.

Lake, Marilyn, *The Limits of Hope: Soldier Settlement in Victoria 1915-38*, Oxford University Press, Melbourne, 1987.

Lakin, Shaune, *Contact: Photographs from the Australian War Memorial Collection*, Australian War Memorial, Canberra, 2006.

Land Conservation Council Victoria, *North-Eastern Area (Benalla-Upper Murray Review*, Land Conservation Council, Melbourne, 1984.

Langley, George F and Edmee M, *Sand, Sweat & Camels: The Australian Companies of the Imperial Camel Corps*, Lowden Publishing Co., Kilmore, 1976.

Lawrence, Thomas Edward, *Seven Pillars of Wisdom: A Triumph*, Jonathon Cape, London, 1935.

Lucic, Karen, *Charles Sheeler and the Cult of the Machine*, Reaktion, London, 1991.

McCarthy, Dudley, *Gallipoli to the Somme: The Story of CEW Bean*, John Ferguson, Sydney, 1983.

MacDonald, Dougal, 'A Vision of National Film-Making', *Canberra Times*, 8 June 1991.

McGoldrick, Prue, *"Yallourn Was . . . ": A Historical and Pictorial Record of the Functions, Life and People of this "Deceased" Town*, Gippsland Printers (Morwell) Pty. Ltd., 1984.

McGregor, Alasdair, *Frank Hurley: A Photographer's Life*, Viking, Camberwell, 2004.

McIntosh, Robert, 'The Great War, Archives, and Modern Memory', *Archivaria*, Number 46, 1998, pp. 1-31.

McKernan, Michael, *Here is Their Spirit: A History of the Australian War Memorial 1917-1990*, University of Queensland Press in association with the Australian War Memorial, St.Lucia, Queensland, 1991.

McQuilton, John, *Rural Australia and the Great War: from Tarrawingee to Tangambalanga*, Melbourne University Press, Carlton South, 2001.

Maddern, Ivan T., *History of Cowwarr 1866-1971*, Back to Cowwarr Committee, Cowwarr, 1971.

Magarey, Susan and Round, Kerrie (eds.), *Living History: Essays on History as Biography*, Australian Humanities Press, Unley, South Australia, 2005.

Malcolm, Janet, *The Silent Woman: Sylvia Plath and Ted Hughes*, A.A. Knopf, New York, 1994.

Manne, Robert, 'A Turkish Tale: Gallipoli and the Armenian Genocide', *The Monthly: Australian Politics, Society & Culture*, February 2007, pp. 20-8.

Martin, Allan, 'Elements in the Biography of Henry Parkes', in James Walter, and Raija Nugent (eds.), *Biographers at Work*, Griffith University, Institute of Modern Biography, 1984, pp. 11-16.

Masson, Sophie, 'People's Photographs', *Quadrant*, May 2005, Number 416, Volume XLIX, Number 5, pp. 51-3.

Matthews, Brian, *Louisa*, McPhee Gribble and Penguin Books, Fitzroy and Ringwood, 1988.

Middleton & Maning's Gippsland Directory 1884-85

Millar, David P., *Charles Kerry's Federation Australia*, David Ell Press, Sydney, 1981.

Mitchell, Elyne, *Light Horse: The Story of Australia's Mounted Troops*, Macmillan, Melbourne, Sun Books, 1982.

Mitchell, W.J.T. (ed.), *Landscape and Power*, University of Chicago Press, Chicago and London, 2002.

Modjeska, Drusilla, *Stravinsky's Lunch*, Picador, Sydney, 1999.

Morgan, Patrick, *The Settling of Gippsland: A Regional History*, Gippsland Municipalities Association, 1997.

Mulvaney, D.J. and Calaby, J.H., *'So Much That Is New': Baldwin Spencer 1860-1929 – A Biography*, Melbourne University Press, Carlton, 1985.

Murray, Robert, *The Confident Years: Australia in the Twenties*, Allen Lane, Penguin Books Australia, Ringwood, 1978.

Murray-Smith, Stephen, *The Tech: A Centenary History of the Royal Melbourne Institute of Technology*, Hyland House, South Yarra, Melbourne, 1987.

Nasht, Simon, *The Last Explorer: Hubert Wilkins Australia's Unknown Hero*, Hodder Australia, Sydney, 2005.

Newton, Gael, *Shades of Light: Photography and Australia 1839-1988*, Sydney, Canberra, 1988.

Newton, Gael, *Silver and Grey: Fifty Years of Australian Photography 1900-1950*, Angus and Robertson, Sydney, 1980.

Northern Territory of Australia, Report of the Administrator for the Year 1912, Parliament of the Commonwealth of Australia, 1913.

Oakman, Daniel, 'Canberra Air Crash: Tragedy at Home', *Wartime: Official Magazine of the Australian War Memorial,* Issue 33, January 2006, pp. 14-17.

O'Donnell, E.E., *Father Browne's Australia*, Wolfhound Press, Dublin, paperback edition, 1999.

Palmer, Nettie, *Henry Bourne Higgins: A Memoir*, George G. Harrap & Co., Sydney, 1931.

Pavils, Janice, *Anzac Day: The Undying Debt*, Lythrvm Press, Adelaide, 2007.

Perkin, Corinne, (with essays by Les Carlyon and Colin Harding), *A Camera on the Somme*, Bendigo Art Gallery, Bendigo, 2009.

Perry, Roland, *Monash: The Outsider Who Won a War*, Random House Australia, paperback edition, 2005.

Perry, Roland, *The Australian Light Horse*, Hachette Australia, Sydney, 2009.

Piggott, Michael, 'The Australian War Records Section and its Aftermath, 1917-1925', *Archives and Manuscripts*, Volume 8, Number 2, December 1980, pp. 41-50.

Pitkethly, Anne and Don, *N.J. Caire: Landscape Photographer*, A. and D. Pitkethly, Rosanna, Vic., 1988.

Pitts, Lilian Louisa, *Merrigum Frank*, [compiled by McGillivray, Euan and Nickson, Matthew], Part of The Biggest Family Album in Australia, Museum of Victoria, 1990.

Plowden, David, *Industrial Landscape*, Chicago Historical Society in association with W.W. Norton & Company, New York/London, 1985.

Powell, Alan, *Far Country: A Short History of the Northern Territory*, Melbourne University Press, Carlton, First Edition, 1982.

Price, Mary, *The Photograph: A Strange Confined Space*, Stanford University Press, Stanford, California, 1994.

Read, Peter, *Belonging: Australians, Place and Aboriginal Ownership*, Cambridge University Press, Oakleigh, 2000.

Reid, Richard, *Gallipoli 1915*, ABC Books, 2002.

Rickard, John, *Australia: A Cultural History*, A Pearson Education Print on Demand Edition, 2001, of the Second Edition, Addison Wesley Longman Limited, 1996.

Roberts, Stephen H., *History of Australian Land Settlement*, Macmillan, South Melbourne, 1968.

Robertson, John, *Anzac and Empire: The Tragedy and Glory of Gallipoli*, Hamlyn Australia, Port Melbourne, 1990.

Robin, Libby, *How a Continent Created a Nation*, University of New South Wales Press, Sydney, 2007.

Robinson, Paul, *Film to Digital: The Story of the Victorian Association of Photographic Societies*, Victorian Association of Photographic Societies Inc., Carnegie, Victoria, 2003.

Robson, Leslie Lloyd, *The First A.I.F.: A Study of its Recruitment 1914-1918*, Melbourne University Press, Carlton, Paperback Edition, 1982.

Ross, John, 'Perceptual Worlds', in George Seddon and Mari Davis, (eds.), *Man and Landscape in Australia: Towards an Ecological Vision*, Australian Government Publishing Service, Canberra, 1976, p. 27.

Rothstein, Arthur, *Documentary Photography*, Focal Press, Boston, 1986.

Runyan, William McKinley, *Life Histories and Psychobiography: Explorations in Theory and Method*, Oxford University Press, New York, 1982.

Sanders, Michael L., and Taylor, Philip, M., *British Propaganda during the First World War 1914-18*, Macmillan, London, 1982.

Sassoon, Joanna, 'Becoming Anthropological: a Cultural Biography of EL Mitchell's Photographs of Aboriginal People' [online], *Aboriginal History*; Volume 28; 2004; pp. 59-86.

Sassoon, Joanna, 'Chasing Phantoms in the Archives: The Australia House Photograph Collection', *Archivaria*, Number 50, Fall 2000, pp. 117-24.

Sassoon, Joanna 'E.L. Mitchell and the Imaginary Broome', *History of Photography*, Volume 23, Number 2, Summer, 1999, pp. 149-56.

Sassoon, Joanna, 'Politics of Pictures: A Cultural History of the Western Australian Government Print Photograph Collection', *Australian Historical Studies*, Number 123, 2004, pp. 16-36.

Schirato, Tony, and Webb, Jen, *Reading the Visual*, Allen & Unwin, Crows Nest, NSW, 2004.

Schwartz, Joan M. and Ryan, James R. (eds.), *Picturing Place: Photography and the Geographical Imagination*, I.B. Tauris & Co. Ltd., London, 2003.

Seal, Graham, *Inventing Anzac: The Digger and National Mythology*, University of Queensland Press, St Lucia, 2004.

Seddon, George, and Davis, Mari (eds.), *Man and landscape in Australia: Towards an Ecological Vision,* from a symposium held at the Australian Academy of Science, Canberra, 30 May – June 1974, Australian National Commission for Unesco, Canberra, 1976.

Serle, Geoffrey, *John Monash: A Biography*, Melbourne University Press in association with Monash University, First published 1982, Second paperback edition, 2002.

Sierp, Allan, *Colonial Life in Victoria: Fifty Years of Photography 1855-1905*, Rigby, Melbourne, 1972.

Sinclair, Andrew, 'Vivat Alius Ergo Sum', in Eric Homberger, and John Charmley (eds.), *The Troubled Face of Biography*, Macmillan Press, London, 1988.

Simpson, Cameron, *Maygar's Boys: A Biographical History of the 8th Light Horse Regiment AIF 1914-19*, Just Soldiers, Military Research and Publications, Moorooduc, 1998.

Slater, Don, 'Photography and Modern Vision', in *Visual Culture*, Chris Jenks (ed.), Routledge, London, 1995.

Smith, T., and Bradley, A. (eds.), *Australian Art and Architecture: Essays Presented to Bernard Smith*, Oxford University Press, Melbourne, 1980.

Sontag, Susan, *On Photography*, Penguin, New York, 1979.

Souter, Gavin, *Lion and Kangaroo, Australia: 1901-1919, The Rise of a Nation*, Fontana Edition, Sydney, 1976.

Spaulding, Jonathan, *Ansel Adams and the American Landscape: a Biography*, University of California Press, Berkeley and Los Angeles, California, 1995.

Spurling, Hilary, 'Neither Morbid nor Ordinary', in Eric Homberger, and John Charmley (eds.), *The Troubled Face of Biography*, Macmillan Press, London, 1988, pp. 116-22.

Squires, Debra, Barraclough, Linda, Clothier, Helen, *Gippsland in Focus: A Directory of Photographers to 1950*, Kapana Press, Bairnsdale, 1990.

Stanley, Peter, *Quinn's Post: Anzac, Gallipoli*, Allen and Unwin, Crow's Nest, NSW, 2005.

Stevenson, David, *1914 1918: The History of the First World War*, Penguin Books, London, England, 2004.

Stevenson, Ian R, *The Line that Led to Nowhere: The Story of the North Australia Railway*, Rigby Limited, Adelaide, 1979.

Stokes, Edward, *United We Stand: Impressions of Broken Hill 1908-1910*, Five Mile Press, Canterbury, Victoria, 1983.

Stomberg, John, 'A "United States of the World": Industry and Photography between the Wars', in Kim Sichel, *Icon to Irony: German and American Industrial Photography*, Boston University Art Gallery, 1995, pp. 17-25.

Tenfelde, Klaus (ed.), *Pictures of Krupp: Photography and History in the Industrial Age*, English Edition, Philip Wilson, London, 2005.

The Relics and Records of Australia's Effort in the Defence of the Empire, 1914-1918, Second Edition, 1925, Australian War Memorial Museum.

Thwaite, Ann, 'Writing Lives', in Eric Homberger and John Charmley (eds.), *The Troubled Face of Biography*, Macmillan Press, London, 1988, pp. 16-33.

Trachtenberg, Alan (ed.), *Classic Essays on Photography*, Leete's Island Books, New Haven, USA, 1980.

Travers, THE, 'From Surafend to Gough: Charles Bean, James Edmonds, and the Making of the Australian Official History', *Journal of the Australian War Memorial* 27 (October 1995), pp. 15-25.

Tsokhas, Kosmas, *Making a Nation State: Cultural Identity, Economic Nationalism and Sexuality in Australian History*, Melbourne University Press, Carlton South, 2001.

UNESCO, Annex 8, *List of Nationally and Internationally Significant Collections: Held in each Institution*; '19. Northern Territory Library – Australia; Name of Collections: Photo Album – Parliamentary Visit to Northern Territory of 1912.

Vincent, Phoebe, *My Darling Mick: The Life of Granville Ryrie 1865-1937*, National Library of Australia, Canberra, 1997.

Walter, James, and Nugent, Raija (eds.), *Biographers at Work*, Griffiths University, Institute for Modern Biography, Brisbane, 1984.

Watson, L.C. and Watson-Franke, M.B., *Interpreting Life Histories: An Anthropological Inquiry*, New Brunswick, N.J., 1985.

Wigmore Lionel, *The Long View: A History of Canberra*, Cheshire, 1963, Revised Edition, 1972.

Williams, John F., *Anzacs, The Media and The Great War*, University of NSW Press, Sydney, 1999.

Willis, Anne Marie, *Picturing Australia: A History of Photography*, Angus and Robertson, North Ryde, NSW, 1988.

Wilson, Brigadier General LC, 3rd Light Horse Brigade, AIF, *Narrative of Operations of Third Light Horse Brigade (Including the Egyptian Rebellion 1919) from 27 October 1917 to 11 July 1919*, facsimile from the original, Naval and Military Press Ltd., East Sussex, & Imperial War Museum, London, date unknown.

Wise's Post Office Directory of 1884-85.

Woodward, C.V., *Thinking Back: The Perils of Writing History*, Baton Rouge, 1986.

Zada, Susie, *Memories of the Bramley & Goghill Families*, S. Zada, Melbourne, 1994.

INDEX

www.ingramcontent.com/pod-product-compliance
Lightning Source LLC
Chambersburg PA
CBHW081715220526

45468CB00008B/1852